Uncertainty is an ever-present and ineradicable aspect of politics. It affects all important issues of governance and policy, in both domestic and international contexts. Rather than treating the uncertainty of politics as a mystery, this book provides an original and direct treatment of political uncertainty as a scientifically knowable phenomenon with well-defined principles and substantive properties. Specific applications of this new theory of political uncertainty are demonstrated in diverse areas of politics, examining such questions as when and how wars break out, when and how governments collapse, and when and how political cooperation emerges. The author shows how probability and mathematical modeling can play a central role in understanding such complex and fundamental issues.

Politics and Uncertainty

Politics and Uncertainty

Theory, Models and Applications

Claudio Cioffi-Revilla

CAMBRIDGE
UNIVERSITY PRESS

PUBLISHED BY THE PRESS SYNDICATE OF THE UNIVERSITY OF CAMBRIDGE
The Pitt Building, Trumpington Street, Cambridge CB2 1RP, United Kingdom

CAMBRIDGE UNIVERSITY PRESS
The Edinburgh Building, Cambridge, CB2 2RU, United Kingdom
40 West 20th Street, New York, NY 10011-4211, USA
10 Stamford Road, Oakleigh, Melbourne 3166, Australia

First published 1998

Printed in the United Kingdom at the University Press, Cambridge

Typeset in 10/12 pt Times New Roman [VN]

A catalogue record for this book is available from the British Library

Library of Congress Cataloguing in Publication data

Cioffi-Revilla, Claudio A., 1951–
Politics and uncertainty: theory, models and applications/Claudio Cioffi-Revilla.
    p.   cm.
Includes bibliographical references and index.
ISBN 0 521 58121 4. – ISBN 0 521 58915 0 (pbk.)
1. Political science.   2. Political science – Methodology.
3. Uncertainty.   I. Title.
JA71.C496   1998
320–dc21   97-23646   CIP

ISBN 0 521 58121 4 hardback
ISBN 0 521 58915 0 paperback

Ad memoriam patris mei

That randomness and probability are real phenomena, and therefore are not to be accounted for by our ignorance of true causes, is a proposition that I defend from a variety of perspectives.

Patrick Suppes, *Probabilistic Metaphysics*

One way of theory building is to collect empirical facts and assume that they will somehow speak for themselves, that an obvious classificatory scheme will emerge from their gross and conspicuous aspects. More often it turns out that either the facts by themselves do not suggest an obvious classificatory scheme, or if they do, that the obvious scheme is not very good. A better way is to develop on intellectual grounds what might be a good scheme, try it out and see what happens when empirical data are used.

Karl W. Deutsch, *Integration and the Social System*

The approach we have chosen and the concepts we are using can accommodate a great many theories. Within this framework many apparently unrelated theories and generalizations can be related and their usefulness enhanced.

Gabriel A. Almond and G. Bingham Powell, Jr., *Comparative Politics*

Contents

Figures

Tables

Preface

This book is about uncertainty in politics, about the defining role that this real-world feature plays in political life, and about how political theory is to understand uncertainty in a systematic way that produces new knowledge. Although most readers will not deny the pervasiveness and significance of uncertainty in politics – particularly in this turbulent age of post-Cold War politics – paradoxically, political uncertainty has been traditionally viewed in ways that normally eschew inquiry. That is, either as an unsolvable mystery to be avoided except by the most fearless minds, as if the proposition "political uncertainty = unknowable" were true by definition, or as a statistical nuisance that is best treated as "measurement error" or an "error term" in quantitative models. Few have looked at political uncertainty in order to understand its character. As I argue in this book, however, political uncertainty is a defining quality of politics that cannot be ignored, either by theory or by public policy. Political uncertainty is also mostly a qualitative phenomenon with a well-defined character; only secondarily is it quantitative, and as such it should be directly addressed by contemporary political science using the appropriate tools of inquiry.

The main contribution of this book is to present a theory of political uncertainty applicable to understanding the diverse domains of political life, both domestic and international. I use specific instances of political phenomena related to coalitions, government policy, deterrence, collective action, conflict, and others as running examples to illustrate the broader theory and its potential scope. However, the applications I present are meant only to assist in the interpretation of the theory; they are not meant as in-depth analyses because those would require separate treatment. The theory addresses one of the central dual puzzles in politics: the aggregate behavior of political variables and the individual occurrence of political events, both of which are phenomena that occur with uncertainty. My theory has two branches, a macroscopic part for the explanation of aggregate political behavior in terms of well-defined forces, and a microscopic part for the explanation of individual political events in terms of their occurrence structure. Unified principles provide linkages between the two levels of analysis. The theory attempts to advance the standards of contemporary political science in the areas of deductive formalization and empirical validity. I give greater emphasis to the former goal because my chief interest in this book is in theoretical development, an area that in spite of recent advances is still less well established in political science. Empirical methods are now more familiar in scholarship and in teaching.

On the deductive side, the theory is constructed in the traditional deductivist tradition, by defining concepts, postulating a set of axioms and assumptions, and, most important, deriving results that account for observed phenomena. I call the main theoretical results principles because formally these are either theorems or corollaries; but they are propositions about politics, not mathematical propositions as such (or they would be called theorems). Whereas theorems, lemmas, and corollaries are content-free statements (formal propositions), scientific principles are to do with substantive properties of the real world (a distinction that is often neglected). General principles explain the larger patterns of uncertainty in political behavior and events; special principles explain more specific aspects.

On the empirical side, the two levels of the theory differ in terms of the appropriate evidence and technical procedures used for drawing valid inferences. The macroscopic part of the theory uses predominantly quantitative empirical methods, such as maximum likelihood estimation, survival analysis, and other nonlinear data analysis approaches discussed in chapter 4. By contrast, the microscopic part of the theory uses predominantly qualitative case-oriented methods similar to those used in the empirical application of decision models or game-theoretic models to historical material. I illustrate how both types of methods are used to evaluate the theory, and I also hope that this will help discredit some enduring but false distinctions between qualitative and quantitative approaches, as if these were always mutually exclusive in scientific investigation.

From a methodological perspective I view my main contribution in the area of theoretical methodology as the development and application of appropriate formal tools for constructing political theory. My emphasis on appropriate tools is important because many of the mathematical models available today were developed with other sciences and a different set of questions in mind. Fortunately, many different theoretical tools exist because mathematics today covers diverse formal languages, some of which have been directly inspired by social phenomena (parts of probability theory, decisional calculus, game theory, graph theory). Theoretical methods will attract greater interest in political science, now that empirical methods are better known and established, because only they can directly assist the scholar in the construction – not just in the testing – of viable theories. What is known as political methodology – including those procedures that are ordinarily taught in "methods courses" – should therefore cover tools for theoretic progress at least as much as tools for checking the empirics; otherwise, there will be little to test empirically, and what there will be will not be adequately systematized to benefit the accumulation of scientific knowledge.

This book is addressed to several scholarly communities, mainly academic but also some in policy areas. The book will be of primary interest to political scientists who wish to develop a better understanding of the nature of uncertainty as it operates in various areas of politics. I demonstrate how political uncertainty is uniformly affected by the same principles. Thus, political scientists who study conflict – domestic or international – will find through this theory much in common with those who study coalitions, policy processes, and collective action – areas where I demonstrate the existence of comparable patterns of political uncertainty that are governed by the same laws.

Another audience consists of social scientists and other academic scholars working in allied disciplines who also study politics from perspectives that differ from those of the political scientist, but who nonetheless acknowledge and wish to develop a better understanding of uncertainty in political life. This broader community includes political sociologists, economists, historians, political anthropologists, and archeologists – scholars who acknowledge uncertainty in the origins and historical evolution of political systems in various civilizations. These allied disciplines may use this theory for comparative purposes, exploring the application of principles across a wider range of time and space than is normal in contemporary political science.

A third community consists of philosophers, epistemologists, and other scholars who share an interest in the advancement of formal political theory, particularly an interest in the role played by *fortuna* in influencing the lives, fortunes, and governance of a collectivity. Members of this community may also be interested in my use of probabilistic causality – as opposed to the older deterministic causality used by more traditional political theories – as a newer and more effective epistemic basis for constructing the theory of political uncertainty presented in this book. While I was writing I also frequently had in mind students of politics in all the above disciplines, particularly those who may feel motivated to develop a better understanding of contemporary approaches to political uncertainty based on rigorous and systematic methods. As a university teacher, I am particularly concerned that students develop early on in their investigation of politics a disciplined and truthful understanding of uncertainty in political life, not the more popular misconceptions of political uncertainty as unknowable or haphazard randomness. Pundits in the public arena make their living from political uncertainty; scholars make their living attempting to decipher it.

Finally, the book should be of interest to the more analytically inclined policy analysts who may wish to consider the implications of these principles of political uncertainty for their own areas of policy concerns. Logically, significant areas of public policy – from local government to national security – are endemically affected by political uncertainty, so improvements in our basic understanding of political uncertainty cannot be ignored without risk. As the best engineers know, there is nothing more practical than good theory.

The background needed to read this book is not advanced, but nonetheless may pose a challenge to some readers who share a substantive interest in the subject matter. Most readers will agree with the premise that political uncertainty is not an easily tractable topic. What some find difficult to accept is the obvious conclusion that to analyze politics with uncertainty but without tools that are sufficiently powerful is to require something impossible. There is no wholly satisfactory solution to this dilemma, only a trade-off compromise between how much can be explained about political uncertainty and how much formal power to apply in the investigation; not everything in life can be easily grasped. The approach I have chosen relies mostly on logic, sets, and elementary probability notions, with a minimum of basic calculus (a powerful analytical tool that is widely used in most scientific disciplines, including "softer sciences" such as biology and economics, but still largely underutilized in political theory). However, I have attempted to provide informal interpretations along the way, and the careful reader will note that there are only a few passages in which the precision of the mathematical language simply cannot be replaced by plain English (which was not invented to construct scientific theories, let alone to understand the world of uncertainty). Other analytical tools are reviewed or developed as needed either in the text or in appendix 4.

In terms of formal analysis, I have aimed to strike at a middle range, between basic mathematics (algebra, linear equations), which can contribute little to a theory of political uncertainty, and higher mathematics (advanced calculus, measure theory, stochastic differential equations, topology), which is not well known in political science. I believe this middle range contains many powerful tools that are presently underutilized or neglected in the construction of political theory. I hope to show – primarily through the principles of the theory presented in this book – how mathematical methods can produce new insights that are as true as those derived by more conventional empirical methods (what I call Kline's thesis, discussed in chapter 3).

My recommendation to any reader interested in the subject matter of political uncertainty but who becomes frustrated by the formalism that I use is to plunge ahead anyway – as Claude Shannon (1951) demonstrated in a famous theorem from information theory, the human mind is capable of acquiring a considerable amount of knowledge even when the stream of signals contains gaps and noise. At the same time, I also hope that those who labor at sharpening their theoretical tools and revel in the sight of a beautiful nonlinear equation with an aesthetically pleasing form will find some new insights or applications, particularly concerning those aspects of political uncertainty that can be understood only through the medium of mathematics. These readers may also require a higher level of formalization, something that should be pursued elsewhere in the specialized journals but that I have tried to avoid in this book.

As I explain in greater detail in chapter 1, the book consists of four parts, along with a set of supporting appendices. Each part corresponds to a basic element of the theory. The first part – foundations – contains an introductory chapter in which I present the topic of political uncertainty in a disciplinary light, examining its place in political theory, the way in which it has historically been addressed, and the axioms I propose to use as foundations for the theory presented in subsequent chapters. The next two parts – the two main theoretical branches, called macropolitics and micropolitics for reasons I detail in chapter 1 – each contain three parallel chapters, dedicated to the basic concepts, the general principles, and the more specific results (special principles) in each branch of the theory. The chapters within each part of the theory are strictly sequential, but the two parts are less so. I chose to present the macroscopic part of the theory first because the microscopic part investigates in greater detail what lies within the "black box" of political behavior, so to speak, and so it seemed more natural to deal first with aggregate political behavior (macro level) and only later with the more specific individual events that compose it (micro level). However, readers with a greater interest in individual political events – particularly those political occurrences that are viewed as one-of-a-kind, as many historians think – may wish to read part III immediately after chapter 1. The fourth part contains a single chapter which synthesizes the macroscopic and microscopic analysis of political uncertainty by providing a unified treatment and explaining the linkages across levels of analysis.

I had not looked forward to writing appendices, but in a book of this nature they turn out to solve a number of common problems. Appendix 1 can be used as a dictionary reference to clarify the meaning of some new terms that are necessary in constructing a political theory in largely unexplored conceptual territory. Appendix 2 explains and summarizes the formal notation used throughout the book; it also helps to identify the key concepts, as any system of notation should. I confess to not being entirely satisfied with the present state of notation, and I suspect that some more creative work along these lines will be necessary to provide the analysis of political uncertainty with a theoretically efficient set of analytical signs – at present an unappreciated need in political theory. Appendix 3 contains the proofs of theorems and corollaries, which I did not include in the text in order to maintain the flow of ideas. I do feel that something is lost by not showing how I first arrived at the main propositions (as opposed to their subsequent proof), but I also realize that moving the technical proofs to the appendix increases the readability of the book. Appendix 4 contains a summary of some formal tools that are useful in the task of theoretical construction – some of the middle-range tools that I referred to earlier. Its main purpose is to highlight some ideas from theoretical methods, not to provide any sort of formal training.

Acknowledgments

This book required a number of years to acquire scope and coherence. During this time I have received numerous valuable comments and advice from many patient colleagues. I thank my first mentors, Umberto Gori and Glenn H. Snyder, for their support in pursuit of formal political theory, and also Alessandro Bruschi, Paul Diesing, and James A. Stimson for showing me how exciting science can be done in the investigation of politics. Also, all graduates of the Facoltà di Scienze Politiche e Sociali "Cesare Alfieri," my alma mater at the University of Florence, owe our gratitude to the esteemed Italian political theoretician, Giovanni Sartori, the modern founder of the Florentine school. I never met the late John V. Gillespie, one of the greatest but least acknowledged American political scientists, who provided me an inspiring epistemological bridge in my journey from Florence to America.

At the risk of unintentionally forgetting someone, I am very pleased to thank the following colleagues for their comments and advice on various parts of this project: Hayward Alker Jr., Pierre Allan, Fulvio Attinà, †Edward E. Azar, Frank Beer, Steve Brams, Stuart Bremer, Dagobert Brito, Eric Browne, Ron Brunner, †Franco Alberto Casadio, Steve Chan, Harold Chestnut, Maurizio Cotta, Luciano Daboni, Raymond Dacey, †Karl Deutsch, Paul H. Diehl, Lawrence Dodd, Richard Engelbrecht-Wiggans, Donald P. Green, Joseph Grieco, Seif Hussein, Michael Intrilligator, Patrick James, Cal Jillson, Paul Johnson, Roger Kanet, William Keech, Edward Kolodziej, Peter Kopacek, Michael Krassa, Jacek Kugler, Jim Kuklinski, Martin Landau, Russell Leng, Jack S. Levy, Mark Lichbach, Alejandro Lorca Corrons, Urs Luterbacher, Duncan MacRae, Harvey Mansfield, Zeev Maoz, Patrick McGowan, Dwaine Mefford, Manus I. Midlarsky, Alex Mintz, Andrew Moravcsik, James Morrow, †Benjamin Most, Stuart Nagel, †Alan Newcombe, Barry O'Neill, Lin Ostrom, Carlo Pelanda, Brian Pollins, Steve Portnoy, George Rabinowitz, Anatol Rapoport, †William H. Riker, Zvee Ritz, Phil Schrodt, Paul W. Schroeder, Ian Shapiro, Herbert Simon, J. David Singer, Randy Siverson, Duncan Snidal, Erik Solem, Harvey Starr, Walter Stone, Vicky B. Sullivan, Charles S.

Taber, William R. Thompson, Marcello Torrigiani, Luigi Vannucci, Koos Van Wyk, John Vasquez, Michael D. Ward, John A. Williamson, and †Avner Yaniv.

I am particularly indebted to the following colleagues who read versions of the entire manuscript and offered many valuable comments: G. Robert Boynton, Harold Guetzkow, Walter Isard, D. Marc Kilgour, Bruce M. Russett, Michael Nicholson, Richard L. Merritt, Robert G. Muncaster, and Dina A. Zinnes.

Many former students provided me with the challenge of explaining my theory in more understandable terms, for which I shall always be grateful. At the University of North Carolina, Chapel Hill: Jim Dixon, Mark Gasiorowski, Don Haynes, Ed Heyman, Craig Murphy, Doug Nelson, Emilio Rodriguez, Jesse Dent, Abdulmonem Al Mashat, and Abdullah Al Sultan. At the University of Illinois, Urbana-Champaign: Gretchen Hower, Pierangelo Isernia, David Jones, Kelly Kadera, S. Chun Lee, Paul Pudaite, and Charles Taber. At the University of Colorado, Boulder: Clay Bowen, Susan Grubb, Mike Kanner, Sean Kelly, David Lai, Todd Landmann, Mohan Penubarti, and Henrik Sommer.

The National Science Foundation and the Merriam Lab of the University of Illinois provided initial support for this project, followed by support from the Center for International Relations of the University of Colorado.

John Haslam at Cambridge University Press has excelled in his capacity as editor, by managing a truly examplar review and production process. I am also grateful to Sandy Rush and Hilary Scannell, for their careful editing.

Finally, no happily married scholar can write a book like this without the relentless support of spouse and family. My greatest gratitude goes to my wife Jean, who sacrificed a great deal over many years so that I could write this book, to my brother Alfred for his cheerful humor, and to my parents for their loving trust. I dedicate this book to my father, who taught me more than I could possibly teach in any book.

Part I

Foundations

1   Introduction

Uncertainty appears to be a characteristic of all political life. Systematic
political analysis can reduce some of that uncertainty.

Robert Dahl, *Modern Political Analysis*

Uncertainty is ubiquitous, consequential, and ineradicable in political life.
However, since antiquity, the puzzle of political uncertainty has often frustrated progress in social science theory and public policy. Uncertainty is
clearly recognized today, in the turbulent world of party realignments,
foreign regime changes, and post-Cold War politics, but many earlier epochs in the many-thousand years' history of politics have been similarly
affected by political uncertainty. The fall of the ancient Babylonian or Roman empires, the Chinese Warring States period, or the collapse of the
Maya states in Mesoamerica all occurred in periods of similar political
uncertainty.

In this first chapter I introduce uncertainty as a fundamental property
of politics, crossing the traditional sub-disciplinary boundaries of international and comparative or domestic politics, identifying major forms of
uncertainty that invite a unified explanation across different areas of politics. I then lay down a system of axioms and explain the main parts of the
general theory of politics presented in this book. Because this chapter is a
point of departure, the main goal is to air some of the major issues, while
leaving for subsequent chapters the more intricate task of detailing the
theory and its application to various areas of political science. An important property of political uncertainty is its duality across levels of analysis,
a feature that is evident in the main concepts, principles, and applications
discussed throughout this book.

1.1   Politics and uncertainty

1.1.1   *Nature of political uncertainty*

Political uncertainty refers to the puzzling lack of sureness or absence
of strict determination in political life. Elections, wars, governmental

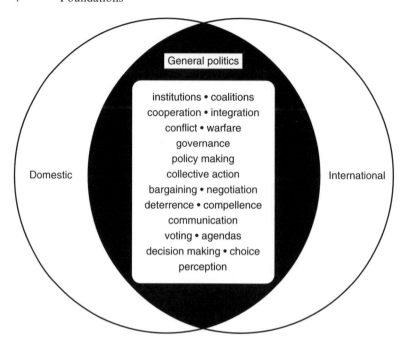

Figure 1.1. General and contextual areas of politics

processes, threats, collective action situations, and other political phenomena identified in figure 1.1 are all inherently uncertain political occurrences. My primary interest in this book is in these core phenomena of general politics, at the rich and fertile intersection of the domestic and international. For example, the uncertainty of coalitions is both domestic (cabinet governments) and international (alliances). The uncertainty of conflict has domestic (civil warfare), as well as international (interstate warfare) manifestations. The fundamental uncertainty of deterrence and compellence threats applies in both national and international contexts, as with other core phenomena in the domain of general politics. Of course, the context-specific details of domestic or international manifestations of these general political phenomena (conflicts, coalitions, deterrence, voting, communication, or others mentioned in figure 1.1) can be important as well, but the core phenomenon must be understood first. So, while often I shall use context-specific illustrations (e.g. interstate war in the next chapter), the main theoretical interest is in understanding the nature of uncertainty in general (context-free) politics.

Politics is fundamentally uncertain because it concerns social behavior "affecting the lives and fortunes of collectivities" or "how they are governed" (Brams 1985: chs. 1–2; Riker and Ordeshook 1973), how political systems are founded (Gerstein et al. 1988: 91; Taylor 1987), how a collectivity of individuals, groups, or states makes an "authoritative allocation of values" (Easton 1965), or how "collective action problems" arise and are managed (Olson 1965). Perhaps the most certain statement that can be made about these and other core puzzles of politics is that we never know for certain that they will happen. This is true in both contexts of politics – domestic and international, as indicated in figure 1.1.

Several extant definitions of politics make the role of uncertainty explicit:

Political decisions can be defined as the "sovereign" collective decisions from which the individual is *less likely* to escape, because of both their spatial extension and their coercive intensity.[1]

Uncertainty means that in politics outcomes are neither predetermined (with probability 1) nor impossible (with probability 0), but lie somewhere in between. *Where* in between, and *how* and *why* are classic puzzles of politics, and the core questions I address with the new theory presented in this book. Were politics not perennially uncertain it would be like the world of eighteenth-century Laplacean mechanics – a world of lifeless pendulums and celestial orbits in which the future is exactly predictable once initial conditions are specified. Politics is fundamentally different because – as Aristotle would have put it – its uncertainty is essential, not accidental.

The fundamental cause of uncertainty in politics lies in the indeterminate nature of individual decisional acts and states of nature (lotteries) that are most commonly beyond the control of political actors, groups, or states.[2] These uncertain acts and events of normal social intercourse have significant effects on the life, fortune, or governance of collectivities – in other words, they are political. Unlike planetary orbits and other simple physical systems, the political behavior of individuals and collectivities is not

---

[1] Sartori (1973: 21), emphasis mine. Uncertainty appears as a constituent feature in numerous other definitions of politics, such as those by Almond (1990: 35), Easton (1965), Gilliant (1987), Masters (1989: 140), Merriam (1970), Moe (1990: 119), or Weber (1949). Uncertainty is also included as a substantive political property in traditional definitions of conflict (Blainey 1973; Howard 1983; von Clausewitz [1832] 1976: 89), as well as being "a noteworthy conclusion" in the cumulative domestic political conflict research program (Lichbach 1992: 348).

[2] By contrast, a classic example of deterministic *metaphor* in politics is the action–reaction model of conflict, where it is assumed that decision makers do not "stop to think" (Richardson 1960a: 12). See also Landau (1979: 78–102), Miller (1979), and Rapoport (1960: ch. 5) on the influence of physicalism on the theory and practice of politics, particularly the use of deterministic models (social physics).

governed by deterministic laws. Note that the indeterminacy of decisional acts and nature's lotteries covers both contexts of general politics – domestic and international.

I view the uncertainty of politics as having three constituent properties that motivate the need and suggest the opportunity for a general unified theory. First, political uncertainty is consequential, because uncertainty causes significant changes in "the lives and fortunes of collectivities" or "how they are governed" – changes that themselves take place with uncertainty from start to finish. Elections, crises, revolutions, public policy processes, wars, and other common political occurrences shown in figure 1.1 have this property, but so do less dramatic political events, such as town meetings, parliamentary hearings, or budgetary appropriations. Political uncertainty, often caused by incomplete information, can cause a coalition to be larger than just "minimum winning," or it can cause a collective action need to become a severe political problem, or it can cause voting agendas to become "multiple-stage" processes. In the area of collective action problems, it has been noted that

the introduction of uncertainty yields a plethora of cases and few general results. Clear cut relationships between group size and collective rationality and/or group asymmetry are especially dificult to establish when uncertainty is present. (Sandler 1992: 90)

A better understanding of political uncertainty – its causes, properties, and consequences – can assist in establishing some general results for understanding collective action and related phenomena.

Recently, the uncertainties of the post-Cold War era have caused numerous changes in the foreign and domestic policies of many countries, as well as other no less significant changes in international institutions.[3] Clearly, uncertainty matters in politics. The principles presented in this book provide some general and specific results to understand the consequences of uncertainty.

Second, political uncertainty is ubiquitous, particularly since the "democratization or massification of politics" (Sartori 1973: 20). No area of politics – none of the themes in figure 1.1 – is immune from chance, just as gravity is everywhere in the physical world, or values pervade the ethical world. Coalitions, governmental policies, and conflict and cooperation are

---

[3] The effects of post-Cold War political uncertainty are numerous, both domestically (Giddens 1995; Gill 1994; Jones 1995; Landy and Levin 1995; Weisberg 1995), and internationally (Rosenau 1992; Russett and Sutterlin 1991; Singer and Wildavsky 1996). Similar uncertainties in politics earlier caused the development of the Concert of Europe (responding to uncertainty over emerging threats to international security) and the League of Nations (responding to uncertainty over the availability of permanent institutions for maintaining peace in times of crisis). Dahl (1984) and Nagel (1975) also use this consequential property of uncertainty in defining political power.

all affected by uncertainty. This property poses a considerable challenge because it can defeat theoretical efforts or lead to only abstract generalities lacking in empirical referents or concrete insights. However, political uncertainty is neither intractable nor all of one form, as I shall demonstrate, and discernible patterns can differ significantly between one form of uncertainty and another. The different patterns of political uncertainty – randomness is not all uniform – which occur within a system of principles constitute an important topic in this book. The ubiquity of uncertainty provides a valuable opportunity, not an obstacle for political theory.

Finally, political uncertainty is ineradicable, because nothing humanly possible can be done to eliminate it. Uncertainty is inexpungible from politics. At best, "systematic political analysis can reduce some of that uncertainty" (Dahl 1984: 6). Rather than ignoring or avoiding political uncertainty, the study of politics should therefore aim directly toward understanding it. My view is that these properties and others that I analyze in this book must be used constructively, as conceptual building blocks, to obtain some new insights into politics based on its inherent uncertainty, and to help integrate the core areas of general political research (the elements in the intersection of politics in figure 1.1) and increase the accumulation of knowledge in our discipline.

1.1.2   *History and political uncertainty*

The core properties of political uncertainty I have just highlighted – consequentiality, ubiquity, and ineradicability – were known to early political thinkers from both Western and Eastern traditions. Thinkers as dissimilar as Aristotle (in the *Politics*), Sun-Tzu (*The Art of War*), and Niccolò Machiavelli (*The Prince* and *Discourses*) recognized these constitutional features of political life and wrote about them extensively, if not theoretically. Also, since antiquity, these properties have been acknowledged in both contexts of general politics – domestic and international. For example, as described by Machiavelli ([1512] 1965: 897) in one of his *Familiar Letters* to Piero Soderini,

Certainly anybody wise enough to understand the times and the types of affairs and to adapt himself to them would have always good fortune, or he would protect himself always from bad, and it would come to be true that the wise man would rule the stars and the Fates. But because there never are such wise men, since men in the first place are shortsighted and in the second place cannot command their natures, it follows that Fortune varies and commands men and holds them under her yoke.

Machiavelli's observation clearly covers both domestic and international politics, being a statement about general politics.

Paradoxically, political uncertainty remained an unsolved mystery throughout the Renaissance, in spite of scientific advances in understanding uncertainty through the concept of probability (Bochner 1966). None of the great classical political thinkers prior to the eighteenth century – occidental or oriental – developed a theory of political uncertainty. Political science might have evolved quite differently had Machiavelli studied Girolamo Cardano's *Liber de Ludo Aleæ* (The Book of Games of Chance), the first treatise on mathematical probability (Ore 1953).[4] Or, shortly after, had Thomas Hobbes (a friend of Galileo Galilei) used the mathematical theory of probability and the fledgling theory of social choice to formalize the *Leviathan* problematique – among sovereigns, state of war, and anarchy (Niou and Ordeshook 1990, 1994; Taylor 1987: ch. 7) – perhaps allowing political science to develop ahead of economics, no doubt with intriguing consequences. Many of the formal elements existed, although clearly not all (game theory). Unfortunately, Cardano's seminal work, unlike *The Prince*, was published posthumously in 1661, more than a century after Machiavelli's death, and probably not early enough for Hobbes to learn and apply.

In the Western world, the uncertainty of politics was first studied scientifically during the time of the French Revolution. This was due primarily to the pioneering work of giants such as Marie Jean de Condorcet, Pierre-Simon de Laplace, and Siméon Denis Poisson.[5] The scientific study of

[4] Machiavelli ([1512] 1965: 954) had a clear (if undeveloped) understanding of decision making under uncertainty, as evidenced by the following observation written to ambassador Francesco Vettori, his benefactor, on December 20, 1514:

> When a prince is forced to take one of two courses, he ought to consider among other things where the bad fortune of either of these can bring him. Then always, other things being equal, he ought to take that course which, if in the end it is bad, will be least bitter.

Similarly, in his second letter to Vettori, he notes:

> All wise men, when it is possible for them not to gamble all their property, are glad not to do so, and considering the worst that can come of it, they consider where in the evil before them the smallest evil appears. Because the things of Fortune are all doubtful, they will join willingly that Fortune who, doing the worst she can, will bring the least harsh end.

These and other observations clearly indicate that Machiavelli had at least an intuitive understanding – if not a formal mathematical grasp – of political decision making under uncertainty. Besides outlining the main structure of a decisional problem (the framework of alternatives, states of nature, utilities, and probabilities), both statements also reflect a clear understanding of risk aversion and what would eventually be formulated by Savage (1951) as the minimax regret criterion.

[5] Political uncertainty had been present much earlier, at least as a concept, in the works of Herodotus (*The History*) and Thucydides (*History of the Peloponnesian War*), both from the fifth century BC. However, it was not recognized as a worthwhile theoretical element in political theory until much later. After Machiavelli's reasoned analysis of *Fortuna politica*, the first scientific seminal works were produced during the Enlightenment, by de Condorcet (1785), de Laplace (1812), and Poisson (1837, 1853). It was no coincidence that some of these scholars were also pioneers in the development of rational choice theories of politics, an area of the discipline with foundations in political uncertainty.

political uncertainty during the French Revolution was no accident, because the explosion in mass popular participation (Ortega y Gasset 1957) increased political uncertainty to what at the time must have seemed an all-time high, so that an unprecedented number of common people for the first time became involved in the affairs of government – the entire nation, as Napoleon would say. It was Poisson's scientific exchange with Laplace concerning the uncertain behavior of the newly formed popular juries that produced the now famous Poisson distribution.[6]

In the twentieth century, many of the seminal works that deal with aspects of political uncertainty have done so in a fragmented way that has overlooked the powerful unifying role of uncertainty in politics.[7] For example, as I show later in this book, the same basic structure and properties of uncertainty are found in political phenomena as diverse as the implementation of government policies (Landau 1973; Pressman and Wildavsky 1973), the problem of collective action (Olson 1965; Sandler 1992), or the onset and development of conflict.[8] In each case the behavioral outcome of these political processes – whether policy implementation, collective action, war, or any of the others in figure 1.1 – is governed by the same pattern of uncertainty and is therefore explained by the same political principles. Similarly, the probabilistic forces (risk hazards) that govern the onset and termination of wars[9] follow analogous principles to the forces that govern the rise and fall of governmental coalitions (Cioffi-Revilla 1984; King et al. 1990). The specific political structures and forces differ across contexts (domestic and international), but only in details. The general principles they obey are uniform.

For as long as politics has existed – during the past five millennia of human history (Cioffi-Revilla 1996; De Laet 1994), possibly longer – uncertainty has played an important causal role in explaining political behavior, often under the guise of "incomplete information" at the individual or group level (Ferejohn and Kuklinski 1990; McKelvey and Ordeshook 1986, 1987; Niemi and Weisberg 1972). Today, in the post-Cold

[6] Unfortunately, modern classic works in probability (e.g. Feller 1968; Parzen 1960) maintain the mistaken impression that the Poisson model was somehow imported into the social sciences from physics (e.g. where it is used to model radioactive decay). In fact the opposite is true. The Poisson model and many aspects of probability theory are mathematical developments inspired by the investigation of social phenomena, similar to deontic logic, game theory, decision theory, fuzzy sets theory, some aspects of graph theory, and catastrophe theory. Regrettably, I am not aware of any comprehensive survey of these branches of mathematics inspired by human (as opposed to physical) phenomena.

[7] Specifically, I refer to the following classic works: Arrow (1951, 1956), Black (1958), de Pietri-Tonelli (1941, 1943), Deutsch (1966), Downs (1957), Pareto (1897), Richardson (1919, 1952, 1960a, 1960b), von Neumann and Morgenstern ([1947] 1972), and Wright (1942).

[8] See Cioffi-Revilla (1987), Cioffi-Revilla and Dacey (1988), Deutsch (1978: 159), and Wright (1942).

[9] See Cioffi-Revilla (1985a, 1985c, 1989), Richardson (1960a), and Weiss (1963).

War age, uncertainty is viewed as "a prime characteristic of turbulent politics" (Rosenau 1990: 8), and continues to play a central role in the production of "collective goods programs" (Baron 1996). Political uncertainty lies at the very foundations of contemporary positive political theory, providing a basis for standard utilitarian choice theories (Lalman et al. 1993) and others based on different mechanisms (e.g. Beer et al. 1987; Quattrone and Tversky 1988; Stone et al. 1995). Mounting empirical evidence also suggests that political uncertainty, or "lack of structural clarity" (Singer 1989), may also be a significant cause of war in the international system (Burns 1958; McClelland 1968; Midlarsky 1975). Uncertainty is just as critical for understanding political cooperation: "Agreements that are impossible to make under conditions of uncertainty may become feasible when uncertainty has been reduced," and "information-rich institutions that reduce uncertainty may make agreements possible in a future crisis" (Keohane 1984: 246–7). Political uncertainty, along with pressure for compromise, causes interest groups to create bureaucracies "that undermine effectiveness and insulate against democratic control" (Moe and Wilson 1994: 5). Fortunately for the continued growth of political science, uncertainty per se does not place politics outside the realm of systematic inquiry. Rather, it provides an opportunity for developing political theory and advancing our understanding.

1.1.3   *Uncertainty and contemporary political science*

Although uncertainty is widely acknowledged as a defining and perennial feature in most areas of general politics (figure 1.1), much of contemporary political science in fact still uses a "variance" paradigm (Casti 1990; Mohr 1982) that tends to overlook uncertainty. Perhaps this is done in order to maximize parsimony at the expense of realism (Occam's razor), consistent with Dahl's epigraph at the beginning of this chapter.[10] In most standard approaches, uncertainty is not accepted as a hard fact of political life, which the political scientist tries to understand in a systematic fashion.[11] Rather, most extant frameworks often equate randomness (behavior governed by probabilistic causality, which is scientifically knowable) with haphazard behavior (behavior not obeying any systematic scientific laws, which is

---

[10] Influential works promoting the variance paradigm have been Blalock (1989), Shively (1989), and Tufte (1974).

[11] Interestingly, the roots of this perspective are also to be found in the Enlightenment. For example, according to Elster (1993: 45), "Tocqueville argued that in democratic societies, stability requires an effort to banish chance, as much as possible, from the world of politics," while "to Veyne's mind, the greatest danger for authoritarian societies is a universalistic system of social mobility in which promotion is by merit rather than by chance." See note 2 above.

unknowable).[12] This common confusion is lamentable, because it effectively diminishes the objective uncertainty of politics to the status of purely artificial statistical entities, such as error terms, measurement errors, or the scientifically unknowable. Today, even in physics – the "mother of causality in science" – the determinism of the traditional covariational framework has long been replaced by probabilistic causality (Bohm 1957), particularly when dealing with the most elementary phenomena (microfoundations). I believe the conclusion to be drawn from these developments is not that a science of politics is impossible simply because uncertainty is so ubiquitous, consequential, and ineradicable; but rather that our choice is between a rigorous understanding of politics, which must include uncertainty, or no understanding at all. God *does* play dice with politics, but the outcomes are patterned, not haphazard.

Informally, the philosopher of history D. H. Fischer has described probabilistic causality as follows:

What is a causal explanation? It is an attempt to explain the occurrence of an event by reference to some of those antecedents which rendered its occurrence probable... A historian, and indeed a natural scientist, can never assert that an effect will always happen but only that it will probably happen. The connection between cause and effect is not necessary but probabilistic. (Fischer 1970: 183–4)

Probabilistic causality involves more than this, as I explain in this book. The task for scientists must be to recognize and explain patterns of politics with all its uncertainty. As I show in this book, the uncertainty of politics contains describable, explainable, and insightful patterns that can be understood scientifically. By contrast, haphazard behavior has neither logic nor pattern, and – by definition – is not knowable. An important goal for political science must be to systematically describe and explain the logic and pattern of political uncertainty across social phenomena.

Three research areas of the "divided discipline" of political science (Almond 1990) acknowledge uncertainty. The first, as I mentioned earlier, is in the use of utility and game-theoretic approaches to construct rational choice theories of politics, in which events, probabilities, utilities, acts, and states of nature provide building blocks for explaining politics.[13] The second area that considers uncertainty also focuses on political choice behavior, but from a variety of nonutilitarian perspectives,

---

[12] This misconception (e.g. Almond and Genco 1977; Singer and Wildavsky 1996: xiv) – that theories must be deterministic to be causal – owes much of its currency to Hempel's (1965) earlier work, in which determinist models were portrayed as the only form of theorizing. I hope to contribute to a better understanding of explanation in politics by using contemporary (post-Hempelian) probabilistic causality.

[13] See, for example, recent overviews by, Brams (1985), Lalman et al. (1993), Morrow (1994), Ordeshook (1986), and Weisberg (1986), based on the earlier pioneering works of Arrow (1951), Black (1958), Downs (1957), and Olson (1965).

including prospect theory (Kahneman and Tversky 1979) and choice mechanisms such as incremental satisfycing (Simon 1955), cognitive balancing (Heider 1958), or priming activation (Anderson 1983).[14] The third is in the use of stochastic approaches to construct probabilistic theories of politics, in which random variables and distribution functions provide building blocks for explaining politics (Casstevens and Casstevens 1989; Cioffi-Revilla 1989; King 1989a; Midlarsky 1981; Schrodt 1985). Studies in these three areas of political uncertainty have significantly but separately advanced our understanding of politics – a contribution that has been noted in some assessments of accumulation of knowledge in political science (Lichbach 1992).

The use of probabilistic causality in understanding uncertainty in some of the core areas of general politics (figure 1.1) has been significant for achieving scientific progress in those areas. For example, the probabilistic study of political coalitions has undergone significant progress using probabilistic causality, as demonstrated by comparing early works (e.g. Blondel 1968) with more recent probabilistic investigations (Cioffi-Revilla 1984; King et al. 1990; Warwick and Easton 1992). Similarly, but in a different area, today we know more than Lewis F. Richardson or Quincy Wright – the first modern scholars to scientifically study war – about conflicts of various magnitudes and their causes, both domestic and international. This has been thanks to numerous probabilistic studies during the past fifty years. Many of these advances in general politics – crossing the traditional sub-disciplinary boundaries of domestic and international politics – have provided valuable premises for the theory presented in this book.

In spite of recorded progress in separate areas of political science using decision-theoretic, game-theoretic, or probabilistic studies, several enduring problems motivate the need for a deeper understanding of political uncertainty that can only be provided by a general unified theory. First, that uncertainty is not simply present in political life, but that it plays a *defining* role in politics, must be more widely recognized and creatively exploited as fertile ground for unifying general core areas of theory and research. This property of political uncertainty also holds considerable promise for improving the design and implementation of policy in the public domain. General principles of political uncertainty must exist or uncertainty could not possibly be so ubiquitous in politics. Probabilistic causality is an epistemology that can protect political theory from extremes

---

[14] The set of decisional mechanisms involved in nonutilitarian political choice is still incomplete, but it is clearly nonempty. Below (section 1.2) I provide a brief inventory for heuristic purposes only, and later (chapter 7) I examine this multimode problem from a more analytical perspective.

such as nihilism and radical utilitarian reductionism; it should therefore be examined.

Second, game and decision theories of politics are rooted in the uncertain occurrence of events, not just in preferences, whether as decisional acts or as states of nature (Jeffrey 1983; Tsebelis 1989), not the reverse. Thus, without general principles that account directly for the substantive uncertainty of politics, politics is reduced to a system of utilitarian reductionism (Suppes 1984, ch. 8), which offers no explanation for political acts down to their causal roots. For example, pure expected-utility models of political decisions can overlook the consequential fact that probability – the prime measure of uncertainty – is *always* a nonlinear property of political events (von Neumann and Morgenstern [1947] 1972: §3, 8–10), and therefore often is counterintuitive as well.[15] By contrast, utility can be linear, even if in most practical situations utilities are nonlinear. Consequently, the uncertainty of events or outcomes in political decisions, particularly when these are viewed as "equilibrium solutions" (Riker 1990: 176), induces greater complexity and potential instability of equilibria than does their utility. Logically, therefore, the probabilistic foundations of politics must take precedence even over other such basic (microfoundational) phenomena as decisions. The explanation of utilitarian political behavior can be informed by a better understanding of its foundations, including other nonutilitarian causal mechanisms that may account for observed decisional acts. Significantly, as Green and Shapiro (1994: 185) emphasize, "to concede this is not to embrace the position that such phenomena cannot be studied scientifically, only that they [decisions] may be governed by causal mechanisms that are qualitatively different from those governing instrumental behavior." Both utilitarian and nonutilitarian foundations can be enriched by a theory of political uncertainty because strict determinism in political choice is a serious alternative only in extreme situations that – by their very nature – usually lack political interest. As I discuss below (section 1.2), the microfoundations of politics lie deeper than the level of decisions; they lie in the outcomes and events that underlie a decision, as well as in the outcomes and events that are framed within it.[16]

Third, while few would deny that the most consequential political phenomena – reforms, domestic turmoil, elections, coalition behavior, crises, or wars – occur with characteristic (diacritic) uncertainty, thus far political science as a discipline has lacked a general and empirically grounded

---

[15] Briefly, the strict nonlinearity of the probability of an event derives from the nature of causal conjunction and disjunction, neither one of which produces linear effects on political uncertainty, as I demonstrate in detail in chapter 6.

[16] As summarized by Maoz (1990: 39), "decision making is a process, not an act of choice," so it is necessarily composed of more elementary events and lotteries.

theory for explaining and testing diverse forms of observed political uncertainty, not just the simple Poisson case.[17] As I demonstrate in this book, political uncertainty has many forms and, remarkably, all of them operate within a uniform and elegant system of principles. While some of this uniformity and elegance may be mathematically induced, one cannot help but wonder whether they also arise from deeper, natural patterns that are found in human behavior, just as uniform and elegant principles exist in the physical world. As I show in each chapter, formal properties such as symmetry, duality, and fractal hierarchy are commonly present across levels of analysis in the study of political uncertainty. Paradoxically, therefore, while uncertainty itself may seem an enigmatic phenomenon, the principles of political uncertainty have remarkable clarity and precision.

Finally, contemporary political science, unlike economics, physics, musicology, or theology, does not yet seem to have a monopoly on the systematic investigation of its own subject matter – politics and government are also studied in anthropology, archeology, geography, sociology, economics, philosophy, and history. Nevertheless, a general theory of political uncertainty with principles that were applicable across different domains of political life in time and space – covering diverse political systems, processes, and events – would be useful in the ongoing explorations of related allied fields that look to political science for guidance. This broader interest regards the uncertain evolution of polities in various historical epochs and societies throughout the world – a vast area of systematic investigation that today is proceeding quite rapidly, independent of developments in contemporary political science. This broader interest in the understanding of political uncertainty extends primarily to the following disciplines:

- political history, investigating the causal logic structure and dynamic evolution of long-term political trends, as evidenced by the empirical record of individuals, groups, or institutions;[18]
- political anthropology and archeology, exploring the uncertain rise and decline of political societies and civilizations since the time of their remote origins in antiquity;[19]

---

[17] The misconception in social science that equates one-on-one the notion of randomness with the Poisson distribution is also common, as illustrated by the following statement based on Richardson's work: "If wars occur at random, one would expect the number of wars beginning each year to conform to the Poisson distribution" (Mansfield 1988: 28). This is a widespread misconception. As I show later in this book (chapter 4), *random* political phenomena are *not* always Poisson distributed (discussed also in Cioffi-Revilla 1985a, 1985b, 1985c; Horvath 1968; Petersen 1987, 1991; Weiss 1963), because randomness has many other interesting forms besides the Poisson case.

[18] See Adams ([1896] 1959), Burns (1960), Dawson (1978), Dray (1960), Floud (1973), Kennedy (1987), Mandelbaum (1942), Quigley (1961), Roberts (1993), Shirer (1960), Teggart (1942, [1925] 1977).

[19] See Binford (1965), Carneiro (1970), Culbert (1973), Flannery (1972), Marcus (1992), Renfrew (1979, 1984), Service (1975), Upham (1990), Willey (1991), Wright (1977).

- political sociology, examining the same uncertain political processes from a broader and more contemporary social perspective;[20]
- political economy, one of the founding social sciences that first recognized the significance of political uncertainty.[21]

These allied disciplines explore important aspects of the uncertain evolution of groups, states, empires, and other polities, but these investigations proceed without much assistance from contemporary political science. Results in these allied fields should also help inform the development of political theory. Thus, reliable insights on the multiple origins (pleogenesis) of the state as a stable form of political system (Carneiro 1970; Eisenstadt 1985; Roberts 1993) and its developmental evolutionary stages (Service 1975; Willey 1991), or findings on the uncertain pattern of rise and fall of states (Culbert 1973; Kennedy 1987; Olson 1982; Renfrew 1979), or inferences on the nature of the collective action problems that are involved in all of the events above (Arrow 1951; Coleman 1973; Olson 1965; Sandler 1992) represent developments that obviously should not be ignored by political science. Conversely, these other allied disciplines should not ignore fundamental developments in political science. A general theory of politics founded on uncertainty could help provide a language for interdisciplinary dialog and further theoretical growth.

1.2   Areas of political uncertainty

How is political uncertainty manifested? What unites and separates its different manifestations? Do types of uncertainty in areas of politics suggest guidelines for theory building? Are some types of political uncertainty more common, and, if so, why? Political uncertainty comes in too many idiosyncratic varieties to specify in full detail, nor is it necessary to do so. However, to begin systematizing this puzzle, it is useful to identify several kinds of uncertainty that occur across areas of political science. Later (section 1.3) I shall use the inventory which follows to develop a more formal typology.

Uncertainty in political probabilities. Uncertainty occurs explicitly in the following important political probabilities: the "probability of winning an election" (Brams 1985), the "probability of integration" (Deutsch 1978), the "probability of policy implementation" (Morgan and Henrion 1990; Pressman and Wildavsky 1973), the "probability of domes-

---

[20] See Blalock (1989), Chase-Dunn and Hall (1996), Coleman (1973), Davies (1962), Eisenstadt (1985, [1963] 1993), Parsons (1969), Skocpol and Somers (1980), Sorokin (1937).
[21] See Arrow (1951, 1956), de Condorcet (1785), de Pietri-Tonelli (1941, 1943), Granger (1956), Olson (1965, 1982), Sandler (1992), Schelling (1978), Schofield (1975).

tic political conflict,"[22] or the "probability of war."[23] Less formally, many ways of expressing our understanding of politics – expressions like "the chance of ..." or "the likelihood that ..." – are common forms of political discourse, although they may not always be exact. If these terms that express political probabilities are to be meaningful, a systematic treatment of the uncertainty involved is necessary, particularly since even experts show considerable errors in their judgment (Chan 1982).

Uncertainty in political "-bilities." Political uncertainty is implicit in another set of classical probabilistic concepts, although the probabilistic character is often hidden by other labels. Examples include "governability," "stability," "credibility," "reliability," "feasibility," or "verifiability." These and other political "-bilities" usually denote some important probabilistic concept that is being defined in the context of some other significant or consequential political event. For example, letting "$\mathbf{P}(\mathbb{Y})$" denote "the probability of the political event $\mathbb{Y}$," one can redefine the above terms as:[24]

> Governability = $\mathbf{P}$(a polity maintains governance capacity)
> Stability   = $\mathbf{P}$(disturbances do not change a given political equilibrium)
> Credibility   = $\mathbf{P}$(a political communication is believed)
> Reliability   = $\mathbf{P}$(political performance is maintained for a given time)
> Feasibility   = $\mathbf{P}$(a policy can be effectively implemented)
> Verifiability = $\mathbf{P}$(an agreement can be ascertained)

Thus, this second form of political uncertainty can be redefined in terms of the first, because each political "-bility" refers to the probability of a political event ($\mathbb{Y}$) that is judged to be significant.

Uncertainty in individual decisions. Uncertainty enters into individual decisions in several ways. First, political choice is affected by uncertainty as to the nature of the precise mechanism used by an actor in a given decisional situation. As summarized in table 1.1, several choice mechanisms are employed in political decision making and not all of them are presently well

---

[22] See, for example, Lichbach (1992) for a comparative review of stochastic models and other mathematical approaches to domestic political conflict.

[23] See, for example, Avenhaus et al. (1989), Bueno de Mesquita and Lalman (1992), Cioffi-Revilla (1987), Cioffi-Revilla and Dacey (1988), Good (1966), Hussein (1987), Nicholson (1989), and Wright (1942).

[24] In appendix 2, I describe the notational system used throughout this book. Thus, I use the symbol $\mathbb{Y}$ to denote these political events as the referent occurrences to be explained (*explananda*), similar to the familiar convention for a dependent (denoted by Y) and an independent variable (X).

Table 1.1. *Mechanisms of political choice*

Mechanism[a]	Original source	Applications	Comments
1 Practical syllogism	Aristotle ([384–322 BC] 1941)	Numerous	"Good reasons" are sufficient causes for chosen acts
2 Deontic logic	14th century AD; von Wright (1951, 1971)	Dacey (1991), Hilpinen (1971, 1981)	Moral obligation. See also Klosko (1990)
3 Economic utilitarian	Bayes (1764/65), Savage (1951)	Arrow (1951), Black (1958), Buchanan (1968), von Neumann and Morgenstern (1947)	Dominant contemporary theory of political choice
4 Instinctive reaction[b]	Richardson (1919, 1960a)	Gillespie and Zinnes (1975), Huckfeldt et al. (1982), Ward (1982)	Uncertainty in parameter values and functional form
5 Satisfycing	Simon (1955, 1956)	Davis et al. (1966)	Also known as political incrementalism, bounded rationality
6 Justified procedure	Suppes (1957, 1984)	Rawls (1971)	Procedural justice not the only application
7 Cognitive balance	Heider (1958)	Abelson (1959)	Lottery among balancing mechanisms
8 Fuzzy logic	Zadeh (1965)	Cioffi-Revilla (1981), Sanjian (1988a, 1988b)	Ambiguity as a form of uncertainty
9 Elimination by attributes	Tversky (1972)	Stone et al. (1995)	Path-dependent uncertainty
10 Prospect theory	Kahneman and Tversky (1979)	Levy (1992), Quattrone and Tversky (1988)	Subjective estimates
11 Priming activation	Anderson (1983)	Beer et al. (1987, 1995)	Multiple aspects of uncertainty

[a] Listed in chronological order by approximate date of invention. These mechanisms are neither exhaustive nor mutually exclusive.

[b] Arrow (1956: 34–5) and Harsanyi (1962: 696–7) were among the first critics of Richardson's action–reaction model (mechanism 4). Brito (1972) provided the first explicit derivation of Richardson's model based on a generalized quadratic utility function from an economic model (mechanism 3).

Source: prepared by the author. Thanks to Francis A. Beer, Raymond Dacey, Jon Elster, Donald P. Green, Amnon Rapoport, Ian Shapiro, and Walter Stone for their comments.

understood.[25] Moreover, the choice of a specific decisional mechanism can be a matter of intrinsic political interest – as, for example, the choice between a deontic mode based on moral obligation and a utilitarian mode based on pure self-interest. Second, uncertainty exists within each decisional mechanism, even within those that seem the most deterministic (e.g. table 1.1, mechanism 4, instinctive reaction).

Thus, in the standard Bayesian decision model (mechanism 3), uncertainty can exist in a political decision situation in two primary ways: (i) with regard to the outcomes or consequences of acts, given various conditions or states of nature (decision making under risk); or (ii) with regard to the probabilities or desirability-utility values themselves (decision making under uncertainty). Both kinds of uncertainty are common in political decisions. Again, Machiavelli ([1512] 1965: 897) had an early understanding of the effects of uncertainty on the outcomes of individual decisions:

> Because times vary and affairs are of varied types, one man's desires come out as he had prayed they would; he is fortunate who harmonizes his procedure with his time, but on the contrary he is not fortunate who in his actions is out of harmony with his time and with the type of its affairs. Hence it can well happen that two men working differently come to the same end, because each them adapts himself to what he encounters, for affairs are of as many types as there are provinces and states. Thus, because times and affairs in general and individually change often, and men do not change their imaginings and their procedures, it happens that a man at one time has good fortune and at another time bad.

Uncertainty can also exist in other aspects of individual political decision making, such as in the nature of outcomes (political or other consequences), in the variety of relevant states of nature (contingencies), in the interaction between probabilities and utilities (interdependence), in cognitive phenomena, and through kinematics (changes in any of the above).[26]

Besides utilitarian mechanisms, uncertainty is also present in other mechanisms of political choice identified in table 1.1. For example, uncertainty is commonly present in cognitive balancing (e.g. how is balance attained – by differentiation, transcendence, bolstering, or denial?); in elimination by attributes (which attributes are decided first?); or in pros-

---

[25] Interestingly, only mechanisms 4 (instinctive reaction) and 5 (satisfycing) in table 1.1 originate directly from the study of politics. Perhaps also mechanism 1 (practical syllogism) and 6 (justified procedure) were closely inspired by politics. All the others originated outside of politics.

[26] Uncertainty originating from cognitive phenomena concerns subjective perceptions of decisional elements (probabilities and utilities). See Levy (1992), Tversky and Kahneman (1992) and, more generally, Graber (1993) on political communication and information processing.

pect mechanisms (how are the weighting functions determined?). Each decisional mechanism in table 1.1 is affected by some form of uncertainty.

Uncertainty in interactive decisions. When decisional conditions or states of nature are produced by the acts (strategies) of other individuals (players), then a game situation exists (interdependent decision making). Uncertainty enters into these decisions in even more ways than in those already indicated for an individual decision situation, primarily as incomplete information. A player may not know the exact preferences or even the strategies of the other player(s), as in electoral competitions with "probabilistic voting."[27] The duration of the interaction (length of game) may be uncertain, as well as some of its most important consequences.

Uncertainty in collective outcomes. Beyond the decisional level, collective consequences are another type of common uncertainty in politics, often involving the joint effects of decisional acts and states of nature. For example, in any two-person 2×2 game each of the four outcomes occurs as a collective outcome, not as a unilaterally determined choice. (Formally, each player choses a lottery of disjunctive outcomes, not an outcome uniquely determined by an act.) Accordingly, uncertainty exists because neither choice is made under certainty. Uncertainty typically increases as the number of players, the length of the game, or lack of information increase. Voting cycles, preference intransitivities, multiple equilibria, strategic uncertainty, and coalition indeterminacy are among the common effects of uncertainty in collective outcomes. An intriguing aspect of uncertainty in collective outcomes has to do with their "resultant" or "emergent" properties (Eulau 1996; Landau 1969, 1979; Lasswell 1935, 1936).

Uncertainty in collective action. Collective goods are particularly important political outcomes with inherently uncertain occurrence and diversity (law and order, national defense, other governmental and collective goods which have a social or collective purpose). Political conflict (revolutions and wars) and cooperation (coalitions and institutions) involve many significant, albeit uncertain, aspects of collective action and public goods. Which members will join a coalition? When will it form? How long will it last? These and other questions always have uncertainty as part of the answer.

Uncertainty in political processes. Uncertainty exists in many important

---

[27] See, for example, Coughlin (1992), Enelow et al. (1993), Enelow and Hinich (1984), Erickson and Romero (1990). See also Green and Shapiro (1994: 159–66) for a critical evaluation of the probabilistic voting research program.

large-scale political processes, such as the evolution of political culture and beliefs, institutions, public opinion, political participation, or processes of international systemic structure and balance of power. These processes containing uncertainty can represent a significant source of political tension, with its own set of consequences. In the classic domestic process of democratic governance (Almond et al. 1996), uncertainty exists throughout the entire "circular flow of influence characteristic of representative government" (Bendor and Moe 1985: 757), such that:

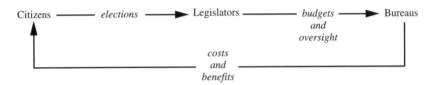

where arrows represent types of influence and each stage contains decisions and lotteries with their own uncertainty. Institutional structures can also affect decisional outcomes (structure-induced equilibria, as opposed to preference-induced equilibria).

In the case of balance of power processes in world politics, analysis indicates that the relationship between power distribution and war probability depends critically upon, inter alia, a set of uncertainties, including the probability of enforcement and other subjective probability estimates (Wagner 1994). These recent results parallel earlier results (Selten and Tietz 1966a, 1966b) on the uncertainty of international security equilibria as conditioned by power distribution and other contextual data (structure-induced uncertainty).

Note that the large-scale (macroscopic) nature of these social processes does not seem to detract much from their uncertainty. By contrast, in physical processes the large scale often induces a fair amount of predictability. Uncertainty is common in both small- and large-scale political phenomena.[28]

Uncertainty in political change. Uncertainty exists in the magnitude and direction of significant forms of political change, an important situation commonly found in domestic or comparative and international politics. Uncertainty in political change differs from contextual uncertainty. Changes in voter turnout, party alignment ("realignment"), government policy, domestic regime transitions, changes in levels of conflict, interna-

---

[28] Computational modeling approaches offer a promising strategy for modeling uncertainty in political processes (Taber and Timpone 1994, 1996).

tional alliance shifts, or global institutions are commonly accompanied by uncertainty, yet their magnitude and direction remain clearly significant for theoretical and policy reasons.

Uncertainty in governmental policy. Uncertainty exists at every stage of the governmental policy process (stages model), as well as in the context or environment of policy. Every stage – problem identification, policy formulation, adoption, implementation, evaluation, and others – whether organized as a seemingly simple sequence (Pressman and Wildavsky 1973) or as a complex iterative process with learning (Morgan and Henrion 1990; Ostrom 1991; Sabatier 1991; Schlager and Blomquist 1995) – presents uncertainty. Moreover, this seems true of governmental policy at all levels, be it local (urban, metropolitan), state, national, regional (e.g. European Union regional policy, Group of Seven), or international (e.g. global, GATT policies, Law of the Seas). Policy uncertainty shows little regard for the concept of national sovereignty. Creating institutions is a common strategy for reducing policy uncertainty.

Uncertainty in policy analysis. Uncertainty exists not only in the real-world policy process, but is also part of the analysis of policy conducted by analysts, as a meta-problem. The real (as opposed to formal) source of a policy problem often presents uncertainty, or the real goals can be uncertain. The impacts or effects of policy can be uncertain. The choice of appropriate measures to evaluate performance can be unclear. The analysis of empirical data related to the policy problem (or to the policy process itself), as discussed next, includes numerous standard considerations of uncertainty. In other words, the analysis of policy is itself an uncertain process, just like any other process of inquiry. A similar type of uncertainty affects intelligence analysis (domestic or foreign), aimed at extracting reliable information from collected data.

Uncertainty in empirical analysis. Uncertainty is present in numerous ways in empirical political research, from observational issues of measurement and data collection, to problems of inference and interpretation (Dacey 1995; King 1989a; King et al. 1994; Viertl 1996). Uncertainty affects general classic problems like data validity and reliability (Carmines and Zeller 1979; Leege and Francis 1974), issues of type I and II errors, as well as more specialized problems of estimation and inference (Morgan and Henrion 1990: ch. 5). One way to view the purpose of data-reduction techniques (from factor analysis to regression) is as precisely aiming to reduce uncertainty – about relationships in the recorded data. Tests of estimates (point and interval) are designed to assess the uncertainty involved in inferring population parameters from sample values. The distribution and properties of the error term (stochastic component) in an empirical equation are also a model of uncertainty (King 1989a).

The summary above highlights the importance and centrality of uncertainty for political science, consistent with the earlier claim that uncertainty is ubiquitous, consequential, and ineradicable in political life.[29] A more parsimonious typology is presented below (section 1.3.1, axiom 1).

As I show in this book, political uncertainty can be unambiguously defined, and different types of uncertainty can be related to one another. The areas of political uncertainty discussed in this section, and others identified later, are fundamentally similar in several important respects. What is more important, they can all be treated within a unified general theory under a common set of principles deduced from a set of basic postulates on political uncertainty. I next turn to the foundations of such a framework.

1.3   General theoretical framework

If politics is inescapably and perennially uncertain, how can it be systematically described, explained, and predicted? How can it be rationally understood without denying its uncertainty? How can a general theory of politics be developed on foundations that are explicitly grounded on political uncertainty? What would be the scope of such a theory, and how would it relate to other concepts and theories in political science? In this book I present a new general theory of politics that accepts uncertainty, causal indeterminacy, and probabilistic causality – cardinal properties of politics well known to scholars and practitioners alike – as substantive features of political life. Although causal – well-defined causes (independent variables/ events) are used to explain politics (dependent variables/events) – the theory is realistic, to explain politics with all its natural uncertainty.[30]

---

[29] Other cases exist, which are not detailed here. For example, uncertainty in hermeneutic analysis occurs with respect to the original meaning or intent of historical sources (Cioffi-Revilla 1996: 4–8), including the possibility of type I and II errors. Uncertainty in chaos models (nonlinear differential equations with some special properties) is examined from a deterministic perspective (Aracil and Toro 1984; Brown 1995; Devaney 1987; Ornstein 1989; Pool 1989), where small variations in initial conditions can produce pseudorandom behavior (butterfly effect). Uncertainty in political discourse is reflected by terms such as "likely," "even-odds," or "somewhat improbable" (Beyth-Marom 1982; Maoz 1990; Wallsten et al. 1986).

[30] Bronowski (1978) and Suppes (1984) provide excellent discussions of causation in different deterministic and probabilistic frameworks, including the history of how each developed. See also Bohm (1957), Brand (1976), Bunge (1979), Cohen (1942), McIver (1942), Olinick (1978: 239–41), and essays by Suppes, Dupré, and others in French et al. (1984). A different approach, using fuzzy mathematics for capturing the *ambiguity* of politics, has significant potential but remains largely undeveloped in political science (Cioffi-Revilla 1981; Nowakowska 1977; Nurmi 1984; Saaty and Khouja 1976; Sanjian 1988a, 1988b, 1989; Zadeh 1965, 1968, 1973). Note that uncertainty and ambiguity are different concepts. The former

Methodologically, the new framework I propose involves the use of tools such as Boolean logic, nonlinear and maximum likelihood estimation, survival and event history analysis, and other techniques that go beyond ordinary least squares and standard correlational methods, as I illustrate in the following chapters. The use of these methods has two important objectives. The first is to explain and expand the theoretical foundations of these new methodological approaches in political science. The second is to promote the use of mathematics as a strategy for discovery in the investigation of politics, based on the thesis that formal methods are used in science to obtain new empirical insights, in addition to their more traditional role in building formal theory – what I call Klein's (1985) thesis.

The theory that results from this new framework is general, because it is applicable to classes of political events and classes of variables, as these are defined in general terms, meaning social behavior that affects the lives, fortunes, or government of collectivities. I use empirical phenomena from the study of conflict, coalition politics, political communication, integration, and other areas of political science as running examples to illustrate the general theory and to derive new and testable propositions, some of which can unite, revise, or challenge earlier findings in the literature. Variables such as the onset, magnitude, or duration of conflict (in domestic or international contexts) are emphasized, because war is a concrete case where uncertain political behavior is manifest, as well as a behavioral response to political uncertainty.[31] In the case of war, multiple causes are themselves an explanation for the uncertainty of war, so "any theory of the causes of war in general or of any war in particular that is not inherently eclectic and comprehensive ... is bound for that reason to be wrong" (Brodie 1973: 339).[32] In broader disciplinary terms, I believe the value of this theory should be judged by three classic standards: generality across areas and contexts of political science, or broad scope; fertility, or ability to yield deductive and testable propositions; and parsimony, or capacity to describe and explain a broad spectrum of political behavior in domestic and international contexts using a limited base of conceptual building blocks and principles.

As illustrated in figure 1.2 and table 1.2, the theory has two main branches, both of which are based on the common set of axioms described

deals with indeterminacy, whereas the latter deals with vagueness or imprecision. As qualitatively distinct traits, uncertainty and ambiguity are formalized by different formal languages – probability and fuzzy sets, respectively (Gaines 1978).

[31] See Garnham (1985), Midlarsky (1974), Rosenau (1990: 12), Snyder (1971: 19).

[32] One can also concur that "the central problem in strategic analysis is to deal with the pervasive uncertainty that is an unavoidable element in the link between 'real world' deterrence and the hypothetical ways by means of which we evaluate our deterrent posture. So far, this uncertainty has not received the analytical attention it deserves" (Sienkiewicz 1982: 217–18). I am grateful to David Goldfischer for bringing Sienkiewicz's work to my attention.

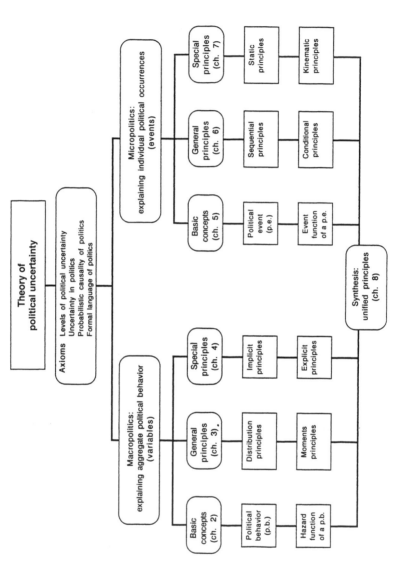

Figure 1.2. Theoretical framework

Table 1.2. *Theoretical framework and causal relations*

	Dual puzzles of political uncertainty	
Variables	Macropolitics: uncertain behavior of aggregate political variables	Micropolitics: uncertain occurrence of individual political events
Dependent	*Political behavior*	*Political occurrences*
Examples:	Time of occurrence, size, support, duration, and other dimensions of a coalition process	Coalition formation, dissolution, countercoalition challenge
Independent	*Risk hazards*	*Prior events*
Examples:	External challenges, internal dissent, socioeconomic (environmental) stress	Necessary events (linked by Boolean AND logic), or sufficient events (OR)
General causal model	*risk hazards →* *political variables,* *political variables* *= f(risk hazards)*	*prior events →* *political events,* *political events* *= f(prior events)*

below. The puzzle of uncertainty in politics presents dual aspects, depending on the level of analysis, each dealing with the uncertain behavior of aggregate political variables (the macro level of politics) and the uncertain occurrence of individual political events (micro level of politics). The former is caused by risk factors or hazard forces at the macro level; the latter is caused by decisional acts and states of nature at the micro level. I explain each level of analysis using concepts and principles within a unified framework based on probabilistic causality.

1.3.1   *Axioms for a new theory*

The traditional covariational approach to political inquiry has a deterministic orientation, based on two forms. In static form, given a dependent political variable Y (e.g. voter turnout at an election) and some independent "covariate" X (e.g. rate of inflation in the economy), the goal in a variance approach is to find a function ("specify" a model, possibly linear) such that each value y of the dependent variable Y can be predicted by a value x of the independent variable X, "plus or minus error." In kinematic form (e.g. as in a Richardsonian action–reaction model) the goal is to construct a model (dynamic system of differential equations) such that, given a set of initial conditions, all future states (political trajectories) are exactly predictable, as if actors behaved like inert masses obeying the rules of eighteenth-century Laplacean mechanics (Huckfeldt et al. 1982; Rapoport 1983; Richardson 1960a). The problems with this common form of determinism when applied to politics are well known and should not be ignored (Casti 1990: ch. 5). Many of them have been demonstrated elsewhere so I will not repeat them here, except to identify and challenge the basic assumptions of political determinism and propose a more appropriate scientific approach based on uncertainty as a fundamental property.[33]

My theory is based on four axioms or "core statements" (Moe 1979). I call these propositions "axioms," in the standard classical sense, because they state the most elementary positions on which I base my theory. These positions concern four key theoretical issues: the substance of politics according to levels of analysis, the role of political uncertainty, the nature of probabilistic causality in politics, and the formal language of political theory. As a system, the four axioms complement each other and jointly define a new view of politics. I believe these axioms are defensibly true propositions (realistic), as opposed to being "as if" postulates à la Friedman (1953) and von Mises (1957).

Levels of political uncertainty. The first axiom I propose addresses the uncertainty of politics by postulating two levels of analysis for understanding political phenomena.

Axiom 1 (on the levels of political uncertainty). *Politics is fundamentally uncertain at two distinct levels of analysis: political variables associated with aggregate macropolitical behavior* (e.g. "intensity of a riot," "duration of a coalition," "time of war onset," "length of legislative process," "size of a political coalition," "level of domestic instability") and *political events associated with individual micropolitical occurrences* ("a collective action problem is solved," "a revolution fails," "a new government is formed," "a crisis occurs," "deterrence fails," "war breaks out").

This first axiom establishes the basic orientation I take toward the nature of things that are called "political" – my conceptual orientation toward what operationally constitutes social behavior that "affects the lives, fortunes, or governance of collectivity." Axiom 1 indicates how I shall describe and explain politics at the most elementary analytical level that concerns uncertainty: by means of variables and events, not by other categories, corresponding to aggregate-macro and individual-micro politics, respectively. Accordingly, I view political systems, processes, institutions, policies, and other major substantive entities in political life as

---

[33] See, for example, Beck (1991), Conybeare (1990), King et al. (1994: ch. 3), Suppes (1984).

knowable in terms of variables and events, the most basic conceptual building blocks at the macro and micro levels of analysis.

The "level-of-analysis" perspective I adopt – distinguishing and relating political phenomena at various scales of aggregation that lie on a continuum between relatively small-scale individual occurrences and large-scale societal processes – is based on a classical paradigm of contemporary political science (Eulau 1963: 19–24, 123–7; 1996; Kaplan 1969; Lasswell 1935; Singer 1961; Waltz 1955), with both ancient and modern roots in scholastic and systemic approaches, respectively. With Eulau (1969: 17), I agree that "rather than thinking of micro and macro in dichotomous terms, the political scientist is better off if he thinks of a 'micro-macro continuum.' What in this continuum is micro and what is macro depends on the point of the micro–macro scale where the observable 'dips in,' where he fixes his object unit of analysis." And yet, even when viewed as a continuum, "the micro–macro gap" persists as an enduring puzzle in contemporary political science (Eulau 1996).

As a general political puzzle, the level-of-analysis perspective also raises an important problematique, concerning the linkages which exist across levels of analysis (the so-called "action–structure" or "agent–structure" problem), a puzzle present in diverse areas of politics (Lalman et al. 1993; Lichbach 1995; Russett and Starr 1996).[34] A viable approach to solving the classical puzzle of linking levels of analysis – albeit without claim to providing a unique solution – is outlined in the final chapter.

Axiom 1 represents a step in the direction of clarifying which rules of aggregation are necessary to calculate political behavior as uncertainty crosses analytical levels (as in the so-called "synergetic" problem; Haken 1978). Variables assume values, whereas events occur, so explanations of politics logically admit to these dual perspectives (macro and micro, respectively), depending on the focus of investigation.[35] Moreover, the two levels of this duality are related, as I demonstrate in the last chapter, because when an aggregate political variable assumes a given value (macro level) – for example, a political coalition forms with a given size, or has a given duration – this is an event (micro level). Conversely, when an individual political event occurs (micro level) this means that a corresponding

---

[34] The level-of-analysis problematique is also addressed by Coleman (1975: 13–15), Eulau (1969), Kaplan (1969: 8, 11, 28–33), Lasswell (1935, 1936), Maoz (1990), Schelling (1978), and Snyder (1996), among others. The most recent is found in Eulau (1996). Elster (1989: 3) postulates an equally fundamental dichotomy between *events* and *facts* in the social sciences. However, the dichotomy between variables and events is arguably more appropriate for understanding political uncertainty, because from the point of view of uncertainty facts can be related to both variables and events.

[35] A rare acknowledgment of this basic but important distinction – variables assume values, events occur – is found in Duvall (1976).

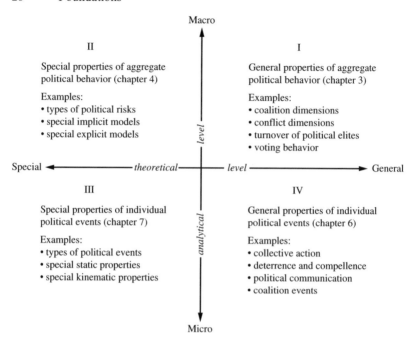

Figure 1.3. Typology of political uncertainty by analytical and theoretical levels

aggregate political variable (macro level) has realized a given value (e.g. coalition size = 3 allies, duration = 4.1 years). The equivalence between the two levels of this duality is key to understanding how the two main branches of my theory – the macropolitical part (chapters 2 through 4) and the micropolitical part (chapters 5 through 7) – are related and linked (chapter 8). Axiom 1 establishes these building blocks and, because the levels are related, this logically guarantees that the main parts of the theory are also related.

Besides providing the first theoretical building block, the level-of-analysis perspective also provides foundations for a more succinct typology of political uncertainty, shown in figure 1.3. When joined by the classic scientific distinction between general and special theoretical levels of analysis, these two types of levels yield four distinct areas of inquiry with well-focused concepts and principles:

1 general properties of aggregate political behavior (figure 1.3, upper-right, quadrant I), focusing on the macropolitical uncertainty of phenomena such as dimensions of coalition or conflict behavior (onsets, magnitudes, durations) and others;

2 special properties of aggregate political behavior (upper-left, quadrant II), focusing on narrower aspects of macropolitical behavior, such as types of political risk factors and their causal or functional form;

3 general properties of individual political events (lower-right, quadrant IV), focusing on the macropolitical uncertainty of phenomena such as the occurrence of a collective action event, deterrence and other threats, or events in the life of a coalition (formation, membership change, or dissolution); and

4 special properties of individual political events (lower-left, quadrant III), focusing on narrower aspects of micropolitical occurrences, such as distinct types of events, special static and kinematic aspects.

Each of these areas of inquiry on political uncertainty is treated in chapters 3, 4, 6, and 7, respectively, with chapters 2 and 5 serving as introductions to macro and micro branches of the theory. As illustrated in figure 1.2, general principles are presented in chapters 3 and 6 – these contain the core results of the theory – while special principles are presented in chapters 4 (macro) and 7 (micro). In spite of their formal name, special principles have numerous applications and extensions. I put forward some integrative results in chapter 8.

This typology of political uncertainty has several advantages. First, it reduces to four fundamental types the many kinds of uncertainty discussed in earlier sections of this chapter. For example, the kinds of uncertainty involved in processes or in political changes discussed in section 1.2 refer to aspects of uncertainty that pertain to aggregate behavior ("macropolitics"). In this case, as indicated earlier in table 1.2, various hazards or risk factors act as causal independent variables. The uncertainty involved in the "error term" of a statistical regression model is also of this type, representing the aggregation of departures from mean behavior. By contrast, the uncertainty involved in most "political probabilities" or in many collective outcomes of individual choice is commonly concerned with distinct occurrences that should be treated as individual events ("micropolitics"). The uncertainty of outcomes involved in decisional situations usually belongs to this class. In this case, several other necessary or sufficient events act as causal independent variables.

Second, the typology yields four classes of macro and micro types of political uncertainty, each with general and specific properties marked by basic concepts and principles in figure 1.2. This serves as a fertile heuristic framework to organize theoretical and empirical research over a relatively broad substantive domain. For example, the four areas in the typology of political uncertainty enable us to examine and compare, say, models of coalition behavior with models of conflict behavior, treating both within the same class of models when their pattern of uncertainty is similar.

Similarly, this enables us to understand the uniform principles of uncertainty that underlie, say, events of deterrence failure, collective action failure, coalition dissolution, and others. Axiom 1 establishes that the political uncertainty at each level of analysis, macro and micro, is similar.

Uncertainty in politics. The second axiom states my position on the nature of politics along the causal spectrum that ranges from the deterministic to the haphazard. This is an ontological issue with implications for how politics is to be understood.

Axiom 2 (on uncertainty in politics). *Politics – the behavior of aggregate political variables and the occurrence of individual political events as posited in axiom 1 – has consequential, ubiquitous, and ineradicable uncertainty, unlike deterministic phenomena.*

Put differently, axiom 2 states that the uncertainty of politics is essential, not accidental, to use Aristotelian terminology. From this perspective, axiom 2 also underlies those areas of general political science research highlighted earlier – decision making models and stochastic process models – where uncertainty is viewed as one of the fundamental puzzles (section 1.1.3).

The first implication I draw from axiom 2 for theory building is that a general theory of politics must directly address and be founded on substantive uncertainty, not on deterministic "as if" assumptions that avoid uncertainty. Eliminating the uncertainty of politics – the extreme in Dahl's epigraph – would be like depriving ethics of values, or taking wealth out of economics, because it would fundamentally denature the object of political science. Politics without uncertainty is like a flat Earth. It *can* exist in an abstract sense (as in the story in the two-dimensional world of Abbott's classical *Flatland*), but it is not part of the real world (Abbott 1952). Deterministic politics are purely hypothetical, although they may serve a heuristic purpose for technically exploring selected properties of the real political (and forever uncertain) world. For example, some of the first voting models were deterministic (Green and Shapiro 1994: 151–9), although recent models now include uncertainty (see note 22). Interaction dynamics between government and opposition have been modeled deterministically to explore instability or revolution as abstract possibilities.[36] But political turbulence is nothing abstract (Gaddis 1992; Rosenau 1990). Similarly, the longevity of cabinet coalitions in parliamentary democracies

---

[36] See, for example, Cortés et al. (1974), Huckfeldt (1989), Tsebelis and Sprague (1989), as well as others reviewed by Lichbach (1992).

has been studied deterministically.[37] But the uncertainty of cabinet durations remains incontestable and is now empirically well established (King et al. 1990). In world politics, arms accumulation processes between states in the international system have been modeled deterministically for more than half a century to understand what would happen "if statesmen did not stop to think" (Richardson 1960a: 12). But statesmen *do* think, so, logically, the inferences of deterministic models must apply to unreal statesmen.[38] In sum, deterministic approaches ("as if" simplifications of politics that emulate classical mechanics) may form a part of theoretical politics, just as the nonexistent *Amphioxus amoeba* inhabits the abstract world of theoretical biology (Ashby 1956), or similar to the way in which imaginary systems are studied in rational mechanics. But the behavior examined by deterministic models at best bears only coarse resemblance to real-world politics, missing the most interesting part. My position for a long time has been that real political life – with all its extant uncertainty – is and must remain the core concern of political science, and must resist the misleading lure of certainty.

Probabilistic causality. The third axiom addresses the nature of causal explanation most appropriate for the study of politics, or what I view as the form of causality that governs political phenomena.

Axiom 3 (on the probabilistic causality of politics). *The causality of politics – how to explain the uncertain behavior of aggregate political variables and the uncertain occurrence of individual political events – is probabilistic, not deterministic.*

As a prelude to my more detailed treatment of probabilistic causality in subsequent chapters, consider a simple bivariate relationship between a dependent political variable Y and some independent variable X, such that "X accounts for (causes) Y." To understand how explanation works in probabilistic causality, it may be useful to first recall how causation works in the more traditional case of deterministic "variance" causality in mainstream political science (correlational or regression models).[39] In essence,

---

[37] De Swaan (1973), Dodd (1976), Sanders and Herman (1977), Taylor and Herman (1971), Taylor and Laver (1973), Warwick (1979).

[38] See Schrodt (1976) for one of the earliest reformulations of arms race models in probabilistic terms, and Rapoport (1960, ch. 5) for an earlier critique of social physics.

[39] The epistemology of probabilistic causality – the successor to Hempel's older Laplacean determinism – is still relatively new in political science. The following standard references are useful: Bronowski (1978), Good (1961a, 1961b, 1962, 1972, 1980), Reichenbach (1956), Salmon (1971, 1980), Suppes (1970, 1984), and essays by Forge, Salmon, Glymour, and van Fraassen collected in McLaughlin (1982). Modern scientific theories use probabilistic causality when fundamental (substantive) uncertainty, not merely measurement error, is involved – as in particle physics (quantum mechanics), psychology (learning), biology (genetics), anthropology (cultural stability), and sociology (social mobility).

given Y with values in a given range $\{y\}$, and X with values in a domain $\{x\}$, there exists a function $Y(X)$ – the specified regression model – such that for every value x one can calculate an exact value y, plus or minus some measurement error. Note that in spite of the "error term" introduced by measurement inaccuracy (the error term in this type of model is *not* meant to capture any substantive political uncertainty because it is primarily a residual category that "does not fit"), the essence of these earlier approaches to causality – inspired by macrophysics and econometrics (Blalock 1964, 1989) – was to map a *single* value y for each value x. This is what a regression equation such as

$$Y = \alpha + \beta X + \varepsilon$$

means. Examples of this approach abound in the search for simple laws of politics, and some rare isolated cases of success do exist.[40] But as a general disciplinary ontology the deterministic project has largely failed. For example, in the study of conflict (dependent variable Y in the regression model) many analyses have searched in vain for the variance-deterministic relationship between dimensions of conflict and structural attributes (Midlarsky 1974; Lichbach 1989; Ostrom and Hoole 1978; Singer et al. 1972), or between war and alliances (Bueno de Mesquita 1978), war magnitude and duration (Cioffi-Revilla 1991a; Wilkinson 1980), and others (Vasquez 1993). Well-known anomalies that remain unresolved through this approach include: data violations of the model (values are not normally distributed), the use of theoretically unjustified transformations (ignoring the nonlinearity of logarithmic and other transformations), nonsignificant statistical results, large standard errors of estimates, parameter instabilities, and unstable functional forms.[41]

Probabilistic causality works differently and is more appropriate for explaining the complex, unstable, and inherently uncertain phenomena of politics. At the aggregate macro level, the first difference concerns the way in which dependent variables are defined in a theory that is based on probabilistic causality – as *random variables*, not as deterministic vari-

---

[40] Duverger's law is perhaps the best known example of a validated deterministic law in domestic politics (Duverger 1954; Taagepera 1986; Taagepera and Grofman 1985). In international politics, some possible candidates are the following bivariate relationships: (i) systemic polarity and war frequency (Midlarsky 1974); (ii) warfare duration and fatalities (Voevodsky 1969a, 1969b; Weiss 1963; Wilkinson 1980); (iii) trade/GNP ratio and country size (Taagepera and Hayes 1977); and (iv) conflict behavior and trade (Polacek 1980). Interestingly, none of these laws is linear and at least one of them, (ii), derives from Midlarsky's probabilistic theory of structural uncertainty (Cioffi-Revilla 1986; Midlarsky 1986).

[41] See Bremer (1995), Eberwein (1981), Singer (1981), for some recent reviews and critiques of standard regression approaches.

ables.[42] The second difference lies in what exactly is being explained – variable distributions and event distributions, not individual realizations. Although individual political realizations may remain unpredictable, their aggregate distribution is predictable with notable accuracy. These two differences are the cornerstones of probabilistic causality at the macro level, so I examine them carefully in this book. For example, using war as an empirical illustration, I show how probabilistic causality models a dependent variable such as war onset with an associated distribution of observed values. The distribution is then causally explained – as discussed in chapter 2 – by a set of substantive political forces acting on belligerents. The resulting theory provides a causal explanation that accounts for political behavior, and includes – does not ignore as plain "measurement error" – the fundamental uncertainty of politics.

At the individual micro level, probabilistic causality is explained by a causal structure of necessary and sufficient conditions for the occurrence of political events. This approach is probabilistic because such conditions may or may not occur. For example, using the collective action problem as an empirical illustration, in one solution (Schofield 1975; Schlager 1995) a leadership coalition and a set of followers are necessary for collective action to occur, and these in turn require other uncertain event occurrences. Although the mechanism is causally precise, the outcome is still uncertain because the entire process remains probabilistic. My theory explains this class of political occurrences at the individual micro level using probabilistic causality.

Political uncertainty does not have a single or unique form, but has different patterns with identifiable causal properties. Different well-defined patterns of political uncertainty include, but are not limited to, the well-known (and over-used) Poisson distribution, the Weibull distribution, and others.[43] The reader can think of this variety as being analogous to the

---

[42] Technically, this is also true in the case of a regression model $Y = f(X)$, whether univariate or multivariate, and the best empirical research manuals indeed point out that X and Y are defined as random variables, not as deterministic variables. However, in practice most political scientists ignore the real mathematical structure of the standard regression equation because this would mean treating the function f in a regression equation *not* as a simple linear function but as a function of random variables. I am not aware of any political theory based on functions of random variables with well-defined range spaces, equivalent events, and other features of functions of random variables. Any such theory would logically be based on probabilistic causality, by the definition of a function of random variables. Therefore, in a strict technical sense – not the practical norm – my theory based on probabilistic causality is fully compatible with the standard regression approach, albeit in a rather narrow technical sense. See Meyer (1970: ch. 5) for an introduction to the theory of functions of random variables, and Cioffi-Revilla (1989), King (1989a), and Midlarsky (1981) for substantive interpretations of random variables in political science.

[43] References to political science applications of probability distributions are given in chapters 2 and 4.

many different forms of deterministic relations (e.g. linear, quadratic, exponential) used by traditional regression models. As I will demonstrate, different causal situations produce different patterns of political uncertainty that require explanation under a common set of principles. For example, I will show how the Poisson distribution captures only one case of uncertainty, and a rather special one at that, whereas political phenomena often occur with different forms.

Formal language of politics. The fourth and last axiom addresses the choice of appropriate formal language for theory building purposes, consistent with the previous three axioms.

Axiom 4 (on the basic formal language of politics). *The primary language for understanding political uncertainty consists of formal logic, sets, and probability.*[44]

My reason for including this last axiom, which has the character of a methodological rule, is based on four considerations. First, the fundamental aspects of political uncertainty are causal and probabilistic, not measurement related, consistent with axiom 2. As I discussed earlier, this is because politics concerns occurrences (either decisional acts or states of nature) that either (i) have yet to occur (so they are uncertain in the future), or (ii) have already occurred but were only one of several possibilities (so that they were uncertain before they happened). Second, probability is not an object but a measure defined on political events when these are understood as point sets, as price is a measure defined on goods, or temperature and mass are measures defined on physical objects. Numerous measures can be defined on political events, such as their time of occurrence, location within a society or system, utility, social cost, and others. The probability of a political event measures the uncertainty of the occurrence, so logically probability provides a basic natural language for political theory. Third, a political event is defined by its causal logic – that is, by a specifiable combination of observable decisional acts or states of nature that cause the event – and not just by a nominal label. Therefore the definition of a political event cannot prescind from the use of set theoretic propositions or formal logic clauses. Fourth, these three types of mathematical languages are related because macropolitical behavior modeled as a random variable uses probability, where distributions consist of events, each of which is defined as a set by means of elementary logic

---

[44] On the formalization of uncertainty using probability, see Bruschi (1990), King (1989a), Lindley (1987), Nicholson (1989), Suppes (1981, 1984), and von Neumann and Morgenstern ([1947] 1972).

connectives. The chapters which follow explicate these formal methodological issues.

Axiom 4 has many implications. For instance, if basic laws of politics do exist, then they must be in the form of nonlinear probabilistic expressions, as I demonstrate in this book. On the empirical side, nonlinear models require maximum likelihood estimation, not ordinary least squares procedures, unless the model to be estimated can be linearized. Another implication of axiom 4 is that any political probability – and expressions such as "the probability of political change," "the probability of war," and others discussed in section 1.2 – is meaningless without a properly defined event (the occurrence of "political change" and "war," respectively). Also, from a purely pedagogical perspective, axiom 4 implies a need for some changes in the standard research methods sequence taught in political science curricula, with greater emphasis on set theory, formal and Boolean logic, and probability theory with calculus. These are essential tools for the theoretical and empirical investigation of macro- and micropolitical uncertainty. In this book I explore these and other implications.

I do not believe any other axioms are needed for the foundations of a theory of politics, although obviously a few more specific premises (formally, auxiliary assumptions) are needed to begin to derive the first theoretical propositions (principles). The four axioms I have proposed are a point of departure. As a system, they are complementary and consistent – they are not mutually contradictory – so they provide a valid and realistic foundation for theory building. Most of all, I believe these axioms make feasible a direct assault on the natural uncertainty of politics. For example, axiom 1 (levels of political uncertainty) and axiom 2 (substantive uncertainty) postulate that political variables and events are both fundamentally uncertain, at different levels of aggregation, without contradicting the other two axioms. As a set, these axioms also differ from those that have been more commonly used in political science. For example, by positing the duality of politics simultaneously as variables *and* as events, axiom 1 departs from the prevailing view that treats the two as unrelated entities, with only variables as the legitimate concern of political science, and events as the preferred territory of pundits. This standard view has contributed, inter alia, to producing a "divided discipline" (Almond 1990). By contrast, axiom 1 views both variables and events as necessarily complementary for a science of politics, albeit at different levels of analysis. Similarly, axiom 3 differs from the mainstream practice because most causal approaches in political science today are deterministic, at least implicitly if not explicitly, contrary to the essence of politics. Finally, the new approach I present in this book differs from other mainstream approaches because it is causal, or process oriented, not merely correlational (Dessler 1991; Elster 1989). As with other systems of axioms in political science, its validity should be assessed primarily in terms of the resulting theory and the understanding it can provide.

1.3.2   Theory and puzzles of political uncertainty

The theory I present in this book represents an attempt to address the dual puzzles of political uncertainty (axiom 1), as shown earlier in figure 1.2 and table 1.2, using theoretical principles illustrated with applications. Notwithstanding the faith of John Stuart Mill in enlightened social engineering (a goal whose importance I find exaggerated), my exposition of the principles of political uncertainty parallels the following idea expressed in Mill's essay *On Liberty* (ch. 5):

The principles asserted in these pages must be more generally admitted as the basis for discussion of details, before a consistent application of them to all the various departments of government and morals can be attempted with any prospect of advantage. The few observations I propose to make on questions of detail are designed to illustrate the principles, rather than to follow them out to their consequences. I offer, not so much applications, as specimens of applications; which may serve to bring into greater clearness the meaning and limits of the two maxims which together form the entire doctrine of this essay, and to assist the judgment in holding the balance between them, in the cases where it appears doubtful which of them is applicable to the case.

In the case of my theory, one puzzle contains questions regarding the macro explanation of the uncertain behavior of aggregate political variables. The following questions exemplify this part of the dual puzzle. What is the probability of conflict initiation on (or a coalition enduring until) date τ, given δ time units (say, years) since the previous onset, and the action of political influences $X_1, X_2, X_3, \ldots, X_n$ that have operated since then, such as changes in voter preferences, macroeconomic performance, international conditions, or other forces? How exactly is the probability of such an event calculated, given available historical data? How do such events – that is, the uncertain behavior of political variables such as war onsets or durations – depend on causal forces? How are behavioral forces defined to meet the necessary theoretical and empirical requirements? How would such factors give shape to different distributions of political uncertainty? How are different distributions explained? Traditionally, most of these questions have remained unanswered, because the application of probability distributions has taken place without much theoretical justification. My approach is theoretical and therefore different. In chapters 3 and 4 I present the macropolitical principles that address these and related questions, together with applications. This is the first broad political puzzle of explaining the behavior of aggregate political variables at the macro level.

The other puzzle in the duality contains questions regarding the micro explanation of the uncertain occurrence of individual political events. How does collective action occur by leadership initiative? How does political integration occur by spillover? How does war occur by deterrence failure? How is the probability of such an event calculated? How do the operational occurrence and the probability of a political event depend on its causal logic? How does the probability of a political event change over time as underlying causes change? What causes political turbulence, and what are its properties? Traditionally, most of these questions have been addressed in an ad hoc, fragmented way, largely ignoring the significant common elements contained in each case. In chapters 6 and 7 I derive the micropolitical principles that answer these and similar questions. The micropolitical principles of the theory explain the occurrence of individual political events in terms of their causal structure.

Besides operating within each level of analysis, probabilistic causality also links both levels of the puzzle of political uncertainty, consistent with axiom 3, so knowledge about the uncertain behavior of aggregate political variables (macropolitical principles) is important for understanding the uncertain occurrence of individual events (micropolitical principles), and vice versa. Macropolitical principles explain the set of values of a political variable (e.g. the distribution of war onsets in history), whereas micropolitical principles "open up the black box" of values and explain the "realization" of a value as the occurrence of an individual event (e.g. war by deterrence failure). Probabilistic causality links observed patterns of aggregate political behavior to underlying causal factors, so knowledge about one is needed to understand the other. To develop "progressive problem shifts" along various stages of this research program (Lakatos 1973; Landau 1979), I first use the system of axioms to derive general principles, and then I use the latter and additional specific assumptions to derive special principles. Each set of principles (macro and micro, general and specific) is used to explore more advanced properties of political uncertainty, so principles are produced in all four quadrants of the typology of political uncertainty in figure 1.3.

As a research program, the theory offers a new integrative framework that I hope will assist in uniting our "divided discipline" (Almond 1990). This may happen in several ways. First, the concepts and principles that comprise this theory can be applied in a variety of seemingly unrelated areas of politics, crossing the traditional sub-disciplinary boundaries of domestic or comparative and international politics. In this book I use some of these as running examples, but the interest should remain focused on general politics (figure 1.1). Second, the theory offers a more rigorous treatment of common but previously ill-defined political concepts such as "events," "potentials for change," or "social forces." These important political ideas can now be explored in a more reliable way to obtain valid inferences. Third, formalization by means of probability and the other related languages (logic, sets) makes possible a set of new interpretations concerning earlier paradigms. For example, I offer new interpretations of several classical theories and other influential ideas that first appeared as "islands of theory" (Guetzkow 1996) in the history of political science but had little or no formal development. If the conceptual foundations of these frameworks contain valid arguments, then the formalizations I propose with this theory can yield new insights. Fourth, the theory offers new foundations for the systematic classification of political behavior using well-defined independent variables and their causal effect on corresponding observable patterns of political uncertainty. Thus, previously distinct types of aggregate political behavior, or diverse types of political events, that were thought to be unique, may be shown to obey similar principles. As I demonstrate at several points in my theoretical development, Hempelian "covering laws" indeed do exist in politics – but they are probabilistic, not deterministic. Finally, from a methodological perspective, the theory offers a new interpretation of earlier determinist regression models from the "variance" approach, explaining their frequent empirical "instability" (Newbold and Bos 1985) and how they may be reformulated within a more appropriate framework based on probabilistic causality. In the chapters that follow I show how, rather than being a source of ignorance, imprecision, or mystery, uncertainty provides an insightful, rigorous, and fertile framework for a theory of politics.

1.4   Conclusions

In this chapter I focused on uncertainty as a defining or constitutional property of politics, a sine qua non for understanding the nature of governance and the effects of decisions on collectivities – the political life. I argued that rather than being treated either as a property of politics that is impossible to penetrate (uncertainty *qua magnum mysterium*), or as a trivial entity that is often ignored as measurement error (uncertainty *qua res indesiderata*), political uncertainty can and should be used as a rigorous cornerstone for a new general theory of politics with wide empirical scope and explanatory power.

After linking the essence of politics to the property of uncertainty, and explaining the cause of uncertainty in politics, I then provided a brief historical survey. The purpose of my historical discussion was to show how uncertainty is an ancient classical idea in politics, one found in early occidental and oriental works, and to note some important scientific developments that have been important for understanding political uncertainty, particularly regarding the development of probability as a key mathematical concept. An important goal of that discussion was to highlight that the development of mathematical probability theory in the late eighteenth and early nineteenth centuries was in part inspired by the European politics of the time (the Laplace–Poisson model of jury behavior, or Condorcet's model of voting), so political science need make no apologies for drawing on ideas from probability and related modeling areas (set theory and formal logic) for developing viable theories founded on political uncertainty. My brief historical survey concluded with a summary on the status of uncertainty in contemporary political science and some current misunderstandings.

In section 1.2 I developed the first systematics of my theory by presenting an initial classification of political concepts that reflect substantive uncertainty in the real world. This classification was drawn up with several classes and had only heuristic value to start focusing attention on the concept of political uncertainty. I identified political uncertainty as present in political probabilities, individual decisions (including nonutilitarian mechanisms of choice), interactive decisions, collective outcomes, political processes, government policy, and empirical analysis, among the most salient. The significant issue – admittedly only a conjecture in this chapter, but a feature that I demonstrate in the following chapters – was that the various types of political uncertainty are amenable to rigorous theoretical treatment under a common set of probabilistic principles founded on uncertainty.

In section 1.3 I began to develop the general framework of my theory by laying down a system of basic axioms, followed by a discussion of what I see as one of the most basic puzzles in political theory – explaining the behavior of aggregate political variables and the occurrence of individual political events. What makes this a political theory, and not merely a restatement of well-established mathematical ideas lacking in substantive content (I view this book only secondarily as a contribution to the development of political methodology), is that the subject matter – uncertainty in politics – is treated as a substantive phenomenon with sui generis significance. Dual manifestations of uncertainty – as variables that behave (aggregate macro level) and as events that occur (individual micro level) – are present across diverse areas of political life. The system of axioms described my position on a set of elementary epistemological issues, such as the levels of political phenomena (axiom 1), the role of uncertainty (axiom 2), political causality (probabilistic; axiom 3), and the basic formal language for establishing foundations in political theory (axiom 4). In the chapters that follow I show how this system of axioms produces a theory of political uncertainty with general and specific applicability to domains of politics (domestic and international). As shown in figure 1.2 and table 1.1, the general theory has two related branches based on levels of analysis, one to explain the aggregate behavior of political variables (I call this the macropolitical part of the theory) and the other to explain the individual occurrence of political events (micropolitical part of the theory). Macro and micro properties of political uncertainty are also linked by unifying principles (chapter 8).

Part II

Macropolitics

2   Behavior of political variables

Men everywhere, especially those who have reflected on the vicissitudes
of politics and war, have from the beginning recognized the central place
of chance in human affairs.

Patrick Suppes, *Probabilistic Metaphysics*

2.1   Introduction

This is the first chapter on the uncertain behavior of political variables,
so my focus is on concept formation and systematics – that is, defining
and classifying the main dependent and independent variables as the
building blocks for understanding uncertainty in macropolitics. In every
theory – probabilistic or otherwise – variables require careful conceptualization and definition; otherwise the framework will not stand. This is
especially so for understanding how probabilistic causality works in explaining political behavior. My focus on defining and classifying the first
building blocks in this chapter means that I will not address the causal
link between the building blocks themselves – what analytically connects
political behavior (dependent variable) and causal hazard forces (independent variables) – until the next chapter, when I will have identified
the precise nature of political uncertainty as it is defined in each type of
variable.

I take some common concepts such as variables, their values, decisional
acts, and states of nature as primitive or axiomatic terms (Jeffrey 1983;
Tsebelis 1989). However, other important but less familiar concepts are
based on random variables, probability functions, and hazard rates; these
I define with greater care because they play a key role in the theory.[1] An
important result from this first conceptualization is in systematics – the

---

[1] The reader should also recall that appendix 4 contains a summary of the main methodological tools used in theoretical analysis. Although not all of them are used in this chapter, a
review of these tools is useful to appreciate the theoretical potential of the ideas presented in
this chapter. For example, theoretical methods can be used to derive additional preliminary
theorems (lemmas) concerning the formal properties of political variables and hazard rates
when these are defined in terms of probability functions.

classification of macropolitical behavior into temporal and intensity domains, along with their statistical measures, special values, and hazard rates. Another concerns the dynamic interpretation of the hazard rate concept as a causal force to account for macropolitical behavior. The ideas introduced in this chapter are also used in later chapters to derive principles and other results.

2.2   Aggregate political behavior: defining dependent variables

2.2.1   *Dimensionality*

What are the basic properties of aggregate political behavior that are useful for constructing a theory of politics with uncertainty? At the macro level, aggregate political behavior is a complex phenomenon that concerns not one but many dimensions of social life affecting the lives, fortunes, or governance of collectivities. Elections, conflicts, government reforms, and party realignments are familiar forms of multidimensional political behavior. Multidimensionality means that phenomena such as coalition processes, wars, elections, or revolutions always occur as n-tuples of variables in a hyperspace – a space with dimensionality greater than three. Dimensions of political behavior are also measurable when they are operationally defined, using systematically recorded data. Some political dimensions are also observable, when they occur as political decisional acts or as states of nature witnessed by observers, a distinction that is also important later on for independent variables (section 2.3). Notationally, a political variable Y assumes values denoted by y_1, y_2, y_3, ... , on the historical timeline τ.[2] Although these and other basic properties of political behavior are not new (Ordeshook 1986; Shively 1989), many implications of the multidimensional property for understanding the uncertainty of politics have remained unrecognized and unexplored.

The first implication of multidimensionality and other basic properties (measurability, observability) is that political uncertainty exists not only with respect to the occurrence of political behavior, but also with respect to other dimensions shown in the next examples. The second is that a reduced set of aggregate dimensions of political behavior can assist in unifying

---

[2] By convention, variables are written in upper-case italics (X, Y, Z) and corresponding values in lower case (x, y, z). For example, the symbol T denotes time between consecutive political events, or time from one event to the next, measured in units such as days, months, or years. Individual values of T are denoted by lower-case italics, t. A different "time" is calendrical or chronological time τ, which is not a variable but an index. These and other notational conventions are described in appendix 2. All variables are assumed to be measurable (through operationalization) but not necessarily observable (a material physical property). Probabilistic variables are commonly measurable but not observable. Empirical frequencies are often observable.

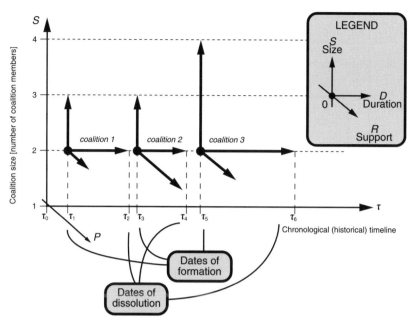

Figure 2.1. Coalitions as an example of multidimensional, observable, and measurable forms of political behavior

diverse areas of politics, as I highlight in the following examples from general political behavior (domestic and international).

Example 2.1 (coalitions: domestic and international). The uncertain process of formation and dissolution of coalitions is a multidimensional political phenomenon described by a set of dependent variables with values that occur on the timeline τ, as shown in figure 2.1. A formal political coalition – a government cabinet or an international alliance – is an n-tuple of observable and measurable realizations $(s, r, \delta, o, \dots)$, as shown in figure 2.1. The n-tuple consists of size $s \in S$, support $r \in R$, duration $\delta \in D$, policy orientation $o \in O$, degree of cohesion $c \in C$, and other dimensions. For example, the West German governmental coalition of Helmut Kohl, which reunited Germany in October 1990, was re-elected for the fourth time in 1994 with the following n-tuple: $\tau =$ AD October 16, 1994, $S = 2$ political parties, $R = 50.3$ percent of votes in the *Bundestag*, and other features.

Example 2.2 (warfare: domestic and international). The "process of war" (Bremer and Cusack 1995; Dessler 1991; Vasquez 1993) is another multi-

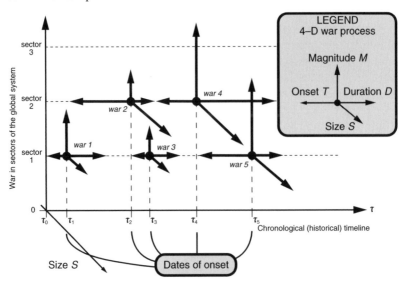

Figure 2.2. Warfare as a multidimensional, observable, and measurable form of political behavior

dimensional political phenomenon described by a set of dependent variables with values that occur on the timeline τ, as shown in figure 2.2. This is a valid conceptualization for both domestic (civil wars) and international warfare (interstate wars). Time of onset (T), magnitude (M), size (S), and duration (D) generate an n-dimensional hyperspace (Duvall 1976). Thus, war is both observable and measurable (Cioffi-Revilla 1990). A single war is an n-tuple of realizations $(t, \mu, s, \delta, \ldots)$, with time of onset $t \in T$, magnitude $\mu \in M$, size $s \in S$, duration $\delta \in D$, and others expressed in appropriate magnitudes. For example, the US Civil War was a political event defined by the following n-tuple: $\tau = \text{AD}$ April 10, 1861, $M = \log(650,000$ fatalities$) = 5.8 \, \mu_R$, $S = 2$ belligerents, $D = 4.0$ years, and other features, where $\mu_R = \log_{10}(\text{fatalities})$, or Richardson's magnitude (Small and Singer 1983: 224).

Example 2.3 (elections: domestic and international). An election (domestic or international, as in the European Parliament) is an n-tuple $(\tau, v, c, o, m, \ldots)$, with realizations for time of occurrence τ, voter turnout $v \in V$, number of candidates $c \in C$, degree of openness $o \in O$, extent of foreign monitoring $m \in M$, and other dimensions of elections. The 1979 US national election, won by President Ronald Reagan and lost by former president Jimmy

Carter, was defined by the n-tuple: $\tau =$ November, 1979, $V = 64$ percent of eligible voters, $C = 2$ contestants, and so forth. Each election for the European Parliament is also an n-tuple $(\tau, v, p, \ldots)$, with realizations for time of occurrence τ, mean (or pan-European) voter turnout $v \in V$, number of parties $p \in P$, and similar dimensions of the European elections.

Although the above examples refer to widely distinct forms of behavior – coalitions, warfare, and elections – they all have important analytical features in common: namely, political behavior is a multidimensional, measurable, and sometimes observable process of n-tuples that occurs with uncertain values on the historical timeline τ. The next step is to define how this process causally occurs.

2.2.2   Uncertainty

How is uncertain political behavior "caused"? How does political behavior "occur"? How are the lives, fortunes, or governance of individuals or groups in a political system (domestic or international) affected by others or by states of nature? How does this occur with uncertainty? Formally, how do dependent political variables assume observed values? What is the nature of this indeterminate but nevertheless causal mechanism? In chapter 1 I laid down the first axiomatic foundations for answering these questions, so I will now continue with more specific assumptions and concepts, specific to political behavior as opposed to events (I discuss political events in the micro part of the theory, chapters 5–7). In the next two chapters I will also show how these assumptions produce new principles (theorems).

The first assumption concerning political behavior – social action affecting the lives, fortunes, and governance of a collectivity – must concern its causality.

Assumption 2.1 (probabilistic causality of political behavior). *Political behavior is governed by probabilistic causality, meaning that each value of a political variable has an associated probability. Formally, a dimension of political behavior (a dependent variable Y with set of values $y_1, y_2, y_3, \ldots$) is a random variable with exact probability values $\mathbf{P}(Y = y)$ in the open interval $(0, 1)$, not a deterministic variable with certain values ($\mathbf{P} = 0$ or 1).*

I view this assumption as a realistic basis for constructing a viable theory of political behavior, not merely as a heuristic postulate. In earlier deterministic frameworks – as I have already discussed in chapter 1 – a dependent political variable Y had a set of values $\{y\}$, with each value y either occurring or not – with nothing in between or more nuanced than this strictly binary situation. In the new framework that I am proposing each dependent variable Y is defined by a set of values $\{y\}$ (just as before) but in addition – this is the first new feature of probabilistic causality – each value y of a dependent political variable Y has an associated probability value, denoted by $\mathbf{P}(Y = y)$ or simply $\mathbf{P}(y)$. Why add this probabilistic dimension to the values of a political variable? Because, as I have argued (axiom 2), in politics each realization y is individually *uncertain* – consistent with assumption 2.1, impossible to predict with deterministic certainty – although the aggregate distribution of values and the probabilities attached to individual values may be well patterned. By contrast, for a deterministic variable all admissible values have probability equal to 1, regardless of their actual likelihood.

The probabilistic causality of political behavior stipulated in assumption 2.1 covers the full range of common political situations regarding feasibility, certainty, and uncertainty, as these distinct political states represent different loci along the probability continuum $[0, 1]$. Symbolically, this property of probabilistic causality means that political behavior is:

1 often feasible, meaning $\mathbf{P}(y) > 0$,
2 never certain, meaning $\mathbf{P}(y) < 1$, and therefore
3 always uncertain, meaning $0 < \mathbf{P}(y) < 1$.

Assumption 2.1 is also consistent with the four axioms I laid down in chapter 1. For example, in the case of coalition duration D (example 2.1, figure 2.1), the individual duration values δ_1, δ_2, δ_3, ..., are governed by probabilistic causality, meaning that each duration value δ has an associated probability $\mathbf{P}(D = \delta)$ that lies between 0 and 1. Coalition duration D is thus a random variable with exact probabilistic values, not a deterministic variable (consistent with axioms 1 and 3).[3] Sometimes (formally, "for some 'realizations'") an individual value δ of coalition duration D may be small (as for a very short-lived government cabinet), and at other times coalition duration may be longer (some West European cabinets headed by Sir Winston Churchill [1940–5, 1951–5], Konrad Adenauer [1949–63], or Alcide de Gasperi [1945–53]); no exact value $\delta \in D$ can ever be predicted with certainty. Only the probability of a value may be exactly calculated and accounted for (consistent with axioms 2 and 4). The same is true for

---

[3] A political variable Y is said to be a random variable (or a stochastic variable) when it may assume each of its possible values y_1, y_2, y_3, ..., with definite probability. The probabilities associated with the values of a random variable need not be the same for all values. I assume all variables to be continuous without loss of generality and to facilitate the presentation. Formal introductions to random variables may be found in classic works such as Feller (1968), Gnedenko (1975), and Parzen (1960, 1962). Applications of random variable models are found in Bishir and Drewes (1970: pt. 4), Bittinger (1976: 324–44), Bittinger and Crown (1981: ch. 6), Chung (1979), King (1989a), Kovalenko et al. (1996), Olinick (1978: 250), and Ross (1985).

other dependent variables of a coalition process, such as time between formations T, size S, or duration D, as well as for similar dimensions of other political phenomena (e.g. wars, elections, or strikes).

This probabilistic view that respects and captures the uncertainty of political behavior is consistent with a classical view of politics. Moreover, bringing out the fundamental uncertainty – concerning when? For how long? With what intensity? And involving whom? – also suggests a new taxonomy with a reduced number of classes of aggregate political variables. From a probabilistic perspective, two orthogonal classes of macropolitical behavior are of primarily theoretical interest: temporal (diachronic) variables and intensity (synchronic) variables.[4] Politically, the former refer to aspects of *when* political behavior occurs, locating macro behavior on the historical timeline, whereas the latter refer to aspects of *what* occurs, focusing on theoretically relevant dimensions. In turn, temporal variables can be divided into two basic types: onset (When did the political behavior begin?) and duration (How long did it last?), which are important theoretical and empirical features of coalitions, conflicts, and numerous other domestic and international phenomena. Intensity variables can be divided into magnitude (How severe was it?) and size (Who participated?), another important class of features for political phenomena.

This theoretical perspective yields the following taxonomy:

$$
\text{Political behavior}
\begin{cases}
\text{Temporal variables (diachronic)} & \begin{cases} \text{Onsets} \\ \text{Durations} \end{cases} \\
\text{Intensity variables (synchronic)} & \begin{cases} \text{Magnitudes} \\ \text{Sizes} \end{cases}
\end{cases}
$$

This taxonomy has the following advantages: (i) the classification is consistent with classical theories of politics that view the area of political science inquiry as related to aspects of when (history), who (actors), what (behavior), to whom (targets), and how (policy);[5] (ii) the resulting categories of political behavior are mutually exclusive, a desirable feature for maxi-

---

[4] A locational class of variables can also be defined, assuming some spatial system of reference. I omit locational variables here not because they are unimportant in politics (e.g. the analysis of spatial diffusion is a prominent area of theory and research), but because the discipline of geography (including political geography) has a more specialized focus on spatial variables (Gaile and Willmott 1984). Locational variables (geographic) may be added to the proposed taxonomy of political behavior.

[5] This "when–who–what –how" view of politics is deeply rooted in the study of both domestic and international politics (Almond 1990: app. B; Lasswell 1936). Methodologically, the "events data approach" is based on measuring these dimensions of political behavior (Azar and Ben-Dak 1975; Kegley et al. 1975; McClelland 1961, 1968; Merritt et al. 1993), both domestically and internationally.

mizing the variance across cases in comparative research; (iii) the resulting categories are exhaustive, covering many fields of politics, both domestic and international; and (iv) the taxonomy is inclusive, because onset, duration, magnitude, and size are dimensions of politics that are measured by various levels of precision, not just "quantitative" (ratio scaled). The conceptualization of political behavior as a random variable (and later the conceptualization of risk factors and events) also prevents "conceptual stretching" (Sartori 1991), because a random variable is a precisely defined mathematical concept, as I will explain next.

As shown in table 2.1, temporal variables that concern the onset and duration of political behavior have been analyzed in greater detail than other dimensions of political behavior that pertain to magnitude or size.[6] However, consistent with assumption 2.1, both classes of variables have uncertain behavior and must therefore somehow be covered by uniform principles in a general theory. The only difference between the two is that temporal variables are defined as aspects of political behavior that are viewed as segments of the chronological timeline τ (the horizontal dimensions in figures 2.1 and 2.2, or calendrical time), whereas intensity variables represent aspects of political behavior that have more traditional or substantive meaning – for example, coalition size S, war magnitude M, electoral turnout E, and other variables representing some substantive dimensions of political behavior. Both classes consist of random variables (assumption 2.1).

By assumption 2.1, a political variable is well defined if and only if its values and corresponding probabilities are well defined.[7] This is done by defining the probability functions that are associated with a given dependent political variable Y. For example, consider war onset T, or any other dependent political variable in table 2.1. (I will first use the variable war onset T as a running example, and in the course of the presentation I will also develop the definition of a generic dependent political variable Y. The reader may substitute war onset T for any of the political variables identified in table 2.1.) As a random variable, war onset T is defined by the cumulative density function:

$$\Phi(t) = \mathbf{P}(\text{war will break out } within \text{ time } t)$$

and by the probability density function

$$p(t) = \mathbf{P}(\text{war will break out } at \text{ time } t).$$

---

[6] King (1989a) uses the more statistical term "event count" to denote what I call here a discrete intensity variable (the more common mathematical term used for this type of random variable) associated to either a magnitude or a size. I prefer the common mathematical term because it is more theoretically neutral ("event count" conveys a less general idea), but the two terms mean the same.

[7] See footnote 3.

(Other probability functions can also be used for defining a random variable, these being the most common.) Empirically, the functions $\Phi(t)$ and $p(t)$ are measured (operationalized) by the distribution of observed cumulative relative frequencies (ogive) and by the distribution of observed relative frequencies (histogram) respectively, as I will illustrate shortly.[8]

More generally, a dependent political variable Y is defined as follows.

Definition 2.1 (political variable). *A political variable Y is defined by its cumulative density function (c.d.f., also called the distribution function of Y):*

$$\Phi(y) \equiv P(Y \text{ will have a value within } y) \tag{2.1}$$
$$= P(Y \leq y)$$
$$= 1 - P(Y > y),$$

or by its probability density function (p.d.f.):

$$p(y) \equiv P(Y \text{ will have a value "in the neighborhood of" } y) \tag{2.2}$$
$$= P(y < Y \leq y + dy).$$

Note that since I am using the probability functions $\Phi(y)$ and $p(y)$ of a dependent political variable Y (temporal or intensity, as the case may be) to rigorously define the specific character of political uncertainty – and therefore different functions will define different qualitative and quantitative types of political uncertainty – it is logically necessary to understand the meaning of these functions, not only in a formal sense (mathematically), but above all in a substantive sense (politically). The c.d.f. $\Phi(y)$ defines the probability of Y assuming a value of y or less, as in equation 2.1. The p.d.f. $p(y)$ defines the probability that Y will assume a value of y (or in the neighborhood of y), as in equation 2.2.

Cumulative probability of political behavior. The c.d.f. $\Phi(y)$ specifies the probability of increasing values of political behavior Y occurring, the probability $P(Y \leq y)$ in equation 2.1.[9] For example, in the case of war onset T (a temporal variable), the c.d.f.

$$\Phi(t) \equiv P(T \leq t) \tag{2.3}$$
$$= 1 - P(T > t) \tag{2.4}$$

specifies the probability of war onset occurring *by* time t, or *within* time t

---

[8] Note that formally, logit and probit equations (Liao 1994) are just cumulative probability functions because they model the probability of an event occurring as a function of a set of risk factors (exogenous independent variables).

[9] In the next chapter I will extend the definition of the c.d.f. to introduce the general analytical expression $\Phi(y) = 1 - e^{-\varphi(y)}$, where $\varphi(y)$ is a hazard rate function that must satisfy only some mild conditions.

Table 2.1. *Taxonomy of political behavior*

Political behavior[a]	Measures[b]
Temporal: Onset variables	
Riots (Midlarsky 1978; Olzak et al. 1996)	Time interval T lapsed between calendar
Coups d'état (Li and Thompson 1975)	dates of consecutive onset events,
Terrorism (Heyman 1979)	measured in units such as number of days,
International events (Hayes 1973; Mintz and Schrodt 1987)	weeks, months, or years
International disputes (Cioffi-Revilla and Isernia 1988; Cusack and Eberwein 1982; Maoz 1994)	
Wars (Cioffi-Revilla 1985a, 1985c, 1990, 1991b; Howeling and Kuné 1984; Howeling and Siccama 1985; Midlarsky 1975, 1988a; Petersen 1991; Richardson 1960b; Small and Singer 1983)	
Temporal: Duration variables	
Cabinets (Browne 1984, 1988; Cioffi-Revilla 1984; Frendreis et al. 1986; Grofman and van Roozendaal 1997; King et al. 1990)	Time interval D lapsed between calendar dates of onset and termination events, measured in days, weeks, months, or years
Government agencies (Casstevens 1980; Casstevens and Casstevens 1989)	(same units as onset T)
Strikes (Horvath 1968)	
Politicians' tenure (Casstevens 1970, 1974)	
International disputes (Diehl 1998; Gochman 1995)	
Interstate rivalries (Cioffi-Revilla 1997)	
Alliances (Hopmann 1967; Job 1976; McGowan and Rood 1975)	
Wars (Horvath 1968; Weiss 1963)	
Intensity variables	
Trust in government	Boynton (1980: 44–51)
Conflict of interest	Axelrod's (1967) or Reich's (1968) indices
Partisanship	Boynton (1980: 37–40)
Party polarization	Sartori (1976)
Party support	Kramer (1971)
Presidential popularity	Stimson (1991)
Political fractionalization	Lijphart (1994), Rae (1971), Taylor and Jodice (1983: vol. II)
Power as capability	Numerous indices in Stoll and Ward (1989: 11–77)
Interaction or transaction	Flows of trade, mail, or communications
Political conflict or cooperation	Events data (COPDAB, CREON, WEIS)[c]
Integration	Indices by Savage and Deutsch (RA), Clark and Merritt (RS), Brams, Rabier

Table 2.1. *cont.*

Political behavior[a]	Measures[b]
Political instability and violence (Midlarsky 1975, 1978; Spilerman 1970, 1971, 1972)	Taylor and Jodice (1983, vol. II)
Systemic polarization and polarity	Indices of capability distribution and concentration (Sabrosky 1985; Levy 1983)
Size of alliances (Horvath and Foster 1963)	Number of members belonging to an alliance
War intensities (Cioffi-Revilla and Mason 1991; Weiss 1963)	Fatalities, magnitude, extent, and other war indicators (Small and Singer 1983)

[a] References in this column are to studies of political variables modeled as random variables. See also Lichbach (1992), Midlarsky (1981), and Schrodt (1985) for reviews of some of the studies cited.
[b] References in this column are to measures or data sources for the corresponding variables.
[c] COPDAB is the Conflict and Peace Data Bank; WEIS is the World Event Interaction Survey.
Source: Prepared by the author.

since the previous war (equation 2.3). By complementarity, this is the same as the probability of war *not* occurring *after* time t (equation 2.4). Similarly, for coalition size S (an intensity variable), the cumulative density function

$$\Phi(s) \equiv \mathbf{P}(S \leq s) \qquad\qquad [2.5]$$
$$= 1 - \mathbf{P}(S > s) \qquad\qquad [2.6]$$

specifies the probability of coalition size being s, *or* smaller (equation 2.5), which is the same as coalition size not being greater than s (equation 2.6).[10]

Probability density of political behavior. Alternatively, the p.d.f. $p(y)$ (whether Y is a temporal or an intensity variable of political behavior) uniquely specifies the amount of probability distributed in the neighborhood of a specific value y, or the expression $\mathbf{P}(y < Y \leq y + \mathrm{d}y)$ in equation 2.2. For example, for war onset T, the density function

$$p(t) \equiv \mathbf{P}(t < T \leq t + \mathrm{d}t) \cong \mathbf{P}(T = t) \qquad\qquad [2.7]$$

specifies the probability of war onset at (or "in the neighborhood of") time t. Similarly, to use a different example, for the probability density function of coalition size S, the expression is

$$p(s) \equiv \mathbf{P}(s < S \leq s + \mathrm{d}s) \cong \mathbf{P}(S = s). \qquad\qquad [2.8]$$

---

[10] A c.d.f. $\Phi(y)$ must respect two formal properties: $\Phi(0) = 0$ and $\Phi(\infty) = 1$.

In this case the p.d.f. specifies the probability of a coalition being of (or "in the neighborhood of") size s.[11]

Each probability function provides complementary or canonical perspectives on the uncertainty of political behavior – like different mirrors positioned to reflect different images of a single object. Thus, a variable Y denoting a given dimension of political behavior represents a single entity, and the probability functions $\Phi(y)$, $p(y)$, and others describe the various aspects of Y's uncertainty. Thus, the c.d.f. $\Phi(t)$ specifies "by when a political event will occur," or the probability that the political behavior in question, Y, will assume a value within a given interval (i.e. the occurrence of "$Y \leq y$"). Alternatively, the p.d.f. $p(t)$ specifies "when a political event will occur," or the probability that the behavior will have a given specific value, within an infinitesimal (i.e. the occurrence of "$y < Y \leq y + dy$" or "$Y \approx y$"). Both probability functions provide exact information on the type or pattern of randomness involved.

Relationship between density and cumulative probability. Because the probability functions of a political behavior variable provide different perspectives on the character of political uncertainty, a logical question arises about the relationship between these functions. Density and cumulative probability portray two facets of uncertainty, each from a different perspective. How are these two macro perspectives on political uncertainty related? From definition 2.1, the two functions are related by the following equations:

$$\Phi(y) = \int_{-\infty}^{y} p(u)\mathrm{d}u \qquad\qquad [2.9]$$

$$p(y) = \frac{\mathrm{d}}{\mathrm{d}y}\Phi(y). \qquad\qquad [2.10]$$

This equivalence derives from elementary probability, and it is important to understand its precise political implication. For example, the equivalence means that knowing something about the cumulative probability of war occurring by a given time (the c.d.f.) also allows us to infer some other information about the probability of war occurring at various points in time before then (p.d.f.). In essence, either function is sufficient to derive the other, by integration or derivation.[12]

[11] Consistent with the properties noted earlier for the c.d.f. (see note 9), a probability density function $p(y)$ has the following properties: $0 \leq p(y) < +\infty$, and $\int_Y p(y)\, \mathrm{d}y = 1$.

[12] Note that this is also true empirically: given a set of empirical values, a distribution of relative cumulative frequencies (ogive) can always be used to construct a distribution of relative frequencies (histogram), and vice versa.

2.2.3   Measurability

How do the preceding concepts translate into measurable dimensions of political uncertainty? Which rules of equivalence may be established between theoretical terms and observational data, given a set of recorded realizations $\hat{y}_1, \hat{y}_2, \hat{y}_3, \ldots$ for a political variable Y? As I have already noted (section 2.2.2), the probability density function $p(y)$ is measured by the observed (empirical) relative frequencies of realized values, whereas $\Phi(y)$ is measured by the observed cumulative relative frequencies. The empirical functions are denoted by $\hat{p}(y)$ and $\hat{\Phi}(y)$, respectively, and each is graphed by a histogram depicting a distinct type of political uncertainty. Although in principle these measurements and transformations – equivalencies of the form $\hat{p}(y) \leftrightarrow \hat{\Phi}(y)$ – appear straightforward and unproblematic, several problems often do arise in practice. Therefore I will now turn to aspects of measurability and illustrate some solutions. I will use a concrete example – the onset of world war, with significant domestic and international political consequences – in the hope of demonstrating the links between theory and observation. Moreover, I have chosen this example deliberately, to show how the general theory is applicable even when the particular form of political behavior has relatively few realizations – fortunately so, in the case of world war onset. Inferences derived from a small number of cases must logically be more cautious; they are valid inferences only when subject to a larger margin of error. The extension to situations with larger number of cases is natural. It is hoped that my analysis will help dispel the incorrect but commonly held view that probability distribution functions are meaningful only when there are large numbers of realizations. However, the main thrust remains that of establishing a general theory; the example is not intended to provide an in-depth analysis of the onset of world war.

Generally, the empirical function $\hat{\Phi}(y)$ is constructed immediately from ungrouped observed values $\hat{y}_1, \hat{y}_2, \hat{y}_3, \ldots$, ranked in increasing order, and therefore presents no problems. However, as shown in figure 2.3, measuring a density function $\hat{p}(y)$ is not as straightforward. This is primarily because, following equation 2.10, the values of an empirical density function are measured by the slopes of segments that connect consecutive values of $\hat{\Phi}(y)$.[13]

To which value y should one assign a calculated slope of Φ in figure 2.3? To (i) the terminal value y_i, or (ii) the initial value y_{i-1}, or (iii) some other value that lies within the interval Δy? As with all purely inductive problems, there is no logically compelling answer. The most neutral method,

---

[13] Silverman (1986) and Stuart and Ord (1991) provide introductions to the estimation of empirical density functions. See also King (1989b) and King et al. (1990) for a Gauss-based algorithm that produces an estimated density function $\hat{p}(y)$.

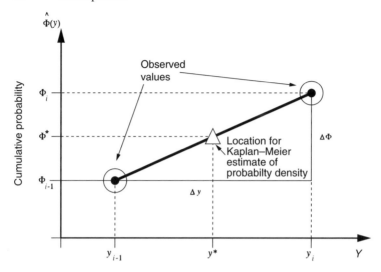

Figure 2.3. Values of an empirical cumulative relative frequency function $\hat{\Phi}(y)$ and estimated values of probability density measured by the slope between consecutive observed cumulative values

called the Kaplan–Meier estimate (Kaplan and Meier 1958), assigns a calculated slope $\hat{p}$ (measured over the interval Δy) to the midpoint y^* in Δy, such that $\hat{p}(y^*) = p(y + \Delta y/2)$. In example 2.4, I show how this measurement procedure works.

Example 2.4 (onset of general world war). Consider the onset T of general world war, one of the most consequential and uncertain forms of political behavior that occurs in the world politics system, with significant domestic and international effects (Levy 1983; Midlarsky 1988a; Thompson 1988). Using Levy's criteria, there have been ten such events in the past five hundred years. Table 2.2 lists dates (τ) and observed values t of T (i.e. the realizations 123, 54, 16, … measured in years) for the epoch that began with the 1495 Treaty of Venice and ended with World War II, the most recent onset of general world war. The raw data consisting of onset dates seems just haphazard. What can be learned about the uncertain onset of general world war? Does it have a precise pattern that is not haphazard? Can such a pattern be explained?

Observed values of T in table 2.2 are first used to construct the empirical c.d.f. $\hat{\Phi}(y)$ by the usual procedures, as reported in table 2.3 and figure 2.4. The resulting values of $\hat{\Phi}(y)$ describe the rising historical probability of

Table 2.2. *Onset of general world war, 1495–1939*

Event	Onset date τ	Onset times $\hat{t}$ (years)
Treaty of Venice (τ_0)	1495	–
Thirty Years' War	1618	123
Dutch War of Louis XIV	1672	54
War of the League of Augsburg	1688	16
War of the Spanish Succession	1701	13
War of the Austrian Succession	1739	38
Seven Years' War	1755	16
French Revolutionary and Napoleonic War	1792	37
World War I	1914	122
World War II	1939	25

Source: Onset dates are from Levy (1983: 75), where a general world war is defined as a war "involving at least two-thirds of the Great Powers and an intensity exceeding 1,000 battle deaths per million population."

general world war, counting from the previous onset. This portrays a precise pattern in political uncertainty, not at all the haphazard impression conveyed by the raw onset data in table 2.2. Thus, using estimates in table 2.3 or figure 2.4, the historical probability of general world war onset by the year 2000, which is 61 years after the previous onset (the World War II onset in 1939), is $\hat{\Phi}(61) \approx 0.79 \pm 0.10$.[14] The present era of "long peace" (Kegley 1991) is not as long as some have argued (Levi 1981; Mueller 1989). Two "long peaces" in table 2.2 – i.e. the pre-Thirty Years' War era of 123 years, and the post-Napoleonic War (Concert of Europe) era of 122 years – lasted much longer.

Table 2.4 and figure 2.5 show values of the empirical density function $\hat{p}(t)$ measured by the Kaplan–Meier procedure shown earlier in figure 2.3. The irregular form of the empirical density function in figure 2.5 is not uncommon, given the relatively small number of available observations ($N = 9$ interwar onset values). King et al. (1990: 854) show how irregular some political density functions can be, even when N is large.

The bottom part of table 2.4, for the calculation of the slope $\hat{p}$, shows empirical values of probability density for general world war onset T.

---

[14] This estimate is sensitive to the number of observations, which is relatively small in this case. However, the fact that table 2.2. lists a population of cases and not a sample (a common situation with political events data) means that this is also a best estimate, based on a complete historical record. The fact that the population is small implies that the estimate is sensitive to minor differences which (only hypothetically) could have occurred in past history (but which did not) and, therefore, should not be interpreted with the same confidence as an estimate resulting from a much larger population. The standard error (± 0.10) is also graphed below, in figure 2.7, to highlight these precautions.

Table 2.3. *Empirical cumulative distribution of general world war onset* T

Observed values of onset time $\hat{t}_i$	Raw frequency	Cumulative frequency	Relative cumulative frequency $\hat{\Phi}(t)$
13	1	1	0.111
16	2	3	0.333
25	1	4	0.444
37	1	5	0.556
38	1	6	0.667
54	1	7	0.778
122	1	8	0.889
123	1	9	1.000

Source: Calculated by the author.

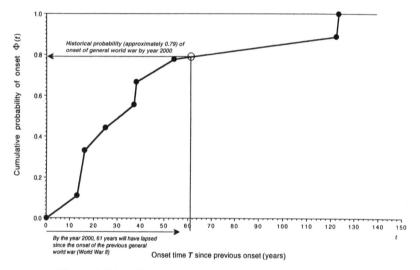

Figure 2.4. Empirical cumulative frequency histogram of general world war onset

These empirical distributions (tables 2.3 and 2.4, figure 2.4) define a specific pattern of uncertainty associated with general world war onset, a distinct pattern not shared by all types of wars. The main theoretical question is: what has caused this specific pattern of uncertainty and not some other? More generally, what has caused general world war onset to have a well-defined pattern at all? I shall answer these questions a little later, because the answer requires a more complete discussion of political behavior as a dependent variable.

Table 2.4. *Measurement of (Kaplan–Meier) empirical density distribution of general world war onset*

	Calculation of horizontal values for the slope $\hat{p}$		
Onset time $\hat{t}_i$ (years)	*t*-interval $\Delta t = t_{i-1}$	$\Delta t/2$	*t*-value at midpoint $t^* = t_i + \Delta t/2$
13	13	6.5	6.5
16	3	1.5	14.5
25	9	4.5	20.5
37	12	6.0	31.0
38	1	0.5	37.5
54	16	8.0	46.0
122	68	34.0	88.0
123	1	0.5	122.5

	Calculation of vertical values for the slope $\hat{p}$		
Values of Φ_i (probability)	Φ-interval $\Delta\Phi = \Phi_{i-1}$	$\Delta\Phi/2$	Φ-value at midpoint $\Phi^* = \Phi_i + \Delta\Phi/2$
0.111	0.111	0.056	0.056
0.333	0.222	0.111	0.222
0.444	0.111	0.056	0.389
0.556	0.111	0.056	0.500
0.667	0.111	0.056	0.611
0.778	0.111	0.056	0.722
0.889	0.111	0.056	0.833
1.000	0.111	0.056	0.944

Calculation of the slope $\hat{p}$	
t-value at midpoint $t^* = t_i + \Delta t/2$	Density $\hat{p}(t^*) = \Delta\Phi/\Delta t$
6.5	0.009
14.5	0.074
20.5	0.012
31.0	0.009
37.5	0.111
46.0	0.007
88.0	0.002
122.5	0.111

Source: Calculated by the author.

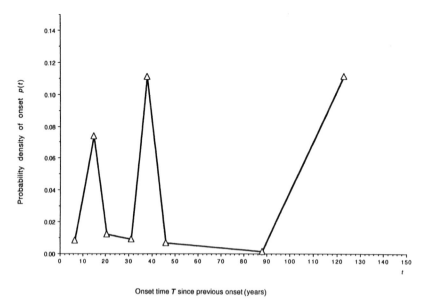

Figure 2.5. Kaplan–Meier estimate of probability density of general world war onset

2.2.4   Variety

As I noted earlier, definition 2.1 allows for political uncertainty with different patterns – the variety of politics – to be represented by different probability functions. This is an important theoretical and empirical point because the uncertainty of political behavior – unlike haphazard chaos – is *not* all of the same form. A political theory that admits to only one form of randomness (e.g. in the common econometric shorthand "ε is the error term") is quite useless for understanding the structure of uncertainty.

Figure 2.6 shows the graphs of three different and distinct patterns of political behavior, all three of which are uncertain, and each of which is uniquely specified by the functions $\Phi(y)$ and $p(y)$ of a given political variable Y. My approach focuses directly on the variety of shapes in political randomness, distinguishing the characteristic uncertainty of politics from merely haphazard phenomena. Note that these functions obey the following properties. In each case the top graph in figure 2.6 depicts the cumulative distribution of the bottom graph (in calculus terminology, the top graph represents the integral of the bottom graph), and the bottom graph is the slope of the top graph (the derivative), consistent with equa-

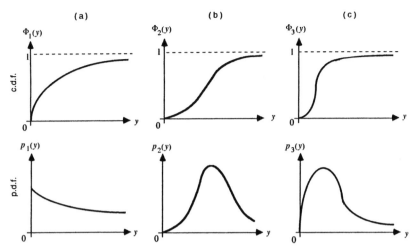

Figure 2.6. Different forms of uncertainty specified by the probability functions of a political variable Y (top: cumulative density functions $\Phi(y)$; bottom: probability density functions $p(y)$)

tions 2.9 and 2.10. Also, $\Phi(y)$ ranges over all possible values of Y as y increases, so $\Phi(y)$ is always monotonically increasing and asymptotic to $\Phi = 1$. However, $p(y)$ can increase *or* decrease but cannot be constant (because the area under $p(y)$ would be > 1, in violation of the concept of probability).

To understand the political characteristics modeled by this qualitative and quantitative variety in patterns of behavioral uncertainty, consider the three probability density functions in figure 2.6 (bottom graphs). Each case represents a distinct form of random political behavior that is *not* haphazard. For example, in case (a) (bottom left) the uncertainty of a political variable Y has the following distinctive features:

1 Many relatively small values of the political variable are observed most often, because the value with highest probability density (the modal or maxiprobable value) is the smallest ($Y = 0^+$). This is how many coalitions, riots, wars, and other political onsets are observed over a long and heterogeneous historical epoch containing many cases, and how many political elites turn over.[15]

2 There is no reversal in decreasing probability density with increasing values of behavior Y, because density decreases monotonically as values

[15] Casstevens (1970, 1974, 1980), Casstevens and Casstevens (1989), Cioffi-Revilla (1985a, 1989), Hayes (1973), Job (1976), McGowan and Rood (1975), Mintz and Schrodt (1987), Moyal (1949), Richardson (1941, 1945a, 1945b, 1960b), Singer and Small (1972), Small and Singer (1983).

increase ($p \to 0$ as $y \to + \infty$). In this case large values of Y are increasingly unlike.

3 The rate of decrease in probability density at a given value is proportional to the value itself ($dp/dy = - ky$), because density in this case has the simple exponential form:

$$p(y) = k\, e^{-ky}, \qquad\qquad [2.11]$$

where k is a constant frequency denoting the number of events per unit of time.

In the next two chapters I will discuss other unique properties of this political situation (case [a] in figure 2.6) because this is a common and highly significant form of political uncertainty. Indeed, this case finds strong empirical support in a remarkable number of areas of political behavior – including *coups*, cabinet durations, war onsets, and alliance formations (see references in table 2.1) – and corresponds to the Poisson distribution. Also, I believe case (a) in figure 2.6 is interesting because, as I will explain later in greater detail (chapter 4), this is the only pattern of political uncertainty that is caused by exactly constant (stationary) risk of occurrence or pressure-to-act operating on individuals and groups. Nothing other than a constant behavioral force can produce this form of political uncertainty (Poisson); all other situations produce political behavior significantly different from case (a).

Cases (b) and (c) in figure 2.6 differ from (a). Both cases represent more complex distributions which specify yet other forms of political uncertainty. For example, case (b) has a clearly marked modal value, indicating greater behavioral regularity (weak periodicity) and somewhat less variability (approximately Gaussian density). Some types of conflict magnitude M and other intensity variables in table 2.1 behave with this form of uncertainty (Cioffi-Revilla and Mason 1991), as I will show in chapter 4. Case (c), on the other hand, is asymmetric, with sharply rising density toward a modal value that is smaller than in case (b).

Uncertainty therefore varies across different types of political behavior, a variation that is both qualitative (by probabilistic modes) and quantitative (by probabilistic values). Randomness is not all of one form. What unifies different types of political behavior under a common set of principles, and is therefore key to theoretical progress, is that each case of uncertainty is uniquely defined by the probability functions $\Phi(y)$ or $p(y)$ in definition 2.1, and – as I show in the next chapter – each pattern is caused by specific behavioral hazards or risks that act under general uniform principles. The randomness of political behavior – politics' fundamental uncertainty – is clearly not all of one form (Poisson's, or case [a] in figure 2.6), as many previous studies have assumed. *Coups,* coalitions, wars, and other political phenomena have different patterns of uncertainty concerning their onset, magnitude, duration, and other dimensions in table 2.1. Moreover, as some have correctly noted, "one should not confuse 'random' with 'haphazard'" (King 1989a: 7). I believe it is a remarkable political fact – and an important foundation for the science of politics – that a relatively small number of patterns of uncertainty play a powerful role in explaining and understanding a large class of political behaviors, including those in table 2.1.

2.2.5   *Special values*

One of the ideas I have established thus far is that a political behavior variable Y can take on any value y over the interval in which it is defined, although the occurrence of a single individual value cannot be exactly predicted (axiom 1); only the probability $\mathbf{P}(Y = y)$ of individual values is exact (definition 2.1). On the basis of this idea, I will now identify a set of special values that help define in a more precise and insightful way the uncertainty pattern of any given political variable Y.

Besides the moments of a distribution (mean, variance, and so forth) other special political values are also useful, each representing a significant property associated with the probability functions $\Phi(y)$ and $p(y)$ that define Y. Because both functions are always nonlinear (see figure 2.6), these values mark special thresholds of political uncertainty, such as maxima, minima, or inflections of probability. Two such values are the median (or semiprobable) value ψ and the modal (or maxiprobable) value ω, as these are defined below. As I discussed earlier for the probability functions, different special values portray different characteristics of political uncertainty. Taken as a whole, the set of special values provides a more composite and precise representation than may be portrayed by any single value. Jointly these special values draw out the nature of political variables as statistical measures.

Moments of political behavior. Because I have defined a dimension of political behavior as a random variable (by assumption 2.1) the first special values to consider are naturally the moments.[16]

Definition 2.2 (first moments of a political variable). *Given a political variable Y with probability density function $p(y)$, the first two moments of Y are the expected value*

---

[16] The symbols $E(Y)$ and $V(Y)$ denote the expected value (arithmetic mean) and the variance of variable Y. More generally, I use the symbol $\sum(Y)$ to denote the set of special values of a political variable Y.

$$E(Y) = \int_{-\infty}^{+\infty} y\, p(y)\, \mathrm{d}y \qquad\qquad [2.12]$$

and the variance

$$V(Y) = E[y - E(Y)]^2. \qquad\qquad [2.13]$$

The common empirical interpretations of these values are as the average (arithmetic mean, $\bar{y}$) and the square of the standard deviation (dispersion from the mean, σ^2), respectively. For example, the moments of the onset T of general world war (example 2.4) are $\bar{t} \approx 49.33$ years and $\sigma \approx 43.51$ years, as calculated from data in table 2.2. One implication of this is that the onset of general world war is somewhat uncertain, more than just moderately so, because the two moments are relatively close to each other, $\bar{t} \approx \sigma$. By contrast, general world war would have greater regularity (and logically be more predictable) if the value of σ were much smaller than 43 years. These empirical political features are not apparent from plain observation, or from reading history; they are derived from the application of theory to the observed facts.

More generally, the relationship between the first two moments of political behavior provides a measure of uncertainty, as shown in the following three cases.

Case 1 (exponentially distributed variables). When

$$E(Y) = V(Y) \qquad\qquad [2.14]$$

a political variable has a Poisson distribution, corresponding to the density function of equation 2.11, or case (a) in figure 2.5. Empirically, in this case $\bar{t} = \sigma$. I believe this equilibrium result is not commonly known (Cioffi-Revilla 1985a; McGowan and Rood 1975; Rood 1978): a political variable that is Poisson distributed has the same expected value and variance, and (sometimes) vice versa. The onset of general world war, as the onset of most other types of wars, is *not* Poisson distributed (because $\bar{t} \neq \sigma$); it is only by mixing all types of wars into a heterogeneous population that one gets a good Poisson fit (Richardson 1960b). Nor are many other political events in table 2.1 Poisson distributed, in spite of a common belief to the contrary.

Cases 2 and 3 (hyperexponential and hypoexponential variables). When

$$E(Y) < V(Y) \qquad \text{(hyperexponential)} \qquad\qquad [2.15]$$

and when

$$E(Y) > V(Y) \qquad \text{(hypoexponential)} \qquad\qquad [2.16]$$

political uncertainty is high and low, respectively. This is because when the expected value of political behavior Y is smaller than its variance (as in case 2, inequality 2.15), knowing the former does not help diminish uncertainty as to how Y will behave. More generally, political uncertainty increases as variance increases relative to expected value $E(\cdot)$. Conversely, political uncertainty decreases as variance decreases relative to $E(\cdot)$. Logically, political behavior becomes deterministic as $V(\cdot) \to 0$, an abstract limit that is never reached. Cases 2 and 3 are called "hyper-" and "hypoexponential," respectively, because they have higher and lower than Poissonian uncertainty. The onset of general world war during the past five hundred years has therefore been hypoexponential ($\bar{t} > \sigma$, or $\bar{t} = 1.13\ \sigma$), indicating a slight tendency toward onset regularity of about once every 49 years. This pattern is similar to case (b) in figure 2.6. Knowing this does not detract from the uncertainty of world war onset, but it does distinguish its uncertainty from both (i) other patterns of uncertainty, and (ii) mere randomness. Other important properties are uncovered later.

The significance of the Poisson distribution as a baseline for judging the character of political uncertainty should be clear from the three cases just examined. The ratio $\bar{t}/\sigma$, a coefficient of variability, is a useful measure of political uncertainty that can be easily calculated from observed data.

Median value of political behavior. The moments of a political behavior variable Y provide the first natural characterizations of its uncertainty. However, in some cases, the expected value may not exist. Other special distribution values highlight additional qualitative and quantitative properties of political behavior. These are the mediam value ψ and the modal value ω, as defined below. The median exists for all distributions.

Definition 2.3 (median value ψ of a political behavior). *The median value $\psi(Y)$ of a political variable Y is the value of behavior that has cumulative probability equal to 0.5 (even-odds chance of occurring). Formally,*

$$\psi(Y) \in Y, \text{ such that } \Phi[\psi(Y)] = 0.5. \qquad [2.17]$$

The median value is insightful for temporal variables such as coalition duration, conflict onset, and others in table 2.1.[17] For example, for conflict

---

[17] Following the terminology used in physics, some political scientists have used the term "half-life" to denote the quantity $\psi(T)$. I prefer the standard term "median value" because the formal political idea is unrelated to any physical phenomenon and, moreover, is not limited to temporal variables alone (as is the half-life in physics). Accordingly, in this theory the median value is as well defined and meaningful for intensity variables as it is for temporal variables.

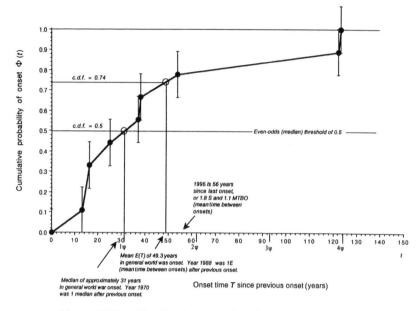

Figure 2.7. Special values (mean and median) in the onset of general world war

onset (or coalition duration) the median value ψ is the time beyond which conflict (or the coalition) is more than likely to break out (or to form). For war expansion, ψ is the time beyond which new additional belligerents are more than likely to join an ongoing war; or for coalition expansion, ψ is the time beyond which new additional allies are more than likely to join an existing coalition. For war duration, ψ is the time beyond which war is more than likely to terminate. In general – for both temporal and intensity variables – the median value $\psi(Y)$ marks the value of Y beyond which the cumulative odds of occurrence are greater than even and the next event (i.e. the value $T = \psi(Y) + dy$) is more than likely to occur. For example, for conflict magnitude, $\psi(M)$ is the even-odds magnitude of conflict. Any war magnitude $\mu > \psi$ has greater than even-odds of occurring. Similarly, $\psi(S)$ is the even-odds coalition size.

Example 2.5 (onset of general world war: mean and median). Figure 2.7 shows the mean $E(T)$ and median $\psi(T)$ values for the onset of general world war, using the same data and analysis presented earlier (example 2.4). The error bars in figure 2.7 are based on the standard error of the observed c.d.f. values. The median value ($\psi = 31$ years) is 37 percent smaller than the mean value ($E = 49.3$ years), so the odds for general world war become greater than even ($\Phi > 0.5 \pm 0.1$) almost 20 years before the expected (mean) time of onset. (Note the margin of uncertainty expressed by the standard error of the c.d.f. values, ± 0.1.) I believe the difference in these two values – elsewhere I have called this difference the "war ledge" (Cioffi-Revilla 1989) – is not commonly considered in the analysis of political uncertainty, although it plays an important role. The difference in the two special values of onset T can explain why highly devastating wars, such as general world wars, are said to arrive "by surprise," as many have said of World War I. Surprise is naturally caused by the fact that such wars may be expected at 49.3 years (mean political behavior), but they tend to occur any time after 31 years (median political behavior).

In general, as shown in example 2.5, the even-odds (median) value $\psi(Y)$ and the expected (mean) value $E(Y)$ are not the same (i.e. $\psi \neq E$), although both represent politically meaningful aspects of what may be called the "the most likely behavior" of Y. The difference between these two measures of uncertainty ($E - \psi$) provides an indicator of what may be called "political surprisability" – the potential for political surprise – because E is the "expected (mean)" value, and ψ is the "even or greater-than-even odds" (median) value. Thus, when $E > \psi$ (as in example 2.5), political behavior occurs in a way that is in some sense overdue according to the probabilistic odds alone, although not according to the historical record. Conversely, when $E < \psi$, political behavior occurs in a way that is premature by the odds alone, although not by the historical experience. History and odds provide the same expectation only when $E = \psi$, a special and arguably rare case. These concepts provide new insights and tools for understanding political uncertainty.

Modal value of political behavior. Another special value of uncertain political behavior concerns when or how the behavior in question is most likely to occur. I define this as follows.

Definition 2.4 (modal value ω of a political behavior). *The modal value $\omega(Y)$ of a political behavior variable Y is the value of the behavior that has the highest probability density. Formally,*

$$\omega(Y) = y, \text{ such that } dp(y)/dy = 0. \qquad [2.18]$$

The modal value offers insights for both temporal and intensity variables, such as coalition size, conflict onset, or others in table 2.1. For example, for coalition size, $\omega(S)$ is the most likely size to occur, or, according to Riker's (1962) theory, the "minimal winning" size. For conflict onset, $\omega(T)$ is the time when conflict is most likely to break out. Generally, $\omega(Y)$ marks the most frequent value of Y.

Note that, in general, the modal value is not necessarily the same as the other special values. For example, when political behavior is Poisson-distributed (figure 2.6, bottom left, case [a]), as happens for the onset of wars of all magnitudes measured over a long (heterogeneous) period of history, then clearly $\omega(T) = 0^+$. This low modal value is always necessarily lower than either $E(T)$ or $\psi(T)$. An important step in understanding the uncertainty of politics lies in recognizing that "average" political behavior (E) usually differs from that which is "most likely" (ω). The two are equal if and only if $E = \omega$, an intriguing but rare coincidence.

This concludes for now my treatment of dependent variables of political behavior as statistical measures, the first building blocks in the theory of political uncertainty. I will next address the second set of building blocks – the forces or risk factors of politics (independent variables) that cause the various patterns of political uncertainty.

2.3   Hazard rate force: defining independent variables

Which types of independent variables cause aggregate political behavior to emerge, changing the lives, fortunes, or governance of collectivities? What causes political behavior? Although at first glance these questions may seem too general to even be useful to consider, in other sciences similar questions have been raised and given precise answers. In economics, consumers and producers react to supply and demand and other well-defined independent variables. In thermodynamics, gas molecules behave according to defined conditions in temperature, volume, or pressure. In psychology, individuals respond to perceived stimuli. What causes political behavior?

More precisely, if the uncertainty of political behavior is governed by distribution functions, what causally governs these functions? What gives shape to – what fundamentally patterns – the uncertainty of political behavior? Can exact answers be given to these questions? What insights may be gained for the understanding of politics in general, and specific areas like coalitions, conflict, and others in particular? The answer lies with hazard forces (independent variables) acting on individuals or groups as causal risk factors that produce aggregate political behavior (dependent variables). An understanding of this concept is necessary in order to use distribution models in a causal and theoretically constructive way, not merely for descriptive curve-fitting (off the shelf estimation) without theoretical justification or causal interpretation.[18]

---

[18] The increasing availability of computer software packages for estimating hazard rate models and other distribution functions (LIMDEP, SAS, SPSS), provides an opportunity to develop more theoretically informed models, with insightful causal interpretation. However, the application of any given probability model should always be informed by an

The history of political science documents many proposals of independent variables and mechanisms of causation to explain aggregate political behavior. Institutions, societal attributes, socioeconomic structures, expected utility, individual or collective instincts, historical events, and others have been proposed as causal explanations of diverse forms of observed macropolitical behavior. In general, the earlier covariational approaches, using these and other independent variables in regression or correlational studies, have yielded mixed results, for reasons already discussed in chapter 1. The approach I will take to this issue is based on a new causal concept that has theoretical potential and can be empirically measured, as well as having some other properties.

2.3.1   *Forces of political behavior*

Aggregate political behavior is caused by situational or risk factors that can be interpreted as causal "hazard forces." I will first discuss hazard forces informally, and then provide a more precise treatment based on the hazard rate concept. Intuitively, the causal forces of political behavior consist of psychological, social, demographic, economic, political, technological, or strategic drives that act on decision makers and members of a collectivity. These are the causal agents of observed political behavior. Some forces originate from decisional acts (from political decisions), whereas others may originate from states of nature. Although the forces that govern political behavior may not be directly observable – many useful theoretical terms are not – they may be measurable. Also, their effects are often both observable and measurable.

The existence of political forces is accepted by most political scientists, traditionalists and behavioralists alike, although few books on politics actually list the term "force" in the table of contents or in the subject index as a separate, well-defined concept. For example, "nationalist forces" have been said to create war (Richardson 1960b: 15). According to others, "our problem is to find the best equilibrium among swiftly moving forces which otherwise may find solutions and balances by violence and destruction!" (Merriam 1945: 256). "Field forces" are said to explain political change because decision makers "are forced under pressure of necessity to improvise policies whose long-run effect is to augment the causes of war" (Wright 1942: 1278). Today, "turbulent forces" (Rosenau 1990) affect both domestic and international political behavior in the post-Cold War era: these are "forces of integration," such as communications, trade, or democracy, and "forces of fragmentation," such as nationalism, religious extremism, or protectionism

understanding of its theoretical properties, mathematical derivation, and substantive interpretation. In turn, these require foundations in probability modeling, which differ in basic orientation from covariational regression modeling.

(Gaddis 1992). "Electoral or democratic forces," "historical forces," "forces of corruption," "institutional forces," "forces of rivalry," "forces of revenge," "armed forces," or "forces of war and peace" are other examples.

Do these forces have any scientific meaning? Do they mean anything as causal independent variables? *Can* a force concept have a valid scientific meaning in explaining the uncertain occurrence of political behavior? With others, I view these forces as the basic drives of political behavior – the causes of change in "the lives, fortunes, or governance of collectivities." As situational risk factors, some forces operate at the individual agent level (instinct, values, expected utility, power drive, fear, or aggression), whereas others operate as aggregate or structural forces that act on domestic or international groups or collectivities (power balances, coalition structures, institutions, cultural norms). For example, using an economic utilitarian mechanism (table 2.1), a force that can operate at the individual level of decision making is the difference between (i) the expected utility of a leading alternative (subjective desirability of a decisional act) and (ii) the expected utility of the second best. The greater the expected utility of the best alternative over the others, the more probable it becomes that such an alternative will be chosen, because the difference will be greater. Thus, $P(\mathbb{A}_i$ is chosen over $\mathbb{A}_j)$ is proportional to $[EU(\mathbb{A}_i) - EU(\mathbb{A}_j)] > 0$, which has the character of a causal force or intensity to chose $\mathbb{A}_i$ over any other $\mathbb{A}_j$ (for $i \neq j$). Causally, $\mathbb{A}_i$ is chosen over $\mathbb{A}_j$ because (if and only if) it has superior expected utility, or $EU(\mathbb{A}_i) >$ all other $EU(\mathbb{A}_j)$.

Over time, or across different political regimes, forces or risk factors can grow, decline, remain constant, or undergo various qualitative changes, depending on social, political, economic, technological, or even physical conditions (like droughts or other natural disasters). From a dynamic perspective, it is desirable to define the concept of force in such a way as to render it analytically tractable, theoretically fruitful, and empirically measurable. The hazard rate concept provides a useful solution to understanding aggregate political behavior in terms of causal force, providing a dynamic explanation that is both insightful and rigorous.

2.3.2   *Properties of causal force*

Consistent with a probabilistic understanding of politics, I view the forces of political behavior as having three fundamental conceptual properties: (i) they can be numerous,[19] (ii) they vary from one realization of political

---

[19] For example, many forces influence the formation, size, or duration of a coalition cabinet government. Similarly, other forces affect the onset of an international crisis, the escalation to war, or the duration of war because "there are many domestic [and international] forces which pressure a nation's foreign policies into particular channels" (Guetzkow 1996: 77).

behavior to another,[20] and (iii) they have a direct causal effect on the aggregate pattern of political uncertainty – on the distribution of observed values – not on individual values (otherwise political behavior would be deterministic, in violation of the axioms presented in chapter 1). These properties may also explain why so much parametric instability has been reported in cross-sectional and longitudinal analyses of political behavior using conventional regression and other deterministic approaches (Beck 1983; Newbold and Bos 1985).

Aggregate risk factors act as hazard forces that give form to the distribution of dependent behavior variables such as conflict onset, magnitude, or duration, explaining the pattern of uncertainty; they do not determine individual values of onset, or else political behavior would be deterministic. Forces change with historical evolution, and so must patterns of uncertainty and the corresponding forms of distributions. If anything is "determined" by these forces it is only the distribution of political variables – the form of political uncertainty – not individual values, which remain fundamentally uncertain. A causal link between dimensions of political behavior (dependent variables) and risk factors acting as hazard forces (independent variables) exists – political behavior *is* caused – and it is probabilistic (by axiom 3), as mediated by distribution functions. In general functional form,

political behavior = f(risk factors or hazard forces),

such that

f: (risk factors or hazard forces) → political behavior,

where the function f represents a probabilistic (not a deterministic) mapping.

2.3.3 Defining hazard force

The required causal concept for explaining aggregate political behavior may seem intuitive. However, a theoretically powerful and empirically tractable definition is not trivial to define in this case because I am requiring that the concept be causal but at the same time not deterministic, consistent with axiom 3 (probabilistic causality). I will illustrate how this can be done by first using the example of the onset of conflict and then showing how the idea can be generalized.

[20] The forces that caused the onset or magnitude of the Los Angeles riots differed from those which caused the earlier 1960s riots (Midlarsky 1978; Spilerman 1970, 1971, 1972). These also differed from the forces which caused the signing of the Maastricht Treaty on European union. Likewise, the forces that determined the onset of World War I differed from those that determined the collapse of the Soviet Union or the fragmentation of former Yugoslavia.

Consider first the nature of two events that are defined with respect to the dependent conflict onset variable T:[21]

W_1: war onset will occur at time t

and

W_2: war onset will not occur by time t,

where t may be any span of time from the previous onset, say 20 months. Thus,

W_1: $T = 20$ months

and

W_2: not $T \leq 20$ months $= T > 20$ months.

Next, consider the corresponding probabilities:

$\mathbf{P}(W_1) = \mathbf{P}$(war onset will occur at time t) $= \mathbf{P}(T = 20$ months),

and

$\mathbf{P}(W_2) = \mathbf{P}$(war onset will not occur by time t)

$= \mathbf{P}(T > 20$ months).

Note the key difference that exists between these two probabilities. The probability $\mathbf{P}(W_1)$ is about war onset occurring at a specific instant of time, t, whereas $\mathbf{P}(W_2)$ is about onset occurring some time after such a point in time. The former is a point-event related to the war onset variable T, whereas the latter is an interval-event defined on the same variable T. Both probabilities concern a single behavioral phenomenon: war onset.

Finally – this is the critical step in understanding the hazard rate as a causal force concept to explain the occurrence of political behavior – consider the ratio of these two probabilities. Informally, this ratio stands for "the chance that war will occur at 20 months" in relation to "the chance that war will not occur by 20 months." In other words, I interpret this ratio (increasingly called the hazard rate in political science, but more precisely the instantaneous occurrence rate) as the tendency, intensity, or propensity – or other synonyms – for the occurrence of war onset at that given time (20 months), given that war has not occurred by then. A tension for behavioral occurrence, for the next realization to occur, is created by the ratio of the two probabilities. The hazard rate concept is therefore also similar to the occurrence of "war in the next instant, given that it has not broken out up

---

[21] Recall that the conflict in question may be domestic, like a civil war, or international, like an interstate war, there being no difference in the essential aspects that are relevant in defining the hazard force concept.

to now." This quantity – the hazard rate $P(\mathbb{W}_1)/P(\mathbb{W}_2)$ – can be meaning-fully interpreted as a probabilistic force of war onset at time t – because it is consistent to call force ("the force for occurrence") that which directly concerns a propensity, drive, or intensity for war to break out at time t, given that it has not broken out by then. Thus, the term hazard force proposed in this theory. Accordingly,

$H(t)$ = hazard force rate of war onset at time t

    = force acting on belligerents to produce a war onset at time t

$$= \frac{P(\text{war onset will occur at time } t)}{P(\text{war onset will not occur by time } t)}.$$

More generally, beyond the specific case of conflict onset T, the hazard force function $H(y)$ is defined as follows:[22]

Definition 2.5 (hazard force). *The hazard force $H(y)$ producing political behavior Y is the ratio of the probability that the value of Y will be y (or "in the neighborhood of y"), relative to the probability that Y will have value greater than y. Formally,*

$$H(y) \equiv \frac{P(\text{political behavior } Y \text{ assumes a value in the neighborhood of } y)}{P(\text{political behavior } Y \text{ assumes a value greater than } y)}$$

$$= \frac{P(y < Y \leq y + dy)}{P(Y > y)}. \qquad [2.19]$$

Note that the hazard force is defined explicitly in terms of probabilities that concern directly the occurrence of political behavior with a given value, so the force interpretation is not a mere metaphor. The function $H(y)$ defines a behavioral force (the force for the event $Y = y$ to occur, such as "conflict will break out at time $T = t$") because a tension, intensity, or propensity for a behavioral event is captured by the ratio of the two probabilities in equation 2.19: the probability that the value of Y be y (i.e. that war will break out at $T = t$), versus the probability that the value of Y will be greater (that war break out after t, or $T > t$).

For the special case of a temporal variable T or D (table 2.1), this ratio of the "at-probability" relative to the "not-by-then-" or "after-probability" (i.e. the probability ratio $P(\mathbb{W}_1)/P(\mathbb{W}_2)$) is known by other names in various disciplines that also study uncertainty using random variables. The following terms denote the same ratio $H(t)$, when the dependent variable

---

[22] Later in this chapter (section 2.3.5) I extend the definition of the hazard force function to the common analytical form, $p(y)/[1 - \Phi(y)]$, which I apply to measurement. The emphasis here is conceptual and logically precedes the relationships between $H(y)$ and $p(y)$ and $\Phi(y)$. The latter play an important role in the next chaper, as general principles.

Y is a time dimension of political behavior: (i) dissolution rate in comparative politics (for modeling cabinet duration); (ii) force of exit in organizational sociology (for modeling time between firings, resignations, or retirements of members); (iii) intensity function in stochastic processes (for time between events); (iv) instantaneous failure rate in systems reliability (for time between system failures); (v) instant mortality rate in demography (for human life span); or (vi) Mill's ratio (economics).[23] I use the term hazard force because it includes both probabilistic (hazard) and dynamic (force) components.

Ultimately, a definition is only as good as the theoretical and empirical benefits it provides. The following are significant benefits that arise from the definition given above of the hazard force of political behavior. First, just as the uncertainty of politics is real and ineradicable, so is the presence of hazards, risk factors, or forces that may be as diverse as anarchy, stability, escalation, integration, and other conditions that act probabilistically upon individuals and groups. These may never determine individual realizations of political behavior, but they do influence the occurrence, evolution, and termination of behavior. Second, the probabilistic ratio contained in this concept captures the classical dynamic concept of force that connotes a drive, tension, intensity, or propensity for change (the occurrence of a new realization). The hazard force concept therefore has the same connotation as the classic scientific concept of "force-as-an-agent-of-change." When used to explain realizations of political behavior – as in the next chapter – the hazard force concept produces a dynamic theory in the classic sense because of the force interpretation. Third, the hazard force concept is analytically powerful and mathematically precise because all the probabilities on which it is based are well-defined *definientia*.

Fourth, definition 2.5 makes the hazard force measurable – meaning that force is no longer a rhetorical or metaphysical mystery – by using observed frequencies. This property means that hazard force can also be used for comparative research purposes, investigating patterns across time, across actors, or across types of political behavior. Finally, this definition allows for a well-defined class of specific functions (formal specifications of the

---

[23] See Bartholomew (1982), Cioffi-Revilla (1984), Cox and Lewis (1966), Gross and Clark (1975), Kaufmann et al. (1977), King et al. (1990), Murthy (1974). Many social science studies now use the term "hazard rate," borrowed from engineering (Allison 1984; Bienen and van de Walle 1989; Vuchinich and Teachman 1993). Since 1985 I have used the term "behavioral force," not wishing to borrow extraneous terms, because the ratio $P(\mathbb{W}_1)/P(\mathbb{W}_2)$ defines a probabilistic concept that is dynamic, causal, and politically meaningful as a propensity for occurrence, independent of whatever other interpretations the same mathematical definition may have in other fields. The general political force in question may assume different specific names in different political contexts, such as force of coalition termination or force of war, the root concept remaining the same.

hazard force function) that must satisfy only the mild mathematical conditions:

$$H(y) > 0$$

because equation 2.19 defines the ratio of two probabilities (both > 0), and the condition

$$\int_Y^r H(y)\,dy = \infty$$

because

$$\int_Y^r \Phi(y)\,dy = 1.$$

Clearly, the set of mathematical functions that satisfy these conditions is by no means empty, so the theory provides options for modeling the hazard force of political behavior.

2.3.4   Interpreting hazard force

Since the force interpretations of the hazard rate are essential for establishing a dynamic theory of political uncertainty – every dynamic theory requires the explicit treatment of how force affects behavior – I will next discuss these interpretations in specific political domains.

Consider the interpretation of the hazard rate in coalition duration, war onset, coalition size, and revolutionary violence. Based on the taxonomy established earlier (table 2.1), the first two of these refer to temporal variables (onset T and duration D), where the hazard force is easier to understand because it operates intuitively over time. The other two are intensity variables (size S and magnitude M) and require a greater conceptual effort.

Example 2.6 (force of coalition dissolution). Consider the case of coalition behavior, where each coalition lasts with durations δ_1, δ_2, δ_3, ... , as in example 2.1 and figure 2.1. Applying definition 2.5 and equation 2.19, let $H(\delta)$ denote the hazard rate for coalition dissolution at time δ, or

$$H(\delta) \equiv \frac{P(\delta < D \le \delta + d\delta)}{P(D > \delta)} \qquad [2.20]$$

where:

$$P(\delta < D \le \delta + d\delta) = p(\delta) = \text{probability of coalition dissolution}$$

at ("in the neighborhood of") time δ, or probability density of dissolution at δ

and

$P(D > \delta) = 1 - \Phi(\delta) =$ probability of dissolution after δ, or the probability that the coalition will not dissolve by δ.

First, consider the conditional probability $P(\delta < D \leq \delta + \Delta\delta \mid D > \delta)$, where $\Delta\delta$ is small. This is the probability of coalition dissolution in the next $\Delta\delta$ units of time, given that the coalition has lasted until time $\delta \in D$. Now, by definition,

$$P(\delta < D \leq \delta + \Delta\delta \mid D > \delta) \equiv \frac{P(\delta < D \leq \delta + \Delta\delta)}{P(D > \delta)} \qquad [2.21]$$

$$= \frac{\int_{\delta}^{\delta + \Delta\delta} p(y) \, dy}{P(D > \delta)} = \frac{\Delta\delta \; p(\lambda)}{1 - \Phi(\delta)}, \qquad [2.22]$$

where $\delta < \lambda \leq \delta + \Delta\delta$. The last term in equation 2.25 is approximately equal to $\Delta\delta H(\delta)$, so the fraction $p(\lambda)/[1 - \Phi(\delta)]$ represents the proportion of coalitions that will dissolve between δ and $\Delta\delta$ (the numerator), out of those that will not dissolve by δ (the denominator). This ratio represents a propensity or intensity – a disintegration force – for coalitions to dissolve at time δ.

Example 2.7 (force of war onset). Consider the hazard rate $H(t)$ of war onset at time t. In terms of equation 2.19, this is expressed as

$$H(t) \equiv \frac{P(t < T \leq t + dt)}{P(T > t)}, \qquad [2.23]$$

where:

$P(t < T \leq t + dt) = p(t) =$ probability that war breaks out at ("in the neighborhood of") time t, or probability density of war breaking out at t

and

$P(T > t) = 1 - \Phi(t) =$ probability of war breaking out after t, or the probability that war will not break out by t.

Again, similar to the previous example, consider the conditional probability $P(t < T \leq t + \Delta t \mid T > t)$, where Δt is small. This is now the probability that war will break out in the next Δt units of time, given that peace has endured until time $t \in T$. By definition,

$$P(t < T \leq t + \Delta t \mid T > t) \equiv \frac{P(t < T \leq t + \Delta t)}{P(T > t)} \qquad [2.24]$$

$$= \frac{\displaystyle\int_{t}^{t + \Delta \psi} p(y) \, dy}{P(T > t)} = \frac{\Delta \delta \; p(\lambda)}{1 - \Phi(\delta)}, \qquad [2.25]$$

where $t < \lambda \leq t + \Delta t$. The last term in equation 2.22 is approximately equal to $\Delta t \, H(t)$, so the fraction $p(\lambda)/[1 - \Phi(t)]$ represents the proportion of wars that will occur between t and Δt (the numerator), out of those that do not occur by t (the denominator). The proportion is therefore akin to a propensity or intensity – a belligerent force – for war to occur at time t.

The preceding examples illustrate the interpretation of $H(t)$ as a force acting on temporal variables of political behavior (onset T and duration D), using the earlier taxonomy presented in section 2.2.2, table 2.1. However, hazard force is not confined to the time-domain alone (temporal variables). The next two examples consider hazard forces applied to cases of political behavior that model size or magnitude (intensity variables).

Example 2.8 (force of coalition size). Consider the size S of a coalition, and the hazard rate $H(s)$, acting on a given collectivity of actors to produce a given size s. The force-like quality of $H(s)$ can be interpreted by examining the expression

$$H(s) \equiv \frac{P(s < S \leq s + ds)}{P(S > s)} \qquad [2.26]$$

where:

$P(s < S \leq s + ds) = p(s) =$ probability that a coalition will be ("in the neighborhood of") size s, or probability density of coalition size being s

and

$P(S > s) = 1 - \Phi(s) =$ probability of coalition size being greater than s, or the probability that size will not be smaller than s.

Consider the conditional probability $P(s < S \leq s + \Delta s \mid S > s)$, where Δs is small. This is the probability that coalition size will be within the next Δs units of size, given that size is within a value of $s \in S$. Again, by definition, this conditional probability is

$$\mathbf{P}(s < S \le s + \Delta s \mid S > s) \equiv \frac{\mathbf{P}(s < S \le s + \Delta s)}{\mathbf{P}(S > s)} \qquad [2.27]$$

$$= \frac{\displaystyle\int_{s}^{s+\Delta s} p(y) \, dy}{\mathbf{P}(S > \delta)} = \frac{\Delta \delta \; p(\lambda)}{1 - \Phi(\delta)}, \qquad [2.28]$$

where $s < \lambda \le s + \Delta s$. The last term in equation 2.28 is approximately equal to $\Delta s H(s)$, so the fraction $p(\lambda)/[1 - \Phi(s)]$ represents the proportion of coalitions that will have size between s and Δs (the numerator), out of those that are greater than s (the denominator). Such a proportion is akin to a propensity or intensity – the force of coalition size – for coalitions to have size s.

Example 2.9 (force of revolutionary violence). Finally, the behavioral force interpretation of the hazard rate can be examined in the context of domestic or revolutionary violence W, with

$$H(w) \equiv \frac{\mathbf{P}(w < W \le w + dw)}{\mathbf{P}(W > w)} \qquad [2.29]$$

where:

$\mathbf{P}(w < W \le w + dw) = p(w)$ = probability that revolution will have a violent level w (or "in the neighborhood of" w), or probability density of violence being w

and

$\mathbf{P}(W > w) = 1 - \Phi(w)$ = probability of violence being greater than w, or the probability that violence will not be smaller than w.

Considering the conditional probability $\mathbf{P}(w < W \le w + \Delta w \mid W > w)$, where Δw is small, this is the probability that violence will be Δw units greater than w. By definition,

$$\mathbf{P}(w < W \le w + \Delta w \mid W > w) \equiv \frac{\mathbf{P}(w < W \le w + \Delta w)}{\mathbf{P}(W > w)} \qquad [2.30]$$

$$= \frac{\displaystyle\int_{w}^{w+\Delta w} p(y) \, dy}{\mathbf{P}(W > w)} = \frac{\Delta \delta \; p(\lambda)}{1 - \Phi(w)}, \qquad [2.31]$$

where $w < \lambda \le w + \Delta w$. The last term in equation 2.31 is approximately equal to $\Delta w H(w)$, so the fraction $p(\lambda)/[1 - \Phi(w)]$ this time represents the proportion of revolutions that will have violence between w and Δw (the numerator) out of those that have violence greater than w (the denominator). This proportion is akin to a propensity or intensity – a force of violence – for revolutions to have a level of violence w.

The preceding examples illustrated the dynamic interpretation of the hazard rate concept in diverse political contexts. In each case, for temporal and intensity variables alike, the hazard rate appears as a tension, a propensity, or a marked tendency for political behavior to manifest a given value – a behavioral force. Given this theoretical conceptualization, I now turn to empirical aspects that link the hazard force concept to observational data.

2.3.5 Measuring hazard force

It is essential for using the concept scientifically to be able to measure the hazard force, otherwise the concept remains purely theoretical. Measuring the hazard force also allows us to obtain a new empirical measure, as I will show in the next example. A measurable hazard force would also yield policy-related benefits because, at least in principle, the measurement of hazard forces could allow analysts to diagnose an operating political system or an ongoing process.

The hazard force can be measured by operationalizing equation 2.19 in definition 2.5. First, note that the numerator and the denominator are

$$\mathbf{P}(y < Y \le y + \mathrm{d}y) = p(y) \qquad \text{(by eq. [2.2])}$$

and

$$\mathbf{P}(Y > y) = 1 - \mathbf{P}(Y \le y) = 1 - \Phi(y), \qquad \text{(by eq. [2.1])}$$

respectively. Using the empirical interpretation of these probability functions and substituting these into equation 2.19 yields the following empirical expression:

$$\hat{H}(t) = \frac{\hat{p}(t)}{1 - \hat{\Phi}(t)} \qquad [2.32]$$

where $\hat{p}(t)$ and $\hat{\Phi}(t)$ are the empirical p.d.f. and c.d.f. respectively. To understand how the empirical measurement of the hazard force works in practice, I shall resume the analysis of world war onsets and now measure the underlying hazard force of onset, which can be interpreted as a "martial

Table 2.5. *Measuring the hazard rate (martial force) of general world war onset*

Variables	Measured values							
t (years)	6.5	14.5	20.5	31.0	37.5	46.0	88.0	122.5
$\hat{H}(t)$	0.009	0.095	0.020	0.019	0.286	0.025	0.010	2.000

Source: Calculated by the author. Plotted in figure 2.8.

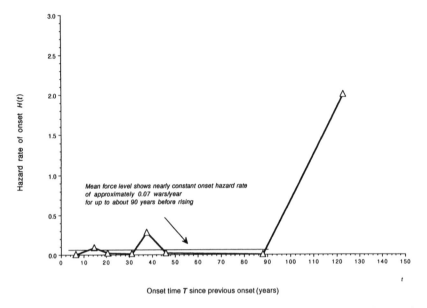

Figure 2.8. Empirical hazard rate of general world war onset (K–M estimate)

force." Parallel examples can be developed for other forms of political behavior, such as coalition formation, size, or duration, or the other variables in table 2.1 (temporal or intensity).

Example 2.10 (historical hazard force of general world war onset). Table 2.5 and figure 2.8 report values of the hazard force $H(t)$ of general world war onset, calculated with equation 2.32 and historical data from tables 2.3 and 2.4. These empirical values of hazard rate (martial force) represent the propensity (conditional probability) for general world war occurring at time t since the previous onset, given that war has not broken out by time t. Informally, this is akin to the notion of "the force or pressure for general

Table 2.6. *Historical special values of onset* T *of general world war*

Special value	Symbol	Time (years)	Remarks
Mean ± s.e.	$E(T)$	49.3 ± 14.5	Longer than one generation of leadership
Standard deviation	$\sigma(T)$	43.5	Shorter than the mean; $\sigma < E$
Uncertainty	E/σ	1.13[a]	Hypo-Poissonian, weak tendency toward regularity; weakly contagious
Median	ψ	31.1[b]	Approximately one generation; shorter than the mean
Surprisability	$(E - \psi)$	18.2[c]	Mean onset overdue

[a] Uncertainty (E/σ) is a pure number, not years.
[b] Calculated from the empirical function $\Phi(t)$ in figure 2.7, following the classical analytical definition of the median (Parzen 1960). Alternatively, $\psi = 37$ years, using the observed values in table 2.2, assuming a discrete distribution.
[c] Based on $\psi = 31.1$ years, assuming the theoretically continuous distribution of time. Alternatively, $(E - \psi) = 12.3$ years, assuming the empirically discrete distribution of time.
Source: Calculated by the author.

world war in the immediate future." As shown in figure 2.8, for about the first 88 years after an onset, this onset force is relatively weak and approximately constant, thereafter escalating to much greater intensity in just a few years. These findings can provide new insights on the onset of world war, and shed new light on its uncertainty. They also suggest new questions. What causes this force (hazard rate) to be initially so weak? Is it fear induced by a previous onset? Why is this force initially constant, besides being weak, as opposed to variable? Why is it not decreasing, as a reaction to the previous onset? What causes the final 88-year escalation that comes as "the beginning of the end" prior to the next onset? Which dynamics that were inoperative earlier are initiated after 88 years? Questions such as these and others had not arisen before because the uncertainty of onset seemed so forbidding to analyze. Historically, the theoretical perspective of political uncertainty indicates that the seeds for large-scale world war start germinating at approximately 80 years (subject to the earlier precautions on margins of error), after which a sharp escalation occurs in the probability of imminent world war onset. In relation to other special values of onset defined earlier (section 2.2.5), this pre-escalation period has the following characteristics:

$$88 \text{ years} = 1.6\,E \qquad \text{(mean value)}$$
$$= 1.8\,\sigma \qquad \text{(standard deviation)}$$
$$= 2.6\,\psi \qquad \text{(median)}$$

According to these estimates, "the beginning-of-the-end" for our current 88-year era – our "long peace" that began after World War II – will therefore occur around 2019, after which time the conditional probability of general world war would begin to escalate rapidly if the current age is similar to past history. Table 2.6 summarizes the special values of onset T of general world war.

In the preceding example I showed how the hazard force is measured using the operational equation 2.32. The application to measuring the hazard force in other cases of political behavior proceeds similarly, after measuring the empirical distribution functions (table 2.4). The empirical measurement of hazard force concludes the macro foundations of the theory. Using these building blocks, the next step is to derive testable principles of aggregate political behavior.

2.4   Conclusions

This was the first chapter that focused on uncertainty at the macro level of politics, the first branch of the theory. I addressed the first two building blocks of macropolitics: political behavior as the dependent variable and hazard force as the independent variable.

I defined political behavior as multidimensional, uncertain, measurable, multiform, and with special values that portray the structure of uncertainty in political behavior. The multidimensionality of political behavior offers a unifying perspective for covering diverse areas of politics under the same general theory, such as conflict, coalition processes, elections, and others identified in table 2.1. The uncertainty of political behavior required the introduction of concepts from probability distributions. The focus on the distributions of political behavior, as opposed to their specific individual values, is a defining feature that distinguishes this theory from earlier deterministic approaches based on covariational models. I showed how, based on the use of distributions to define political behavior, uncertainty is not all of one form ("random" does not mean the same as "haphazard"), but has different forms that can be specified by various distributions grounded on the substantive politics of the situation. I showed how the uncertainty of political behavior is also measurable, using empirical distributions that are constructed directly from recorded data. Specially defined values of political behavior, such as moments, median, mode, and surprisability provided more exact characterizations of the structure of uncertainty for understanding political behavior.

I defined the other building block of the macro part of the theory – the hazard force – as the propensity, intensity, or drive (formally, the conditional probability) that political behavior of a given form will assume a precise value as opposed to a lesser value. For temporal variables of political behavior, the onset (or duration) force refers to the propensity for a political event to occur at precisely time t (or terminate at exactly time δ), given that it has not done so until then. Unlike different distribution functions, which can be importantly different at the tails, the behavioral force function can distinguish between different distributions of behavior based on substantive political conditions.

The main running example I used in this chapter was the onset of general world war, a significant form of political behavior characterized by great uncertainty, major domestic and international consequences, and repeated recurrence throughout the centuries. I analyzed the onset of general world war as a random variable T with well-defined probability functions and governed by onset hazard force. In the next chapters similar examples will be used to demonstrate the theoretical link between political behavior and causal hazard forces.

The main focus of this chapter was on concept formation – to define political variables and the hazard forces that govern their behavior. I therefore did not extend my analysis beyond what was minimally sufficient to proceed with the principles in the next two chapters. However, it is possible to explore other ideas immediately connected with those presented in this chapter, such as theorems that explore the properties of distributions, special values, and so forth. For example, an analysis of the sensitivity of each of the special values to changes in some property of the underlying distribution is of intrinsic political interest, even if such topics are not commonly explored in standard mathematical works on probability. The building blocks established in this chapter serve as a guide in future explorations.

3 General macropolitical principles

> Contrary to the impression students acquire in school, mathematics is not just a series of techniques. Mathematics tells us what we have never known or suspected about notable phenomena and in some instances even contradicts perception. It is the essence of our knowledge of the physical world. It not only transcends perception but outclassses it.
>
> Morris Kline, *Mathematics and the Search for Knowledge*

3.1 Introduction

Kline's thesis on the powerful role of mathematics for establishing new principles applies a fortiori to the political world, where intuitive perceptions are plentiful but often provide *un*reliable foundations for theory.[1] In this chapter I derive the first set of core theoretical propositions on political uncertainty – the general macropolitical principles – using the concepts of political behavior and hazard force developed in chapter 2. The main goal here is to derive the linkage between political behavior and hazard force – called the distributions principle – and to use this aggregate principle to derive additional general results. These principles are the analytical core of the macro part of the theory of political uncertainty because they address the causal relationship that exists between political behavior and the hazard forces just examined in the previous chapter. Consistent with my approach thus far, I have solved this puzzle using the framework of probabilistic causality.

Formally, the principles contained in this chapter have the logical status of theorems, because they are propositions based on the axioms and

---

[1] Briefly stated, the Kline–Wigner thesis states that there are significant aspects of the real world – I extend this to the political world – that can be discovered exclusively through the medium of mathematical analysis (Kline 1985; Wigner 1969). Moreover, such mathematically uncovered features are as real or truthful as those discovered through direct empirical observation, only more reliably so because they are never distorted by measurement imprecision (error, misperception, incompleteness, and so forth). Mathematical inference – used in various modes, such as analysis, synthesis, bootstrapping, transformations, approximations, induction, and deduction – is a powerful engine for empirical discovery, not just for formalization.

assumptions that I introduced earlier (chapters 1 and 2). Mathematically, the main equations contained in these principles are composite functions, given the unspecified character of the hazard force function $H(y)$. The reader will note the relative complexity of the first set of equations contained in these theorems. I cannot apologize for this complexity because such seems to be the nature of political uncertainty – a complex phenomenon that only theory can help explain but that cannot be artificially reduced by imposing convenient but arbitrary simplifications. Interestingly, however, the pattern of mathematical complexity is repetitive or canonical (using different but specifiable combinations of accumulation, decay, interaction, and so on), with similar forms arising in different combinations in each principle. I interpret this to mean that the deep nature of political uncertainty has an elementary code constituted by more fundamental elements that recur in various canonical forms – the atoms of political behavior, so to speak. To assist in the understanding of these first principles, I present a new helpful method for visualizing the mechanism of probabilistic causality, based on the associated input–output relation or function machine of each macro principle when viewed as a system with comparable components and well-defined structure. The elements of this method are outlined in appendix 4. Although the view of a mathematical function as an input–output system is well established, I believe my use of this approach to explicate the probabilistic causality of political uncertainty is original, helpful, and provides a basis for other extensions.[2] These new representations of political behavior also lead to an additional set of simpler canonical forms for expressing the general macro principles. My exposition of these principles is only a first step toward subsequent theoretical developments. Most of the equations for these general principles are simplified further in chapter 4, but only after the hazard force function has been specified. However complex the mathematical form of the general macro principles may appear, their theoretical power – their explanatory value – is immediately apparent from the explicit linkage that they establish between political behavior and causal hazard forces.

The principles contained in this chapter have a number of theoretical and empirical properties. They are *general*, because they account for large classes of real-world political behaviors – recall the classes of temporal and intensity variables introduced earlier in the taxonomy of section 2.2 (table 2.1) – regardless of the specific form of hazard forces that are operating on political actors. This parsimonious property alone justifies the importance

---

[2] On the input–output system view of a mathematical function, see Bittinger (1976: 21), Bittinger and Crown (1982: 22–3), Thomas (1992: 18). My use of formal input–output systems analysis to model the uncertainty of aggregate political behavior at the macro level of the theory represents an extension of these standard methods.

of these principles, beside their capacity to generate more specific results, which I explore in chapter 4. These principles are also *dynamic*, based on the force interpretation of the hazard rate, because they treat hazard force – as opposed to some other property of political behavior – as the causal independent variable. Finally, these principles also have other substantive and formal properties, such as being *probabilistic* (explaining uncertainty), *nonlinear* (counterintuitive), and *universal* (applicable *erga omnes*).

To set the proper tone for the presentation of general principles, I shall first discuss the necessary requirements of a macro causal explanation of political behavior, consistent with the axioms and assumptions of probabilistic causality stated earlier. After outlining the general framework, I then present each of the general macro principles followed by a brief discussion with political interpretations. These are important to understand in full detail how and why political uncertainty occurs at the macro level of analysis as a result of hazard forces acting on individuals and groups. The formal proof of each principle is given in appendix 3. In the section following the presentation of principles I discuss some of their most salient properties, given their somewhat high level of abstraction and the relative paucity of these types of principles in contemporary political science. In subsequent chapters I derive more specific, less abstract results that are applicable to historically concrete domains of political behavior.

This chapter parallels chapter 6 in the second part of this book, which deals with the set of general micro principles for political events. Both chapters rely on Morris Kline's thesis to derive new insights on political uncertainty. I realize that in both chapters the level of abstraction is substantially higher than some readers would prefer, particularly in the case of some mathematical expressions that cannot be simplified further without destroying the essential political meaning of the relationship. However, the nature of general principles inherently requires a certain distance from empirical detail, and in the case of political uncertainty some of the basic complexity of the phenomenon seems to carry over into the formal principles. As noted by Suppes (1984: 70):

Axiomatic methods are seldom used at the same time that any detailed data or experimental evidence are considered. Those parts of theoretical science that do proceed axiomatically, as for example in parts of modern economics, are usually not set forth in conjunction with any complex and subtle consideration of data.

For this reason the orientation of this chapter is primarily axiomatic. As I argue here, I believe the complex manner in which hazard forces affect political behavior goes a long way in explaining why politics is always uncertain to the common observer – and at the very least puzzling to the political scientist attempting to understand it.

The main innovations in this chapter are – in order of presentation – the explicit application of the Kline–Wigner thesis in political science theory; the detailed treatment of probabilistic causality linking hazard force (independent variable) to aggregate political behavior (dependent variable) explicitly through the distributions principle; the input–output analysis of general macro principles to better understand political uncertainty; the derivation of explicit general principles that specify the relationship between hazard forces acting on agents of political behavior and the moments and other special values of such behavior; and the canonical forms for these principles to reduce their mathematical complexity and appreciate the underlying order – as an elementary code of political uncertainty at the macro level of analysis.

3.2   Macropolitical framework

The following theoretical elements provide a minimal set of analytical requirements for a causal framework suitable for explaining political behavior: (i) a set of well-defined dependent variables (Y) representing political behavior (*explanandum*); (ii) a set of independent variables (X) representing the causes of behavior (*explanans*); and (iii) a well-specified causal mechanism directly linking a dependent variable Y to one or more independent variables X. The first two of these components have already been defined (chapter 2). In this chapter I derive the third component. Each component must be treated in a manner consistent with the four axioms of the theory – on the duality, uncertainty, causality, and formalization of political uncertainty (axioms 1–4, section 1.3.1). Taken together, the three components of a causal explanation are formally expressed as a mapping

$$f\colon X \to Y$$

or as a function

$$Y = f(X)$$

where f specifies the causal mechanism that accounts for Y given X.

Scientifically, political behavior (Y) and its principal properties (the special values defined in chapter 2 and other characteristics of political uncertainty) must logically obtain as the deductive result of independent variables (X) acting through one or more general principles (f). A more specific requirement – because I wish to construct a macro theory to causally explain political behavior – is to use hazard force as the independent causal variable, as opposed to a different (nonforce) independent variable, as well as a specific mechanism that connects hazard force to observed political behavior.

I note that hazard force is not the only type of causal independent variable that is suitable for explaining politics. Other nonforce or static factors such as institutional structure, societal indicators, or socio-economic attributes have been used earlier. However, my thesis is that these macro parameters are only causally contextual to political behavior, and may help in describing the circumstances of behavior but not in explaining its causes. This is because using these static, macro conditions (which are not by themselves force-like entities) as independent variables to attempt to explain variable realizations of political behavior (like using "regime type" to explain political instability, or "systemic polarity" to explain international war fluctuations) is theoretically incoherent. How can a constant factor explain an observed change? Using static macro attributes to construct an explanation of time-varying behavior is analogous to the way the ancient Greeks explained why a body falls: because a body's essence makes it be (or "correlates with being") on the ground. The Greek research program in science ultimately failed because a macro constitutional essence is, by definition, always static, and therefore cannot simultaneously be a cause of behavioral change. Having said this, I should also add that certain contextual factors can indeed be significantly associated with certain macro patterns of aggregate political behavior (e.g. regime type to explain political behavior). The technical implementation of this is discussed in the next chapter (section 4.4). Thus, although contextual factors cannot explain particular changes in political behavior (individual realizations) they can be a relevant factor in terms of distribution patterns.

Consider how a changing phenomenon is explained by modern science: a body falls because it is acted upon by some force. The difference between the ancient Greek and the modern scientific explanations clearly lies in the nature of the causal process or mechanism that is proposed to account for the observed behavior. The scientific explanation of behavior is always essentially dynamic. The two explanations are not equally causal because they invoke different agents of change: location and force, respectively. Only the modern explanation goes beyond the search for mere correlation – by providing a causal mechanism based explicitly on a behavioral force (the force of gravitation in the case of a falling object, or hazard force in the case of political behavior). The Greek explanation remained at the level of mere correlation and omitted any process.[3]

When force is used to explain political behavior, however, it must be a

---

[3] There is a vast literature on causal explanations in ancient Greek and in modern science, as well as on the role of mathematical development in solving the puzzle of explanation in physical science. Two of my favorite works in this area are Bochner (1966) and Bronowski (1978).

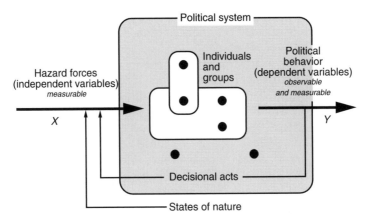

Figure 3.1. Causal effect of hazard forces (independent variables X) acting on individuals and groups producing political behavior (dependent variables Y)

well-defined concept; otherwise, it fails to play a productive scientific role and instead remains just a mythical or rhetorical term (as "force" has in dialectical Marxism, liberalism, historical romanticism, and other philosophical "-isms" that have previously used the term force to explain political behavior). In this theory hazard force is a substantive independent variable, rigorously defined, and consisting of the probabilistic pressures or tensions for change discussed in the previous chapter (section 2.3). The precise political meaning of hazard force is given by the concrete form of behavior being explained (e.g. coalition size, war onset) as I illustrated in section 2.3.4. The hazard force I have defined is therefore intended as an explanatory agent in the classic dynamic sense.

As illustrated in figure 3.1, the macro level of this theory is explicitly dynamic. I view the observable patterns of political behavior (dependent variables Y) as being caused by hazard forces (independent variables X) that operate on individuals, groups, or collectivities. Accordingly, changes in socioeconomic structures, societal attributes, policy changes, or other factors – formally these are referred to as states of nature and decisional acts – play a causal role in explaining political behavior only when these are formally defined as hazard forces. Recall that states of nature and decisional acts were already identified as important sources of uncertainty in section 1.2. Here I am relating both to the process which underlies the origin of hazard forces in the real world. For example, the onset of World War I and the fall of the Berlin Wall both resulted from measurable hazard forces acting on nations and groups of individuals.[4] The hazard forces active in politics are generated in two ways: (i) by decisional acts (themselves forms of political behavior) performed by individuals or groups, or (ii) by new states of nature (politically significant events unaccounted for by decisional acts, such as changes in economic, social, or even physical conditions). Each general principle details the structure of this probabilistic causality from a different perspective, as shown below.

Why are hazard forces causal? First, because they make political behavior occur, whereas correlates merely co-occur with behavior and do not make it occur. Second, as I show with the general principles below, because the hazard forces I have defined (definition 2.5) are capable of shaping political behavior into specific patterns of uncertainty (distributions). When hazard forces change so do the uncertain patterns of political behavior manifested by actors. Logically, this proves that behavioral force causes and not merely correlates with political behavior. Moreover, as the principles in the next section indicate, the changes in political behavior that are caused by changes in hazard force all take place with predictable and testable properties that are governed by unified probabilistic mechanisms.

3.3   General macropolitical principles

How exactly do hazard forces govern political behavior? For example, recalling the analysis of conflict in chapter 2, how does war force "determine" the onset, magnitude, or duration of conflict in history? Or, how do various political forces "determine" the formation, duration, or dissolution of governmental coalitions? In other words, how does this new probabilistic approach produce a viable framework of truly dynamic laws that go beyond the unstable correlations and weak linear models obtained through the earlier standard regression approaches?

The answers I provide to these questions are reached primarily by theoretical deduction, supported secondarily by empirical inferences. In turn, deductive principles lead to testable propositions. Using the building blocks already established and the proofs in appendix 3, it may be shown

---

[4] I discussed the measurement of the hazard rate force in section 2.3.5. In the case of the onset of World War I and the fall of the Berlin Wall, the behavioral forces that caused these events could be measured by the same general procedure already shown for the onset of world war, adapted to the specific characteristics of the corresponding dependent (random) variable Y. For example, to measure the hazard force that destroyed the Berlin Wall, one would first assemble an events dataset to obtain an accurate description of the prior process according to a set of common observational dimensions such as time between events T, level of conflict C, and so on. The associated hazard force would then be measured using the same procedure that I demonstrated in example 2.10.

that the following five macro principles of political behavior hold true as general relationships:

- distributions principle (theorem 3.1);
- moments principle (theorem 3.2);
- expectation principle (theorem 3.3);
- median principle (theorem 3.4);
- modal principle (theorem 3.5).

The first of these macro principles – the distributions principle – establishes the core link that exists between political behavior and hazard force. The other four principles provide the connection between each of the special values of political behavior (E, V, ψ, ω, and others; see section 2.2.5) and the underlying causal forces modeled by the hazard rate or intensity function. Following the distributions principle, each of the other principles is obtained as in a bootstrapping procedure, to explore core aspects and properties of macropolitical uncertainty.

3.3.1   Distributions principle

Recall that $H = H(p, \Phi)$, by definition 2.5, and $p \Leftrightarrow \Phi$, by the relationship that exists between the definitions of probability density and cumulative probability (equations 2.9 and 2.10). Therefore it also follows that the relationships $H \rightarrow p$ and $H \rightarrow \Phi$ must exist. This first principle can be stated as follows.[5]

Theorem 3.1 (distributions principle). *The general causal relationship between hazard force $H(y)$ and political behavior Y is given by the equations*

$$p(y) = H(y) \exp\left[-\int_0^y H(u)du \right] \qquad [3.1]$$

and

$$\Phi(y) = 1 - \exp\left[-\int_0^y H(u)du \right]. \qquad [3.2]$$

Informally, this principle states that the probability density of political behavior, $P(Y \approx y)$, is given by the interaction of the hazard force (behav-

---

[5] The reader is encouraged to closely examine the proof of this theorem in appendix 3 because it involves the use of various probability functions. Understanding the various steps involved in the proof can assist the reader to gain a better understanding of the role that probability functions play in defining the uncertainty of political behavior.

ioral propensity) and the cumulative effect of the unrealized propensity up until that point (the integral taken from 0 to y), with the latter decreasing with increasing values of cumulative effects. Put differently, the frequency with which political behavior of value y occurs is caused by an interaction between the hazard force and the discounted cumulated hazard up to that point. The latter component is given by the expression

$$\exp\left[-\int_0^y H(u)du \right],$$

which in turn consists of a hazard force accumulation process (a build-up in occurrence propensity), represented by

$$\int_0^y H(u)du$$

and a decay or discounting process, represented by

$$e^{-f(\bullet)}.$$

The distributions principle states that the political uncertainty portrayed by the density function $p(y)$ is accounted for by the interaction of these more elementary component processes.

Further insights on the uncertainty of political behavior are gained by examining the companion equation 3.2 in the distributions principle. To see this, consider the expression

$$S(y) = 1 - \Phi(y)$$
$$= P(Y > y)$$

called the survival function, representing the probability of a value larger than y being realized. When Y is a time variable, such as coalition duration or war onset, then S represents the probability of lasting longer than δ, or $P(D > \delta) = 1 - P(D \le \delta)$. Then, rewriting equation 3.2, we obtain

$$S(y) = \exp\left[-\int_0^y H(u)du \right],$$

which again consists of a combination of hazard force cumulation

$$\left[-\int_0^y H(u)du \right],$$

followed by simple exponential decay from $S(0) = 1$ to $S(\infty) = 0$ and median (half-life) value when $S(\psi) = 0.5$. The uncertainty of survival is therefore governed by these two processes, which provides a new insight into the nature of political uncertainty, telling us exactly how such uncertainty is caused. For example, for coalition duration D, this means that surviving beyond time δ, $S(\delta) = \mathbf{P}(D > \delta)$, is determined by a process that discounts or forgets (political memory loss) the hazard force (all the tensions to terminate the coalition) that has build up until δ. However, unlike the process that governs the probability density, $p(\delta) = \mathbf{P}(D \approx \delta)$, this process is not dependent directly on the hazard force acting alone, $H(\delta)$. Therefore, the structure of political uncertainty involved in accounting for survival is different (and simpler) than that which is involved in accounting for turnover (frequency). The specifics of probabilistic causality involved in each general case differ in ways that are important, albeit unobservable.

Note that the hazard force in both equations 3.1 and 3.2 appears explicitly as the independent causal agent that explains the exact form of the distributions $p(y)$ and $\Phi(y)$ of political behavior Y (dependent variable).[6] This important property satisfies the dynamic requirement that I discussed earlier, namely the need for an explicit treatment of force in successfully accounting for political behavior. In addition, equations 3.1 and 3.2 provide the required specification of the general mappings or functional forms discussed in the previous section.

I view the meaning of this first principle (theorem 3.1) as fundamental to understanding the dynamic character of macro uncertainty in political behavior. As shown by the associated input–output system in figure 3.2, the principle specifies the exact link of probabilistic causality that exists between (i) a given type of hazard force (with precise form, intensity, and other characteristics defined by the function $H(y)$) acting on individuals or groups, and (ii) the exact distributions of political behavior those actors will produce (equations 3.1 and 3.2).[7] As shown in figure 3.2, hazard forces (input) are transformed as in equations 3.1 and 3.2 to produce the distributions of political behavior (output). Thus, by measuring or postulating the hazard forces that operate on actors, it becomes possible to derive, predict, and test all properties of the distributions of a given political variable Y.

---

[6] Mathematically, equations 3.1 and 3.2 are functions of functions (composite functions), so the hazard force function $H(y)$ needs to be specified in order to obtain complete explicit solutions for the distribution functions $p(y)$ and $\Phi(y)$, as I demonstrate in chapter 4. However, it is precisely the statement of these principles as functions of functions that guarantees their generality. The rate of change of $p(y)$ and $\Phi(y)$ with respect to y can be obtained by applying the chain rule, since $p = f(H)$ and $H = g(y)$, where f and g are both assumed to be differentiable.

[7] The method and notation for representing an equation as an input–output system are summarized in appendix 4.

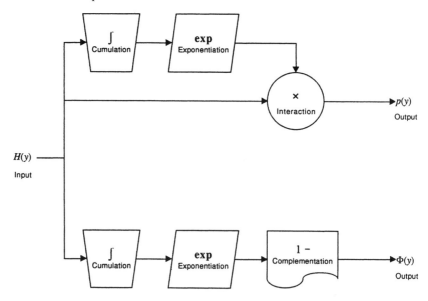

Figure 3.2. Distributions principle of political behavior

Rather than suppressing or avoiding uncertainty this core principle – by addressing the puzzle of why, how, when or with what intensity political behavior of a given type occurs – makes the uncertain behavior of Y rigorously derived from $H(y)$, and therefore fully explained, not arbitrary.

The distributions principle is important because it provides the primary means for this macro level of the theory to investigate the root causes of uncertain political behavior. This is because: (i) the principle uses a mechanism of probabilistic causality, not determinism, to explain political behavior (probabilistic hazard forces cause political change); (ii) the principle requires one to model the specific causal hazard forces that produce a given dimension of observed behavior (like coalition duration D or war onset T); and (iii) the principle is used to deductively derive the set of expected patterns or observable properties that are empirically testable. As I will show in chapter 4 in greater detail, when I introduce additional special principles to specify the form of hazard force, these new theoretical results methodologically imply moving away from more traditional regression models, toward more robust research methods involving the use of non-linear models, maximum likelihood estimation (MLE) procedures, event history analysis (EHA), and time-dependent (nonstationary) parameter estimation.

Because I have defined political behavior as a random variable, and in turn a random variable is defined in terms of its associated probability functions (the p.d.f. and the c.d.f.), it follows that the distributions principle must contain within it several other deductive results. This is especially useful regarding the set of special values of political behavior, the n-tuple $\sum(Y) = (E, V, \psi, \omega, \ldots)$ defined earlier in section 2.2.5. What other general relationships may exist between hazard force and the set of special values of political behavior? What new insights can such relationships provide for understanding political uncertainty? The distributions principle provides the theoretical cornerstone for the other four general macro principles that follow.

3.3.2 Moments principle

The moments of a political behavior variable (section 2.2.5) constitute the first set of special values in the n-tuple $\sum(Y)$. In the case of a random variable, as I have defined political behavior Y (assumption 2.1, definition 2.1), the moments originate from a source called the moment-generating function. This is an entity akin to what may be called the "character" of uncertainty.[8] The political interpretation of the moment-generating function is theoretically and empirically interesting because as a single expression it encapsulates all the moment-related properties of Y, so it is in fact a synthesis of Y's political uncertainty. In this context, the moment-generating function defines the character of uncertainty for a given dimension of political behavior Y. The distributions principle (theorem 3.1) leads to the following result in terms of the moment-generating function:

Theorem 3.2 (moments principle). *Given a hazard force H(y) producing political behavior Y, the moment-generating function of Y, denoted by M(α), is*

$$M(\alpha) = \int_{-\infty}^{+\infty} H(y) \exp[\alpha y - \int_{0}^{y} H(u)du] \, dy. \qquad [3.3]$$

Informally, this principle states that a general relationship exists between the hazard force H and the source (the moment-generating function) that generates the set of moments of political behavior Y (i.e. the expected

---

[8] The moment-generating function is a basic probabilistic concept and is discussed in the works cited in chapter 2, note 3. An alternative approach is to use the characteristic function $\phi(y)$, defined as the Fourier–Stieltjes transform of the distribution function $\Phi(y)$. Although the characteristic function is mathematically more elegant, I prefer the moment-generating function because its political interpretation is more immediate and its use requires less technical treatment.

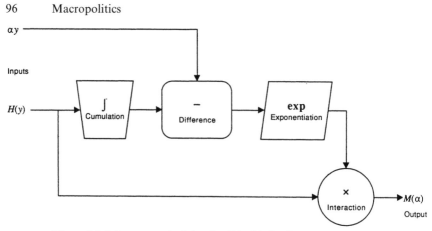

Figure 3.3. Moments principle of political behavior

value, variance, and others). More specifically, as detailed in equation 3.3 and the associated input–output system in figure 3.3, the moments principle contains the accumulation of hazard force (integrals) and other complex processes (exponentiation, interaction, second-order accumulation, and so on). Although a simple ordinary-language paraphrase of this principle is impossible (which is why mathematical language is used) the main idea is that hazard force determines the defining parameters of uncertainty in much the same way as the ambient forces acting on a population (demographic pressure, resource availability, outside influences, and so forth) determine its aggregate behavior. For example, the war onset hazard function $H(t)$ determines the moment-generating function for onset T, from which one can then derive all moments and properties of war onset. Thus, the complicated form of equation 3.3 may be excused by the amount of deductive information it contains!

To interpret equation 3.3, note that this is a function of a point of reference $\alpha \in Y$, as well as being a function of hazard force. More specifically, $M(\alpha)$ is produced by the cumulation of two interactive components, the hazard force $H(y)$ and a discounted value of cumulative hazard, taken over all values of the political behavior variable Y. Again, this is a complex but unique and fully specified process which accounts for the uncertainty in producing the moments of political behavior.

3.3.3   Expectation principle

Given the prominent role of the expected value (mean or arithmetic average) and the variance in characterizing a pattern of uncertainty in political behavior, the first two special values (moments) are of natural interest. I

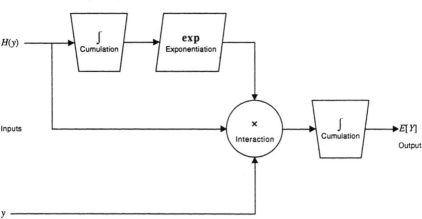

Figure 3.4. Expectation principle of political behavior

call the relationship between hazard force and these first moments the
expectation principle.

Theorem 3.3 (expectation principle). *Given a hazard force H(y) producing
political behavior Y, the first two moments are*

$$E(Y) = \int_{-\infty}^{+\infty} y\, H(y) \exp\left[-\int_0^y H(u)\mathrm{d}u \right] \mathrm{d}y \qquad [3.4]$$

and

$$V(Y) = E[y - E(Y)]^2. \qquad [3.5]$$

The expectation principle states how hazard force determines the expected value and variance of a given political behavior. As can be easily
seen from the form of equation 3.4 (a composite-exponential-integral equation that is only slightly less complicated than equation 3.3) and the
associated system in figure 3.4, the exact effect that hazard force has on
average political behavior (and on its variance) is again complicated and
anything but linear, although it is fully specified. It goes without saying that
to expect common intuition to grasp the effect of hazard force on average
political behavior – let alone on a single realization – is to confuse human
intelligence with something approaching godly omniscience. The expectation principle adds to the explanation of why political behavior *is* factually
uncertain: because the effect of hazard force on even average political
behavior is highly complex and cannot be grasped by intuition alone.

Notwithstanding this complexity, however, theorem 3.3 is totally unambiguous in stating the exact way in which expected political behavior depends on hazard force. And this, like the other principles, is a net gain in understanding. Other moments of the random variable Y are similarly derived.

Interpreting equation 3.4, it says that the expected value $E(Y)$ of political behavior Y is accounted for by the cumulation of three interactive components, taken over all values of Y. The first component is simply the value y; the second is hazard force H; the third is the discounted cumulative hazard force; and all three components interact. The complexity of this process accounts for another aspect of political uncertainty, albeit within a fully defined process.

3.3.4   Median principle

Recall that the median value always exists, while this is not true for the expected value. The median value is also determined by hazard force. As defined in the previous chapter (section 2.2.5), the median value of political behavior Y, denoted by $\psi(Y)$, is the value of political behavior Y beyond which there is a greater than even-odds of another realization (the next event). The median principle specifies exactly how ψ is dependent on the hazard forces $H(y)$ that are acting on political behavior Y.

Theorem 3.4 (median principle). *Given a hazard force $H(y)$ producing political behavior Y, the median value ψ of Y is given by the solution to the equation*

$$\int_0^{\psi} H(y)\mathrm{d}y = \zeta, \qquad\qquad [3.6]$$

where $\zeta = \ln 2 \approx 0.69$.

The median principle is stated as an implicit expression because it refers to a threshold value that is subject to a political condition (viz., $\Phi = 0.5$ when $y = \psi$), whereas the other special values E and V refer to exact quantities.[9] Besides its intrinsic significance in stating the relationship between hazard force and median value, the median principle is also instrumental for expressing the "uncertainty ledge," or difference between the special values E and ψ, as discussed earlier for war onset (section 2.2.5). Equation 3.6 can

---

[9] The proof of theorem 3.4 explains how equation 3.6 is derived, why the equation contains the median value ψ as a limit, and how the constant ζ originates. The associated input–output system for this principle cannot be represented explicitly because equation 3.6 cannot be solved for ψ until $H(y)$ is specified (chapter 4).

be solved for ψ as soon as $H(y)$ is specified, so the relationship between behavioral force and semiprobability value is unambiguous.

3.3.5 Modal principle

The fourth special value of political behavior is the modal value, denoted by $\omega(Y)$. Recall that ω is the most probable value realized by a political behavior variable Y (section 2.2.5). The modal principle states how this value of political behavior depends on the hazard force $H(y)$ operating on actors.

Theorem 3.5 (modal principle). *Given a hazard force $H(y)$ producing political behavior Y, the modal value ω of Y is given by the solution to the equation*

$$(1 - [H(y)]^2) \exp\left[- \int_0^y H(u)du \right]\left[\frac{dH(y)}{dy}\right] = 0 \qquad [3.7]$$

letting $y = \omega$.

A simple informal paraphrasing of this principle is not practical, for obvious reasons, although the associated input–output system is represented in figure 3.5. Note that the complexity of the modal principle is caused mostly by the nature of the modal value itself. Although superficially the notion of a modal value does not seem to pose any problem of interpretation (after all, "the most common political practice" is a concept that seems easy enough to understand), in reality this value has very special properties as a maximum of the probability density function (where, by definition, $dp/dy = 0$). Significantly, the complexity of equation 3.7 reflects the fact that the causal process involved in moving from the action of a hazard force to the occurrence of a modal value of political behavior is very intricate, so the result is logically uncertain although its mathematical expression is exact (theorem 3.5).

Interestingly, the modal principle also shows how hazard force affects modal political behavior in two contrasting ways: on the one hand, there is a cumulative hazard force that builds up like a stress or rising tension (the integral exponential function); on the other hand, there is a change in hazard, a second-order dynamic (the derivative). Moreover, both components interact (the product), and all this still leaves out the first term before exponentiation (the complement of the squared hazard force). The complexity of this relationship is qualitatively consistent with that of the other principles.

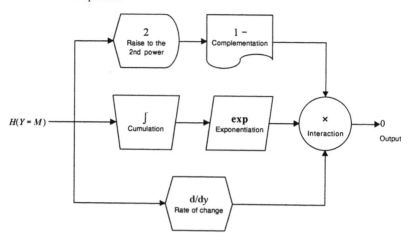

Figure 3.5. Modal principle of political behavior

3.4   Canonical macropolitical principles

Each of the macropolitical principles represents a general theoretical proposition on the relationship between the uncertain behavior of measurable
variables and the underlying causal hazard forces. The principles are
general because the precise form of the hazard force function $H(y)$, the
dynamic cause of political behavior, is not yet specified. Thus, the five
macro principles show how the relationships that exist between hazard
force and political behavior are independent of the specific form of hazard
force. Each principle therefore holds universally, as a true covering law
must.

The causal form of these general macro principles can also be examined
more closely to understand in greater depth the character of political
uncertainty. This can be seen by focusing on the invariant structure of the
input–output systems that define each case of probabilistic causality. Such
a structure is shown by the system represented in figure 3.6, which synthesizes the invariant part that was shown in the earlier systems (cf. figures
3.2–3.5). As indicated by this general system, political behavior (output Y
as the dependent variable) is produced by two types of inputs: a force input
that is always transformed by the operations of accumulation and exponentiation (the L-transform in the shaded area) and other inputs (the
I-transform in the lower part).[10] The former input is invariant across the

---

[10] Note that these two transformation functions are useful shorthand expressions to represent
more cumbersome equations and therefore to be able to extract the essential structure of
political uncertainty at the macro level of analysis.

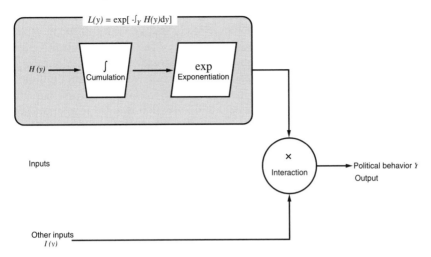

Figure 3.6. Probabilistic causality of political behavior

general principles and is not a commutative process because accumulation and exponentiation are not reversible operations. The latter input varies because its precise form depends on the specific general principle and the structure of its probabilistic causality; this can include untransformed hazard force (H), values of behavior (y), or parameters (α). The two inputs that define general and particular probabilistic causes interact with one another (formally, the two functions multiply) to produce political behavior.

By way of synthesis, the above discussion leads to the following theoretical result. From the perspective of the probabilistic causality of political behavior, each general macro principle represents a canonical variation on the equation

$$Y = L(y)\,I(y), \qquad\qquad\qquad\qquad [3.8]$$

where $L(y)$ represents the transformation of the hazard force function $H(y)$ by the recurring familiar operator

$$\exp\left[-\int_Y H(y)\mathrm{d}y \right],$$

interpreted as the discounted cumulative hazard force, and $I(y)$ is given by the structure of probabilistic causality in a specific general principle. Equation 3.8 is the simplest possible expression for representing how the uncertainty of political behavior is generated and explained through the mechanism of probabilistic causality. The political interpretation of this result in plain English is perhaps not as straightforward because the concepts are new and our thinking habits are too simple or intuitive for probing this far into the deep probabilistic nature of political uncertainty. Roughly speaking, this canonical result (equation 3.8) means that political behavior always results from a combination of hazard forces that are always processed in the same way (cumulation followed by decay; they are not direct or untransformed forces) and other well-defined causes that depend directly on the aspect of political behavior being examined. Accordingly, the former are universal (nomothetic) forces, whereas the latter are specific (idiographic).

Based on this result, the previous equations of the general principles (theorems 3.1–3.5) can now be rewritten in the following simple canonical forms:

$$p(y) = L(y)\, I(y), \qquad \text{(p.d.f. principle)} \qquad [3.1']$$

letting $I(y) = H(y)$;

$$\Phi(y) = 1 - L(y), \qquad \text{(c.d.f. principle)} \qquad [3.2']$$

$$M(\alpha) = \int_Y [(I(y)/L(y)]\, dy, \quad \text{(moments principle)} \qquad [3.3']$$

letting $I(y) = H(y)\exp(\alpha y)$;

$$E(Y) = \int_Y I(y)\, L(y)\, dy, \qquad \text{(expectation principle)} \qquad [3.4']$$

letting $I(y) = y\, H(y)$; and

$$L(y)\, I(y) = 0, \qquad \text{(modal principle)} \qquad [3.7']$$

letting $I(y) = \{1 - [H(y)]^2\}\, dH(y)/dy$.

In every principle, hazard force is treated explicitly as the primary theoretical cause (independent variable) of political behavior (dependent variable). The theorems presented in this chapter are therefore true dynamic principles in the classical scientific sense established earlier, not metaphoric propositions as in much of the extant literature that rhetorically appeals to the action of "political forces" to explain behavior. Significantly, these principles also prove that remarkable unity also exists among seemingly diverse political dynamics (domestic and international), with hazard force acting as a unifying concept (theorems 3.1–3.5). The uncertainties of onset, magnitude, or duration – for such diverse political phenomena as government coalitions, revolutions, riots, wars, international alliances, or other political events detailed by the taxonomy in table 2.1 –

are uniformly governed by the macro dynamical principles founded on well-defined behavioral force.

None of these general macro principles of political behavior (theorems 3.1–3.5) is causally linear; none of them even remotely resembles the linear world of traditional regression models. The interpretation of the nonlinear property of these principles must be worded with caution because counter-intuitive effects are commonly present whenever nonlinear behavior is involved. Whereas linear behavior is always intuitive, nonlinear behavior is often (albeit not always) counterintuitive.

The nonlinearity of these principles means that a change in hazard force usually has neither an intuitive nor a predictable effect on the pattern of resulting political behavior.[11] This is consistent with fundamental political uncertainty. Only the canonically transformed principles are linear in form, but the linearity created by the transformation is formally induced, not natural. As I showed with each theorem, the nonlinearity involved in these behavioral principles involves a combination of mathematical exponentiation (a transformation from a level scale to a magnitude scale), integration (from level to accumulation), differentiation (from level to rate of change), and interaction (product of terms). Moreover, the first three of these transformations are not commutative. When hazard forces change, as is common in history, political behavior will change in the ways expressed by these principles – ways that are far too complex for any observer to comprehend and predict, or for political actors to understand. This is the fundamental reason why only the distributions of aggregate political behavior – as opposed to individual values – offer viable areas for scientific inquiry.

Perhaps more than any other property, I view this probabilistic non-linearity as the principal cause of uncertainty in political behavior. Later I will show that probabilistic nonlinearity is also the main cause of uncertainty for the occurrence of political events. The basic laws of political behavior are all written in the language of nonlinear probability equations. Theoretically, these basic principles only scratch the surface of a much larger area of investigation. If the proper scientific procedure is for method to usually follow substance, and not the opposite, then macro models of political behavior could profit significantly from the mathematical theory of stochastic differential equations.

Clearly, the next step is to model the hazard force more specifically

---

[11] My demonstration of the nonlinear property should not be interpreted as an endorsement of the "chaos" models recently in vogue. Chaos models are deterministic (nonlinear differential equations) and therefore I view them as rather problematic for establishing the foundations of political theory. However, they are valuable "as if" (heuristic) models, following the traditional scientific practice of analyzing simple deterministic models that approximate phenomena that are known to be inherently indeterminate.

because this is the key to deriving testable theoretical results about observable patterns of political behavior. The hazard force is modeled specifically by making substantive assumptions about the basic causal dynamics of political behavior – such as the effect of martial and peaceful forces on the onset, magnitude, and duration of war – as I demonstrate next in chapter 4.

3.5   Conclusions

The purpose of this chapter was to present the first set of general macro principles that govern the behavior of aggregate political variables. The material in this chapter was based on the conceptual building blocks established in chapter 2. I began by describing the macro framework of my theory by focusing first on the relationship between political behavior (dependent variable) and the causal hazard forces that produce such behavior (independent variables). This relationship governs the various macro level forms of uncertainty in politics, including the distribution characteristics, the set of special values, and other properties. In introducing this macro framework, I also distinguished this from other alternative frameworks, including earlier frameworks that did not exploit the causal role of forces in accounting for behavioral change (ancient Greek science).

I presented five general macro principles that account for patterns of uncertainty in aggregate political behavior. These first results are called the distributions principle (theorem 3.1), the moments principle (theorem 3.2), the expectation principle (theorem 3.3), the median principle (theorem 3.4), and the modal principle (theorem 3.5). Although other general macro principles can also be derived by methods similar to those described in appendices 3 (proofs) and 4 (methods), these five principles provide an initial core with inherent theoretical value and also a set from which to derive other more specialized results (in chapter 4). The most important of the general macro principles is by far the first – the distributions principle – because it provides the exact form of the distribution functions for any form of political behavior, given the form of the hazard force acting on the agents that produce the behavior. The distributions principle is not intuitive from the observation of political behavior and constitutes the main result of the macro part of this theory of political uncertainty. For these reasons, I called attention to its formal proof in appendix 3. The other four general macro principles derive from this basic proposition.

The general property of these principles also led to their representation as input–output systems and to the derivation of simpler canonical forms. The nonlinear property contributes greatly to the explanation of uncertainty in many forms of political behavior. By being general, dynamic, and nonlinear, these principles of political behavior stand in marked contrast to prevailing models from the regression literature, which are rather more particular, static, and mostly linear.

The set of general macro principles of political behavior is rich in implications, given the properties discussed above. Additional results beyond those that I have focused upon can be derived by applying additional methods of theoretical analysis (appendix 4). For example, for each principle it is possible to derive sensitivity results on how dynamical changes (variations in the causal hazard force) affect observed properties of political behavior (special values, distributions). Most of these results would be nonintuitive, given the complicated structure of the input–output systems.

An important methodological thrust in this chapter was the use of mathematical analysis to discover previously unknown features of political uncertainty, features that are as real as those that are actually measured by standard empirical approaches (Kline's thesis expressed in the epigraph at the beginning of this chapter; Cioffi-Revilla 1989). I highlight this because although this is a powerful idea, which is known and practiced in many disciplines and particularly in theoretical science, it remains largely unknown in political science, where I hope to show that it can have a promising and exciting future. The idea of using mathematical analysis as a heuristic for discovery is equally valid for the remaining chapters, including those in part 3, which deal with the occurrence of political events.

4   Special macropolitical principles

Our problem is to find the best equilibrium among swiftly moving forces which otherwise may find solutions and balances by violence and destruction!

Charles E. Merriam, *Systematic Politics*

4.1   Introduction

In this chapter I present the special principles of macro political behavior. These are propositions derived from the earlier general principles under more specific assumptions regarding the qualitative and quantitative properties of hazard force operating on actors. Modeling hazard force by means of specific equations – by modeling the exact form of the hazard rate function $H(y)$ in each of the general macro principles that I already established in the previous chapter – is the key to deriving testable theoretical results about observable patterns of political behavior. A specific set of hazards acting on a given political variable yields (using the general macro principles) specific distributions, special values, and other significant properties. Hazard forces are modeled by making substantive assumptions about the basic causal dynamics of political behavior to capture the type and variety of causal forces at work – such as the effect of anarchy, stability, or escalation on the onset, magnitude, and duration of conflict.

As I have discussed so far, many types of hazard forces potentially affect political behavior; logically too many to consider without some prior systematization. Political hazard forces can sometimes be as intangible as those feared by Charles Merriam in the epigraph to this chapter, or they can be as concrete as the residential segregation forces that cause racial riots in urban centers (Olzak et al. 1996). In this chapter I shall first develop some systematics to obtaining a viable taxonomy of political forces, a task similar to the systematization of political variables for the analysis in chapter 2 (table 2.1). I shall then use the new taxonomy of hazard forces as a guide in the subsequent theoretical development of special macro principles. Using the taxonomy as a navigational chart for the course of the investigation will permit me to advance the research program through a sequence of "progressive problemshifts," in the sense used by Lakatos (1973). I examine some of the more insightful models individually, and show how each generates a set of new special principles based on particular political conditions, and how in each instance these special principles are derived from the broader general principles that I established earlier in chapter 3.

Besides serving as a heuristic for developing the research program at the macro level of analysis, another advantage of the taxonomy I propose is to help systematize and integrate the emerging technical literature on probabilistic causality that is based on the application of hazard rate or survival models, logit and probit models, Poisson regression, event history analysis, and others in the same tradition.[1] As I hope to show by the theoretical and empirical analysis in this chapter, these recent approaches refer mostly to formal or technical variations on a central theme that has much deeper theoretical significance for understanding political uncertainty. This is because these recent statistical approaches are all reducible to the framework of special macro principles of hazard force. The conceptual affinity between my theory and these other approaches – founded on the common use of core probability concepts such as the density function and others – helps in relating the principles I develop in this chapter to both the traditional probabilistic literature that focused almost exclusively on fitting distributions to empirical political behavior, and to the fledgling literature on probabilistic causality.

To illustrate the application of the special macro principles developed here, I shall use the widely available data on international conflicts, as well as examples from applications to domestic violence and coalition governments. However, my presentation and theoretical development remain focused on the core themes of general politics identified in chapter 1, table 1.1, covering both domestic and international domains. Indeed, the principles explored in this chapter present valuable opportunities for modeling the diverse environments and hazard forces which operate in the different domains of domestic (structured) and international (anarchic) politics. Recall that the general principles developed in the previous chapter cover both of these diverse domains because hazard force (dependent variable) is unspecified in the form of general principles. However, the special principles explored in this chapter are specific with respect to the form of hazard force(s), so the dynamics of a precise political domain – domestic or international – can be modeled more accurately. As a result, as these principles become better understood and applied, we may begin to uncover

---

[1] References are given in tables 4.1–4.2 and throughout the chapter.

more fundamental similarities and differences between domestic and international politics – not just in terms of the political centralization–anarchy dimension, but in more insightful ways that explore more complex dynamic properties. A foundation for this is given by the special macro principles discussed in this chapter.

4.2   Modeling hazard forces

How should a model of hazard force be developed or specified to account for political behavior? Which political features of the real world should be enhanced on empirical grounds and which should be suppressed on grounds of parsimony? In chapter 2 I already introduced the idea that hazard forces act in many forms (section 2.3). Here I will develop a more systematic treatment of hazard forces, by providing a taxonomy and a related sequence of models ranging from simple to complex. This is needed in order to make theoretically disciplined use of the general macro principles – otherwise their mathematical complexity can confound the theory and produce only a disarray of special results lacking in meaningful cohesiveness.

4.2.1   *Taxonomy of hazard forces*

Intuitively, as exemplified by Charles Merriam's admonition, it would seem that the hazard force involved in this theory can have as many forms as the variety of political behaviors it can produce, subject only to a few formal constraints (section 2.3.3). In fact, at least for now, there is no logically compelling basis for classifying hazard forces on purely inductive grounds. In addition, many hazard forces commonly mentioned in everyday political language (e.g. "electoral force," "technological forces," "colonialist forces," and so forth) are only allegorical metaphors, so they cannot seriously be used for systematic purposes.

To systematize hazard forces into a tractable class of cases, I postulate two different criteria for classifying political dynamics: (i) according to their theoretical specificity, hazard forces can be implicit or explicit; and (ii) according to their complexity, they can be caused by a singular hazard force (monocausal) or by multiple hazard forces (multicausal). This two-by-two classification generates the fourfold taxonomy shown in table 4.1.

The four classes of political dynamics specified in table 4.1 – implicit–monocausal (class 1), implicit–multicausal (class 2), explicit–monocausal (class 3), and explicit–multicausal (class 4) – are exhaustive and mutually exclusive, as a true taxonomy must be. I highlight the following features of this taxonomy:

Table 4.1. *Taxonomy of hazard forces*

	Implicit $H = H(y)$	Explicit $H = H(y; x_1, x_2, x_3, \ldots)$
Monocausal (single hazard force) $H = H(f)$	Class 1 models: *Implicit–monocausal* A single aggregate hazard force governs political behavior $$H = \begin{cases} k & \text{(model I)} \\ \alpha y^b & \text{(model III)} \\ \text{others} \end{cases}$$ Published applications cited in notes 6 and 9, and table 4.3	Class 3 models: *Explicit–monocausal* A single explicit force governs political behavior $H = \exp[-f(x)]$, where $$f(x) = \begin{cases} k \\ ax^b \\ \text{others} \end{cases}$$ No known published applications
Multicausal (several hazard forces) $H = H(f_1, f_2, f_3, \ldots)$	Class 2 models: *Implicit–multicausal* Several aggregate hazard forces govern political behavior $$H = \begin{cases} \phi + \rho y \,\text{(model II)} \\ a + b/y + cy \\ \alpha y^\beta + \gamma/y \,\text{(model IV)} \end{cases}$$ See Cioffi-Revilla (1985a, 1985b), Cioffi-Revilla and Lai (1995), Cioffi-Revilla and Landman (1996), Cioffi-Revilla and Mason (1991), Cioffi-Revilla and Sommer (1993)	Class 4 models: *Explicit–multicausal* Several explicit hazard forces govern political behavior $H = \exp[-f(x_i)]$ where $i = 1, 2, 3, \ldots$ Models V, VI, VII See Berry and Berry (1990), Bienen and van de Walle (1989), King et al. (1990), Olzak et al. (1996)

Source: Prepared by the author.

1 The four classes cover many existing applications of probability distributions in political science (stochastic processes, when time is the referent random variable), so the taxonomy provides a theoretically based framework for a broad range of other investigations. As I will show, all applications of the Poisson and Weibull distributions, as well as more recent logit and probit models (variations on the Poisson distribution), fall under class 1. Also recent models from event history analysis – as these models are called in sociology and demography – are the simplest special cases (log-linear models) within class 4.

2 The taxonomy identifies additional hazard force models that thus far have remained unexplored for developing viable macro explanations of political behavior. For example, little research has been done with class 2, 3, and 4 models. The overwhelming effort in political science has been on class 1 (Poisson) models, the simplest and most parsimonious, but also the most theoretically limited. The taxonomy highlights the significant variety of other forms of randomness for understanding political uncertainty at the macro level of analysis.

3 The taxonomy shows that the concept of hazard force is well chosen because it yields a viable and fruitful variety of macro political cases that is coherently organized. Rather than being based on a classification that is purely formal or mathematical (content-free) – for example, a classification of cases based purely on type of distribution (Emerson 1986; Kovalenko et al. 1996) – the taxonomy is based on the hazard force for behavioral occurrence as a substantive political concept.

4 The taxonomy offers a theoretically based system for rigorously classifying previously unrelated areas in political science, namely different forms of political behavior, actors, and historical time periods (eras). I will demonstrate this property using the case of political coalitions and war.

5 From a policy perspective, the taxonomy can be used for identifying and ranking different operational situations – in domestic or international domains – that may call for different approaches to political or conflict management. For example, political behavior governed by class 4 hazard forces (a variety of separate hazard forces affecting political uncertainty) requires vastly more complex intervention policies than situations governed by class 3 hazard forces (monocausal), although the former could be more readily identifiable from an empirical standpoint. It may remain a truism that the successful performance of public policies can never be guaranteed with certainty, but policy designs may be improved by conducting an appropriate diagnostic identification of the probabilistic hazard forces at play and designing the intervention accordingly.

6 Finally, the taxonomy offers a framework for planning various research programs to explore sequences of hazard force models to explain political behavior. In the next section I will identify a sequence of models that progresses from implicit-monocausal (relatively simple political case to analyze and understand) to explicit-multicausal (more complex).

4.2.2   *Progressive problemshifts*

In table 4.2 I summarize a sequence of problemshifts based on the four basic classes identified by the taxonomy in table 4.1. The progressive

Table 4.2. *Progressive problemshifts through successive macro models and empirical methods*

Model	Equation	Empirical estimation and testing
Implicit hazard force models		
I Constant hazard force (equilibrium model)	$H(y) = k$	Empirical estimation of implicit hazard models is based on standard statistical methods for duration data (e.g. Bartholomew 1982; Elandt-Johnson and
II Linear hazard force model	$H(y) = a + by$	Johnson, 1980; Gross and Clark 1975; Meyer 1970), generalized for other measurable dimensions
III Nonlinear forces	$H(y) = \kappa \alpha \, y^{\alpha - 1}$	such as intensity or extent (King 1989a). All models should be estimated using maximum likelihood estimation because a specific hypothesis (equation) is being tested. OLS approximations are also available (Morgan and Henrion 1990: ch. 5)
IV Multiple hazard forces	$H(y) = H_1 + H_2 + H_3$	
Explicit hazard force models		
V: Log-linear additive hazard forces	$\ln H = \kappa + \sum \beta_i x_i$	Empirical estimation is based on methods of event history analysis (Allison 1984; Blossfeld et al.
VI Nonlinear additive hazard forces	$\ln H = \kappa + \sum_i \beta_i x_i^{\gamma_i}$	1989; Blossfeld and Rohwer 1995; Coleman 1981: ch. 5; Tuma and Hannan 1984). See Berry and Berry (1990), Bienen and van de Walle
VII Interactive hazard forces	$\ln H = \kappa \prod_i \beta_i x_i^{\gamma_i}$	(1989), and King et al. (1990) for political science applications

Source: Prepared by the author.

problemshifts advance in two directions that yield special macro principles based on implicit and explicit hazard forces, $H(y)$ and $H(X_1, X_2, X_3, \ldots)$, respectively. Other specifications of the hazard force equation are possible, based on different political assumptions and the constraints discussed earlier (chapter 2). I use these because they represent a viable progression from simple to more complex. All explicit distribution models (e.g. event history analysis or hazard rate models with covariates) are based on implicit models from the classical theory of distributions, so an understanding of implicit models (classes 1 and 2) takes priority over explicit models (classes 3 and 4). So far I have developed, tested, and analyzed mostly implicit models in three main areas of domestic and international political science: in the study of domestic government coalitions, international rivalries, and wars (references are cited in table 4.1). These are followed by explicit models discussed later in this chapter.[2]

Large-scale political change occurs when conditions affecting the lives, fortunes, or governance of a collectivity are significantly altered by hazard forces. Because political conditions can often be measured, and significant changes can be detected by several criteria, it follows that a number of propositions concerning the pattern of hazard forces are testable. The following are testable theoretical expectations, some of which are illustrated in this chapter in the context of coalition behavior and war:[3] (i) In a heterogeneous population of political behavior occurrences (e.g. all governmental coalition durations between 1960 and 1990; or all interstate wars worldwide during the past five centuries), relatively "simple" hazard forces should be detected (as in table 4.2, models I and V; monocausal dynamics). This is because many different hazard forces (some promoting political behavior, others inhibiting behavior), acting on many different actors (individuals, groups, or larger collectivities), will produce a mostly stationary net result (a "political wash out"). (ii) By contrast, in a more homogeneous population (e.g., only Italian government coalitions with center-left support; only those European wars that occurred between the end of the fifteenth century and the 1648 Peace of Westphalia), more complex forces should be detected (for instance, models IV or VII; multicausal dynamics). This is because fewer hazard forces acting on fewer types of actors will tend to produce more clearly distinctive features and a weak or absent statistical equilibrium. (iii) Large-scale political changes (such as domestic regime changes or foreign hegemonic transitions) are preceded by increasingly severe hazard force (i.e. dH/dy increases as major change approaches).[4] In general, longer historical periods and more diverse politi-

---

[2] See also Cusack and Eberwein (1982) and Williamson et al. (1988) for applications to disputes among nation states in the international system. The last column of table 4.2 provides references to the empirical method used for each class of models. In general, these methods begin by calculating the empirical hazard force values (the hazard rate values) from the observed data, using equation 2.32 and the Kaplan–Meier method. After obtaining these values, conventional curve-fitting methods are used to estimate each hazard force model. Ordinary least squares (OLS) estimation is normally used for the linear models, whereas maximum likelihood (MLE) estimation is used for the nonlinear models. These methods are illustrated later in this chapter.

[3] Because the main thrust of this book is theoretical, the generally supportive tests reported in this chapter should be viewed only as illustrative, not as definitive tests. All empirical results reported in this chapter are based on OLS estimation for linear and linearized models, and MLE for nonlinear models.

[4] Other testable hypotheses are as follows: (iv) developing political systems (like a new or emerging domestic regime or international order) are governed by decreasing hazard force ($dH/dy < 0$); (v) decaying political systems (such as a disintegrating polity) are governed by increasing hazard force ($dH/dy > 0$); (vi) stationary political systems have approximately constant hazard force.

cal conditions compose a more heterogeneous set of realizations, whereas a shorter and less diverse set of political conditions compose a more homogeneous set of realizations. These and other hypotheses lead to a progression of models, starting with the first and simplest implicit-monocausal model of political behavior (constant or Poissonian hazard force).

4.3 Implicit models

4.3.1 Single implicit hazard

Politics governed by constant hazard force: model I. The simplest implicit model of political behavior is based on the following assumption.

Assumption 4.1 (constant hazard force). *The hazard force $H(y)$ producing political behavior Y is constant over all $y \in Y$. Formally,*

$$H(y) = k \qquad [4.1]$$

where $k > 0$ is a constant.

Examples of constant hazard forces in domestic politics include popular mass demands on government (in democratic systems), incumbent politicians' desires for re-election (in elective systems), and resource scarcity (in all political systems). Another example of constant hazard force is found in world politics, in what realists call the "anarchy condition" in the international system,[5] the concept derived from Hobbes's *Leviathan* and Rousseau's allegorical metaphor in the stag hunt. Anarchic force in the international system changes only in the long run (glacially so) – if it changes at all. In general, political conditions described as "background forces" are constant.

The following special principle obtains from applying assumption 4.1 (equation 4.1) to the general macro principles (theorems 3.1–3.5):

Theorem 4.1 (principle of political behavior by constant hazard force). *A political variable Y produced by constant hazard force k has the following properties*:

$$p(y) = k\,e^{-ky} \qquad \text{(by [3.1] in theorem 3.1)} \qquad [4.2]$$
$$\Phi(y) = 1 - e^{-ky} \qquad \text{(by [3.2] in theorem 3.1)} \qquad [4.3]$$
$$M(\alpha) = \frac{k}{k - \alpha}, \text{ for } \alpha < k \quad \text{(by [3.3] in theorem 3.2)} \qquad [4.4]$$

---

[5] Chatterjee (1975), James (1993), Herz (1957), Morgenthau and Thompson (1985), Snyder (1971), Waltz (1955).

Table 4.3. *Model I estimates (MLEs) of hazard force* k *(level of anarchy) for war onset* T *in the international system, 1500–1965*

Type of War	Hazard force[a] k (months^{-1})	Historical era $\Delta\tau$	Data source
Deadly quarrels[b] $3.5 \leq \mu \leq 4.5$	0.045	1820–1929	Richardson (1960b)
Wars of modern civilization[c]	0.050[d]	1500–1931	Wright (1942)
International wars	0.052[e]	1816–1965	Singer and Small (1972)
Interstate wars	0.028[e]	1816–1965	Singer and Small (1972)
Reciprocated military actions	0.032[f]	1815–1965	Siverson and Tennefoss (1982)

[a] Background anarchy. All estimates are significant at the 0.05 level.
[b] $1\mu = \log_{10}$(combatant and civilian fatalities).
[c] See Wright (1942: app. 20) as revised by Richardson (1960b: 129).
[d] Wright's estimate calculated from data reported in Richardson (1960b: 129).
[e] Calculated by Urs Luterbacher.
[f] Reported in Cioffi-Revilla (1985a: table 2).
Sources: Cioffi-Revilla (1985a), Richardson (1960b), Singer and Small (1972).

$$E(Y) = V(Y) = 1/k \quad \text{(by [3.4] and [3.5] in theorem 3.3)} \quad [4.5]$$
$$\psi(Y) = \zeta/k. \quad \text{(by [3.6] in theorem 3.4)} \quad [4.6]$$

Model I has widespread empirical support in politics, including most of the applications in table 2.1 (taxonomy of political variables). For example, table 4.3 shows applications of model I for war onset T, following Lewis F. Richardson's seminal work. However, most scholars are familiar only with parts of this model, primarily equations 4.2 and 4.5, and usually know it by a different name: the Poisson distribution.[6] Three features of model I shed new light on the nature of political behavior that conforms to this model:

1 For hazard force to be constant (i) it must be a single aggregate hazard force (monocausal dynamic) that is steadily influencing actors to produce Y, which seems improbable if not impossible (e.g. many hazard forces other than constant anarchy act on potential belligerents to produce crisis or war onsets); or (ii) the hazard rate value of k is actually

[6] All estimates in table 4.3 and later are MLEs unless otherwise noted. See Brookshire and Duncan (1986), Browne (1984, 1988), Browne et al. (1986), Callen and Leidecker (1971), Casstevens and Casstevens (1989; and works cited therein), Cioffi-Revilla (1984, 1985a), Frendreis et al. (1986), Hopmann (1967), Job (1976), King et al. (1990), Li and Thompson (1975), Mansfield (1988), McGowan and Rood (1975), Midlarsky (1975, 1981, 1983a), Mintz and Schrodt (1987), Moyal (1949), Richardson (1941, 1945a, 1945b, 1960b), Singer and Small (1972), Siverson and Duncan (1976), Small and Singer (1983), Ulmer (1982), and Wallis (1936). For recent evidence invalidating the constant hazard force model for war onset, see Cioffi-Revilla (1985a), Howeling and Kuné (1984), Howeling and Siccama (1985), and Petersen (1987, 1991).

an equilibrium value resulting from deeper forces other than anarchy, H_1, H_2, H_3, ..., such that their combined resultant appears to be constant. For example, a constant war onset force, $H(t) = k$ (as reported in table 4.3 for wars in history), can be the result of belligerent hazard forces (H_B) and pacifying forces (H_P), such that $k = H_B - H_P$. Either of these new possibilities (multicausal dynamics) is intriguing and worth pursuing. Although this second mechanism is politically more plausible, yet another possibility – perhaps even more plausible – is that other hazard forces are active but at a much lower magnitude than the single hazard force of anarchy, so an essentially constant result is detectable. The resulting hazard force is mostly composed of anarchy.

2 Because probability density in this model is the simple negative exponential function (equation 4.2), all political behavior conforming to model I is Poisson distributed (e.g. all the wars in table 4.3). Many political events are known to occur with this distribution when they are examined over a sufficiently long time period: turnover in legislative, bureaucratic and elite systems, as well as patterns of *coups d'état*, strikes, coalitions, and wars. However, before model I was developed there was no substantive deductive account of *why* so many kinds of political behavior show this as opposed to other forms of uncertainty. Given a constant hazard force $H = k$ pressuring actors to produce these political events – *coups*, wars, and others – the theory accurately predicts that the probability density of observed events (in general, a political variable Y) will be the simple negative exponential, as in a Poisson process. Previous applications of the Poisson distribution are therefore now explained and unified by this principle (theorem 4.1).

3 Previous applications of model I have misinterpreted the model's empirical success in politics as *un*interesting, reducing its use to mere "evidence of randomness," as if randomness had all the same form (Poisson). Model I suggests otherwise: political hazard force must necessarily be constant for Y to be Poisson distributed. In logic form,

$$[H(y) = k] \Leftrightarrow [p(y) = k\, e^{-ky}]. \quad \text{(by [4.2] in theorem 4.1)} \quad [4.7]$$

Rather than being uninteresting ("plain random"), it is remarkable to discover that highly consequential forms of political behavior (such as elite turnover or conflicts) are governed by forces that are constant – forces seemingly as complex as those that cause individuals and groups to act politically. However, what seems more likely is that the constant hazard rate is the net result of deeper variable forces (such as H_B and H_P earlier), so an intriguing and previously unknown dynamic equilibrium process (multicausal) is arguably at work. This new insight has implications for other forms of human behavior (beyond politics) that obey this same model (e.g. innovation diffusion or personnel turnover in organiz-ations).[7]

Other results in model I shed new light on properties of politics not accessible through other approaches or through plain observation. For example, although the onset of domestic or international political conflicts may be governed by a constant force (for heterogeneous populations, like those in table 4.3), the cumulative probability of onset over t not only increases, but does so asymptotically (nonlinearly). On average, political events in this model (such as conflict onsets) occur after their cumulative probability has passed the even-odds threshold (because $E(Y) > \psi$, by comparing equations 4.5 and 4.6), so when hazard force is constant, events such as war onsets, expansions, or terminations occur when they are "overdue" or "ripe for occurring." This represents a previously unknown property for a large class of political behavior, and one worthy of further investigation.

Politics by variable hazard force: models II and III. The next progressive problemshifts within implicit models – advancing beyond model I of constant hazard force – consider political behavior caused by variable force. I will consider two implicit models, one governed by vari-able linear hazard force (model II), the other governed by variable non-linear hazard force (model III).

Model II (Politics by linear hazard force). Empirical tests show that al-though many political variables behave approximately like model I (par-ticularly in heterogeneous populations which cover longer historical per-iods or more diverse political conditions), *variable* hazard forces are more realistic and should fit and test better in a more homogeneous set of realizations (relatively shorter or less diverse). Model II has the simplest variable hazard force.

Assumption 4.2 (linear political hazard force). *The hazard force $H(y)$ acting on a political variable Y varies linearly over all $y \in Y$. Formally,*

$$H(y) = \phi + \rho y, \qquad\qquad [4.8]$$

where $\phi > 0$ is the threshold hazard force for political behavior to occur, and $-\infty < \rho < +\infty$ is the amount by which hazard force varies over values of Y (since ρ is the slope of H with respect to y).

---

[7] Midlarsky (1981), Rapoport (1983).

For example, for war onset T, the slope ρ specifies the change in hazard force over time between onsets, reflecting the combined changes in stability and escalation hazards, and ϕ is the background onset hazard force that models anarchy at $t = 0$. Special principles similar to those for model I can be derived for model II by applying assumption 4.2 (equation 4.8) to the general principles (theorems 3.1–3.5). Model II is methodologically progressive because it contains all properties of model I as $\rho \to 0$, plus new properties when anarchy is not the sole hazard force (i.e. when $\rho \neq 0$). For example, theorem 3.4 (equation 3.6) predicts that when escalation prevails over stability ($\rho > 0$), as during unstable periods, the median value ψ of political behavior will be smaller than the expected value $E(Y)$, making political events (in this case onsets) occur with "greater surprise" or "before they are expected." However, the opposite is true – political events will seem "overdue" – when stability forces prevail ($\rho < 0$). This hypothesis can be tested using data on surprising versus expected political events (such as governmental changes, riots, or wars).

Empirically, this model should fit and test better than model I when a long period of history (or a heterogeneous population of realizations) is divided into politically more homogeneous (shorter and less diverse) eras, during which time equilibrium properties are less likely to emerge. This is confirmed by findings shown in table 4.4 for the onset of "large wars" before and after the Treaty of Westphalia (i.e. before and during the modern nation state system).[8] Model II is superior in the more homogeneous era, as theoretically anticipated, when hazard forces other than anarchy are observed as a consequence of the shorter and less diversified period.

Model III (politics by nonlinear hazard force). Although model II is progressive with respect to model I, it is conceptually and technically flawed because it allows hazard force to become negative (violating the definition of probabilistic force) whenever $\rho < 0$ (during an unstable era) and the value of Y grows large ($y \to \infty$). The problemshift to model III solves this problem by considering qualitatively different nonlinear hazard forces.

Assumption 4.3 (qualitatively variable political hazard force). *The hazard force $H(y)$ producing political behavior Y varies qualitatively by decreasing,*

---

[8] I use the term "large war" as a shorthand for "a war involving one or more 'great powers'" (as in Levy 1983). Some large wars are the Thirty Years' War, the Crimean War, and all world wars. "Great power wars" (wars involving at least one great power on each side) are more restrictive and, like other wars, are likely to be governed by other hazard forces. Note that in terms of the theory of self-organized criticality (Bak and Chen 1991), a political system subject to increasing hazard force (i.e. when $dH(y)/dy > 0$) should exhibit "flicker noise," or the $1/f$ noise spectrum, indicative of significant dependence on past events.

Table 4.4. *Linear hazard force model estimates (MLEs) for large war onset, model II:* $H(t) = \phi + \rho t$

ϕ	$\rho\,(\times 10^{-3})$	F-ratio	R^2	Comments
Whole era: 1495 to present				
0.163*	0.969	0.315	1.9%	Heterogeneous population; only constant anarchy is significant, as expected
(0.029)	(1.7)			
Pre-Westphalian era: 1495–1648				
− 0.364	184.770*	7.50*	55.5%	Homogeneous population; escalation forces other than anarchy (positive slope) are significant, as expected
(0.371)	(67.5)			
Post-Westphalian era: 1648 to present				
0.112*	2.609	2.22	13.7%	Heterogeneous population; only constant anarchy is significant
(0.030)	(1.8)			

Notes: Numbers in parentheses are standard errors.
*$p < 0.05$
Source: Compiled by the author.

increasing, or remaining constant, linearly or nonlinearly, over all $y \in Y$. *Formally*,

$$H(y) = \kappa\, y^{\alpha}, \qquad\qquad [4.9]$$

where $\kappa > 0$ and $-\infty < \alpha < +\infty$ are parameters describing the qualitative adversity (α) and quantitative intensity (κ) of hazard force H.

As shown in figures 4.1 and 4.2, the adversity parameter α captures the qualitative nature of force acting on individuals or groups, making $H(y)$ decrease, increase (linearly or nonlinearly), or remain constant. Model III

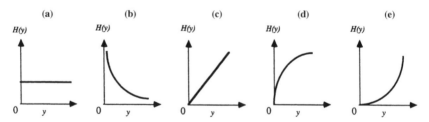

Figure 4.1. Qualitatively different forms of hazard force in model III (from left to right: [a] constant hazard force [$\alpha = 0$]; [b] decreasing [$\alpha < 0$]; [c] steadily [linearly] increasing [$\alpha = 1$]; [d] increasing with decreasing margin [$0 < \alpha < 1$]; or [e] increasing with increasing margin [escalation, $\alpha > 1$])

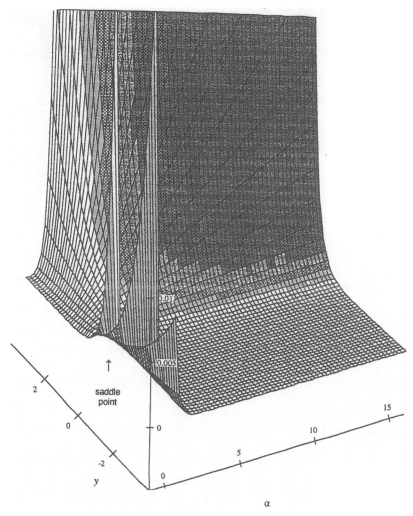

Figure 4.2. Graph of hazard force $H(y, \alpha)$ in model III (note the saddle point on the vertical plane $\alpha = 0$)

captures five qualitatively different behaviors of hazard force, each generating a special pattern of political uncertainty: constant (encompassing all properties of model I as $\alpha \to 1$, and of model II as $\rho \to 0$), concave decreasing (stable status quo), linear (hazard rate increases steadily, as in model II when $\rho > 0$), convex increasing (time dampens the propensity for the next realization to occur), and concave increasing (escalating propensity toward change).

Table 4.5. *Nonlinear hazard force model estimates (MLEs) for large war onset, model III*: $\ln H(t) = \ln \kappa + \alpha \ln t$

$\ln \kappa$	α	F-ratio	R^2	Comments
Whole Era: 1495 to present				
− 1.710*	− 0.068	0.168	1.0%	Heterogeneous population; only
(0.390)	(0.165)			the anarchy constant is significant, as expected
Pre-Westphalian Era: 1495–1648				
− 3.031*	1.400*	25.6*	81.0%	Homogeneous population; escala-
(0.436)	(0.277)			tion (instability) slope significant, as expected
Post-Westphalian Era: 1648 to present				
− 2.278*	0.078	0.165	1.2%	Heterogeneous population; only
(0.451)	(0.191)			constant anarchy is significant, as expected

Notes:
Numbers in parentheses are standard errors.
*$p < 0.05$.
Source: Compiled by the author.

For example, consider again war onset T. When $H(t)$ behaves as in figure 4.1(e) we have a political situation in which hazard forces acting on potential belligerents escalate rapidly, as when emerging tensions and conflicts go unresolved, causing war onset to be governed by equations 4.10–4.14 below with $\alpha > 2$. Historically, this is how war occurred in the pre-Westphalian European system (see table 4.5 for supportive evidence; note the decreasing fit for the more heterogeneous population of wars in the present era, as $\alpha \to 0$), as well as in Asia thousands of years earlier (Cioffi-Revilla and Lai 1995). The collapse of Communist regimes in East Central Europe may again have generated similar forces (Brzezinski 1989, 1993) – a proposition that can be tested – as in the case of the Yugoslavian civil war and other cases of disintegrative warfare.

The following special principle is derived in the same way as model I, by applying the assumption of variable hazard force (equation 4.9) to the general principles (theorems 3.1–3.5).

Theorem 4.2 (political behavior under qualitatively different nonlinear hazard force): *A political variable Y under qualitatively different hazard force* (equation 4.9) *has the following properties*:

$$p(y) = \kappa \, y^\alpha \exp\left(-\frac{\kappa}{\alpha} y^{\alpha} + 1 \right) \qquad \text{(by [3.1] in theorem 3.1) [4.10]}$$

$$\Phi(y) = 1 - \exp(-\frac{\kappa}{\alpha} y^{\alpha+1}) \qquad \text{(by [3.2] in theorem 3.1)} \quad [4.11]$$

$$E(Y) = \left(\frac{\kappa}{\alpha}\right)^{-1/(\alpha+1)} \Gamma\left(1 + \frac{1}{\alpha+1}\right) \text{(by [3.4] in theorem 3.3)} \quad [4.12]$$

$$V(Y) = \left(\frac{\kappa}{\alpha}\right)^{-2/(\alpha+1)} \left\{\Gamma\left(1 + \frac{2}{\alpha+1}\right) - \left[\Gamma\left(1 + \frac{1}{\alpha+1}\right)\right]^2\right\}$$
$$\text{(by [3.5] in theorem 3.3)} \quad [4.13]$$

$$\psi(Y) = \zeta^{\alpha/\kappa(\alpha+1)}. \qquad \text{(by [3.6] in theorem 3.4)} \quad [4.14]$$

where $\Gamma(\xi)$ is the value of the gamma function evaluated at ξ.

Because model III covers five qualitatively distinct hazard forces (figures 4.1 and 4.2), each generating its own special probability functions and predictions (using theorems 3.1–3.5), this model also captures diachronic historical change – the nonstationarity and epochal dependency of political dynamics. Although monocausal, model III allows political variables to show a given pattern in one era and a different pattern in another – while maintaining the same general model and varying the single parameter α. This qualitative and quantitative variety in model III is shown in figure 4.3, which illustrates the exact correspondence between the form of the hazard force (left) and the corresponding form of uncertainty in political behavior (right). The figure also shows how model III subsumes model I (top) as well as model II when $\alpha = 1$ (middle).

Recall the case $Y = T$ (general temporal variables; table 2.1), when the referent behavior is time between political events. Figure 4.4 illustrates the correspondence between these properties of hazard force and distributions on the one hand, and the equilibrium properties of the underlying political process on the other. These principles apply to the class of political processes where the question of stability or instability is significant, such as the duration of coalitions (alliances, governmental coalitions), international ("enduring") rivalries, warfare, and other temporal variables discussed earlier (chapter 2). Model III therefore takes a similar approach to macropolitical behavior as social choice theory (Lichbach 1996: vii) by asking whether equilibrium exists and, if so, whether it is stable.

Domestic and international dimensions of political violence sometimes conform to model III in spite of its monocausal nature (Cioffi-Revilla 1989; Horvath 1968). For example, empirical tests of model III confirm that it fits well in different eras of world history which have been governed by different hazard forces (different special dynamics), consistent with political change. As shown in table 4.5, from the end of the fifteenth century to the

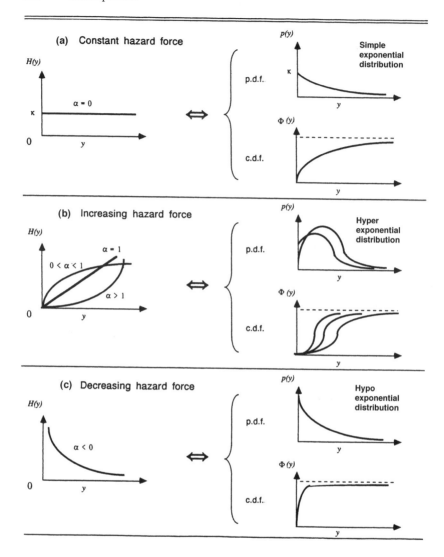

Figure 4.3. Graphs of hazard force $H(y, \alpha)$ and political behavior in model III (derived from the distributions principle, theorem 3.1)

time of the Thirty Years' War, the qualitative form of war hazard force acting on the European great power system was escalating between onsets ($\hat{\alpha} > 1$, as in figure 4.1(e)), indicative of a highly unstable system which was perhaps about to change into a new structure (the modern nation state system). By contrast, as theoretically expected, in modern times (after 1648)

Equilibrium case[a]	Hazard function $H(\delta)$	Graph of hazard force	Variability coefficient $c = \sigma/\mu$	Distribution $p(y)$ of political behavior Y
Indifferent	Constant $(\alpha = 0)$	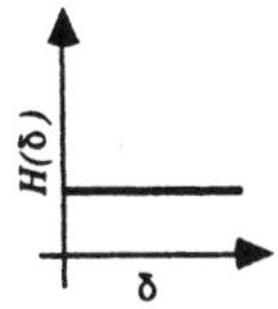	1.0	Exponential (Poisson)
Stable	Decreasing $(\alpha < 0)$	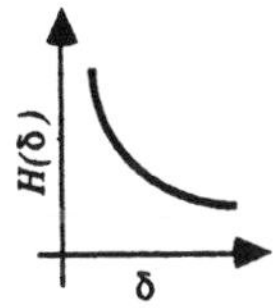	> 1.0	Hyper exponential
Unstable	Increasing $(\alpha > 0)$	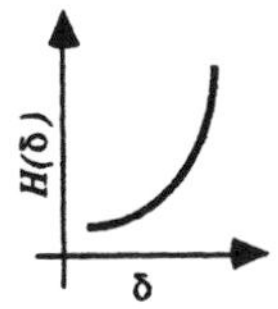	< 1.0	Hypo exponential (Erlang)

Figure 4.4. Hazard force and equilibrium of political behavior
[a] These cases are stationary. When the equilibrium is dynamic (i.e. non-stationary; not shown in this figure), the hazard force is time varying and the graph, the variability parameter c, and the form of the distribution will all vary accordingly.
Source: adapted from Cioffi-Revilla (1985a).

the war hazard force has been approximately constant (closer to figure 4.1(b) and to model I estimates in table 4.3), consistent with the more heterogeneous post-Westphalian era. The most consequential wars (hegemonic wars and global wars; Gilpin 1981; Midlarsky 1988a; Thompson 1985) are probably preceded by the rise of massive hazard forces similar to those that restructured the system after 1648 (so $\hat{a} > 1$, as in figure 4.1(e)), explaining their capacity to achieve large-scale transformation in international order. This theoretical idea is testable. Empirical applications of model III to other political variables should show a similar variety and epochal variation in the single causal hazard force that is producing political behavior – all within the special principles of this model.

4.3.2   Multiple implicit hazards

In spite of their progressive superiority, the three preceding implicit hazard force models are flawed by assuming that hazard force is always unitary or monocausal (without components), particularly models I and III, whereas politics is arguably governed by different hazard forces acting simultaneously. Model IV solves this problem by shifting the focus toward multiple hazard forces simultaneously acting to produce political behavior (multicausal dynamics), while remaining within the domain of implicit models.

Assumption 4.4 (multiple simultaneous hazard forces). *The hazard force* $H(y)$ *producing political behavior* Y *has three components:* (i) *a background hazard force with constant intensity* a, (ii) *an inhibiting force of political behavior* (conceptually the opposite of hazard force), *inversely proportional to* y; *and* (iii) *a hazard force promoting political behavior, exponentially proportional to* y. *Formally,*

$$H(y) = H_{\text{background}} + H_{\text{inhibiting}} + H_{\text{promoting}} \qquad [4.15]$$

$$= a + \frac{b}{y} + c\, e^y. \qquad [4.16]$$

To interpret this multicausal model, consider the onset of conflict. For example, in the domain of international wars, three independent hazard forces may be operative to cause onsets: (i) a background stationary force (systemic attributes that promote war and are constant between onsets, such as political culture, long-standing grievances, polarity, territorial features, strategic location, or technology); (ii) a decreasing hazard force (the inversely proportional force of stability in assumption 4.4, part 2) caused by the occurrence of the preceding onset; and (iii) an escalating exponential hazard force caused by the synergistic interaction of naturally accumulating conflicts of interests in a fundamentally anarchic system. A similar theoretical argument can be made in the multicausal domain of domestic politics for the onset of severely disruptive violent events, particularly in weak regimes.

Table 4.6. *Multicausal hazard force model estimates (MLEs) for large war onset, model IV*: $H(t) = a + b/t + ce^t$

a	b	$c\ [\times\ 10^{-3}]$	F-ratio	R^2	Comments
Whole era: 1495 to present					
0.173*	− 0.034	0.000	2.54	15.4%	Heterogeneous population;
(0.026)	(0.113)	(0.0)			constant anarchy is
					significant, as expected
Pre-Westphalian era: 1495–1648					
0.353	− 0.362	0.314*	19.5*	84.1%	Homogeneous population;
(0.209)	(0.569)	(0.1)			exponential escalation
					force is significant, as
					expected; anomaly for c
Post-Westphalian era: 1648 to present					
0.142*	− 0.053	0.000	3.72	36.4	Heterogeneous population;
(0.027)	(0.115)	(0.0)			constant anarchy is
					significant, as expected

Notes: Numbers in parentheses are standard errors.
*$p < 0.05$.
Source: Compiled by the author.

Table 4.6 shows the results of applying model IV to the onset of large wars. Again, the most heterogeneous eras show approximately constant hazard force and poorer fit, whereas the homogeneous era before 1648 shows significant variable hazard force with better fit, consistent with our theoretical expectations. The exponential (escalation) force component in the former era confirms a similar finding for model III earlier ($\alpha > 1$ and $c > 0$, consistent across models). An empirical anomaly in table 4.6 is that the second hazard force component – the decreasing (stability) force – is not significant. The onset of these large wars apparently has not been affected by conflict resolution efforts between onsets, but perhaps even larger wars (such as great power wars or global wars) will show a significant inhibiting component because of bigger stakes, greater effort, and higher systemic impact.

Analysis thus far has confirmed the following conclusions across the three variable implicit models (models II–IV):[9]

[9] Mathematically, equations 4.10 or 4.11 define the Weibull distribution (Cioffi-Revilla 1985b, 1989; Horvath 1968; Petersen 1987, 1991 [and Petersen's references to the Weibull distribution cited therein]; Weiss 1963). Also, political behavior in model III is exactly Rayleigh distributed as $\alpha \to 1$, and approximately normal or Gaussian distributed $N[\bar{y}, \sigma]$ as $\alpha \to 3.5$. Empirical tests have also generated some purely methodological innovations. Rather than merely fitting distributions to data, the aim has been to detect and analyze fluctuations in time-varying parameters indicative of diachronic change.

1 The fit of variable multicausal hazard force models – "background hazard force plus" models – is strongest and most significant for the more homogeneous populations of realizations or eras of history, as anticipated by the theory. As the focus increases (increased homogeneity), it is possible to see that there is more to account for political behavior than only the single cause of background anarchy.

2 Moreover, the greater the heterogeneity of the population the stronger the fit of the constant hazard force (Poisson) model, which explains why none of the variable hazard force models fits the largest eras of history, as expected.

3 Each consecutive model contains a greater variety of hazard forces, and does better empirically, as measured by total variance accounted for (the R^2 statistic for linear forces, and small standard errors for nonlinear models).

4 All four implicit models deductively generate and explain patterns of observed political uncertainty. The power of general principles (theorems 3.1–3.5) is therefore confirmed by being able to derive new special principles within each model. This is key to understanding the causal links between specific hazard forces (like anarchy or stability), political behavior, statistical properties of politics, and political uncertainty within a unified theory.

5 Each successive model contains all the properties of the simpler models plus new qualitative and quantitative properties, as required in a progressive problemshift.

4.4   Explicit models

The next progressive problemshifts use explicit hazard forces (table 4.1, right side; table 4.2, lower part). As I discussed earlier (section 2.3), political behavior can be explained through probabilistic causality using specifiable hazard forces which account for observable macro level distributions. For example, in the domestic political domain, relative deprivation (Gurr 1970; Lichbach 1995, 299 et seq.), increased interactions (Olzak et al. 1996), and other contextual factors have been analyzed as specific forces which account for urban violence and unrest. In the international domain, a traditional hypothesis in the study of world politics is that "the recurrence of war is explained by the structure of the international system" (Waltz 1989: 44). Most of the current literature (e.g. Bremer and Cusack 1995; Sabrosky 1985) uses regression approaches to search for the effect of structural variables such as systemic polarity, assuming that these had a direct deterministic effect on war variables. Results have been notoriously weak and mixed – as anticipated by this theory based on probabilistic causality – with numerous reports of parameter instability, cross-century differences, and other anomalies already discussed in chapter 1 (Eberwein 1981; Singer 1981, 1989). Probit and logit methods, as probabilistic approaches that respect and model uncertainty, offer improved but partial solutions, as indicated below.

Perhaps the most famous unexplained anomaly in world politics research is the cross-century correlational reversal between war and systemic variables, first discovered by the Correlates of War Project of the University of Michigan in 1968 (Ostrom and Hoole 1978; Singer et al. 1972; Singer and Small 1968). This theory explains these and other time-dependent reversals: they are caused by deeper dynamic changes in the hazard forces that produce war. Political behavior variables, such as war onset, *are* governed by systemic forces such as shifts in polarity, in alliance patterns, or in transaction flows (such as migration and commerce), but not in the way the earlier variance models imagined. Patterns of war do change as these and other "glacial" forces change.

Explicit models in this theory provide new perspectives on earlier regression analyses. First, causal variables such as systemic polarity, power concentration, alliance bonds, and others must be viewed as probabilistic hazard forces (as in definition 2.2), not as common deterministic variables. Second, these explicit hazard forces may produce distributions of observed war behavior (not individual values as assumed by the traditional regression approach), as governed by the general distributions principle (theorem 3.1). Third, the fundamental uncertainty of political behavior is respected – through probabilistic causality – while explicit hazard forces play a viable causal role in explaining distributions of behavior and their long- and short-range historical evolution. Estimating an explicit model requires empirical methods from event history or transition data analysis, as indicated in table 4.2 (Aalen 1978; Allison 1984; Blossfeld et al. 1989; Blossfeld and Rohwer 1995; Cox and Isham 1980; Cox and Oakes 1984; Kalbfleisch and Prentice 1980; Rohwer 1993). The same general principles apply, only now the special principles derived for these models contain explicit hazard forces and parameters.

4.4.1 *Single explicit hazard*

The simplest explicit model of aggregate political behavior relies on a single-component hazard force (monocausal). In domestic politics, depending on the structure of a political system (parameters such as political culture, regime type, elite accountability, institutional stability, and organizational complexity, among others) an individual hazard force may be demand for reform, governmental control, resource scarcity, elite cohesiveness, foreign interference, and so forth. In international politics, single explicit hazard forces include systemic polarity, alliance aggregation, population pressure, balance of power, "imperialism," and other causal forces.

Various political ideologies and normative frameworks often have this explicit monocausal character, consistent with class 3 models, and generally claim to provide single-variable explanations of political behavior. Thus, for Marxist-Leninists the cause (explanation) of political change through conflict lies in class struggle (conflict among social classes); for liberal-rationalists the single cause of all political behavior lies in the maximization of expected utility (a force independent of any other human drive, including ethical motives); for extremist pacifists it is mostly armaments that cause war.

Common to all explicit monocausal models of political behavior is the reliance on a single hazard force. Thus,

$$H(y) = \exp [-f(x)],\qquad\qquad [4.17]$$

where x is the single hazard force chosen. Although empirically implausible (behaviorally rare) this model of macropolitical behavior is theoretically significant because it yields its own set of meaningful special principles. In addition, the monocausal model is important because it contains many of the fundamental properties of more complex models that have a larger number of explicit hazard forces (independent variables). For example, when

$$\ln H(y) = \alpha + \beta X,\qquad\qquad [4.18]$$

which represents the simplest explicit monocausal form, then

$$p(y) = \exp [- (\alpha + \beta X + y\, e^{-(\alpha + \beta X)})]\qquad\qquad [4.19]$$

and

$$\Phi(y) = 1 - \exp [- (y\, e^{-(\alpha + \beta X)})]\qquad\qquad [4.20]$$

by applying the general distributions principle (theorem 3.1). In turn, as before, special principles follow for each individual moment and special value.

These specific principles in turn can be used to explore macroproperties of political behavior Y as caused (via probabilistic causality) by, say, the background hazard force α (parameter) and the specific hazard force X (independent variable). For instance, specific results can be derived by exploring the effect of α and X on $p(y)$, $\Phi(y)$, $E(Y)$, $V(Y)$, ψ, and ω. Comparative statics, normalized to α and X to control for different units, can provide new insights concerning the sensitivity of macropolitical behavior Y (dependent variable) to changes in the specific hazard force X

(independent variable) or to changes in parameters α and β. This is the approach of probabilistic causality for exploring the effect of hazard force X on political behavior Y while respecting the fundamental political uncertainty.[10]

4.4.2   Multiple explicit hazards

From simple to more complex, the research program can examine three basic types of explicit multicausal situations (recall table 4.2): linear additive (model V), nonlinear additive (model VI), and interactive (model VII), all of them included in class 4 (explicit multicausal models in table 4.1). With the appropriate caution for the fact that we are dealing with probabilistic causality, not with deterministic causality, this progression is somewhat similar to the standard progression in the multivariate regression literature (e.g. Judd and McClelland 1989; Shively 1989; Tufte 1974).

Note immediately that the meaning of the causal variables is now fundamentally different. Independent variables X_1, X_2, X_3, ..., are now properly defined as hazard forces that give form to the distribution of values of a political variable Y (by theorem 3.1), not as the traditional deterministic variables that are meant to predict exact values of Y. In this sense, the independent variables X_1, X_2, X_3, ..., in a multicausal hazard function may be called *conditionants* rather than *determinants*. Causally, what these variables do – the effect they have – is to condition individual values of political behavior to occur with a certain probability; in no sense do they determine individual values. If anything is "determined" by the independent variables X_1, X_2, X_3, ..., it is the set of distribution properties (by the general distributions principle).

Before exploring explicit multicausal models in some detail, I note that the difference between these models and a logit or probit equation lies in the dependent variable. Whereas a probit or logit equation attempts to model probability directly (as a simple hypothesis, without requiring any deductive theoretical justification), in the models which follow the hazard force produces a distribution of probability values (equations 3.1 and 3.2 of the general distributions principle), doing so by means of the causal explanatory principles discussed in the previous chapter. Although both

---

[10] Surprisingly little is understood about the theoretical properties of these explicit monocausal principles of political behavior (class 3). However, the research journals are beginning to publish studies that move directly into the statistical application of explicit multicausal models (class 4) almost as if these were a simple extension of traditional multivariate regression techniques of the general form $Y = f(X_1, X_2, X_3, ..., X_n)$. Clearly, further theoretical research on the basic properties of explicit monocausal principles is needed in order to develop proper foundations for the multicausal principles and their corresponding statistical models.

approaches are probabilistic, only the hazard force model is arguably causal and not merely correlational. Being based on the log-odds, rather than the hazard rate, probit and logit models are also simpler and more descriptive implementations of probabilism, closer to traditional regression approaches in conceptual orientation.

Independent hazards model. The essence of these models can be understood by examining the simplest log-linear additive case (model V):

$$H(y) = \exp\left(\alpha + \sum_{i=1}^{n} \beta_i X_i\right), \qquad [4.21]$$

where X_i is the ith explicit hazard force and $i = 1, 2, 3, \ldots, n$. This is sometimes called an exponential hazard rate function because the resulting distribution has exponential form. When log-linearized, α and the β coefficients represent the intercept and slope of the log-hazard, ln H. (I write equation 4.21 in this untransformed way on purpose, to highlight its fundamentally nonlinear character, in spite of the seemingly linear apearance – unfortunately similar to a regression equation – when log-transformed.) Applying the distributions principle (theorem 3.1), we obtain

$$p(y) = \exp\left[-\left(\alpha + \sum_{i=1}^{n} \beta_i X_i + y \, e^{-(\alpha + \Sigma i \, \beta i \, Xi)}\right)\right] \qquad [4.22]$$

and

$$\Phi(y) = 1 - \exp\left(- e^{-(\alpha + \Sigma i \, \beta i \, Xi)}\right) \qquad [4.23]$$

as the special distributions principle for explicit functions of multicausal hazard forces X_1, X_2, X_3, ..., acting to produce political behavior Y. Hence, probabilistic causality is accounting for the way in which the hazard forces (independent variables) affect the distributions of political behavior Y (dependent variable). The other properties (moments and special values) and principles of this independent multicausal hazards model are derived by similar procedures to those already outlined for the monocausal models (section 4.4.1).

Model V is theoretically applicable to a broad class of political phenomena whose aggregate behavior is affected by a linear combination of independent hazards. Such is the case for the duration D of governmental coalitions in parliamentary democratic systems. For example, in a comprehensive empirical study, King et al. (1990) have estimated model V (equation 4.21) and obtained a good fit for $\alpha = 3.57 \pm 0.32$ and several distinct independent hazards, such as party fractionalization and polarization. As King and collaborators point out in discussing their model 2.4, this class of models provides a unified approach to combining the constant hazard force (Poisson) acting on coalitions (Browne 1984; Browne et al. 1986; Cioffi-Revilla 1984), with a set of other independent hazard forces (Strom 1988). Both sets of causal factors (implicit and explicit forces) operate within a mechanism of probabilistic causality to explain aggregate coalition behavior.

Other important insights may be obtained in the domain of international poitics with a similar class of models. For example, consider model VI for the hazard force H producing war *onset* T. Some studies (e.g. Midlarsky 1974; Polacek 1980) have suggested that onset frequency may be proportional to the magnitude of systemic polarity (log P), and inversely proportional to the flow of trade transactions (Θ). These and other multivariate hypotheses from the earlier regression literature can be reinterpreted and formalized by this new framework using the following testable model with explicit hazard forces in the log-transformed equivalent to equation 4.21:

$$\ln H = \alpha + \beta_1 S + \beta_2 P + \beta_3/\Theta \qquad [4.24]$$

where S is system size, P is polarity, and Θ is the volume of transactions. (Recall that none of these relationships is truly linear; only the log-transformed of the original equations are linear for typographical or for estimation purposes.) War onset is assumed to be independent of time in this model, because time appears nowhere on the right-hand side of the equation, consistent with the earlier Poisson assumption (so α is the constant hazard force in equation 4.21). Accordingly, a theoretical affinity exists between this model (equation 4.21) and the monocausal constant hazard force model I (section 4.3.1), the difference being the additional independent variables and the log $\leftrightarrow$ exp transforms needed to respect the condition $H > 0$ (section 2.3.3) whenever the effect of independent variables is negative.

Another example applying this type of multicausal hazard model IV (equation 4.21) is to the duration D of international conflicts (so-called interstate rivalries; Diehl 1998). A model IV for the hazard force h of rivalry duration d has the following form:

$$\ln H = \alpha + \beta_1 N + \beta_2 W, \qquad [4.25]$$

where N = the number of disputes that occurred during each rivalry; and W = the number of wars that occurred between participating rivals, both as explicit independent variables (covariates). In a preliminary analysis of forty-five enduring rivalries (Cioffi-Revilla 1998) using the standard SPSS estimation algorithm (log-likelihood), results show that $\beta_1 = -0.15$ and $\beta_2 = -0.42$, both estimates significant at the 0.01 level. Such empirical results seem worth exploring further from a theoretical perspective, because they indicate that the frequency of disputes and wars has an effect on the distributions and macro properties of rivalry duration.

Dependent hazards model. A theoretically important extension of equation 4.21 is the case when the hazard force $H(y)$ is allowed to change with respect to values of Y. This is a common political situation when Y is a temporal variable and onset T or duration D have hazard rates proportional to time lapsed (see table 2.1). These are time-dependent hazard forces. In this case the hazard force function takes on the form

$$H(y) = \exp\left(\alpha + \sum_{i=1}^{n} \beta_i X_i + \gamma Y\right),$$
[4.26]

where γ is the coefficient of dependence proportionality. This is sometimes called a Gompertz hazard rate function, because it gives rise to a Gompertz distribution.

Finally, taking the progression one step further, we reach the politically significant case where the hazard force is affected by the magnitude of the values of Y – when H is affected mostly by the largest values – and not simply by the untransformed values (the previous case). In this case

$$H(y) = \exp\left(\alpha + \sum_{i=1}^{n} \beta_i X_i + \gamma' \ln Y\right),$$
[4.27]

where γ' is now the coefficient of dependence proportionality on $\ln Y$ (the magnitude of Y, not merely the scalar value of Y). This is sometimes called a Weibull hazard rate function, because it gives rise to a Weibull distribution. Empirical studies seem to indicate that domestic racial violence has this form, only slightly complicated by a higher-order term in the exponent function. In the most current comprehensive study of race riots in American urban areas, Olzak and collaborators (1996) report strong support for a hazard force model of the form

$$\ln H = \alpha + \beta_1 N + \beta_2 N^2 + \beta_3 R + \gamma' \ln T,$$
[4.28]

where N = number of previous riots, R = residential segregation, and T = time since the previous riot onset. The theoretical foundations for these and other empirical studies require further exploration in the light of the special macro principles presented in this chapter.

To close my treatment of explicit models, particularly those in the multi-causal category of the taxonomy (class 4), I highlight the following points:

1 Event history analysis, Poisson regression, and other fledgling techniques supported by statistical packages provide the statistical imple-

mentations of the theoretical principles I have discussed, so these empirical techniques must always be grounded on and interpreted in the light of the principles discussed in this chapter, not the reverse. An understanding of these principles is assumed in any statistical application. Not all statistical packages provide the same quality estimates (Olzak et al. 1996).

2 The explicit hazard force models discussed in this chapter (section 4.4) and others in the same category (classes 3 and 4 in the taxonomy in table 4.1; models V–VII in table 4.2) are used when the hazard force $H(y)$ acting on an aggregate variable of political behavior Y is a function of explicit variables that are somehow measurable (called "covariates" in sociology), such as socioeconomic conditions, systemic structure parameters, or some event frequencies. The theoretical framework of these models differs fundamentally from the more traditional framework of multivariate regression models. Therefore a multicausal hazard function must never be interpreted in the same way as a multivariate regression model, even if research publications unfortunately employ virtually identical table formats for reporting parameter estimates (intercepts, slopes, standard errors, and so forth) for these two different types of models.

3 None of the explicit independent variables that are specified in a hazard force function can be accurately called a "determinant," because the models being considered are all based on probabilistic causality (consistent with axiom 1.3), not deterministic causality. Elsewhere (Cioffi-Revilla 1996) I have suggested the term "conditionants," rather than the traditional term "determinants." The term conditionant conveys the idea that in these causal models the explicit hazard factors (independent variables) affect the conditional probability of values of political behavior Y being realized, by modeling the hazard rate H; they do not determine the actual values of the behavior variable Y. Therefore, in a strict sense, hazard force H conditions – does not determine – political behavior Y, which is the meaning of probabilistic causality.

4.5   Conclusions

In this chapter I applied the set of general macro principles developed in chapter 3 to a succession of specific cases of hazard force commonly found in political situations. From a systematic perspective, I distinguished between implicit and explicit models, as well as between political situations governed by a single hazard force (monocausal dynamics) and those based on several hazard forces (multicausal dynamics).

Implicit models explain macropolitical behavior in terms of aggregate causal hazard forces, such as anarchy, stability, or escalation, without specific reference to their substantive origin (economic, demographic, social, or other observable indicators). Empirically, these models are estimated using statistical methods from point process estimation or survival analysis. Several progressive problemshifts were examined, using the onset of war in recent centuries as a running example. Hazard force was shown to be approximately constant for large, heterogeneous populations of realizations (explaining the widespread applicability of the Poisson model to social behavior), but variable for smaller, more homogeneous populations (associated with different, non-Poisson patterns of uncertainty).

Explicit models explain macropolitical behavior in terms of individual substantive causal forces, such as economic, demographic, social, or other – as when specific systemic forces are hypothesized to produce patterns of war behavior. Empirically, explicit models are estimated using statistical methods from event history analysis and hazard rate with covariates or competing risks. These models are also used to explain earlier anomalies reported in the literature, such as the famous cross-century reversal in the correlates of war.

Part III

Micropolitics

5 Occurrence of political events

Fischer, Mayer, and the Marxists insist that war did not just happen, but was caused. This is true, but so is the converse. Until 1914 peace did not just happen, but was caused.

Paul Schroeder, *World War I as Galloping Gertie*

5.1 Introduction

This is the first chapter on the uncertain occurrence of political events – the lower level of analysis that I postulated in chapter 1 (axiom 1) – so my focus returns to the tasks of concept formation and systematics. This chapter on the occurrence of individual political events parallels chapter 2 on the behavior of aggregate political variables. Accordingly, in this chapter I define and classify the building blocks for understanding uncertainty in micropolitics, consistent with the axioms in chapter 1: political events and the causal logics that produce them. To maintain overall theoretical consistency with respect to previous chapters, my treatment in these chapters will parallel my earlier treatment of behavioral distributions and political variables in the macropolitical part of the theory. My interest remains focused on core aspects of general politics, as identified in figure 1.1. Again I should stress that these conceptual building blocks require careful definition. The goal is to understand the subtle workings of probabilistic causality at the micro level of political event occurrences, after having seen the way probabilistic causality operates at the macro level of aggregate political behavior. I shall address the links between the building blocks in the micropolitical part of the theory – what analytically binds together political events (defined as *explananda*) and causal logics (*explanans*) – in the next chapter, after defining in this chapter the nature of each and how they combine to produce political uncertainty.

I take some purely formal concepts such as sample points, sets, sample spaces, decisional outcomes, and states of nature as primitive or axiomatic (Chung 1979; Feller 1968; Goldstein et al. 1991). However, I provide a more extensive treatment of other politically significant but less well understood concepts that play a key role in this part of the theory, such as events and event functions. This focus on events and their causal logics – the main sections of this chapter – parallels my earlier focus on the macropolitical concepts of the random variable and distributions as the formal basis for the *explanandum* and the *explanans* of political behavior, respectively. An important result from this conceptualization is obtained again in the area of systematics, with the result this time in the form of a new classification of the logics of micropolitics. In the next two chapters I use the ideas introduced in this chapter to derive general principles, special principles, and other results, similar to the theoretical development I presented in earlier chapters for macropolitical behavior.

In this chapter I also ground the occurrence of political events on states of nature and decisional outcomes, thereby providing microfoundations for the theory of political uncertainty. However, as a precautionary note, I should point out that reference to decisional outcomes or choices must be taken in the light of my earlier discussion of political decisions (section 1.2.4), where I highlighted the significant variety of choice modes. Among these, the expected utility model is only one among several causal mechanisms (see table 1.1). Grounding the theory on microfoundations means simply that the most minute elements of political events are specified, and these consist of states of nature and decisions – a procedure which accepts the existence of various concrete decisional mechanisms.

5.2   Individual political occurrences: defining events

In general, how does one define a political occurrence? How does one do so in terms of events? More specifically, what is required to explain the occurrence of a political event? Although questions such these may seem obvious or unnecessary to some – after all, who cannot describe a generic political event? – definitional accuracy is important because the common-language meaning of these terms, sometimes even when used in scholarly works, is too often taken for granted. Lack of attention in defining the occurrence of political events can lead to significant oversights in terms of causal understanding of political uncertainty at the micro level of analysis. As I demonstrate in this section, there is nothing trivial about defining political occurrences with the systematic rigor that is necessary for founding a viable theory of politics at the micro level of analysis. The alternative can only produce a weakly founded theory, particularly when events and their uncertain occurrence (or failure to occur) are the principal objects of explanation (the *explananda*). In addition, my definitional treatment of the concept of political occurrence as an event is intended to clarify the differences that exist between the political and the formal aspects of the term "event," corresponding to the substantive and mathematical aspects, respectively. To understand the former – my primary objective in this and in the next two chapters – it is necessary to appreciate some of the technical (or even philosophical) properties of the latter.

5.2.1   Meanings of political occurrence

Like many other social science terms, the term "political event" has several language meanings that are widely used, besides the more specialized meaning I assign to it shortly in this chapter. Before stating the meaning I use, I believe it is insightful – even prudent, given the goal of this general theory – to highlight some of the other meanings of the term (the semantic *definientia* of "political occurrence"). This is useful in a scientific study because the meaning I will stipulate should not be too far removed from the common-language usage, otherwise we would develop a science of politics so detached from historical political experience that its principles would become difficult to interpret in the real world. Keeping common-language semantics in mind when one is defining political events with rigor is also consistent with a view of scientific language as an improvement upon – not an orthogonal departure from – common language (Bruschi 1990).

Common language. The common individual – mass culture in general – sees political events more or less as social situations that are often controversial or open to contentious debate, with or without actual violence. Indeed, for many people, including journalists, some of whom occasionally act in the political world as consequential actors, politics means basically a controversy that is polemic or conflictual (Gilliant 1987). This meaning of a political event is in some contrast with the far more pacific conception of politics favored by contemporary political science scholars, for whom political occurrences are related to the core social issues of value allocation, redistribution, and governance.

Partisanship, in a broad sense, also provides another common-language meaning. Accordingly, for the common person those situations that are designated as "political" – as in the terms "political maneuvering" or "political manipulation" – are usually seen as founded upon, or even caused by, biased or value-laden perspectives – so much so that they sometimes involve decisions by other people who are more often than not seen as "more powerful." Socially divisive events, such as the passage of a controversial legislative bill, intervention in an ongoing foreign conflict, or a change in the composition of a long-standing coalition are some examples of recurring situations that share this common-language meaning of the term "political event."

History. Another class of meanings of the term "political event" – meanings that are no longer common but scholarly – is to depict a important historical occurrence which produces collective consequences, such as an election, a *coup d'état*, an arms embargo, or a constitutional reform. In this sense, political events are those most commonly found in history books, the discrete components of historical evolution. Some of these political events, such as the 1989 downfall of Communism in Eastern Europe and the former Soviet Union, have complex causes and equally complex consequences. In this sense, large-scale political events often imply changes that affect people individually as well as collectively. Also in this sense, political events happen all the time in every collectivity that endures under some form, and occurrences are usually recorded because they are worth remembering. Indeed, in this historical sense, it can be said that a collectivity exists if and only if it produces political events – otherwise, it is dead *qua communitas.*

Informally, political events such as elections, party realignments, or wars are therefore situations or occurrences that happen (i.e. they are "realized") somewhere in the space–time of history. What makes these events specifically political is the verifiable fact that such occurrences empirically affect a group of individuals (a "collectivity") that is commonly larger than the group of individuals who made the decisions which caused the changes. Political events in a historical sense will differ in numerous particulars, but all of them share these common properties.

Empirical social science. In most social science research, the concept of a political event is often taken for granted, as if it were a primitive or axiomatic term. The term is not even defined as a distinct concept in the major extant scholarly lexicons or in state-of-knowledge compendia in political science,[1] although the term is used often in these works. Perhaps this is because the concept of an event seems so basic to an understanding of any social phenomena that no serious definitional effort seems necessary.

The most notable exception to this in social science is in the area called events-data research (Plano et al. 1982, 49–50), where the analysis is based on the statistical count and analysis of individual political occurrences, an approach practiced in both domestic and international domains, and the

---

[1] Finifter (1983, 1993), Plano et al. (1982), Polsby and Greenstein (1975), Shils (1968), Weisberg (1986).

use of more rigorous definitions becomes unavoidable.[2] Accordingly, political events are often systematically recorded for longitudinal and comparative purposes using measurement instruments commonly called events-data scales. Well-known examples of such scales are those developed by the Conflict and Peace Data Bank (domestic and international COPDAB scales; Azar 1980), the World Event Interaction Survey (WEIS; McClelland 1978), the Behavioral Correlates of War Project (BCOW; Leng 1993), and other similar dataset projects that record primarily day-long, so-called "fine-grained" events. Alternatively, political events that have a longer time-scale, or so-called "coarse-grained" episodes such as government coalitions, revolutions, crises, or wars, are recorded by means of operational definitions (see, e.g. Cioffi-Revilla 1990 and 1991b for international crises and wars). Time of onset, duration, actor, political content (substance as described by verbs), and other historically distinct characteristics represent separate dimensions of political occurrences that are recorded using scales and operational definitions. An events-data scale – also called an ethogram in behavioral science (Cairns 1979) – sometimes also makes it possible for political events to be measured according to some intensity (e.g. "level of conflict" or "level of cooperation," as in COPDAB). When an episodic (coarse-grained) political event is measured by means of an operational definition, sometimes this also allows the recording of some intensity (e.g. "coalition size" or "war fatalities" when measuring government coalitions and warfare, respectively). The dimensional property of political behavior variables at the macro level (section 2.2.1) also applies to political events at the micro level, because events have attributes such as time of occurrence, magnitude, duration, and so on.

Theoretical social science. Political events defined in the events-data tradition mark a major scientific improvement over the common-language and historical use of the term, primarily because of the increase in precision and systematic use. In turn, this provides a more solid basis for making valid inferences. However, several theoretically insightful properties of political events – properties which are essential for explaining their uncertain occurrence – remain hidden unless a more formal definition is propounded. Also, as the term indicates, events-data always imply a large set of events, never a single datum. I believe this is because events-data measurement was originally developed primarily for descriptive purposes (and for providing early

---

[2] For example, individual political events, such as a "government sanction," an "armed attack," a "demonstration," or a "political change" are carefully defined in Taylor and Jodice (1983). However, the generic term "political event" is defined only in terms of the nation state, and then only by exclusion (not "criminal" and not "economic"). See Cioffi-Revilla (1990: ch. 3; 1991b) and Vasquez (1993: chs. 1, 2, and 3) for recent analyses of the concept of war and related war events.

warning), not for explaining individual political occurrences. In particular, the desired theory of political events based on uncertainty requires a definition that is not restricted to classes of events which occur only in large-number aggregations (as in events-data research), but is applicable to the occurrence of individual, one-of-a-kind events which are commonplace in general political life, as identified earlier in figure 1.1.

I define a political event as follows.

Definition 5.1 (political event). *A political event* $\mathbb{Y}$ *is a state of the world containing a specific combination of more elemental occurrences (sample points) from the sample space* Ω *of decisional outcomes and states of nature which "affect the lives and fortunes of collectivities and how they are governed."*[3]

Accordingly, a political occurrence is well defined if and only if the following two components are also specified: (i) a set of more elemental real-world events (the sample points consisting of decisional outcomes and states of nature which concern "collective lives, fortunes, or governance"), and (ii) an operational rule that causally links such events. The use of decisional outcomes and states of nature as elementary occurences also grounds the theory on microfoundations.[4] Logically, a deficiency in either component causes a political event to be ill defined.

In table 5.1, I illustrate these ideas using examples from various domains of politics, and two examples from simple probability theory (bottom) to provide a helpful analogy.[5] For instance, consider the event "die turns up odd," or event $\mathbb{O}$. This occurs when either 1, 3, or 5 occurs (elemental

---

[3] As a notational convention, I write an event using upper-case hollow letters (e.g. $\mathbb{Y}$), in order to respect the conceptual distinction between events and variables. I write the latter in upper-case italics, following the standard convention. Accordingly, $\mathbb{Y}$ denotes a political event and Y denotes a political variable. Obviously the two are conceptually related (axiom 1 in chapter 1) but each has a distinctive set of constitutional properties (an event is defined on a sample space of points; a variable is defined on a set of values). Each realization of a variable constitutes an event; a variable is a set of realizations. These conceptual remarks are also important for developing a unified theory linking macro (variables) and micro (events) levels of analysis.

[4] Recall that by this I do not mean to equate microfoundations with expected utility models. Consistent with my earlier discussion in section 1.2.4, political choice can occur in a variety of modes, most of them not by expected utility calculation.

[5] The background sample space (where events come from) is not commonly considered by most extant probability models of politics. This oversight can lead to problems that are commonly found in the literature (e.g. Hussein 1987). Also, note that a political event may consist of states of nature (situations unaccounted for by human acts) or decisional outcomes (act-dependent events resulting from other actor(s) choice or game-strategic equilibria). This distinction is also discussed by Tsebelis (1989), along with some consequences of ignoring the distinction, and by Jeffrey (1983) in his act-dependent decision theory. I am grateful to Raymond Dacey for introducing me to Jeffrey's theory.

Table 5.1. *Political events, elemental events (sample points), and sample space*

Political event	Symbol	Elemental events (*sample points*)	Sample space Ω
"Party A wins an election"	$\mathbb{E}$	Party A nominates a candidate, voters cast sufficient votes for party A, etc.	All possible electoral outcomes
"Government coalition forms"	$\mathbb{G}$	One coalition forms from a set of winning coalitions	All possible coalitions in the polity
"Collective action occurs"	$\mathbb{A}$	Collective action need is recognized, leaders coordinate, followers follow, and so forth	All possible states of the political community
"*Coup d'état* occurs"	$\mathbb{P}$	Constitutional leader is forcefully removed from office, usurper takes over, and so forth	All possible states of a domestic political system
"Crisis occurs"	$\mathbb{C}$	A state undertakes threatening action, another state resists	All possible states of the international system
"War occurs"	$\mathbb{W}$	Belligerents fight, fatalities occur, national leadership assumes special powers, economic system experiences effects, and so on	All possible states of the international system
"Die turns up odd"	$\mathbb{O}$	1 or 3 or 5 occurs	1, 2, 3, 4, 5, 6
"Die turns up even"	$\mathbb{E}$	2 or 4 or 6 occurs	1, 2, 3, 4, 5, 6

Source: Prepared by the author.

events), from among the six possible outcomes (sample space). The "rule" which produces $\mathbb{O}$ using 1, 3, and 5 is the notion of disjunction, expressed by the statement "... when either...". Axiomatically (theoretically), the elemental events (sample points) which are in the sample space of all possible outcomes (1, 2, 3, 4, 5, 6) play the same role in defining the referent event $\mathbb{O}$ as decisional outcomes and states of nature in defining a referent political event $\mathbb{Y}$. In each case they provide the substance which forms the referent event as a distinct realization.

Turning to the political events in table 5.1, consider the event "party A wins an election," denoted by $\mathbb{E}$. This political event is defined in terms of a set of more elemental events, such as "party A nominates a candidate," "voters cast a sufficient number of votes for party A," and so on, some of which are states of nature (e.g. favorable macroeconomic conditions) while others are decisional outcomes (e.g. voters participating). The elemental events (sample points) can vary depending on the specific definition that is used, but what matters most in terms of maintaining rigor is that the elemental events be precisely identified. The elemental events in $\mathbb{E}$ are causally linked in such a way as to make $\mathbb{E}$ distinguishable from other political events that can be formed from the same sample space or from other sample spaces. For example, $\mathbb{E}$ is different from the event $\mathbb{B} =$ "Party B wins an election," which can be defined on the same sample space as $\mathbb{A}$. Different electoral outcomes ("party A wins an election," "the election was a landslide for party C," and so forth) are defined by using different elemental events (all drawn from the sample space Ω) to compose another electoral outcome.

Similarly, different types of war events ("great power war," "civil war," and so forth) are defined by using different elemental events (all drawn from the sample space Ω) to compose another war event. Another event in table 5.1, "crisis occurs" ($\mathbb{C}$), may originate from a similar sample space, but will have a different set of elemental events or a different causal structure, such that $\mathbb{W} \neq \mathbb{C}$. Accordingly, a crisis event $\mathbb{C}$ shares some elemental points with a war event $\mathbb{W}$, so the intersection of the point sets of the two events is not empty. There are also some unique events in $\mathbb{W}$ that are not in $\mathbb{C}$, such as the occurrence of a significant number of combat fatalities, without which $\mathbb{W}$ would be politically indistinguishable from $\mathbb{C}$. Or, as another example, some elemental events of collective action, $\mathbb{A}$, are unique to that event while others may be shared, say, with event $\mathbb{W}$.

Note that in elementary probability theory the sample points (e.g. 1, 3, or 5) which are used to define an event ("die turns up odd") are left undefined (what causes 3 to turn up?). Similarly, at some point, the elemental events which compose a political event must be left undefined. At which point? At a point beyond which we do not care (just as we do not care to know why or how 3 turns up in the die event). Given that politics results mostly from human decisions, as opposed to being mostly the result of states of nature, a natural resting place for modeling and explaining the occurrence of political events and their uncertainty is at the level of decisional outcomes. In turn, the elements of a choice situation are generally – albeit not always – considered to be states of nature, no longer decisional outcomes. This approach also allows the theory of political uncertainty to rest on microfoundations of decision making, consistent with the axioms in chapter 1.

The main idea to be drawn from the preceding discussion of definition 5.1 is that a political event – or a class of political occurrences which have some significant trait in common – can be said to have a diacritic composition with respect to both the set of component elemental occurrences (sample points) and the relation among elemental component events (combination of sample points).[6] In addition, table 5.1 parallels table 2.1 (taxonomy of political behavior) in illustrating the potentially broad scope of this part of the theory, including the uncertain occurrence of events in both domestic and international domains. On the basis of definition 5.1, the differences between domestic and international occurrences seem to be mostly accidental (with different levels of situational anarchy) – without, of course, denying that different levels of situational anarchy can be so quantitatively different as to practically constitute a qualitative difference.[7] The main reason for this broad empirical scope – a desirable theoretical feature as defined by the focus on general politics in chapter 1 (figure 1.1) – is due to the way in which I have defined a political event: as a collection of more elemental points (a topological point-set) emerging from a background sample space of states of nature and decisional acts, and not just as a plain occurrence that has no further detail or causal structure to it, as in the other meanings of common language, history, and event-data research. The earlier meanings (common language and history) did not permit this.

Axiom 1 (section 1.3.1) postulated the duality of politics in terms of variables and events as distinct levels of analysis. Comparing definition 5.1 with definition 2.1, we can see that a political event is quite a different conceptual category – a theoretical building block made of different substance (decisional outcomes and states of nature from a sample space, as opposed to values from a domain) and of different form – from a political behavior. Whereas at the macro level of analysis a political behavior is defined by random variables (chapter 2) that assume values from a given set (domain), at the micro level a political event is defined by other, more elemental events (sample points) that occur (or fail to occur) from among a larger set of possible events (sample space). It is important to highlight and keep in mind these categorical differences across levels of analysis – events are to the micro level as variables were to the macro level – just as it is important to understand the parallel similarities that exist between these concepts. From a causal perspective, political events occur in a sample space, whereas variables assume values in a given domain. In the previous

---

[6] Note that the last two examples in table 5.1 are the classic cases of tossing a die, as this experiment is commonly used in elementary probability theory. The purpose is to make clear the political (substantive) and mathematical (formal) parallels between the following categories: events, sample points, and sample spaces. Obviously, the greater complexity of political events compared to die-rolling events must be acknowledged (they are caused by the presence of decisional outcomes and states of nature), but the fundamental parallelism holds, making all the cases in table 5.1 (and others) subject to the same mathematical principles.

[7] See Cioffi-Revilla and Starr (1995) for a more detailed analysis of this commonality.

chapters I discussed how hazard forces cause variables of aggregate political behavior to produce a precise distribution of values, with all its well-defined properties. The next task is therefore to explore how a political event causally occurs in a sample space constituted by other more elemental events.

5.2.2   Event function of a political occurrence

What explains the uncertain occurrence of a political event $\mathbb{Y}$? For example, in reference to the events in table 5.1, what explains the occurence of a coalition formation, a crisis or a conflict onset? More generally, how do elemental events (sample points) in the political sample space combine to form recognizable events? Although seemingly too abstract to answer with the necessary degree of precision, this question does have a precise answer based on the causal logic which links those related uncertain occurrences – that is, the more elemental events denoted by $\mathbb{X}_1$, $\mathbb{X}_2$, $\mathbb{X}_3$, ..., $\mathbb{X}_n$ in the sample space – that make $\mathbb{Y}$ occur at a given time, have a given magnitude, or last a given duration.

In other words, what explains the occurrence of a political event is the causal logic which makes the event occur based on how other causal events from the background sample space of politics occur or fail to occur. Thus, for a candidate to win an election, other related events – for example, events connected with campaign funding, constituent support, the nomination process, electoral laws, state of the economy, and so on – must occur or fail to occur in a given combination, or sometimes in one of several equally effective combinations. Similarly, for a conflict to terminate, other related events – for example, events connected with strategic objectives, force planning, alliance dynamics, domestic support, and so on – must occur or fail in nonarbitrary ways. For collective action to take place, a critical combination of causal events must occur in a specific way, otherwise the collective action will not take place. I note that this type of causal explanation for the occurrence of political events is also the one referred to in Schroeder's epigraph at the beginning of this chapter – World War I and the peace that preceded it both occurred because they were caused (they did not just simply happen). Similarly, paraphrasing Schroeder, the fall of Communism beginning in 1989 did not just happen, but was caused; until 1989 Communism did not just happen, but was caused. Today – as well as thousands of years ago – the process of state formation is caused by a specifiable set of events; it does not just happen. In general, political events are caused by more elementary and sometimes unobservable states of nature and decisional outcomes.

This reasoning leads to the next conceptual building block, called the event function, which operationally (i.e., causally) produces a political event.

Definition 5.2 (event function of a political event). *Given a political event* $\mathbb{Y}$ *and a set of other events* $\{\mathbb{X}\}$ *causally connected to the occurrence or failure of* $\mathbb{Y}$, *the mapping* Ψ: $\{\mathbb{X}\} \to \mathbb{Y}$ *is called the event function of* $\mathbb{Y}$. *Thus,* $\mathbb{Y} = \Psi\{\mathbb{X}\}$.[8]

Informally, the event function (e.f.) of a political occurrence refers to the causal rule or mechanism that specifies how the events related to the main occurrence are to combine – how $\mathbb{Y}$ forms out of the undifferentiated uncertainty of different possibilities consisting of states of nature and decisional outcomes (the background sample space). The term "mechanism" (Elster 1989) may be used to describe an event function, so long as it is understood as being devoid of any deterministic connotation – the logic of an event function is probabilistic, consistent with the axioms of political uncertainty in chapter 1. Formally, as I will demonstrate in the next two chapters, the argument of an e.f. spells out in specific detail the exact causal logic explaining how a political event $\mathbb{Y}$ is produced.

Unlike the events in simple parlor games (e.g. events produced by plays of die, roulette, or cards), many common and therefore seemingly simple political events – for example, policy implementation, coalition formation, or war onset – can have a complicated event function that must be modeled and explained to understand the uncertainty of occurrence (or of failure). Only the standard pedagogical events like those used in elementary probability textbooks, such as "die turns up even" or "coin lands tails," seem to have a very simple event function – this is why they also have a significant pedagogical value. What is more important, as I will show, a reduced class of relatively simple event functions can be used to explain the uncertainty of a remarkably large class of political events.

Which event functions exist and how do different event functions explain the occurrence of a political event? Which properties of event functions determine the uncertainty of political events? How does an event function determine the probability of a political event? In the next two chapters I provide answers to these questions by deriving a set of general and specific

---

[8] Given the rules of isomorphic equivalence between set theory, formal logic, events algebra, and Boolean algebra, an event function may be written in any one of the following ways: as a set-theoretic statement ($\mathbb{Y} = \mathbb{X}_1 \cup \mathbb{X}_2$), as a sentential logic proposition ($\mathbb{Y} = \mathbb{X}_1 \vee \mathbb{X}_2$), as an event-algebraic formula ($\mathbb{Y} = \mathbb{X}_1 + \mathbb{X}_2$), or as a Boolean sentence ($\mathbb{Y} = \mathbb{X}_1$ OR $\mathbb{X}_2$). This formal equivalence between these discrete mathematical structures is useful for expressing (modeling) the occurrence of political events in alternative ways, particularly when one approach seems easier than the other, or when comparing deductive results from the formal calculus used in each approach. See Boole (1951), Goldstein et al. (1991), Ragin (1987), Richards (1989), and Rogers (1971).

principles. But before addressing these questions I must complete this introductory chapter on the logics of politics at the micro level by highlighting a distinction between the different causal modes of causal explanation for political events. I shall do so using many of the areas of political uncertainty identified earlier in section 1.2.

5.3   Occurrence of politics: defining causal logics

In the previous section I introduced the idea that political occurrences originate from a set of more elemental events, all of them drawn from a background sample space. The sample space includes many possible events, only some of which are realized, and then only in a specific combination. In this section I use these concepts to systematize the causal occurrence of political events by distinguishing two basic logics for explaining how the combination of sample points forms into a singular political event. I call these two fundamental logic modes sequential and conditional because these terms capture quite well the mode of causal reasoning involved in each case. It is interesting to see how both modes are commonly used in political thinking, although to my knowledge their individual logic has not been investigated in the literature. Each mode gives rise to a set of general and special principles for understanding individual political events and their uncertain occurrence at the micro level of analysis, to parallel the earlier general and special principles for aggregate political behavior at the macro level. Given their importance, I dedicate the rest of this chapter to providing an intuitive introduction to the two causal logics supported by some simple examples that give a preliminary flavor of sequential and conditional political explanations. This is necessary in order to proceed from the more familiar to the less familiar area of general and special principles. The next two chapters explore the main implications with greater rigor and depth. Later I also demonstrate how both logics are combined, to advance our understanding of political uncertainty in a unified way (switching logics back and forth), and to bring out the full bimodal structure of political uncertainty in event occurrences at the micro level of analysis.

5.3.1   *Sequential logic*

In sequential logic mode, the occurrence of a political event is explained by providing a temporal succession or path of prior events that leads to occurrence. Informally speaking, this type of causal explanation is related to – albeit not identical with – the common language expression "what lies ahead," or what "leads to" a political occurrence, hence the causal designation "sequential." Sequential logic generally places most of the explanatory emphasis on a process-oriented causal argument with several intervening contingencies, looking toward the future from the vantage point of the past. The occurrence of a political event in sequential logic mode is explained more as a possible outcome, among several alternative outcomes, rather than as a given that must occur.

For example, consider the event "a two-party government coalition is formed." A sequential logic explanation of this event would use the successive occurrence of a series of events, such as "the previous coalition is dissolved," "party A communicates willingness to form a government with B," "party B responds with similar willingness," and so on, including all the required constitutional and extra-constitutional procedures, up to the outcome event "a new government forms." In this case all the prior events in the sequence would be contained in the argument of the event function. Similarly, a sequential logic explanation of the event "war breaks out" generally relies upon the successive occurrence of a "chain" of events "leading to war." In this framework such events are viewed as "the process that leads to war," or that can lead to war if the process does not change. Accordingly, in terms of the event function for the occurrence of "war breaks out," the events that occur prior to onset would be contained in the argument.

In general form, using the notation I established earlier (definition 5.2), a political event $\mathbb{Y}$ explained in a sequential causal logic mode is represented by

$$\mathbb{Y} = \Psi_s\{\cdot\},$$

where the argument $\{\cdot\}$ of the e.f. Ψ is given in sequential logic mode. The sequential logic mode of causal explanation is used implicitly in the following areas of political science:

- electoral processes, where the nomination of each canditate prior to the final vote is contingent upon prior decisions by voters in primary elections or caucuses (Stone et al. 1995);
- legislative processes, where the passage of a bill is the outcome of a multistage evolution, going through several caucuses, parliamentary committees, or assemblies, and finally the bill becomes law;[9]
- public policy implementation when this phenomenon is viewed as a "trickle down" process (Pressman and Wildavsky 1973);

[9] I do not provide any specific scholarly references in this area because this is the standard process prescribed by national constitutions, with some modifications allowed for more purely political, extraconstitutional events (e.g. party consultations; Truman 1951). I am grateful to Calvin Jillson and John W. Kingdon for their comments on contemporary legislative process research in American politics.

- international crises, dispute escalation, and war onset;[10]
- input–output systems analyses that view policy responses or failures as the result of political events caused by environmental disturbances (Almond and Powell 1978);
- functionalist process of international integration that relies on the "spill-over" effect as the mechanism for obtaining political development (Mitrany 1948, 1966, 1975; Haas 1964); and
- political interactions that can be represented as a game in extensive form.

The fundamental causal feature shared by these and other separate disciplinary themes is that each relies on a set of event sequences and paths – the explicit consideration of time is essential in these topics, although the scale of time units may remain undefined – to explain the occurrence of political events. This feature calls for a common set of principles based on the sequential logic mode. Such principles can then be used to explain and gain new insights on the uncertain occurrence of political events.

The sequential logic explanation of a political event is also used in works by historians (e.g. Kennedy 1987; Rotberg and Rabb 1989: 149–248; Schroeder 1972) and in historically oriented works by political scientists.[11] This is due to the inherently evolutionary form of causal explanation in the sequential logic mode. In sequential mode the uncertain occurrence of a political event (e.g. the political collapse of the former Soviet Union) often involves moving from some prior event that is singled out as "the origin" (e.g. the abolition of Communist constitutional monopoly on political power in the USSR), through a sequence of "critical events" (e.g. the victory of the anti-Communist Solidarity movement in Poland) and other events which are viewed as "turning points" (e.g. the non intervention by the USSR in Poland, the collapse of the Berlin Wall and the East German regime) to "final outcomes" (the political collapse of the former Soviet Union) (Dunlop 1993; Wiegel 1992). Indeed, as I will show in the next two chapters, the analysis of politics by sequential logic principles – including empirical and theoretical aspects – offers a fertile terrain for interdisciplinary collaboration between history and political science.

5.3.2   Conditional logic

In the conditional logic mode, the occurrence of a political event is explained by providing necessary or sufficient conditions. Informally speak-

---

[10] Cioffi-Revilla (1987), Cioffi-Revilla and Dacey (1988), Russett (1962), Snyder and Diesing (1977), Vasquez (1993), Wright (1942).
[11] For example, Gilpin (1981), Jillson (1981, 1994), Midlarsky (1988a), and Thompson (1988).

ing, this type of causal explanation is related to – albeit not identical with – the common-language expression "what lies behind" a political occurrence; hence the causal designation "conditional." Conditional logic places most of its explanatory emphasis on the structure of a causal argument, looking toward background conditions from the vantage point of the present. The occurrence of a political event in conditional logic is explained more as a given that must somehow be accounted for, rather than as a possible outcome.

For example, a conditional logic explanation of the event "deterrence works" is based on the joint occurrence of "credibility of intent" and "credibility of capability". In the classical theory of deterrence these two causal events (conditions) are viewed as necessary and sufficient. Accordingly, in terms of the event function for the occurrence "deterrence works," both events would be contained in the argument of the event function. Similarly, consider the event "a two-party government coalition is formed." A conditional logic explanation of this event could be based on the two elemental events (conditions) "party A agrees to form a coalition with party B" and "B agrees to form a coalition with A," both included in the argument of an associated event function.

In general form, using the notation I established earlier (definition 5.2), a political event $\mathbb{Y}$ that is explained in a conditional causal logic mode is represented by

$$\mathbb{Y} = \Psi_c\{\cdot\}$$

where the argument $\{\cdot\}$ of the e.f. Ψ is now given in conditional logic mode. The conditional logic mode of causal explanation is used implicitly in the following areas of political science:

- collective action situations (Olson 1965; Lichbach 1996), where the core puzzle lies in exploring when, how, or why collective action occurs through a variety of causal conditions;
- political coalitions, detailing the conditions under which political coalitions (whether domestic coalition governments or international alliances) will form, endure, and dissolve (Riker 1962);
- the general "opportunity-willingness" framework for explaining general political behavior;[12]

[12] The conceptual framework for the opportunity-willingness framework was first established by Sprout and Sprout (1969), followed by Starr (1978, 1977), Most and Starr (1989), and Cioffi-Revilla and Starr (1995). Consistent with my focus on general politics, I interpret the opportunity-willingness framework as a general political proposition obviously covering both domestic and international politics; not just the latter.

- political or social systems that are based on specifiable sets of structural-functional conditions for attaining and maintaining system performance (Easton 1979; Kaplan 1957; Levy 1950);
- deterrence and compellence, both threats which are based on the assumption that credibility of intent and credibility of capability are necessary conditions for these threats to work (Brodie 1959; Cioffi-Revilla 1983);
- theories of world politics formulated on the basis of necessary or sufficient conditions for given forms of war or peace, such as the "democracies-don't-fight" hypothesis (Russett 1993), the power transition hypothesis (Organski and Kugler 1980; Kugler and Organski 1989), or models based on expected utility.[13]

In this case the fundamental causal feature shared by these and the other areas of political science research that I identify in the next two chapters is the reliance on a system of uncertain necessary or sufficient conditions – some may be decisional outcomes while others may be states of nature – for explaining the occurrence of political events. Although the phenomena may be empirically distinct, from a theoretical perspective this feature calls for a common set of principles based on the conditional logic mode. Such principles are then used to explain political events and their uncertain occurrence.

5.3.3   Integrated logic

Hume's classic reservation about attributing causes to the occurrence of empirical events – in the physical as well as the political world – is insightful for what it implies with regard to the two logics. In essence, neither logic individually provides a complete scientific explanation for the occurrence of political events. Informally, this is because a political event is always fundamentally and deeply embedded within both causal modes, and the scientific understanding of politics requires both, perhaps unlike the more basic scientific understanding that is deemed to be sufficient in macrophysics. In the next two chapters I shall develop a formal treatment of how the two logic modes combine to explain the uncertainty of political occurrences, after treating each logic separately. In chapter 6 I will also demonstrate how sequential logic can be seen as a special and important case of conditional logic, while maintaining the two logic modes separate for analytical purposes.

Perhaps the complementarity between these two micro modes also

---

[13] See, for example, Bueno de Mesquita (1981), Bueno de Mesquita and Lalman (1987), Harsanyi (1962), Hernes (1975), Nicholson (1992), Saris and Saris-Gallhoffer (1975).

explains why – enduring academic disputes over quantitative versus qualitative methods notwithstanding – the most causally inquisitive political
scientists and historians will continue to read each other's scholarship with
interest. This is because the events contained in a conditional causal
explanation – the investigation of necessary or sufficient conditions that is
generally preferred by political scientists – always "come from somewhere";
indeed, they do so from prior events in history that originate in the
sequential mode. Conversely, the events contained in a sequential causal
explanation – the investigation of antecedent events along a causal path,
generally preferred by historians – must also have to come from somewhere
or "be caused," as in the conditional mode. In chapter 7 I explore how this
causal integration works, along with other special micropolitical principles
that explain the uncertain occurrence of a political event. First, however, I
must establish the general governing principles for each micro mode in
chapter 6.

5.4   Conclusions

This was the first chapter that focused on uncertainty at the micro level of
politics, the second branch of the theory. In this chapter I addressed the
first two building blocks of micropolitics: political occurrences as the main
explanandum (similar to the status of a dependent variable, but in reference
to events) and other event occurrences and their causal interrelationship as
the *explanans* (similar to independent variables).

I defined the first building block, a referent political occurrence, after
first examining various meanings of the term "political event" in common
language, history, and empirical research in social science. The latter
meaning is defined mostly in terms of the events-data tradition. The
definition of a political event that I proposed is theoretically motivated,
designed to have deductive value, by offering a unifying perspective for
examining political occurrences in diverse areas of politics under the same
general theory, such as events that occur in elections, coalition processes,
warfare, and others. The uncertainty of political occurrence required the
introduction of several axiomatic concepts such as sample space and
elemental events from probability theory. I interpreted the elemental
events or sample points from probabiity theory as elementary decisional
outcomes or states of nature that are political – because they have effects
on the lives, fortune, or governance of a collectivity. This focus on the
composition of a political occurrence based on more elementary events, as
opposed to the uniqueness of each event, is another defining feature that
distinguishes this theory from earlier idiosyncratic approaches. I showed
how, depending on the type of composition that is used to define a given

political occurrence, its uncertainty can be of one type or another. Political uncertainty is not all of one form but can have different forms that can be specified by the substantive politics of a given situation.

I defined the other building block of this part of the theory – the occurrence structure itself – as the probabilistic mechanism responsible for the production (formally, the event function) of a political occurrence with a given form. Two such modes for event occurrence exist, called sequential and conditional, each with its own form of probabilistic causality. For each mode I provided examples of political occurrences in diverse political domains – including both domestic and international politics – such as collective action, coalition formation, deterrence, war onset, public policy, and political communication. Note that some of these events also regard topics already examined at the macro level of analysis (e.g. coalition formation, war onset), but are now examined at the micro level of analysis to demonstrate how the theory shifts levels depending on our perspective on political uncertainty. Unlike other causal approaches, which focus on the empirical statistics of event models (e.g. in the logit approach), the event function focuses on the exact mechanism of probabilistic causality to better understand uncertainty. In the next chapters I use similar examples to demonstrate the theoretical link that exists between the occurrence of political events and their causal logic as expressed by an event function.

The purpose of defining these concepts is to construct a causal explanation of political uncertainty at the micro level which parallels the causal explanation of political uncertainty at the macro level. As outlined earlier in table 1.2 and shown in this chapter, elemental events and event functions play a role in explaining political events at the micro level of analysis, similar to the role played by hazard forces and distribution functions in explaining political variables at the macro level. The details of this causal framework are explored in greater detail in the next two chapters to derive general and special principles.

Because the main focus of this chapter was on concept formation – to define political events and the logic modes that govern their occurrence – I did not extend my analysis beyond that which was minimally required to proceed with the micropolitical principles in the next two chapters. Accordingly, it is possible to explore further a set of other ideas that are closely linked to those presented in this chapter. For example, a more detailed analysis of the character of the political sample space has inherent interest, particularly in terms of decisional outcomes and states of nature, given the fundamental importance of a sample space in defining any of the events derived from it. This could also shed further light on the meaning of what is "political" as distinct from, say, social, economic, or cultural – obviously a critical issue for understanding political events. Another narrow topic of foundational interest would be the properties of a political sample space – in which events affecting the large class of issues of governance occur – with regard to the axiomatic definition of probability measures in such a space. Perhaps the building blocks established in this chapter will serve as motivation for such future investigations.

6   General micropolitical principles

There is no point in using exact methods where there is no clarity in the concepts and issues to which they are to be applied.

– John Von Neumann and Oskar Morgenstern,
Theory of Games and Economic Behavior

6.1   Introduction

In this chapter I continue to construct the micropolitical part of the theory of political uncertainty by using sequential and conditional modes and the main building blocks introduced earlier – events defined as sets of elemental occurences (sample points) drawn from a background of possibilities (political sample space), and event functions, defined as causal mappings which link elemental occurrences to compose the referent political event of interest.

In this chapter I derive the general principles for understanding the uncertain occurrence of political events. As such, this chapter parallels chapter 3, in which I derived the general macropolitical principles for understanding the uncertain behavior of political variables. As I will show in detail in this chapter, general micropolitical principles for understanding political events exist in two modes, sequential and conditional. Commenting on the onset of World War I, historian Charles Morris once observed that "every event in history has its roots somewhere in earlier history, and we need but dig deep enough to find them" (Morris 1914: 1). The core puzzle I address in this chapter concerns the causal link between these conceptual blocks, a puzzle that I continue to solve in the framework of probabilistic causality.

Similar to chapter 3, the nature of the principles I establish in this chapter is general, because these principles govern a large class of more specific real-world political events that may occur in domestic or international domains (recall figure 1.1), similar to those identified earlier in table 5.1 and the research areas identified in sections 5.3.1 (sequential) and 5.3.2 (conditional). As was the case earlier with the general macropolitical principles, the general micropolitical principles derived in this chapter also hold their validity irrespective of the substantive content of the particular political events that appear in a causal explanatory argument. This parsimonious property is one of the reasons why they are important. Another reason lies in the capacity of these general principles to generate more specific results and new insights that are explored in this and the next chapter. I have called these principles logic because central to their content is always a set of causal arguments involving necessity and sufficiency, as opposed to other features associated with the occurrence of causal events, such as the time when they occur, their magnitude, or duration (i.e. the various behavioral variables that I already examined at the macro level). I also intend the micropolitical status of these principles, based on individual events, to parallel the macropolitical status of the earlier principles, based on aggregate distributions. These micropolitical principles also have other substantive and formal properties that parallel similar properties that I established earlier for macropolitical principles, such as probabilism (capturing and explaining the uncertainty of political occurrences), nonlinearity (counterintuitive behavior), and universality (applicable *erga omnes*).

As I discussed in section 5.3, the two logic modes that explain the occurrence of a political event are sequential (or "forward") and conditional ("backward") logic, both of which are used to causally define a political event $\mathbb{Y}$. Both modes are also used to specify the associated event function Ψ, and to derive the probability of main political interest, $\mathbf{P}(\mathbb{Y})$ to understand the uncertainty involved in the occurrence of the political event $\mathbb{Y}$. In turn, these first general results are used for deriving further inferences, as detailed in this and the next chapter. I shall first establish the set of general sequential micropolitical principles (section 6.2), followed by the general conditional micropolitical principles (section 6.3). However, this order is only for purposes of exposition, going from the more to the less familiar. Conceptually the two modes enjoy equal theoretical status in explaining the uncertain occurrence of a political event. The proof of each principle is given in appendix 3. I follow the presentation of the general principles by a discussion of some of their properties (section 6.4), following an approach similar to that in earlier chapters. In the next chapter I use the general micropolitical principles established here to derive more specific results (special micropolitical principles) to shed additional light on the nature of political uncertainty at the micro level of analysis.

6.2   General sequential principles

6.2.1   *General framework*

In sequential logic the occurrence of a given political event $\mathbb{Y}$ is explained as an outcome – one among several possible events – which takes place in the sample space of a branching process that passes through several nodes (section 5.3.2). The next examples illustrate this causal perspective in greater detail than in the previous chapter; later I expand the focus from these particular examples to a broader class of occurrences drawn from a variety of areas in domestic and international politics. My claim is that, just as the next examples below share some important theoretical similarities, so does the broader class examined in the next section. All political events have essentially the same sequential logic characteristics and must therefore obey the same general principles, so long as we can identify the historic roots and trace out the sequential branching process. In each of the next two examples it is possible to consider more details, but the logic remains fundamentally the same.

Example 6.1 (sequential logic of government policy). Consider the enactment of government policy (referent event $\mathbb{Y}$) as a response for coping with price inflation in a national economic system, as illustrated in figure 6.1.[1] Policy enactment is a state of the world – a probabilistic outcome in a large sample space of decisional acts and states of nature – caused by a set of sequential political changes. The latter include "initiating events" such as inflation increasing, followed by "group demands," and concluding in "government action" as the last event that sets the stage for policy enactment to occur (top-right outcome in the tree in figure 6.1). The causal logic that explains a "policy enactment" outcome in this sequential mode is therefore as follows:

IF "inflation occurs" THEN → ("demands arise" or "do not arise")
IF "demands arise" THEN → ("government responds" or "does not")
IF "government responds" THEN → "policy is enacted"

Thus, at an initial time τ_0 there is a probability that the initiating disturbance and the subsequent political events will occur. The first of these events

---

[1] This example is based on the framework developed by Almond and Powell (1978: 9–10) and other systems theorists who use a similar input–output approach to the analysis of government performance. The case of inflation as the environmental disturbance is incidental, not essential, because the political system's general policy response should be similar under a broad range of environmental or extrasystemic disturbances (e.g. changes in society, technology, demography, or culture).

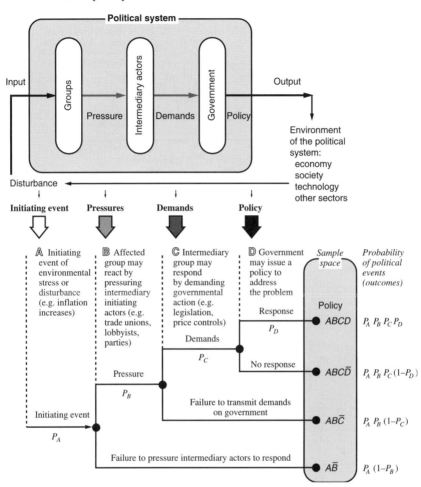

Figure 6.1. Sequential logic of government policy

represent the "seeds" or "origins" of policy enactment. If popular demands arise in response to inflation (system input), then there is a probability – which is not the same as the probability of demands arising in the first place – that government will respond and do something. Here the "potential" for policy being enacted is given by the government responding. Finally, if government does respond then the outcome is policy enactment (system output) in the form of price controls, government subsidies, or other common measures. This analysis also assumes – from observing the way

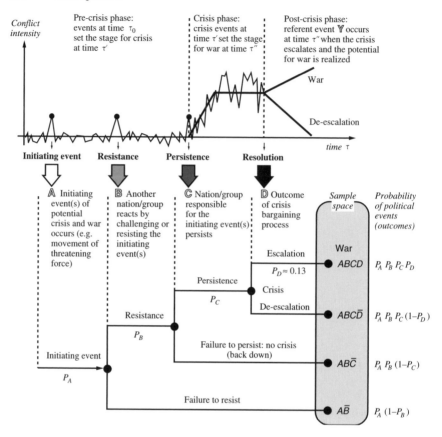

Figure 6.2. Sequential logic of international conflict

government works in industrialized societies – that prior events (e.g. inflation, group demands, lobbying) always set the causal stage for collective
action and policy responses. To paraphrase Schroeder, government policies are caused, they do not just happen; but so are policy failures. The
entire process from start to finish involves a mix of states of nature (e.g.
inflation rising) and decisional outcomes (e.g. demands on government),
but the logic of the situation is uniform – events are events, whether they
originate from human decisions or from states of nature.

Example 6.2 (sequential logic of the onset of war). Consider the onset of war
as a referent event $\mathbb{Y}$, within the conflict process illustrated in figure 6.2.[2] In

this conflict process, war is a state of the world – a probabilistic outcome in a sample space of decisional acts and states of nature – that is caused by political changes that later evolve into crisis events. The political changes are the events labeled as "initiating event" and "resistance," following the terminology of Snyder and Diesing (1977). The crisis events are the "persistence" and the crisis-bargaining events. The latter are the events that "set the stage for war" (top-right outcome in the sequential logic tree). The causal logic that explains the "war onset" outcome in this sequential mode is therefore given by the following multistage, or branching, process:[3]

IF "political changes" THEN → ("crisis" or "no crisis")

IF "crisis" THEN → ("escalation" or "de-escalation")

IF "escalation" THEN → "war"

Here again, as in the governmental policy process (example 6.1), at an initial time τ_0 there is an a priori probability that initiating and resistance events will occur. These events in the early stages of a conflict process may be called the "seeds" or "origins" of war because war onset can later evolve from them. If resistance occurs, then there is another probability that a crisis will occur (note that this probability is not the same as the earlier probability). This second event may be called the "potential" for war, a concept that denotes a more advanced stage of evolution than the "origin" or "seed" of war. Finally, if a crisis escalates, then the outcome is war. Expressed in formal logic form,

persistence ⇔ crisis

and

escalation ⇔ war.

This sequential logic analysis of war onset assumes – as I believe is true in history – that prior causal events always set the stage for the occurrence of

---

[2] In this sequential logic analysis of war onset I propose an alternative framework based on the standard approach in international relations research, as originally put forth in Quincy Wright's (1942) so-called n-crisis problem. See, for example, Cioffi-Revilla (1987), Cioffi-Revilla and Dacey (1988), Gochman and Maoz (1984), Maoz (1982, 1994), Russett (1962), Snyder and Diesing (1976), Vasquez (1993), and Ward (1988). I am grateful to Umberto Gori for introducing me to Wright's problem in Deutsch (1978), and to Raymond Dacey for the collaboration that lead to our new solutions (Cioffi-Revilla and Dacey 1988).

[3] Note that there are 2^n final outcomes in a sequential logic process containing n branching nodes. Therefore, in this example, there are $2^4 = 16$ outcomes. Also note that the sequential logic event tree in the bottom of figure 6.2 is pruned because I have not shown all the events that are logically possible, only those that are politically relevant. The twelve events omitted are politically meaningless (e.g. an escalation to war after the target of hostility fails to resist, or war occurring when the aggressor backs down after resistance by the target). The assumptions used for pruning are useful as a first approximation, because they simplify the political situation by eliminating all the events with zero or very small probability. However, the main political results remain the same when all the events are included and the tree is logically exhaustive (unpruned).

Table 6.1. *Sequential logic of political events*

Event X_{-5} at time $\tau - 5$	Event X_{-4} at time $\tau - 4$	Event X_{-3} at time $\tau - 3$	Event X_{-2} at time $\tau - 2$	Event X_{-1} at time $\tau - 1$	Referent event Y at time τ	References
Domestic politics						
Environmental input (e.g. inflation) enters the political system.	Affected voters place demands on pressure groups, unions, or parties.	Pressure groups respond and pressure policy makers.	Policy makers respond and enact laws and other measures.	Bureaucratic agencies act to implement.	Policy outcomes occur (price controls, welfare measures).	Almond and Powell (1978), functional–structuralist system theorists.
—	Deterioration or change in national economic, social, or political conditions.	Government responds with policy.	Problems persist; government is challenged by opposition.	Coalition crisis occurs, including intense bargaining.	Coalition dissolves (cabinets, alliances).	Browne (1984). Frendreis et al. (1986).
Policy is enacted by law.	Higher agency begins implementation.	Lower agency follows.	Lower agency follows.	Lower agency follows.	Policy is locally implemented.	Pressman and Wildavsky (1973).
—	—	Severe changes in economic, social, or political conditions.	Alternate political leadership develops.	Domestic crisis, crisis of the state, revolutionary potential rises.	Revolution breaks out.	Brinton (1938), J. C. Davies (1962), Gurr (1970), Krejci (1983), Lichbach (1995), Skocpol (1979).
—	—	Changes in social conditions occur.	Need for collection action enters agenda.	Coercion or incentives occur.	Collective action occurs.	J. S. Coleman (1973), Olson (1965).
International politics						
—	Initiating event (e.g. change in threatening force) occurs	Resistance by some other(s) occurs.	Persistence by initiator; crisis occurs.	Crisis bargaining fails to peacefully resolve; crisis escalates.	War onset (civil or international) occurs.	Leng (1993), Maoz (1982, 1994), Russett (1962), Snyder and Diesing (1977), Wright (1942, 1965).
States pursue national growth and expansion policies.	Power imbalance occurs.	Imbalance is politically acknowledged.	Mobilization to restore balance begins.	Power adjusted by alliances or arms race.	Balance of power is restored.	Chatterjee (1972, 1975), Morgenthau and Thompson (1985).
Need for integration is recognized; enters agenda.	Low politics area is defined.	Low politics agreement is reached.	Low politics integration succeeds.	Spill-over occurs.	High politics integration occurs.	Groom (1978), Lew (1989), Mitrany (1975), Nye (1968).
Issue of conflict of interest and common interest enters agenda.	Bargaining and negotiations begin.	Negotiations are successfully completed.	Agreement is signed by each side.	Necessary ratification events occur.	International agreement (treaties, protocols, etc.) becomes law.	Bermann (1989), Jillson (1981), Mancini (1989), Manin (1987), Nadelmann (1990), Plender (1986).

Source: Prepared by the author.

crises and wars. As Schroeder has pointed out (1972), both World War I and the peace that preceded it were caused, they did not just happen (chapter 5, epigraph). Neither crises nor wars occur "out of the blue." As in the earlier case of governmental policy, note that some events "on the road to war" are decisional outcomes while others are states of nature.

The sequential processes in the preceding examples, illustrated in figures 6.1 and 6.2, are somewhat reminiscent of extensive form game trees. The similarity – albeit not the identity – is natural, given that the elemental events "on the way" to each outcome consist (by definition 5.1) of decisional outcomes and states of nature. However, whereas the game-theoretic emphasis is on strategies, my emphasis here is on the uncertainty properties of the process and its outcomes, treating causal events without further detail. Special principles in the next chapter look more closely at the specific nature of causal events, as decisional outcomes or states of nature.

Beyond these idiosyncratic examples, important as policy and war are for understanding an array of political issues, a larger and consequential class of political events obeys the same causal logic, as illustrated in table 6.1 for domestic and international domains of politics. In each area – as I showed in examples 6.1 and 6.2 above – a referent political event $\mathbb{Y}$ (column 6, table 6.1) results as the outcome of prior uncertain conditional events that "set the stage" for the next branching node in a process that unfolds (columns 1 through 5) toward the future leading to the event $\mathbb{Y}$. This is how or why in politics nothing really occurs "out of the blue" – a widely established but largely undeveloped principle in the study of politics. The sequential logic of this process also gives rigorous scientific meaning to political ideas such as "the potential for revolution is growing (or decreasing)" and similar expressions in other areas.[4]

This large class of cases obeys the same causal pattern: political events occur through an evolutionary sequence of prior events. This is a simple but important idea that can be generalized as a theoretical assumption. I state this as follows:

Assumption 6.1 (sequential causal logic of politics). *A political event* $\mathbb{Y}$ *is a future outcome at time* τ *in the sample space of a branching process that begins at* $\tau - n$. *Formally,*

$$\mathbb{Y} \text{ occurs i.f.f. } ``\mathbb{X}_{\tau-1} \mid \text{all necessary events since } \mathbb{X}_{\tau-n}",$$

---

[4] The potential for a political event can be said to exist whenever its probability satisfies the condition $\pi < \mathbf{P}(\mathbb{Y}) < 1$, where $\hat{\pi} = 0.35$ is an experimental estimate for the probability that $\mathbb{Y}$ "cannot be ruled out entirely" (Beyth-Marom 1982: 261). See also Maoz (1990: 252–4) and Zadeh (1968) for other linguistic or qualitative values of probability. I discuss these verbal probabilities in section 7.3.4 in the next chapter.

so

$$\mathbb{Y} \Rightarrow \mathbb{X}_{\tau-1} \Rightarrow \mathbb{X}_{\tau-2} \Rightarrow \ldots \Rightarrow \mathbb{X}_{\tau-n+1} \Rightarrow \mathbb{X}_{\tau-n}. \qquad [6.1]$$

Assumption 6.1 formalizes the main idea discussed thus far, namely that all political events *always* come from prior and uncertain occurrences, as carried out by individuals, groups, or institutions, or as imposed by states of nature beyond human control. Regardless, a political event never comes "out of the blue." Every referent event $\mathbb{Y}$ in column 6, table 6.1, has antecedents in columns 1 through 5. The implications of this first assumption are explored next, as I demonstrate how the apparent simplicity of politics is most often only superficial.

6.2.2   Sequential principle

The first general micropolitical principle that I derive from assumption 6.1 concerns the probability of a political event $\mathbb{Y}$ when this is explained in the sequential mode.

Theorem 6.1 (sequential probability principle of a political event). *A political event* $\mathbb{Y}$ *with event function given by*

$$\mathbb{Y} = \mathbb{X}_{-1} \wedge \mathbb{X}_{-2} \wedge \ldots \wedge \mathbb{X}_{-n+1} \wedge \mathbb{X}_{-n}, \qquad [6.2]$$

where the time index τ *is implicit and each event is dependent on a previous event, has sequential probability given by the product of conditional probabilities*

$$\mathbf{P}(\mathbb{Y}) = p_{-n} \cdot p_{-n+1} \cdot p_{-n+2} \cdot \ldots \cdot p_{-1} = \prod_{i=0}^{n-1} p_i \qquad [6.3]$$

$$= P^{\Lambda}, \qquad (\Lambda = 0, 1, 2, 3, \ldots, n-1) \qquad [6.4]$$

where:

$p_{-n} = \mathbf{P}(\mathbb{X}_{-n})$ for the first event
$p_{-n+1} = \mathbf{P}(\mathbb{X}_{-n+1} \mid \mathbb{X}_{-n})$ for the second event
$p_{-n+2} = \mathbf{P}(\mathbb{X}_{-n+2} \mid \mathbb{X}_{-n} \wedge \mathbb{X}_{-n+1})$ for the third event
. . .
$p_{-1} = \mathbf{P}(\mathbb{X}_{-1} \mid \text{all prior events})$ for the last event prior to $\mathbb{Y}$
$\Lambda = $ *number of prior events leading to* $\mathbb{Y}$, *or length of the process,*

and

$$P = p_{-n} = p_{-n+1} = p_{-n+2} = \ldots = p_{-1}, \text{ when}$$

the individual probability of each event is taken as the same.

Informally, the sequential probability principle states that the chance of a political event occurring depends on two and only two key features of the situation: (i) the chances of the prior events in the chain of events that can lead to the outcome, and (ii) the number of "links" in the chain. Nothing else matters as a separate factor: neither the actors, nor the particular issue, nor the timing, nor any other factor separately considered. All these other situational features are factored into the two variables, P (the chances of the prior events in the chain of events leading to the outcome) and Λ (the number of links).

Equations 6.3 and 6.4 constitute the formal core of the sequential probability principle for political events. The essence of this principle, from a purely qualitative standpoint, lies in the multiplicative form that stems directly from the argument of the sequential event function.

I note immediately that, by equation 6.4, the sequential probability of a political event is nonlinear in both independent variables, P and Λ. This means that, in contrast to the simple appearance of axiom 6.1 or equations 6.2 and 6.3, the sequential probability of a political event always changes in nonintuitive ways when changes occur in the probability of the priors or in the length of the branching process. I will analyze how this works after investigating an important property uncovered by the sequential probability principle – hypoprobability.

6.2.3   Hypoprobability principle

The following result – formally, a corollary – follows immediately from the sequential probability principle (theorem 6.1). The theoretical significance of this principle is that it introduces a new concept to understand political uncertainty. I call this new concept hypoprobability.[5]

---

[5] Consider a compound event $\mathbb{Y}$, produced by n other events, such as those normally given in a sequential logic event function $\Psi_s\{\mathbb{X}_i\}$. In purely formal terms, the property I call hypoprobability consists of the strictly smaller value of the probability of the compound event, $\mathbf{P}(\mathbb{Y})$, relative to the probabilities p_i of the n events that make up the compound argument of $\mathbb{Y}$. The mathematical reason for hypoprobability is straightforward: probabilities are values defined between 0 and 1, so the multiplication theorem for the probability of a compound event (a mathematical axiom) always requires the product of the n component probabilities, thereby decreasing the value of the probability of the compound event. I call this phenomenon of obtaining a reduced value *hypo*probability. This is a politically meaningful property that to my knowledge is not highlighted in the pure mathematical theory of probability because the formal meaning is unimportant. Later in this chapter I will also introduce the dual concept of *hyper*probability, an uncertainty notion with opposite symmetry.

Corollary 6.1 (sequential hypoprobability principle of a political event). *When the prior events of a political event* $\mathbb{Y}$ *have not yet occurred, the a priori probability of* $\mathbb{Y}$ (the "out-of-the-blue probability") *is always*: (i) smaller *than the individual probability P, and* (ii) smaller *than the smallest of the probabilities of the prior events. Formally*,

$$\mathbf{P}(\mathbb{Y}) < \min \{p_{-n}, p_{-n+1}, p_{-n+2}, \dots, p_{-1}\} \qquad [6.5]$$
$$< P. \qquad [6.6]$$

A further implication of this political property is as follows: looking at the probability of any of the Λ prior events leading to the outcome event of interest ($\mathbb{Y}$) is always misleading because such probabilities always overestimate the objective value of $\mathbf{P}(\mathbb{Y})$. Moreover, in sequential logic a political event always occurs with probability lower than the least probable of the priors.[6] The magnitude K of this gap, a general property of uncertainty in real-world politics, can be readily measured by the difference

$$K = P - \mathbf{P}(\mathbb{Y}), \qquad [6.7]$$

where $K < 0$ (hypoprobability), $K > 0$ (hyperprobability), and $K \to 0$ as $P \to \mathbf{P}(\mathbb{Y})$.

Political events explained in sequential mode are always hypoprobable because their occurrence as outcomes is always less likely than any of the prior conditional occurrences. This new phenomenon – an insight derived from theorem 6.1 – is present in the earlier examples of war onset and government policy, although the phenomenon remained hidden. Note that the hypoprobability property is also empirically testable because (or as long as) each probability is well defined and measurable by means of observed relative frequencies.

Example 6.3 (hypoprobability of policy outcomes). Recall example 6.1. Apply the sequential probability principle to derive the probability $\mathbf{P}(\mathbb{L})$ of obtaining a policy outcome from a political system. The result is similar to equations 6.3 or 6.4, where now P denotes the prior events' probability in the policy process. Assuming the four stages in example 6.1 (initiating event $\mathbb{A}$, pressure event $\mathbb{B}$, demands event $\mathbb{C}$, and response event $\mathbb{D}$), this yields

$$\mathbf{P}(\mathbb{L}) = P_A P_B P_C P_D = P^4 \qquad [6.8]$$

as the equation for the sequential probability of a policy outcome, given

---

[6] Note that hypoprobability has nothing to do with incomplete information. Rather, the phenomenon derives from the fundamental character of political uncertainty as expressed by the sequential probability principle. No amount of additional information or intelligence can narrow the gap between the probability of prior events and the sequential probability of an event.

the occurrence of an environmental disturbance ($\mathbb{A}$) and a successful system response (the compound event $\mathbb{A} \wedge \mathbb{B} \wedge \mathbb{C}$). More generally, the probability of successful policy response in a political system with length of process Λ (considering the totality of input events, popular collective action events, legislative requirements, and so forth) is given by

$$\mathbf{P}(\mathbb{L}) = P^\Lambda, \qquad\qquad [6.9]$$

where P is the probability of each processing node functioning successfully. Hypoprobability in the domestic political process occurs because the probability of a policy response eventually occurring is always smaller than the probability of any of the events that are required along the way, even smaller than the least probable of these events (say, attracting sufficient party interest to prepare and introduce a bill).

Example 6.4 (hypoprobability of war). Recall example 6.2. To derive the "out-of-the-blue" probability of war (or the probability of "war on a perfectly peaceful day"), apply the sequential probability principle (theorem 6.1 and equations 6.3 and 6.4) to the "war path" in example 6.2. This yields:

$$\mathbf{P}(\mathbb{W}) = P_A\,P_B\,P_C\,P_D = P^4, \qquad\qquad [6.10]$$

where the probabilities on the right-hand side refer to the events of initiation, resistance, persistence, and escalation, respectively, as in example 6.2, figure 6.2. By the hypoprobability principle (corollary 6.1, equations 6.5 and 6.6), $\mathbf{P}(\mathbb{W})$ must also be lower than the lowest of prewar probabilities. To verify this, consider table 6.2, which reports empirical onset rates for "potentially severe conflict" events (namely, international crises and foreign military interventions) and "severe conflict" events (international wars of various types) in recent history. Using the Correlates of War Project rates as valid relative frequency estimates ($\hat{v}$) of the theoretical probabilities in equation 6.10 (indicated as COW 7 and COW 10 in table 6.2; Singer and Small 1984), and the operationalization "crisis $\equiv$ militarized interstate dispute," then

$$\hat{v}(\mathbb{W}) < \min\{\hat{v}_A,\,\hat{v}_B,\,\hat{v}_C,\,\hat{v}_D\}$$
$$(0.69 \text{ onsets/year}) < \min\{\hat{v}_A,\,\hat{v}_B,\,\hat{v}_C,\,(5.29 \text{ onsets/year})\}$$

This last expression is empirically true because there are many more initiating events ($\mathbb{A}$), resistance events ($\mathbb{B}$), and persistence events ($\mathbb{C}$), than there are crisis events ($\mathbb{D}$), so the inequality holds. The hypoprobability of war consists of the lower probability of war (corresponding to the lower frequency $\hat{v}(\mathbb{W}) = 0.69$ onsets/year) in relation to the probabilities of the component events, the latter being always strictly larger.

Table 6.2. *International conflicts, 1495–1988*

Dataset	Number of events n	Years	Historic range $\Delta t + 1$ (years)	Onset rate $k = n/(\Delta t + 1)$ (events per year)	Mean time between events $1/k$ (years)
Potentially severe conflicts: crises and interventions					
COW 10	> 916	1816–1988	173	> 5.29	< 0.189
Wilkenfeld 5A	323	1929–1985	57	5.67	0.176
Wilkenfeld 5B	698	1929–1985	57	12.25	0.082
Pearson 8	> 200	1946–1988	43	> 4.65	< 0.215
Subtotals	> 2,137	—	330	—	—
Averages[a]	480	—	82.5	> 5.20	< 0.192
Severe conflicts: Wars					
Levy 4A	119	1495–1975	481	0.247	4.042
Levy 4B	60	1495–1975	481	0.125	8.017
Midlarsky 9	154	1495–1815	321	0.480	2.084
COW 7	118	1816–1986	171	0.690	1.449
Subtotals	451	—	1,454	—	—
Averages[b]	130	—	363.5	0.472	2.527
For all events	> 2,588[c]	1495–1988	1,784	> 2.84[d]	< 1.36[e]

[a] The estimates of potentially severe conflict are systemic, so they are calculated without using Wilkenfeld 5B, which contains nation-level events (Wilkenfeld 5A is systemic).
[b] Calculated without using Levy 4B data, which are a subset of Levy 4A.
[c] Total number of international conflict events contained in the eight interstate conflict datasets of the Data Development for International Relations (DDIR) Project.
[d] Average onset rate of international conflict events (counting both potentially severe and severe conflicts).
[e] Mean time between international conflict events (MTBE), counting both potentially severe and severe conflicts.
Source: Adapted from Cioffi-Revilla (1990: 48).

The hypoprobability phenomenon is not easily seen or intuitively understood from plain observation of political events – much as the elasticity of demand for a product (a similarly unobservable but no less real property) is not observable from simply watching consumer behavior. Informally, hypoprobability may be thought of as the additional degree of political difficulty that is involved in implementing or realizing the sequence of prior events required to produce a political event; that extra effort that goes beyond the distinct difficulties of separately producing each prior. The occurrence of a political event is difficult when the event has several priors. This is what I mean by the "political difficulty" that is induced by hypoprobability so long as assumption 6.1 is upheld (Cioffi-Re-villa and Starr 1995). Additionally, such difficulty increases when we con-sider that politics by definition involves coordination, collective action, or other interdependent social situations that are never straightforward. Phe-nomena such as war, elections, coalition formations, treaties, or trade in-volve the production of several (sometimes numerous) interdependent priors not just for a single actor but a collectivity of actors (otherwise the outcome events are not political) whose behavioral responses are necess-ary to produce results. For this class of defining political events the im-pact of hypoprobability is always present and, consequently, the difficulty of producing events is significant.[7] Hypoprobability is a property of politi-cal uncertainty at the micro level of events.

The preceding examples illustrate the application of the sequential probability principle to the occurrence of a political event and the role played by hypoprobability. The following estimate is also made possible by the sequential probability principle.

Example 6.5 (probability of escalation to civil war and to international war). What is the probability of an international crisis escalating to war? Besides having intrinsic theoretical importance, this probability has pol-icy implications for conflict resolution, particularly for different types of crises that involve different types of actors (major powers, minor powers, and so on). The sequential probability principle can be used to estimate this probability by solving equation 6.10 for P_D and then using the empiri-cal onset frequencies as estimates of probabilities. Using the COW esti-mate for the onset of crises involving nation states in the modern interna-tional system, this yields:

$$P_D = \frac{\hat{v}(W)}{(\hat{v}_A + \hat{v}_B + \hat{v}_C)} = \frac{119}{916} \approx 0.13$$

as the estimated probability of war escalation in a crisis. Estimates for other types of crises are similarly derived using the other rates in table 6.2 or other estimates (e.g. Midlarsky 1988a, 1988b). For the onset of civil war there is no parallel concept to that of international crisis as the pre-amble to war onset. However, civil war is just as hypoprobable in sequen-tial logic mode, because its probability is always less than the probability of the events that lead to it.

[7] Most and Starr (1989: ch. 4) have used a similar logical argument to demonstrate that the onset of war is a rare event. My scope here is broader and methodologically supportive of applying rare event distributions, such as the Poisson and the hyperexponential distribu-tions to the analysis of political events (Ruíz-Palá et al. 1967).

The two principles I have presented thus far in this chapter (theorem 6.1 and corollary) explain the remote likelihood of political events – their hypoprobability – before the necessary prior events occur. For instance, war (civil or international) is impossible $[\mathbf{P}(\mathbb{W}) = 0]$ when a crisis has not occurred, but war becomes increasingly likely as the process undergoes the occurrence of each additional sequential event. Formally, $\mathbf{P}(\mathbb{W}) \rightarrow 1$ as $\Lambda \rightarrow 0$, which is consistent with equation 6.4, so long as $P > 0$.[8]

6.2.4   *Sequential sensitivity principles*

Intuitively, we "know" that the probability of political events – the structure of their uncertainty – is constantly changing, making estimates of the life, fortune, or government of a collectivity seemingly impossible to calculate, let alone to maintain currently updated. Thus, the fall of Communism behind the former iron curtain – intrinsically domestic changes in Eastern Europe and the USSR – can also be seen as a branching event for future uncertain warfare (Mearsheimer 1990). Although they will always remain uncertain, such wars may or may not occur with calculable probability as given by theorem 6.1. Similarly, current changes in the political culture of the United States (Brzezinski 1993), along with economic decline (Kennedy 1987), can represent branching events along a long and complex path that may or may not lead to ultimate downfall but which is governed by principles of political uncertainty such as theorem 6.1.

This property of political events – that they are always embedded at some point along a sequential branching process – raises the following question. What is the effect of changes in prior events or in the length of the branching process on the sequential probability of a political event? How is a future political event – such as global war or US decline – affected as history moves down a given path crossing many branching nodes? The general answers I provide to these questions also follow from the sequential probability principle (theorem 6.1).

Corollary 6.2 (dependence of the sequential probability on the probability of priors). *The rate of change in the sequential probability of a political event with respect to change in the probability of the prior events P is given by the expression:*

---

[8] The increased probability of war during a crisis has been noted by some scholars and used as a basis for investigating crises as microcosms of world politics (e.g. Snyder and Diesing 1977). What makes war sometimes loom so prominently since the early stages of the sequential process is that the slope of $\mathbf{P}(\mathbb{W})$ with respect to Λ is initially steep (for small values of Λ), so $\mathbf{P}(\mathbb{W})$ rapidly approaches 1 as $\Lambda \rightarrow 0$. This property is also highlighted by corollary 6.3 below, which states the exact variation in probability.

$$\frac{\partial \mathbf{P}(\mathbb{Y})}{\partial P} = \Lambda P^{\Lambda - 1},$$ [6.11]

which is always positive, so $\mathbf{P}(\mathbb{Y})$ *is concave with respect to P.*

Qualitatively, this result means that changes in the probability of the prior events have a similar effect on the sequential probability of a political event (increasing or decreasing), as intuitively expected. However, what is not intuitive is that the magnitude of the effect will differ, depending on the situation (i.e. depending on the values of P and Λ at the time of change).

Corollary 6.3 (dependence of the sequential probability on the length of the process). *The rate of change in the sequential probability of a political event with respect to change in the length of the process is given by the expression:*

$$D_\Lambda \mathbf{P}(\mathbb{Y}) = P^{\Lambda + 1} - P^\Lambda,$$ [6.12]

which is always negative, so $\mathbf{P}(\mathbb{Y})$ *is convex with respect to* Λ.

Informally, this principle says the opposite of the previous one, namely that changes in the length of the process have an adverse effect on the sequential probability of a political event (increasing → decreasing, and decreasing → increasing). This is also intuitively expected. However, again, the magnitude and behavior of this effect is not intuitive and will differ depending on the situation (i.e. values of P and Λ).

Recall that Λ denotes the number of prior events ("steps") leading to $\mathbb{Y}$, or length of the sequential process. In table 6.1, I have shown how, empirically and conceptually, this is commonly accomplished by five or six steps for a large variety of political occurrences in the domestic and international domains. In general, the process begins with some arbitrarily chosen initiating event (e.g. a socioeconomic change acting as input; a significant change in operating conditions for a governmental coalition; or some other) and ends with the referent political event $\mathbb{Y}$ as an outcome. If the length of the process can be specified as a function of critical stages which must occur, then the value of Λ can be estimated and the convexity property of $\mathbf{P}(\mathbb{Y})$ with respect to Λ (corollary 6.3) always holds.[9]

Both sequential sensitivity principles are nonlinear. Therefore the sequential probability of a political event depends in potentially nonintuitive ways on both the probability of the priors and the length of the process. Moreover, the two independent variables have opposite effects.

Which of the two independent variables has a greater effect on the sequential probability of a political event – the probability of prior events

[9] In the next chapter (section 7.3.3) I present further results for the case when sequential stages are compound events.

or the length of the process? This question is theoretically important because it addresses a nonintuitive property of political uncertainty, namely, the differential sensitivity of the probability of a political event to changes that may occur in the prior events or in the length of the process, for whatever reasons. The question is also important from a policy perspective because in some situations one of these variables may be more manipulable than the other. There is no intuitive answer to this question, except through analysis. The following principle answers the question.

Corollary 6.4 (sequential dominance principle): *The sequential probability of a political event* $\mathbb{Y}$ *is more sensitive to the probability P of prior events than to the length* Λ *of the sequential branching process. Formally,*

$$s_p > s_\Lambda \qquad \qquad [6.13]$$

because

$$\frac{\partial P(\mathbb{Y})}{\partial P}\left[\frac{P}{P(\mathbb{Y})}\right] > \left(P(\mathbb{Y})_{\Lambda+1} - P(\mathbb{Y})_\Lambda\right)\left[\frac{\Lambda}{P(\mathbb{Y})}\right]. \qquad [6.14]$$

This principle states (guarantees) another new insight on the uncertain occurrence of a political event. (I call this a "dominance" principle because it says which independent variable dominates the behavior of the dependent variable.) Applied to war, the principle states that the sequential probability of war is more sensitive to the events that lead up to the onset than to the number of such events.[10] Restated more generally: the probability of a political event, $P(\mathbb{Y})$, is more sensitive to the probabilities of the prior events (P) than to the length of the process (Λ). In politics, in other words, chance counts more than process, although both give form to political uncertainty.

The implications of the sequential dominance principle are also potentially significant for developing an understanding of political occurrences based on "path-dependence" and "lock-in" (Arthur 1989). For example, just as the neoclassical theory of the economy had to give way to a more relevant theory, making economic history relevant once again, results from the sequential logic analysis of political events demonstrate why political

---

[10] Other examples from table 6.1 can also be interpreted considering this principle. The probability of policy output in a political system responding to a disturbance is more influenced by the probabilities of demands, responses, and other political events occurring than by their total number (the Almond–Powell process); or the probability of policy implementation is more sensitive to individual agency-to-agency transmission probabilities than to the total number of agencies or steps involved in the whole sequence (the Pressman–Wildvasky process).

history is as important as decision-making for understanding how a polity works.[11]

Change in the probability of a political event is nonlinearly affected by the probability of prior events. This explains why politics is sometimes surprising – like the onset of the Yugoslavian civil war in July 1991, only days after the new CSCE crisis mechanism had been established:[12] a small change in the probability of priors can boost a larger-than-expected change in the probability of a political event.[13] Exactly when does this occur? Beyond where the slope of equation 6.4 is greater than 45°, when $\partial \mathbf{P}(\mathbb{Y})/\partial \Lambda = \Lambda P^{\Lambda - 1} > 1$, so solving for P yields $P > \Lambda^{-1/(\Lambda - 1)}$. For $3 < \Lambda < 10$, this "booster threshold" is at $0.58 < P < 0.70$, or always higher than even-odds.

The practical or policy implication of the dominance result for effective political action – for boosting the probability of affecting a collectivity – should be clear. Prior events have a strong effect on the sequential probability of a future political event when their probability exceeds even-odds (exactly $\Lambda P^{\Lambda - 1}$, depending on Λ), so they must be planned with at least that chance of succeeding; otherwise they have only a weak effect on political events.

In general, each prior event is a compound event, not a simple event, having its own event function. This leads in two theoretical directions: to the other logic of political events, which I examine in the next section, and to special principles, which I examine in the next chapter.

6.3   General conditional principles

6.3.1   *General framework*

In conditional logic mode, a political event is explained as an occurrence caused by a combination of other necessary or sufficient occurrences (section 5.3.1). The next two examples illustrate this dual nature of the

---

[11] A pure theory of rational choice in politics (like neoclassical theory in economics) does not rely on history for explaining how the polity works because pure rational choice explanations are generally not path dependent.

[12] The Conference on Security and Cooperation in Europe (CSCE), re-established by the 1990 Treaty of Paris, is the fifty-three nation international institution of the new European security regime. The principal political goal of the CSCE is to peacefully manage the repercussions of loss of Communist power in Eastern and Central Europe. The Yugoslavian civil war, which broke out in July 1991, was the first emergency it faced.

[13] This may also partially explain what Rosenau (1990) has called the "turbulence" of contemporary world politics. Note that the same phenomenon does not affect all events. For instance, the result does not hold when $\mathbf{P}(\mathbb{Y}) = p_1 + p_2 = 2p$, where p_1 and p_2 are the probabilities of alternatively sufficient conditions for $\mathbb{Y}$ to occur. In this case $d\mathbf{P}(\mathbb{Y})/dp_1 = d\mathbf{P}(\mathbb{Y})/dp_2 = 2$, which is a constant.

conditional micropolitical causation. Later I will expand the focus from these particular examples to a broader class of occurrences drawn from different areas of general politics. My claim is that, just as the next two examples highlight the causal structures (operations) of necessity and sufficiency in politics, so does the broader theoretical class of phenomena from which these particular examples are drawn. All political events can be viewed from the perspective of necessity and sufficiency in conditional logic, so these basic modes must obey the same general principles – so long as we can identify the causal events, with their connections, and are able to construct an appropriate event function. In each of the next two examples it is also possible to consider more details, but the purpose at this stage is simply to highlight and distinguish the two basic forms of conditional logic.

Example 6.6 (politics by conjunction of necessary causes: deterrence). Consider the case of deterrence, a general political phenomenon (figure 1.1) found in both domestic and international domains.[14] This is a political situation in which some adversary's behavior is prevented by means of a threat that has the following form: "Refrain from doing A or I will punish you with T," where A ("aggression occurs") and T ("threat is executed") are events. In the classical theory, "deterrence works" (event D) when the adversary believes that the defender has the capability to carry out the threat and also the intent to do so if aggression should occur. In other words, D occurs when the following two events occur: "capability is credible" (C) and "intent is credible" (I). Formally,

$$D = \Psi(C, I) \qquad\qquad [6.15]$$
$$= C \cap I, \qquad\qquad [6.16]$$

where $\cap$ signifies the conjunction of C and I. Politically, conjunction means that D occurs only if both C and I occur. In the case of deterrence we speak of necessary conditions, requirements, and similar causal concepts. The significant causal property illustrated by this example is that the referent political event, in this case "deterrence works," occurs as a result of the conjunction of other events.

Example 6.7 (politics by disjunction of sufficient causes: political communication). Consider the case of political communication as another general political phenomenon, in domestic or international domains (figure 1.1).[15]

---

[14] Compellence, the companion concept of deterrence in the theory of threats, can also be used as a parallel example. Deterrence aims at preventing a given form of behavior using a threat of the form: "Do not attack Kuwait, or else…" Compellence aims at inducing a given form of behavior by using a threat of the form: "Withdraw from Kuwait, or else…" Both threats aim at modifying behavior.

[15] Following Shannon's classic theory, a message contains meaning (in fundamental units of

This is a compound political process consisting of events in which the transfer of meaning is most often achieved by using a redundancy of signals to ensure that the correct meaning is understood or inferred by the audience. Thus, an election campaign manager will issue multiple signals, or use several media channels, to communicate a candidate's political platform (e.g. newspaper, television, radio); an actor issuing a deterrent threat will rely on several signals (e.g. several "legs" in a strategic nuclear "triad"); or a treaty negotiator will use redundant means to communicate resolve (at the negotiation table, back-door channels, using third parties). If $\mathbb{R}$ represents the reception of the intended political meaning by the audience, and $\mathbb{A}$, $\mathbb{B}$, and $\mathbb{C}$ are the successful receptions of the alternative or redundant signals, then

$$\mathbb{R} = \Psi(\mathbb{A}, \mathbb{B}, \mathbb{C}) \qquad\qquad\qquad [6.17]$$
$$= \mathbb{A} \cup \mathbb{B} \cup \mathbb{C}, \qquad\qquad\qquad [6.18]$$

where $\cup$ signifies the disjunction of $\mathbb{A}$, $\mathbb{B}$, and $\mathbb{C}$. Politically, disjunction means that $\mathbb{R}$ occurs if $\mathbb{A}$ or $\mathbb{B}$ or $\mathbb{C}$ occur. In the case of political communication we speak of sufficiency, redundancy, alternative or equivalent signals, and similar causal concepts. The significant causal property illustrated by this example is that the referent political event, in this case "political communication succeeds," occurs as a result of the disjunction of other events.

In example 6.6, I explained deterrence in terms of a conjunction of causal events. However, it is also possible to explain deterrence in terms of a disjunction of events, following the explanation in example 6.7 for political communication. Similarly, in example 6.7, I explained how political communication works based on a disjunction of causal events. However, it is also possible to explain political communication based on a conjunction of causal events.[16] Therefore, dual explanations are possible within conditional logic.

---

information), whereas a signal is an encoded message. Only signals are actually transmitted and received, together with noise (Shannon and Weaver 1949). A closely related topic is signal processing in intelligence (Axelrod 1973; Chan 1979; McCalla 1992; Newman 1975).

[16] Indeed, the theory of political communication based on Shannon's model (Cioffi-Revilla 1979; Merritt 1972) is based on the successful occurrence of the following set of conjunctive events: once a decision is made to communicate a given political message to a given audience, "a political message is encoded into a signal" (event $\mathbb{X}_1$), "the signal is transmitted to the audience" ($\mathbb{X}_2$), "the audience receives the signal" ($\mathbb{X}_3$), and "the audience decodes the received signal, separating the intended message from noise" ($\mathbb{X}_4$). Note that some events are compound (e.g. $\mathbb{X}_4$) and all are conditional on the occurrence of a prior event. Political communication can also be modeled in sequential mode, by taking the decision to send a message as the "initiating event" and the successful reception of the intended meaning as the final "outcome event." In either mode conjunction is inherent.

Table 6.3. *Conditional logic of political events*

Referent political event Y	Necessary causal events (AND-based conjunction)	Sufficient causal events (OR-based disjunction)	References
Domestic politics[a] Political systems: "A political system functions or performs," in the sense of structural-functionalist theory.	"Function 1 is successfully carried out" AND "function 2 is successfully carried out," etc.	The disjunctive view is uncommon for this political event.	Aberle (1950), Almond (1960), Davis (1959), Deutsch (1966), Downes (1976), Easton (1979), Eisenstadt (1993), Flanigan and Fogelman (1965), Hempel (1959), Holt (1965), Landau (1968), Mclachlan (1976), Munch (1976).
Elections: "A political party wins an election".	"The party won the votes of group 1" AND "the party won the votes of group 2" AND "the party won the votes of group 3," etc., as many as are necessary to win the election.	"The party won the votes of coalition A" OR "the party won the votes of coalition B" OR "the party won the votes of coalition C," etc., any coalition being sufficient to win the election.	Downs (1957); literature on elections.
Legislation: "A legislative bill becomes law".	"The bill is approved by one house" AND "the bill is approved by the other house" AND "the bill is published in the official gazette".	One of several alternative coalitions passes the bill (and the bill is published).	Kingdon (1984, 1989), Mezey (1979), Shepsle (1979), Shepsle and Weingast (1987).
Coalitions: "A coalition forms".	"Ally 1 agrees to join" AND "ally 2 agrees to join" AND "ally 3 agrees to join," etc.	"Alternative coalition configuration A forms" OR "alternative coalition configuration B forms" OR "alternative coalition configuration C forms," etc.	Chatterjee (1975), Ordeshook (1986), Riker (1962).
Domestic conflict: "Civil war type I breaks out".	"Government forces fight nongovernment forces" AND "nongovernment forces fight government forces".	"A and B fight over political rights" OR "A and B fight over economic rights" OR "A and B fight over other rights".	Brinton (1938), Deutsch (1966), Gurr (1970), Horowitz (1985), Lichbach (1995), Small and Singer (1983), van den Berghe (1990).

Concept	Conjunctive ("AND") form	Disjunctive ("OR") form	References
Domestic conflict: "Civil war type II breaks out".	"Nongovernment forces fight other nongovernment forces" (AND, implicitly, "nongovernment forces fight other nongovernment forces").	Similar to above: "A and B fight over political differences" OR "A and B fight over economic differences" OR "A and B fight over other differences".	Similar to those above.
Domestic conflict: "Civil war type III breaks out".	Government forces fight two or more nongovernment forces that are fighting among themselves.	Similar to a combination of the above two situations.	Similar to those above.
Cooperation: "The state of mutual cooperation ('CC') occurs in a game of prisoner's dilemma".	"Actor A chooses to cooperate" AND "Actor B" chooses to cooperate" (Nash equilibrium).	A and B chose to cooperate for multiple reasons ("fear," "non-myopic optimization," "magnanimity," "altruism," etc.).	Axelrod (1981), Brams (1994), Olson (1965), Rapoport and Chammah (1965), Sandler (1992).
Breakdown of cooperation: "Mutual cooperation ('CC') fails in a PD-game".	"A or B can defect" AND "A or B is willing to defect".	"A defects" OR "B defects".	Same as above.

International politics

Concept	Conjunctive ("AND") form	Disjunctive ("OR") form	References
World politics: "Political behavior occurs".	"Opportunity occurs" AND "willingness occurs".	Equivalent modes of political behavior.	Cioffi-Revilla and Starr (1995), Starr (1978).
Treaties: "An international treaty enters into force".	"The treaty is successfully negotiated by all the parties" AND "the treaty is signed by all the parties" AND "the treaty is ratified by all the parties".	One of several equivalent treaties enters into force (the disjunctive view is uncommon).	Fisher and Ury (1983); references similar to those in table 6.1, last row.
Strategy: "Deterrence works".	"Capability is credible" AND "intent to retaliate is credible".	"Use of retaliatory mode 1 is credible" OR "use of retaliatory mode 2 is credible" OR "use of retaliatory mode 3 is credible".	Brodie (1959), Cioffi-Revilla (1983), M. A. Kaplan (1958), Mearsheimer (1983), Morgan (1983), Raser (1969), Russett (1963), Singer (1958), Snyder (1960), Wohlstetter (1959), Zagare (1987).

Table 6.3. (*cont.*)

Referent political event $\mathbb{Y}$	Necessary causal events (AND-based conjunction)	Sufficient causal events (OR-based disjunction)	References
Strategy: "Extended immediate deterrence works".	"Capability of at least one protector is credible" AND "intent to retaliate by at least one credibly capable protector is credible".	"Retaliation by protector 1 is credible" OR "retaliation by protector 2 is credible" OR "retaliation by the Nth protector is credible".	Huth (1988), Huth and Russett (1984, 1988), Ikle (1973), Morgan (1983).
International conflict: "International war breaks out (between belligerents A and B)".	"Belligerent A attacks B" AND "B counterattacks A".	"A and B fight over territory" OR "A and B fight over political succession" OR "A and B fight to establish hegemony".	Blainey (1973), Holsti (1991), Howard (1983), Midlarsky (1988a), Small and Singer (1983), Vasquez (1993).
International conflict: "International war breaks out (between belligerents A and B)".	"E_A (attack B) $>$ $E_A(\overline{\text{attack B}})$" AND "$E_B(\text{resist A}) > E_B(\overline{\text{resist A}})$", where $E_A(\mathbb{X}) = $ A's expected utility of act $\mathbb{X}$.	"Crisis 1 between A and B escalates to war" OR "crisis 2 escalates" OR "crisis 3 escalates" OR ... OR "crisis n escalates" (Wright's n-crisis problem).	Bueno de Mesquita (1981), Chatterjee (1973), Cioffi-Revilla (1987), Cioffi-Revilla and Dacey (1988), Harsanyi (1962), Wright (1942: 1272).
Balance of power in the international system: "Stability is maintained".	"No great power becomes hegemonic" AND "general world war is avoided" AND "no great power loses its independence".	"The great powers form and dissolve alliances (external mode)" OR "they increase their military capability (internal mode)".	Chatterjee (1972, 1975), Claude (1962), Gulick (1955), Midlarsky (1983b), Petty (1690).

[a] I follow the convention of denoting events with quotation marks.
Source: Prepared by the author.

Theoretically, this causal duality means that alternative modes of explanation are possible in politics – which is itself a cause of political uncertainty – because the events that affect a collectivity (i.e. "political" events) can arise from several operational conditions. A political event can arise from the onset of several necessary conditions, just as it can arise from the onset of one or more sufficient conditions. Each of these situations may be specified in terms of a distinctive conditional logic event function. Politics can therefore be overexplained, in this sense, although this does not detract from its uncertainty.

Beyond the particular examples of deterrence and political communication, a broader class of political events obeys the same conditional logic, as illustrated in table 6.3. In each area – as I showed earlier in examples 6.6 and 6.7 – a referent political event $\mathbb{Y}$ results from the uncertain occurrence of necessary or sufficient events. The main difference between examples 6.6 and 6.7 and table 6.3 is that the examples highlighted only one causal mode (conjunction or disjunction) whereas table 6.3 provides both modes (columns 2 and 3). The causal events are uncertain in that they are never preordained because they all ultimately depend on decisional outcomes and states of nature. This is another way of seeing how or why in politics nothing occurs "out of the blue" – everything is caused. The conditional logic mode also gives rigorous scientific meaning to common political ideas such as "the causes of instability have changed" and similar diachronic expressions in domains of politics.[17]

The conceptual existence of these dual causal perspectives in many areas of politics, a duality based on political necessity (conjunction) and sufficiency (disjunction), provides the basis for stating the following theoretical assumption.

Assumption 6.2 (conditional causal logic of politics). *A political event* $\mathbb{Y}$ *occurs in two ways* (see figure 6.3): *either by the joint occurrence of* necessary *conditions* (intersection of events $\mathbb{X}_1$, $\mathbb{X}_2$, $\mathbb{X}_3$, ..., $\mathbb{X}_n$, *by Boolean logic conjunctive* AND); *or by the occurrence of one among several* sufficient *conditions* (union of events $\mathbb{Z}_1$, $\mathbb{Z}_2$, $\mathbb{Z}_3$, ..., $\mathbb{Z}_m$, *by Boolean logic disjunctive* OR). *Formally*,

$$\mathbb{Y}_X = \Psi_\cap(\mathbb{X}_1, \mathbb{X}_2, \mathbb{X}_3, ..., \mathbb{X}_n)$$
$$= \mathbb{X}_1 \cap \mathbb{X}_2 \cap \mathbb{X}_3 \cap .... \cap \mathbb{X}_n$$
$$= \mathbb{X}_1 \wedge \mathbb{X}_2 \wedge \mathbb{X}_3 \wedge ... \wedge \mathbb{X}_n \qquad [6.19]$$

for a conjunctive (AND-*caused*) *political event* $\mathbb{Y}_X$, *and*

---

[17] The expression "the causes of war have changed" is ambiguous in ordinary language. In the theoretical approach I am proposing, it can mean that a given event function for war has changed, making it then possible to ask how, why, or other precise questions.

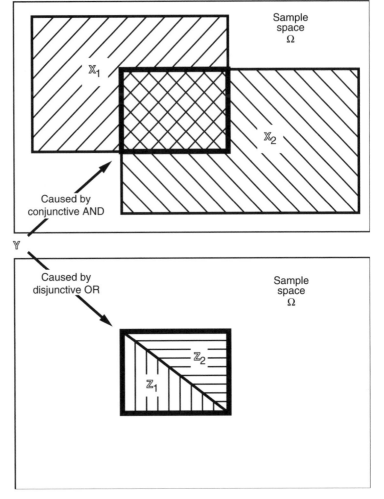

Figure 6.3. Venn diagram for a political event $\mathbb{Y}$ caused by equivalent operations on a sample space Ω (event $\mathbb{Y}$ (thick rectangle set) occurs when necessary conditions $\mathbb{X}_1$ AND $\mathbb{X}_2$ occur (top), or when sufficient conditions $\mathbb{Z}_1$ OR $\mathbb{Z}_2$ occur (bottom))

$$\mathbb{Y}_Z = \Psi_\cup(\mathbb{Z}_1, \mathbb{Z}_2, \mathbb{Z}_3, \ldots, \mathbb{Z}_m)$$
$$= \mathbb{Z}_1 \cup \mathbb{Z}_2 \cup \mathbb{Z}_3 \cup \ldots \cup \mathbb{Z}_m = \mathbb{Z}_1 \vee \mathbb{Z}_2 \vee \mathbb{Z}_3 \vee \ldots \vee \mathbb{Z}_m, \quad [6.20]$$

for a disjunctive (OR-*caused*) *political event* $\mathbb{Y}_Z$.

Assumption 6.2 acknowledges that the sample space of political events can always be partitioned in logically *orthogonal* but canonical ways to produce the same political event $\mathbb{Y}$. These alternate (canonical) partitions can be seen in the Venn diagram in figure 6.3, represented by the union and the intersection of sample points. I call this an assumption because it is not derived from other propositions; however, I view it as a true proposition, not an "as if" hypothetical. I believe this dual property of the conditional logic of politics also contributes to producing uncertainty, because a political event can occur in either way and actors cannot anticipate which way it will occur. However, grasping this phenomenon gives us a better understanding of political uncertainty. For example, assumption 6.2 proposes a solution to a long-standing puzzle in general politics:

> While [scholars] have been posing questions of sufficiency ("If some X_1, X_2, ..., then war") ... they should recognize that their procedure of working conditional from the reports of conflict that appear in various war lists limits their focus to an examination of possible necessary relationships ('Only if some X_1, X_2, ..., then war') (Most and Starr 1982: 835).

This problem of how sufficiency and necessity are to be reconciled is solved by understanding the conditional causal logic I have just discussed. Figure 6.3 illustrates the causal geometry of the problem and its two canonical solutions by conjunction (necessity, equation 6.19) and by disjunction (sufficiency, equation 6.20). In practice, of course, not all partitions on a background sample space will have the same political feasibility (Majone 1975a, 1975b), theoretical parsimony, empirical testability, or deductive power.[18] This is also why some of the cases in table 6.3 are viewed in one prevalent way as opposed to another, or in both ways. For example, the investigation of coalition formation – more generally, the solution to collective action problems – normally focuses more on the necessary conditions than on the (individually) sufficient conditions. However, the study of deterrence or the onset of war frequently addresses both necessary and sufficient conditions.

The duality created by necessary and sufficient conditions for the occurrence of political events gives rise to the following general principle.

Theorem 6.2 (existence and nonuniqueness principle of political event logics). *Given a political event $\mathbb{Y}$ caused by necessary conditions $\{\mathbb{X}\}$, or by*

---

[18] The results that follow assume that the causal events in the argument of an event function Ψ are independent. When the causal events are not independent, other models must be considered, usually requiring the use of conditional, not ordinary, probabilities. However, the probabilities will still multiply in every case of conjunction (and for the disjunction of complementary events). The reason for this is that even when events are conditional, the conjunction of events always requires the product of probabilities. Therefore the results that follow remain valid.

alternative conditions $\{\mathbb{Z}\}$, *there exists at least one* event function Ψ *for producing* $\mathbb{Y}$. *Formally*,

$$\exists\, \Psi \text{ defined on } \Omega \ni (\{\mathbb{X}\} \cup \{\mathbb{Z}\}) \to \mathbb{Y}, \text{ for } (\{\mathbb{X}\} \cap \{\mathbb{Z}\}) \neq \varnothing.$$

The preceding principle gives rise to two branches of the theory of political events based on a conditional logic of occurrences, one based on conjunction and the other on disjunction. The remaining sections of this chapter explore these two sets of results. The two modes are unified in the next chapter, after the principles that govern each are analyzed.

6.3.2   Conjunctive politics

Conjunctive principle. The first general conditional principle I derive concerns the probability of a political event that occurs by conjunction. Applying the theorem for the probability of a compound event to the first part of assumption 6.2 (equation 6.19) yields the following theorem.

Theorem 6.3 (conjunctive principle): *The probability of a conjunctive political event* $\mathbb{Y}_X$ *is given by the product of the probabilities of the n necessary events. Formally*,

$$\mathbf{P}(\mathbb{Y}_X) = \mathbf{P}(\bigwedge \mathbb{X}_i) = \prod_{i=1}^{n} \mathbf{P}(\mathbb{X}_i)$$
$$= p_1\, p_2\, p_3 \cdots p_n = P^{\Theta}, \qquad\qquad [6.21]$$

where Θ *denotes the number of necessary causal events for* $\mathbb{Y}$ *to occur* $(2 < \Theta < n)$ *and P is the probability of these events.*

Informally, the conjunctive principle states that the chance for a political event to occur, when such event is caused by the joint occurrence of other factors or conditions (the causal $\mathbb{X}$'s), equals the chance of the least likely factor, weighted down by all the others that are required. For example, if three political parties are needed to form a coalition, then the chance of the coalition forming will be equal to the chance of the least reliable ally joining, weighted down further by the chances of the other two joining. No matter how pessimistic or counterintuitive this result may appear (perception is a poor guide for understanding political uncertainty), the effect of causal conjunction on political occurrences is real and strongly dampening or inhibitory.

Equation 6.21 constitutes the formal core of the conditional conjunctive principle for political events. The essence of this principle, from a purely qualitative standpoint, lies in the multiplicative form that stems directly from the argument of the conjunctive event function (equation 6.19).

Comparing theorem 6.3 with theorem 6.1, we can see immediately that the sequential logic mode was a special case of conjunction, also called sequential Boolean AND, or conjunction by sequential conditionality. The main implication of this formal equivalence between the two is that sequential logic models of politics and conditional models by conjunction must share similar properties such as nonlinearity, sensitivities, and dominance. In the interest of completeness, I will now present these results.

Note that, by equation 6.21, the conditional conjunctive probability of a political event is always nonlinear in both independent variables, P and Θ. This means that, in contrast to the simple linear appearance of assumption 6.2 or equation 6.19, the probability of a conjunctive political event can change in nonintuitive ways when changes occur in the probability of the causal events P or in the number of the necessary events Θ. I will analyze this further, after examining the role of hypoprobability in conjunctive political events.

Hypoprobability principle for conjunction. The following corollary follows immediately from the conjunctive principle (theorem 6.3).

Corollary 6.5 (hypoprobability principle). *A political event that occurs by the conjunction of other causal events has probability that is always:* (i) smaller *than the probability P of the individual causal events, and* (ii) smaller *than the* smallest *of the separate probabilities of the causal events. Formally,*

$$\mathbf{P}(\mathbb{Y}) < \min \{p_1, p_2, p_3, \ldots, p_n\} \qquad [6.22]$$
$$< P. \qquad [6.23]$$

The hypoprobability of conjunctive political events can be interpreted as follows. Looking at the probability of any of the Θ causal events that are necessary to produce the political event of interest ($\mathbb{Y}$) is always misleading because such probabilities always overestimate the objective value of $\mathbf{P}(\mathbb{Y})$. Note that this is true whether we use the individual probability values p_1, $p_2, p_3, \ldots, p_n$, or the uniform value P. Moreover, in the conjunctive mode a political event always occurs with probability lower than the *least* probable of the causal events.[19] The magnitude K of the gap is measured by the difference

$$K = P - \mathbf{P}(\mathbb{Y}),$$

[19] As I noted earlier, hypoprobability has nothing to do with incomplete information, in this case regarding the probability with which the necessary causal events will occur. Hypoprobability stems from the fundamental character of political uncertainty expressed by the conjunctive principle. Additional information cannot narrow the gap between the probability of the necessary events, the $\mathbf{P}(\mathbb{X})$'s, and the probability of the referent event, $\mathbf{P}(\mathbb{Y})$. Chan (1982) discusses the occurrence of hypoprobability and hyperprobability as a failure in the coherence of expert judgments.

where $K < 0$ indicates hypoprobability, $K > 0$ indicates hyperprobability, and $K \to 0$ as $P \to \mathbf{P}(\mathbb{Y})$.

Political events that occur by conjunction are always hypoprobable because their occurrence is always less likely than any of the causally necessary occurrences. This phenomenon – an insight derived from theorem 6.3 – is present across the domains of politics identified in table 6.3. The hypoprobability property is also empirically testable because (or as long as) each probability is well defined and measurable by means of observed relative frequencies.

Example 6.8 (hypoprobability in a coalition). Consider a political coalition with Θ pivotal members, each having a probability P of remaining in the coalition. Such multiparty coalitions are common in parliamentary systems of government, as well as in legislative bodies for passing laws. Even in the case of single-party government, the appearance of solidarity may only be formal, because internal factions form coalitions with pivotal members (Mershon 1996). Because each of the Θ members is pivotal, all members are necessary to maintain the coalition in power. In this case K measures the gap between the individual parties' probability of adherence P (called loyalty or reliability, in this context) and the probability that the coalition will remain together. Hypoprobability here means that the probability of a coalition remaining together is not only lower than the adherence probability of the allies P, but also lower than the lowest of the individual party reliabilities. I believe one reason why some coalition breakdowns come by surprise is that hypoprobability is always at work but is not observable. Because of hypoprobability, the allied reliability P, or even the lowest of the Θ adhesion probabilities, always overestimates the real probability of coalition survival.

Example 6.9 (hypoprobability in deterrence). Consider a deterrence threat with Θ necessary operational requirements (example 6.6), as is characteristic of power relations in domestic and international domains. Strategically, the Θ operational requirements break down into conditions for achieving credibility of capability and those for the credibility of intent. Safety in operation, affordability, survivability to disabling or countermeasures (e.g. pre-emptive strikes), command and control, and damaging capacity are some examples of these requirements. Note that $\Theta > 1$ always because some events are always necessary to implement the two credibility conditions. (A similar situation is also valid for compellence, when Θ actions are necessary to induce a modification in the adversary's behavior.) In this case K measures the gap between the probability of success of the individual requirements, P, and the probability that the deterrence threat as a whole will prevent the undesired aggression. Hypoprobability here means that the probability of deterrence working is not only lower than the probability of the requirements P, but also lower than the lowest of the individual requirement reliabilities (e.g. command and control when attacked by countermeasures, or in a post-strike environment). Some deterrence failures may seem surprising only because hypoprobability is always at work but most analysts do not recognize it. Because deterrence is affected by hypoprobability, the requirement reliability P, or even the lowest of the Θ requirement probabilities, always overestimates the real probability of deterrence working.

Example 6.10 (hypoprobability in a domestic political system). Consider a domestic political system in the structural–functional framework. Let Θ denote the number of necessary functions to maintain system performance, each function having a probability P of performing. Typically, such functions are related to processes such as resource maintenance and extraction, value maintenance, distribution of authority, legitimation, and other basic functions of governance. Because each of the Θ functions is defined as a sine qua non, all functions are necessary in order to maintain governance in the system. In this case K measures the gap between the individual functions' probability of continuation P (what may be called functional reliability) and the probability that the system as a whole will endure. Hypoprobability in a political system means that the probability of overall system endurance is not only lower than the probability of functional performance P, but also lower than the lowest of the individual probabilities of functional performance. Some political system failures can seem surprising, but this is only because hypoprobability has been at work but unnoticed within the functional structure of the system. Because of hypoprobability, the functional reliability P, or even the lowest of the Θ performance probabilities, always overestimates the real probability of a political system enduring.

Example 6.11 (hypoprobability in the international system). Consider the international political system, where stability and strategic security are maintained by several conditions or requirements in an "anarchic" decisional environment. For example, in the *Realpolitik* tradition, stability is maintained by a balance of power process (arms accumulation processes and alliance formations and dissolution). The system is stable if (i) no great power becomes hegemonic, (ii) global hegemonic war is avoided,[20] and (iii) each great power maintains independence. In general, let Θ denote the

[20] Limited or local wars within an existing stable system can occur. However, global (usually hegemonic) war is a system-transforming event.

number of stability conditions, each condition having a probability P of obtaining or enduring. Because the failure of any one condition makes the system fail (i.e. as an international or global security failure), all conditions are necessary in order to maintain the system. In this case K measures the gap between the probability of continuation of the individual requirements P (what may be called their security reliability), and the probability that the international security system as a whole will endure.

Hypoprobability in the international system means that the probability of maintaining international peace and security is not only lower than the probability of the endurance of each condition P, but is actually lower than the probability of the most difficult condition to maintain (perhaps (i) in the above balance-of-power conditions). Some international system failures can seem surprising, such as World War I (the global war that "no one wanted"), but this is only because hypoprobability, constantly at work eroding the endurance of security conditions, goes unrecognized. Because of hypoprobability, the probability of conditions P, or even the lowest of the least likely of the Θ individual conditions, always overestimates the real probability of maintaining international security in the global international system.

Hypoprobability is neither observable nor intuitively understood from plain observation of conjunctive political events. As noted earlier (section 6.2.3), in this regard hypoprobability is similar to the elasticity of demand for a given product, which is a similarly unobservable but no less real property. A product's elasticity is not observable from simply watching consumer behavior, just as the hypoprobability of a conjunctive political event is not observable from simply observing its occurrence. Informally, this is because hypoprobability may be thought of as the additional degree of political difficulty that is involved in implementing or realizing the necessary events that are required to produce a given political event; that extra effort that goes beyond the distinct difficulties of separately producing each requirement. Logically, the probability of a political event is greatly reduced when it is based on many requirements – hypoprobability explains why. This is what I mean by the "political difficulty" that is induced by hypoprobability under assumption 6.2. Additionally, such difficulty increases when we consider that politics by definition involves coordination, collective action, or other interdependent social situations that are never straightforward for the actors to accomplish. Such phenomena as creating and maintaining coalition governments, deterrence threats, and political systems involve the production of several (sometimes numerous) interdependent requirements involving not just a single actor but a collectivity of actors (otherwise the events are not political). For this class of defining political events the impact of hypoprobability is always present and, consequently, the difficulty of producing events is significant.

The two conditional principles I have presented thus far (theorem 6.3 and corollary 6.5) explain the remote likelihood of conjunctive political events – their hypoprobability – as caused by the necessary requirements. For instance, a coalition is unlikely to endure when the number of pivotal allies is large, but endurance becomes increasingly likely as the number of pivotal allies decreases. Formally, $\mathbf{P}(\mathbb{Y}) \to 1$ as $\Theta \to 1$, which is consistent with equation 6.21, as long as $P > 0$.

Sensitivity principles for conjunction. In the real world it is intuitive that the probability of political events – and therefore the structure of their uncertainty – is constantly changing, making estimates of the life, fortune, or government of a collectivity seemingly impossible to calculate, let alone maintain currently updated. Although they will always remain uncertain, all conjunctive political events occur with calculable probability, as given by theorem 6.3.

This property of conjunctive political events – the fact that their occurrence is governed by the probability of causally necessary events and by the number of such other events – raises the following question. What is the effect of changes in the probability or in the number of the necessary events? How is a conjunctive political event – such as a coalition enduring, deterrence working, or a political system performing – affected as changes occur in the likelihood or in the variety of the requirements that bring it about? The general answers I provide to these questions also follow from the conjunctive principle (theorem 6.3).

Corollary 6.6 (dependence on the probability of requirements *P*). *The rate of change in the probability of a conjunctive political event with respect to change in the probability of the necessary events P is given by the expression:*

$$\frac{\partial \mathbf{P}(\mathbb{Y})}{\partial P} = \Theta P^{\Theta - 1}, \qquad\qquad [6.24]$$

which is always positive, so $\mathbf{P}(\mathbb{Y})$ *is concave with respect to P.*

Qualitatively, this result means that changes in the probability of the causal events have a similar effect on the probability of occurrence (increasing or decreasing), as intuitively expected. What is not intuitive is that the magnitude of the effect will differ, depending on the actual values of *P* and Θ when the changes occur, as in equation 6.24.

Corollary 6.7 (dependence on the number of requirements Θ). *The rate of change in the probability of a conjunctive political event with respect to change in the number of necessary conditions is given by the expression:*

$$D_\Theta \mathbf{P}(\mathbb{Y}) = P^{\Theta+1} - P^\Theta, \hspace{3cm} [6.25]$$

which is always negative, so $\mathbf{P}(\mathbb{Y})$ *is convex with respect to* Θ.

Recall that Θ denotes the number of necessary causal conditions (events) for $\mathbb{Y}$ to occur, where $2 < \Theta < n$. I note immediately that this result (corollary 6.7) depends critically on how Θ is determined. In other words, sometimes there are several ways in which a given political event could be disaggregated into more basic events,[21] but some of these more basic events may themselves remain compound events. In this case, these results are weakened. The number of necessary causal events Θ (and later in this same chapter, the number of sufficient events Γ) makes sense – and therefore these results are meaningful – only if there is a unique such number, ensuring that the most basic types of events have been specified. My solution to this problem, as already discussed in section 5.2.1, is to decompose events down to the level of decisions, as explained in greater detail in the next chapter. Using the individual decisional level as the limit of detail for disaggregation is also consistent with a social choice approach. Below the decision level, in general, we find only states of nature. Therefore, the number of constituent events Θ (and later Γ) is a meaningful variable.

Informally, corollary 6.7 says the opposite of corollary 6.6, namely that changes in the number of necessary conditions have a reverse effect on the probability of a conjunctive political event (increasing → decreasing and decreasing → increasing). This is also intuitively expected. However, once again, the magnitude and behavior of this effect are not intuitive and will differ, depending on the actual values of P and Θ.

Both conjunctive sensitivity principles are nonlinear. Therefore the probability of a conjunctive political event depends in potentially nonintuitive ways on both the probability and the number of the necessary conditions required for it to happen. Moreover, these two independent variables have opposite effects.

Which of the two independent variables has a greater effect on the probability of a conjunctive political occurrence – the probability of necessary conditions occurring or the number of such conditions? This question is theoretically important because it addresses a nonintuitive property of political uncertainty, namely the differential sensitivity of the probability of a conjunctive political event to changes that may occur in the causal events or in their number, for whatever reasons. The question is also important from a policy perspective because in many real-world situations one of these variables may be more manipulable than the other. For example, whereas a political actor may have some control over P (e.g.

---

[21] Formally, this is because, by definition 5.1, each event is defined as a set of sample points from a sample space Ω which can be partitioned in several ways.

increasing the component reliabilities in deterrence, or increasing the performance probability of some functions in a political system), usually actors have little or no control over Θ. Therefore the question of which of the two variables has a greater impact on $P(\mathbb{Y})$ is often important, sometimes critically so. There is no intuitive way to answer this question, except through analysis. The following principle answers the question.

Corollary 6.8 (dominance principle for political conjunction). *The probability of a conjunctive political event $\mathbb{Y}$ is more sensitive to P than to Θ:*

$$s_P > s_\Theta \qquad\qquad\qquad [6.26]$$

because

$$\frac{\partial \mathbf{P}(\mathbb{Y})}{\partial P}\left[\frac{P}{\mathbf{P}(\mathbb{Y})}\right] > \left(\mathbf{P}(\mathbb{Y})_{\Theta+1} - \mathbf{P}(\mathbb{Y})_{\Theta}\right)\left[\frac{\Theta}{\mathbf{P}(\mathbb{Y})}\right]. \qquad [6.27]$$

This principle states (guarantees) a new insight concerning the uncertain occurrence of a conjunctive political event. Applied to coalitions, a leader should be more concerned about maintaining allied reliability (a variable that has attracted little previous attention) and less concerned about coalition size (now the conventional wisdom, following Riker's principle).[22] Other examples from table 6.3 can also be interpreted in the light of this principle. The probability of deterrence working is more influenced by the probabilities of the component requirements than their total number; the probability of maintaining a political system is more greatly improved by improving functional performance than by attempting to reduce the number of functions ("increase individual performance within an existing structure" is a superior policy than "smaller is better so let's reduce the structure"); winning an election that depends on the support of a set of groups is more effectively accomplished by winning the enduring support of a few groups than by winning over as many groups as possible.

Restated more generally: the probability of a conjunctive political event, $\mathbf{P}(\mathbb{Y})$, is more sensitive to the probabilities of the necessary causal events (P) than to the number of such events (Θ). In politics, once again, chance counts more than structure, although both give form to political uncertainty.

Change in the probability of a conjunctive political event is nonlinearly

---

[22] Likewise, a legislator should worry more about the probability of having the voters' support than about increasing their numbers. A propagandist should closely monitor the selection, encoding, transmission, and reception of political information, and be less concerned about problems like source-to-target noise. A peacemaker confronted with a multidimensional conflict should focus on resolving the individual issues and dedicate less effort to reducing their number.

affected by the probability of necessary conditions. This explains why politics is sometimes surprising – such as the defeat of President George Bush in the 1992 presidential campaign, only months after he had enjoyed the highest popularity ratings ever: a small change in the probability of necessary conditions, when the number of conditions is very high, will drastically cause a larger-than-expected change in the probability of a political event. Exactly when does this happen? Beyond the point where the slope of equation 6.24 is greater than 45°, when $\partial \mathbf{P}(\mathbb{Y})/d\Theta = \Theta P^{\Theta-1} > 1$, so solving for P yields $P > \Theta^{-1/(\Theta-1)}$. For a number of conditions in the interval $3 < \Theta < 10$, this "booster threshold" lies within the range of $0.58 < P < 0.70$, or always higher than even-odds.

The practical or policy implication of the dominance result for effective political action – for boosting the probability of affecting a collectivity – should be clear. Policy requisites have a strong effect on the probability of a conjunctive political outcome when their probability exceeds even-odds (exactly $\Theta P^{\Theta-1}$, depending on Θ), so they must be planned with at least that chance of succeeding; otherwise, they have only a weak effect on the occurrence of political events.

6.3.3   Disjunctive politics

Disjunctive principle. The second set of general conditional principles I derive concerns the probability of political events that occur by disjunction. Applying the theorem for the probability of a compound event to the second part of assumption 6.2 (equation 6.20) yields the following principle.

Theorem 6.4 (disjunctive principle). *The probability of a disjunctive political event $\mathbb{Y}_Z$ is given by the following equations*

$$\mathbf{P}(\mathbb{Y}_Z) = \mathbf{P}\left(\bigvee Z_j\right) = 1 - \prod_{j=1}^{m} [1 - \mathbf{P}(Z_j)]$$
$$= 1 - (1 - q_1)(1 - q_2)(1 - q_3)\ldots(1 - q_m)$$
$$= 1 - (1 - Q)^{\Gamma}, \tag{6.28}$$

where Γ denotes the number of sufficient (or "redundant") causal events for $\mathbb{Y}$ to occur $(2 < \Gamma < m)$ and Q is their probability. Alternatively,

$$[1 - \mathbf{P}(\mathbb{Y}_Z)] = (1 - Q)^{\Gamma}. \tag{6.28'}$$

The political interpretation of the disjunctive principle is more intuitive through the alternative equation 6.28′. Informally, this states that the chance for a disjunctive political event to not occur equals the chance that all the sufficient causal events fail to occur. Another possible wording is as follows: the chance of a political event occurring, when such event can be caused by the alternative occurrence of redundant factors or conditions (the causal $\mathbb{Z}$'s), equals the chance of the most likely causal factor occurring, increased further by all the other factors. For example, if three different configurations of political parties (e.g. A–B, A–C, or A–D) are individually sufficient to form a government coalition, then the chance of a coalition forming will be equal to the chance for the most likely coalition, boosted by the chances for the other two. In this case, no matter how optimistic or counterintuitive this result may seem, the effect of causal disjunction on political occurrences is real and, this time, strongly amplifying or stimulating for occurrences to take place.

Equation 6.28 constitutes the formal core of the disjunctive principle for political events, and parallels equation 6.21 for conjunctive political events. The parallelism can best be seen by comparing equations 6.21 and 6.28′, with Θ and Γ as necessary and sufficient conditions, respectively. The political essence of the disjunctive principle, from a purely qualitative viewpoint, lies in the complement of the Γ failures in redundant events – i.e. the political meaning of the expression $1 - (1 - Q)^{\Gamma}$ – that are contained in the argument of the event function (equation 6.28).

In reference to the conjunctive logic of political events, using the equivalence between the operators AND and NOT OR, the main connection is that conjunctive logic models of politics and conditional models by disjunction share exactly opposite properties in terms of their nonlinearity and sensitivity, but – as I will show – they share the same dominance properties.

Note that, by equation 6.28, the probability of a disjunctive political event is always nonlinear in both independent variables, Q and Γ. This means that, in contrast to the simple appearance of assumption 6.2 or equation 6.20, the probability of a disjunctive political event can change in nonintuitive ways when changes occur in the probability Q or in the number Γ of the redundant events.

Hyperprobability principle for disjunction. The following corollary follows immediately from the disjunctive principle (theorem 6.4).

Corollary 6.9 (hyperprobability principle). *A political event that occurs by the disjunction of other causal events has a probability that is always*: (i) larger *than the probability Q of the individual causal events, and* (ii) *larger than the largest of the separate probabilities of the causal events. Formally,*

$$\mathbf{P}(\mathbb{Y}) > \mathbf{max}\ \{q_1, q_2, q_3, \ldots, q_m\} \qquad [6.29]$$
$$> Q. \qquad [6.30]$$

The hyperprobability of disjunctive political events can be interpreted as follows. Looking at the probability of any of the Γ causal events that are sufficient to produce the political event of interest ($\mathbb{Y}$) is always misleading because such probabilities always underestimate the objective value of $\mathbf{P}(\mathbb{Y})$. Note that this is true whether we use the individual probability values $q_1, q_2, q_3, \ldots, q_m$, or the uniform value Q. Moreover, in the disjunctive mode a political event always occurs with probability higher than the most probable of the causal events.[23] The magnitude K of the gap is measured by the difference

$$K = Q - \mathbf{P}(\mathbb{Y})$$

where now $K > 0$ (hyperprobability) only and, just as before, $K \to 0$ as $Q \to \mathbf{P}(\mathbb{Y})$.

Political events that occur by disjunction are always hyperprobable because their occurrence is always more likely than any of the causally sufficient occurrences. As before, this phenomenon – an insight derived from theorem 6.4 – is present across the domains of politics identified in table 6.3. The hyperprobability property is also empirically testable because (or as long as) each probability is well defined and measurable by means of observed relative frequencies.

Example 6.12 (hyperprobability in government organizations). When complex governmental operations succeed, this is not by chance but because redundancy is used to generate hyperprobability. However, the fact that it is used does not mean that it is understood. Consider a governmental organization with Γ redundant agencies, programs, or procedures, each having a probability Q of operating properly (Bendor 1985; Landau 1969, 1973). Such redundancy is generally uncommon because it can be costly to develop and maintain, but sometimes the risk of failure is even higher – particularly in terms of loss of human lives – so the expense is undertaken. For example, disjunctive operations are common in areas such as emergency intervention (e.g. FEMA operations), national security ("permissive action links," or PALS, in launching nuclear weapons), air traffic control (supervisory functions and redundant hardware), and counterintelligence (multiple codes, back-up procedures, poli-verification). Because each one of the Γ components is theoretically sufficient, one is enough to achieve success. In this case K measures the gap between the probability of success

---

[23] Hyperprobability also has nothing to do with incomplete information, in this case regarding the probability with which the redundant causal events will occur. As I showed earlier, hyperprobability stems from the fundamental character of political uncertainty expressed by the disjunctive principle. Additional information cannot narrow the gap between the probability of the redundant events, the $\mathbf{P}(\mathbb{Z})$'s in this case, and the probability of the referent event, $\mathbf{P}(\mathbb{Y})$.

of individual components, Q, and the probability that the operation as a whole will succeed. Hyperprobability means that the probability of success in a disjunctive governmental operation is not only *higher* than the probability of the component stages Q, but even higher than the *highest* of the individual component probabilities. So the reason some governmental successes occur by surprise at times is that hyperprobability has been at work but is unobservable. The component probability Q, or even the highest of the Γ individual probabilities, always underestimates the real probability of operational success when redundancy is built in, because of hyperprobability.

Example 6.13 (hyperprobability of domestic conflict). Hyperprobability can play a role in the onset of large-scale domestic conflict, such as ethnic warfare, insurrection, or outright disintegration of public order. Hyperprobability is particularly prone to inducing violence in formerly orderly states where public authority (and the force to back it up) has lost legitimacy. Consider a society of fragmented and dissatisfied groups with Γ alternative cleavages, any one of which is sufficiently severe to be individually capable of causing the onset of warfare. This type of redundancy is common in societies with deep divisions along ethnic, religious, or economic lines and in which the state has weakened and anarchy has increased. Russia, Romania, Yugoslavia, Sudan, Somalia, Haiti, Iran, Mexico, and Palestine are well-known cases. (Increasingly, the United States may be in this situation, particularly along ethnic lines.) Because each of the Γ cleavages is theoretically sufficient, one is enough to cause the onset of violence. In this case K measures the gap between the individual cleavage's probability of onset Q and the probability that violence will erupt. Hyperprobability means that the probability of eruption in a disjunctive social conflict situation is not only higher than the probability at the level of separate cleavages, Q, but even higher than the highest of the individual cleavage probabilities. So, again, the reason why some social conflicts erupt apparently without warning is that hyperprobability had been at work but is unobservable. The cleavage probability Q, or even the highest of the Γ individual cleavage probabilities, always underestimates the real probability of domestic conflict occurring when redundancy exists in the triggers of violence. Hyperprobability explains this.

Example 6.14 (hyperprobability of deterrence). Hyperprobability also plays an important role in the design and successful performance of deterrence threat systems, for example when such systems are based on a so-called "triad" of threats (strategic weapons), with three "legs." Consider a strategic nuclear triad with three alternative weapons systems (viz., missiles, bombers, and submarines), any one of which is sufficiently threatening to be individually capable of dissuading an adversary from undertaking aggression. This type of redundancy currently exists only for the United States, Russia, and Ukraine, and it exists in two legs for China, Israel and perhaps other powers. Each of the three legs is theoretically sufficient, so one is enough to deter. In this case K measures the gap between the individual legs' reliability Q and the probability that deterrence will work. Hyperprobability means that the probability of deterrence working in this disjunctive system is not only higher than the probability of each leg deterring Q, but even higher than the highest of the individual leg reliabilities. I believe this is an important reason why triadic deterrence worked successfully between the nuclear powers during the Cold War, in spite of all its problems and high economic cost. In any case, the leg reliability Q, or even the highest of the Γ individual leg reliabilities, always underestimates the real probability of deterrence working when such redundancy exists in the means of retaliation. Hyperprobability explains this as well.

Example 6.15 (hyperprobability of political change). Hyperprobability also occurs in political decision-making, which explains why so many political decisions are made even if few of them can be accounted for by the ideal expected utility model. This is because political choice is produced by numerous alternate mechanisms, such as those identified in table 1.1. Any of these mechanisms is sufficient for producing a choice (e.g. obligation, instinct, expected utility). This type of redundancy virtually guarantees that, given the need, some choice will be made, even if the result is suboptimal. Because each mechanism is theoretically sufficient to produce a choice, one is enough to avoid impasse – a rare occurrence. In this case K measures the gap between the separate mechanisms' reliability Q in producing some choice, and the probability that some choice will indeed be made when it is (for any number of reasons) necessary. Hyperprobability means that the probability of a choice occurring in this disjunctive system is not only higher than the probability of each choice mechanism working, Q, but even higher than the highest among the full set of mechanisms. I believe that political features such as these may be an important reason why choices are so common in political life. In any case, the individual mechanism reliability Q, or even the highest of the individual reliabilities, always underestimates the real probability of a political choice. Hyperprobability explains how and why this occurs.

As I remarked earlier for hypoprobability, hyperprobability is neither discernible nor intuitively understood from plain observation of disjunctive political events. My earlier analogy with the elasticity of demand for a given product carries over to this case as well. Informally, hyperprobability may be thought of as the additional degree of political ease that is involved in implementing or realizing the redundant events that are sufficient to produce a given political event; that extra ease that goes beyond the distinct task of separately producing each requirement. Logically, a political event occurs easily when it is based on many redundancies – hyperprobability explains why. This is what I mean by the "political ease" that is induced by hyperprobability under assumption 6.2. Such ease is relatively rare because hyperprobability comes at a high cost and can be politically justified only under a relatively narrow set of circumstances. Such phenomena as the onset of violent social conflict, or creating and maintaining government operations, deterrence policies, and balancing power, involve the production of redundant conditions that operate as multiple efforts. For this class of important political events the impact of hyperprobability is always present and, consequently, such events occur with relatively greater ease.

The two principles I have presented thus far (theorem 6.4 and corollary 6.9) explain the relatively high likelihood of disjunctive political events – their hyperprobability – as caused by the redundant conditions of sufficiency. For instance, governmental performance is unlikely to fail as long as redundancy is sufficiently high, but successful performance becomes increasingly unlikely as redundancy decreases. Similarly, deterrence is unlikely to fail when the number of legs is three, but success becomes increasingly unlikely as the number of legs decreases. Formally, $\mathbf{P}(\mathbb{Y}) \to Q$ as $\Gamma \to 1$, which is consistent with equation 6.28, as long as $Q > 0$.

Sensitivity principles for disjunction. The hyperprobability property of disjunctive political events – the fact that their occurrence is governed by the probability of causally redundant events and by the number of such sufficient occurrences – raises the following questions. What is the effect of changes in the probability or in the number of the sufficient events? How is a disjunctive political event – such as social conflict breaking out, deterrence working, or decisions being made in a political system – affected as changes occur in the likelihood or in the variety of the redundancies that bring it about? The general answers I provide to these questions follow from the disjunctive principle (theorem 6.4).

Corollary 6.10 (dependence on the probability of redundancies Q). *The rate of change in the probability of a disjunctive political event with respect to change in the probability of the sufficient or redundant events Q is given by the expression:*

$$\frac{\partial \mathbf{P}(\mathbb{Y})}{\partial Q} = \Gamma(1 - Q)^{\Gamma - 1}, \qquad\qquad [6.31]$$

which is always positive, so $\mathbf{P}(\mathbb{Y})$ *is concave with respect to Q.*

Qualitatively, this result means that changes in the probability of the redundant events have a similar effect on the probability of occurrence (increasing or decreasing), as intuitively expected. What is not intuitive is that the magnitude of this effect will differ depending on the values of Q and Γ when the changes occur, as in equation 6.31.

Corollary 6.11 (dependence on the number of redundancies Γ). *The rate of change in the probability of a disjunctive political event with respect to change in the number of sufficient conditions is given by the expression:*

$$D_\Gamma \mathbf{P}(\mathbb{Y}) = Q(1 - Q)^\Gamma,$$
[6.32]

which is always positive, so $\mathbf{P}(\mathbb{Y})$ *is concave with respect to* Γ.

Again, recalling the discussion following corollary 6.7, the number of causally sufficient events Γ is meaningful, not arbitrary, when the referent political event $\mathbb{Y}$ is decomposed down to a level where we encounter decisions. This is shown later in greater detail (section 7.3.3). Consistent with definition 5.1 (referent political event $\mathbb{Y}$), the level of decisional outcomes plays a fundamental role in providing microfoundations.

Informally, this principle says something similar to corollary 6.10, namely that changes in the number of redundant or sufficient conditions have a similar effect on the probability of a disjunctive political event (increasing or decreasing). This is also intuitively expected. However, once again, the magnitude and precise behavior of this effect is not intuitive and will differ depending on the actual values of Q and Γ.

Both disjunctive sensitivity principles are nonlinear, so the probability of a disjunctive political event happening depends in potentially nonintuitive ways on both the probability and the number of the sufficient conditions for the event to happen. The two independent variables have similar effects in terms of direction, but not in terms of magnitude.

Which of the two independent variables has a greater effect on the probability of a disjunctive political occurrence: the probability of sufficient conditions occurring or the number of such conditions? This question is theoretically important because it addresses a nonintuitive property of political uncertainty, namely the differential sensitivity of the probability of a disjunctive political event to changes that may occur in the redundant conditions or in their number, for whatever reasons. The question is also important from a policy perspective because in many real-world situations the changes required in one of these variables may have different costs or varying difficulty of manipulation. For example, a political actor typically has to decide between changing the level of Q (e.g. increasing the performance probability of ongoing operations in government, or increasing the reliabilities in the existing "legs" of a deterrence system), or changing the number Γ of operating events. Since, by the dependence principles (corollaries 6.10 and 6.11), increases in Q and in Γ will both increase $\mathbf{P}(\mathbb{Y})$, but generally at different costs, the question of which of the two variables has a greater impact is important, sometimes critically so. There is no intuitive way to answer this question, except through analysis. The following principle answers the question.

Corollary 6.12 (dominance principle for disjunction). *The probability of a disjunctive political event $\mathbb{Y}$ is more sensitive to Q than to Γ:*

$$s_Q > s_\Gamma$$

since

$$\frac{\partial \mathbf{P}(\mathbb{Y})}{\partial Q}\left[\frac{Q}{\mathbf{P}(\mathbb{Y})}\right] > \left(\mathbf{P}(\mathbb{Y})_{\Gamma+1} - \mathbf{P}(\mathbb{Y})_\Gamma\right)\left[\frac{\Gamma}{\mathbf{P}(\mathbb{Y})}\right]. \qquad [6.33]$$

This principle states (guarantees) a new insight concerning the uncertain occurrence of a disjunctive political event. For instance, war onset is more sensitive to deterrence failure (which at least in principle can be controlled by policy) than to the number of alternate failure modes (which is beyond control). Other examples from table 6.3 can also be interpreted in the light of this principle. The probability of deterrence working is more influenced by the reliability of each leg than the number of legs. Therefore, a deterrent system based on multiple threats should seek to increase the credibility of individual legs (as China, France, Israel, and the United Kingdom have sought to do), rather than seek to increase the number of legs (as the United States and the Soviet Union have done). Similarly, a legislative bill should rely more on a small number of highly dependable enforcement measures rather than try to offset noncompliance by a large number of measures. A politician should rely on a small number of reliable supporters rather than a large crowd of dubious followers (except, of course, when a crowd is perceived to be unstoppable). International peace is better preserved through a few dependable security accords (e.g. an effective United Nations Security Council supplemented by a set of regional arrangements such as the CSCE) rather than through a complex regime of bilateral agreements (as Bismarck first engineered but later failed to control prior to World War I).

Restated in more general terms: the probability of a disjunctive political event, $\mathbf{P}(\mathbb{Y})$, is more sensitive to the probabilities of the sufficient or redundant events (Q) than to the number of such conditions (Γ). In politics, once again, chance counts more than structure, although both give form to political uncertainty.

Change in the probability of a disjunctive political event is nonlinearly affected by the probability of the sufficient conditions. This explains why politics is sometimes surprising – like the onset of so much "turbulence" in the post-Cold War international system (Rosenau 1990): an increase in the probability of sufficient conditions (the numerous cleavages discussed in example 6.13), coupled with an increase in the probability of each, will cause a much-larger-than-expected change in the probability of a political event. Exactly when does this occur? Prior to where the slope of equation 6.31 is greater than $45°$, the highest value of Q where $\Gamma(1 - Q)^{\Gamma - 1} > 1$, so $Q > 1 - \Gamma^{-1/(\Gamma - 1)}$. For a number of conditions in the interval $3 < \Gamma < 10$, this "booster threshold" lies within the range of $0.42 < Q < 0.30$, or always lower than even-odds.

The implication of the dominance result for effective political action – for boosting the probability of affecting a collectivity – can be expressed as follows. Redundant events or conditions have a strong effect on the probability of a disjunctive political event when their probability is less than even-odds (exactly $\Gamma(1 - Q)^{\Gamma - 1}$, depending on Γ), so they need not be planned with more than that chance of succeeding; otherwise they will have a diminishing effect on the probability of political outcomes.

6.3.4   "Several-among-some" politics

General political situation. The previous two political situations – pure cases of conjunction and disjunction – are extreme, because the referent occurrence $\mathbb{Y}$ always requires that either *all* conditions from a set of necessary conditions be satisfied, or *one* condition alone be sufficient for occurrence. However, between these two causal extremes lies a significant class of real-world political situations characterized by partial necessity or partial sufficiency. This arises whenever several conditions (more than one) must be met from among a broader set of possible conditions for an occurrence. I call this political situation the "several-among-some" causal structure, as illustrated in the following four examples.

Example 6.16 (collective action). Consider a situation involving a group of individuals that for some reason must act jointly, a situation involving "collective action" (Coleman 1973; Olson 1965).[24] Common cases involv-

---

[24] Formally, achieving and maintaining the state of mutual cooperation in a prisoner's dilemma game (CC, with any number of players) presents a collective action problem. Lichbach (1996: ch. 6) and Taylor (1987: 88–92 et passim) also provide game theoretic analyses of the "several-among-some" situation which I am analyzing here in terms of the

ing collective action are ballot initiatives, mass mobilization processes, the onset of conflict (domestic or international, violent or not), the imposition of international sanctions, and so on. The cessation of violent conflict (ceasefire) also involves collective action. Typically, collective action is initiated not by the totality of the group, or by a single individual, but rather by some core subgroup – which in turn may consist of a single leader plus a few close followers. In short, collective action occurs if several individuals "activate" the group. The "several among some" principle below (theorem 6.5) applies directly to the subgroup solution to the classic collective action problem, offering a new perspective.

Example 6.17 (deterrence). In most real-world deterrence systems it is assumed that some of the redundant threats will not be credible, but it is sufficient for a few to perform in order for aggression to be dissuaded. Thus, during the Cold War, the US (and to some degree also the French) strategic nuclear doctrine had assumed that a single leg of the triad might not be sufficient to deter under a variety of scenarios (an adversary might neutralize a single leg, such as the submarine force) but three legs were overkill (Tsipis 1975; Yost 1981). Thus, a two-out-of-three posture was assumed by some strategists to be the more realistic configuration.

Example 6.18 (coalitions). In most empirical situations a political coalition is "oversized," in the sense of Riker (1962; see also Shepsle 1974). Accordingly, the support of the totality of the allied parties is not strictly necessary in order for the coalition to maintain power, although several of the parties – fewer than the totality – will be pivotal.

Example 6.19 (voting). Consider a voting body, generally a legislature, where unanimity is not required but some minimal set of votes must be positive for a resolution to pass. In the UN Security Council, consisting of fifteen members with each member casting one vote, a substantive resolution must have ten votes to pass. The intriguing feature of this situation is that the ten votes must include those of the five Permanent Members (the United States, Russia, China, the United Kingdom, and France), or veto-powers, so the other five come from the group of ten rotating non-Permanent Members. Now, by the requirement of the five Permanent Members and the five-out-of-ten non-Permanent Members,

$$\mathbb{Y} = (\mathbb{X}_1 \wedge \mathbb{X}_2 \wedge \mathbb{X}_3 \wedge \mathbb{X}_4 \wedge \mathbb{X}_5) \wedge (\text{5-out-of-10 non-Permanent Members}).$$

causal event structure and the resulting political uncertainty. Schelling's (1978) analysis of tipping models and situations in which some members of a collectivity are enough to provide a collective good is also relevant, and incorporated by Lichbach (1996) and Taylor (1987).

It can be easily seen that there are several ways in which the latter of the two conditions on the right-hand side of this event function can be satisfied from among a large number of redundant voting patterns.

The several-among-some situation in the preceding examples can be readily generalized by the binomial combination of a number, denoted by v, of minimally necessary configurations among a larger set of m that are available (generally, $m > v > 1$), or v-among-some situation. That is, the number of political configurations that provide the occurrence – arguably not all of these will have the same political feasibility – is given by

$$\binom{m}{v} = \frac{m!}{(m - v)! \; v!},$$ [6.34]

where $m! = m \times (m - 1) \times (m - 2) \times \; \ldots \times 1$ is the factorial of m. The several-among-some situation therefore represents a highly significant general political class because, formally, the v-out-of-m structure reduces to

(i) the pure conjunctive case as $v \to m$ (by theorem 6.3) and
(ii) the pure disjunctive case as $v \to 1$ (by theorem 6.4).

The theoretical significance of this should be immediate: The quantity v marks an important political threshold, because toward the upper bound $(v \to m)$ the situation will tend to resemble a conjunctive occurrence of necessary conditions, hence subject to hypoprobability, whereas toward the lower bound $(v \to 1)$ the situation will tend to resemble a disjunctive occurrence of sufficient conditions, hence subject to hyperprobability. In sum,

$$1 \leftarrow v \to m$$

disjunction   conjunction
hyperprobability   hypoprobability
$P(\mathbb{Y}) > \max P(\mathbb{X})$ $P(\mathbb{Y}) < \min P(\mathbb{X})$

Empirically, an oversized coalition will experience hyperprobability in proportion to the oversize, and hypoprobability as it is trimmed to minimal winning size. Similarly, a collective action problem can be facilitated by hyperprobability when the leadership core is larger and more efficient than is minimally necessary, whereas it reaches a critical level as the core shrinks and each member becomes more indispensable.

Several-among-some principle. The preceding ideas yield the following general result.

Theorem 6.5 (several-among-some principle). *The probability of a political event that is caused by a minimum of v conditions from among a group of m that are possible or available, with a v-out-of-m event function, is given by the equation*

$$\mathbf{P}(\mathbb{Y}) = \sum_{i=v}^{m} \binom{m}{i} P^i (1 - P)^{m-i}, \qquad [6.35]$$

where P is the probability of the causal events, and $i = 1, 2, 3, \ldots, v, \ldots, m$.

It can be easily shown that this principle reduces to the conjunctive principle and to the disjunctive principle when $v \to m$ and $v \to 1$, respectively. Therefore this is a very general and powerful result with broad applicability to diverse domains of politics.

Although equation 6.35 looks complicated, a direct way to interpret this general result is simply to apply it to some familiar cases. The next examples provide direct applications of the several-among-some principle.

Example 6.20 (deterrence and legislative voting). During the Cold War the United States pursued a nuclear strategy based on a two-out-of-three partial active redundancy (example 6.17). (Alternatively, consider a legislative decision where two-out-of-three votes are necessary to gain approval.) Using theorem 6.5, this yields a probability of overall deterrence given by

$$\mathbf{P}(\mathbb{Y}) = \sum_{i=2}^{3} \binom{3}{i} P^i (1 - P)^{3-i}$$
$$= P^3 + 3P^2(1 - P) = 3P^2 - 2P^3, \qquad [6.36]$$

where $P = \mathbf{P}(\mathbb{X})$ is the probability that each leg individually will work. The graph of this deterrence probability as a function of the individual leg probabilities P is shown in figure 6.4. A number of significant properties are contained in this case, namely: (i) the behavior of the overall deterrence probability differs both qualitatively and quantitatively from the probability P of each leg, because the function is everywhere monotone-nonlinear with respect to P; (ii) the relationship is affected by both hypoprobability (for $0 < P < 0.5$) and hyperprobability (for $0.5 < P < 1$) because it is both concave and convex; and (iii) the cross-level behavior between individual legs and overall deterrence is reversed at the point where both have

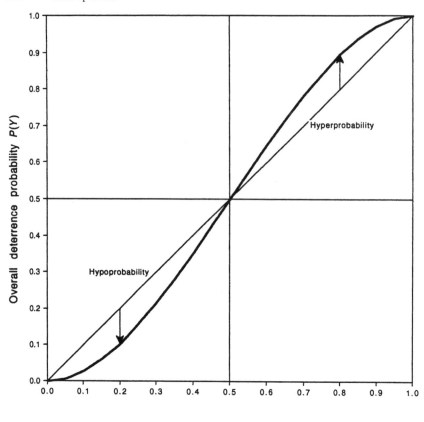

Probability of each triad leg deterring P(X)

Figure 6.4. Deterrence probability for a two-out-of-three strategic triad

even-odds, because the inflection point is at this location. Overall, there-fore, the benefits of redundancy occur only in the upper range of perform-ance (for $0.5 < P < 1$), whereas the costs of the necessary conditions in requiring that at least two legs work are paid for in the lower range (for $0 < P < 0.5$). None of these inferences could be obtained from an intuitive view of the deterrence problem.

Example 6.21 (voting: combining veto power and qualified majority). Recall the voting situation for the UN Security Council, where five affirm-ative votes are required from each of the Permanent Members, plus five others from the remaining ten non-Permanent Members (example 6.19).

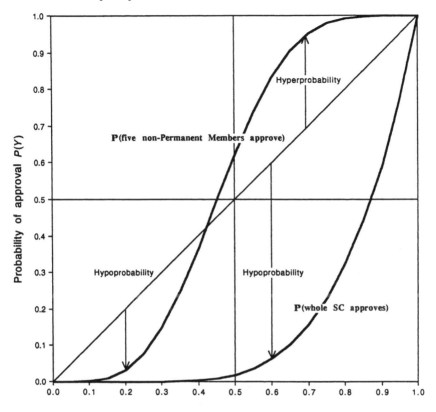

Probability of each member approving P(X)

Figure 6.5. Voting in the UN Security Council

Using theorems 6.3 and 6.5 for each of the subsets of votes, the probability of passing a resolution will be given by

$$\mathbf{P}(\mathbb{Y}) = P^5 \left[\sum_{i=5}^{10} \binom{10}{i} P^i (1 - P)^{10-i} \right] \qquad [6.37]$$

$$= 252P^{10} - 1050P^{11} + 1800P^{12} - 1575P^{13} +$$

$$+ 700P^{14} - 126P^{15}, \qquad [6.38]$$

where P is the probability that each member will approve (not vote against). The graphs of this approval probability as a function of the individual voting probabilities P are shown in figure 6.5. In this case the uncertainty is even more complicated, although still tractable. The lower right curve, $\mathbf{P}$(whole SC approves), is the graph of the entire equation 6.36 (or 6.38), which covers the total situation (i.e. the event "five votes AND five-out-of-ten votes"). Clearly, the presence of the Permanent Members, through the probability function P^5 in the first part of equation 6.36, dominates the overall voting situation, inducing overall strong hypoprobability.

However, the voting behavior of the non-Permanent Members, five of which must approve, is far more politically interesting even if these have no veto power. This is shown by the upper graph, $\mathbf{P}$(5 non-Permanent Members approve), which refers exclusively to the combinatorial term in the second part of equation 6.37. A number of properties similar to the earlier "two-out-of-three" deterrence case recur in this situation of "five-out-of-ten," but are more pronounced: (i) the behavior of the overall approval probability for non-Permanent Members differs both qualitatively and quantitatively from the individual probability P of each member because the function is again everywhere monotone-nonlinear with respect to P; (ii) the relationship between the two probabilities is again affected by both hypoprobability and hyperprobability, because the function is both concave and convex, but this is no longer diagonally symmetric; and (iii) the cross-level behavior between individual non-Permanent Members and their collective voting behavior is surprising because the inflection point is now at less than even odds, at a more complicated location. Overall, therefore, the benefits of redundancy in the voting coalitions among the non-Permanent Members occur earlier than even-odds (approximately at $0.4 < P < 1$), whereas the costs of the necessary number of votes accrue only in part of the lower range (approximately at $0 < P < 0.4$). Again, none of these inferences is apparent from an intuitive discussion of the voting problem in the UN Security Council, not even the relationship between the two probabilities of Permanent and non-Permanent Members.

Numerous political events are governed by the "several-among-some" principle of partial necessity or partial sufficiency (theorem 6.5). In each case, the political occurrence will contain both hypoprobability and hyperprobability, as given by the principles derived earlier. The value of necessity v relative to the value of sufficiency m is what critically determines the threshold where hypoprobability ends and hyperprobability begins (compare the location of inflection points in figures 6.4 and 6.5).

6.4   Conclusions

In this chapter I presented the first set of general micropolitical principles that govern the occurrence of political events at the micro level of analysis.

My treatment was based on the conceptual building blocks that I established in chapter 5. I began by recalling the earlier distinction between sequential logic and conditional logic as general causal approaches that are used to explicate the relationship between a referent political event (viewed as a dependent variable) and the causal events that produce such an occurrence (independent variables). This dual logic relationship – sequential and conditional – governs the various forms of political uncertainty at the micro level, including the probability of the referent political event, the way in which the event is modeled, and the structure of the underlying causal mechanism. For each logic mode I first provided some illustrative examples drawn from general politics (cases such as governmental policy, coalitions, deterrence, war onset in domestic and international domains; figure 1.1), established the general framework, and then proceeded to develop the set of general micropolitical principles for political events. Each set of theoretical results contains a basic principle (theorem) and a subset of further deductive inferences (corollaries) that focus on probabilistic properties.

Empirically, the causal analysis of political events at the micro level means moving toward Boolean techniques (e.g. Ragin 1987) and case methods (George and Smoke 1974; Rosenau 1987; Skocpol and Somers 1980; Snyder and Diesing 1977), appropriate for analyzing the uncertain occurrence of events, as supported by formal logic and related approaches, rather than traditional regression models designed to treat deterministic variables. With few exceptions (Baloyra-Herp 1995), most of this empirical effort has been directed toward international politics, with fewer applications so far in domestic politics. However, the variety of domestic politics examples in this chapter suggests many fertile areas to test and extend the theory. Case studies of collective action should prove particularly fruitful.

At the theoretical level, the first set of political event principles consisted of the sequential principle (theorem 6.1), the sequential hypoprobability principle (corollary 6.1), the sequential dependence principles (corollaries 6.2 and 6.3), and the sequential dominance principle (corollary 6.4). Each of these principles established the sequential logic properties of uncertainty for the occurrence of political events. The main examples I used for these principles were drawn from government policy and the onset of war.

The second set of political event principles was based on conditional logic. This was shown to be a more general approach that analytically (albeit not heuristically) can subsume sequential logic, as shown by the existence and nonuniqueness principle (theorem 6.2). The first set of conditional logic results are based on political conjunction. The main results here were the conjunctive principle (theorem 6.3), the hypoprobability principle for conjunction (corollary 6.5), the dependence principles for conjunction (corollaries 6.6 and 6.7), and the dominance principle for conjunction (corollary 6.8). The second set of conditional results was based on disjunction. These results included the disjunctive principle (theorem 6.4), the hyperprobability principle for disjunction (corollary 6.9), the dependence principles for disjunction (corollaries 6.10 and 6.11), and the dominance principle for disjunction (corollary 6.12). The main examples used to illustrate these principles were from coalition behavior, political choice, general political systems, governmental operations, and deterrence.

After presenting the extreme cases of pure conjunction and pure disjunction, I then focused on the empirically common case of partially and combined conjunction and disjunction – the situation called "several-among-some," or "v-out-of-m," in which a political event occurs whenever several conditions are met (conjunction) among a larger set of some other conditions that are available (disjunction). The main result of this part of the analysis concerned the several-among-some principle (theorem 6.5), a unifying result at the micro level of analysis. Collective action, deterrence, coalition behavior, and majority voting were examined as significant cases.

The most important general micropolitical principle is arguably the v-out-of-m principle, because at one extreme (pure necessity) it generates the conjunctive principle, while at the other (pure sufficiency) it generates the disjunctive principle. The second most important micro principle presented in this chapter is the conjunctive principle, because in one case it gives rise to sequential logic principles and in another to the conditional logic principles.

These principles provide the initial core that has intrinsic theoretical value; other general micropolitical principles can be derived by applying similar methods, as well as those described in appendices 3 (proofs) and 4 (methods). This is also the propositional core from which I derive other more specialized results in the next chapter. These principles (theorems) and their numerous implications (other theorems and corollaries) are not intuitive from the plain observation of political events. They therefore constitute the main result of the micropolitical part of this theory of political uncertainty. Most of the other special micropolitical principles derive from these basic propositions.

The general micropolitical principles for political events are rich in implications. Additional results beyond those that I have presented in this chapter can be derived by applying methods of theoretical analysis (appendix 4). For example, for each principle it is possible to derive additional sensitivity and dominance results, synthesizing these as vector fields for the main probabilities. Many of these additional results would most likely be nonintuitive, given the deeply rooted presence of nonlinear phenomena such as hypo- and hyperprobability.

An important methodological theme in this chapter was again the use of mathematical analysis to uncover previously unknown properties of political uncertainty, aspects that are as real as those that are commonly observed though more standard approaches (Kline's thesis introduced in chapter 3; Cioffi-Revilla 1989). The idea of using mathematical analysis as a powerful theoretical heuristic for discovery is therefore shown to be as valid for the micropolitical part of the theory as it was earlier for the macropolitical part.

7   Special micropolitical principles

History is past politics, and politics present history.
Sir John Robert Seeley, *Growth of British Policy*

7.1   Introduction

The key to deriving additional theoretical results about the occurrence of political events, to better understand their uncertainty at the micro level, is to model events by specifying their event functions. This is done by modeling the causal argument of Ψ in the general principles that I presented in chapter 6. As I will show in this chapter, a specific event function for the occurrence of a given political event yields, using general micropolitical principles, specific properties, and new insights that are otherwise not available through historical observation or statistical analysis. A political event is modeled by making substantive assumptions concerning the causal logic of its occurrence (or failure), such as the effects of conjunction and disjunction of other causal events related to occurrence, endurance, and failure. The result of this procedure is a fully specified analysis of political event occurrences, looking into the micro level of the black box. These results are also essential for linking macro and micro principles in the unified framework presented in the next chapter.

In this chapter I first provide an overview of major theoretical directions for the occurrence of political events. These approaches yield a taxonomy of static and kinematic principles that point to significant new areas for exploration related to structural and temporal variations in political uncertainty, respectively. Static principles explain the occurrence of political events based on the logic structure alone, independent of time. Kinematic principles, on the other hand, focus on the evolution of political occurrences as a function of time. Following a standard convention in comparative analysis (Bartolini 1993), both forms of variation (structural and temporal) may be viewed as orthogonal to each other. Each set of principles is amenable to further investigation beyond that which can be provided in this chapter, so I will limit my discussion to some of the core special principles in order to establish a foundation. In the next chapter I also explore ways of combining these results at the micro level with earlier results at the macro level. As I did for the special macropolitical analysis earlier, I will show how the taxonomy I propose also provides a chart for exploring a broader course of investigation – "a research programme advanced by progressive problemshifts," in the sense of Lakatos (1973). I will then examine some of the individual models in some detail, deriving special principles that shed additional new light on political uncertainty at the micro level. Part of this analysis involves also a new perspective on the relationship between sequential and conditional logic for exploring the occurrence of political events.

The special micropolitical principles presented in this chapter can also assist in systematizing and integrating other emerging topics or middle-range political theories that have thus far remained unrelated, including collective action, policy making, electoral campaigns, political integration, deterrence, and "turbulence" in post-Cold War world politics. As I hope to show with my analysis in this chapter, many ideas that are central to these topics and other topics in general politics (figure 1.1) concern formal variations on a common theme that has deep theoretical significance. This is because many of the basic political ideas concerning occurrences in these areas are reducible to the uniform framework of special micropolitical principles that explain how causal events produce uncertain political oc-currences. The conceptual affinity between this part of the general theory and these other middle-range theories – an affinity based on the causal specification of the main political events – can help in improving the communication among these islands of theory by offering a more general framework with specific applications.

Finally, the presentation and analysis of special micropolitical principles in this chapter is supported by a system of graphic notation for causal event trees (appendix 4). This graphic methodology can be extended further, perhaps even linked to the graphic methods presented earlier for the macro level of analysis (section 3.4). The main purpose of these graphic represen-tations at the micro level is to gain a better understanding of the probabilis-tic occurrence of a referent political event $\mathbb{Y}$ based on the causal elemental events (decisional outcomes or states of nature). Every well-specified politi-cal event should have a corresponding event function and tree.

7.2   Modeling political events

In chapter 5, I introduced the concept that the occurrence of a political event takes place in two modes – conditional or sequential – depending on the causal event function (section 5.3). The several-among-some principle (section 6.3.4) provides a unified treatment of both, but their distinctive causal modes remain intrinsically interesting at the micro level of analysis. For this reason I shall maintain their treatment distinct.[1] I now develop a more systematic treatment of this important idea based on types of causal occurrence by providing a taxonomy and a sequence of models that range from simple to more complex. Although the immense variety of political events in the general classes identified in figure 1.1 and tables 6.1 and 6.3 may appear to endow them with an infinite diversity of causal structures, I demonstrate that a small class of cases is sufficient for understanding a broad range of political complexity. This systematization allows a more productive theoretical use of the general micropolitical principles derived in chapter 6, and at the same time maintains an organized framework.

7.2.1 Taxonomy of political events

Empirical political events – real-world occurrences that have marked consequences for a collectivity or its governance – can have many different event functions. Indeed, political event functions at the micro level can be as varied as the causal forces that govern the many forms of empirical political behavior at the macro level (chapter 4). Moreover, as I remarked earlier for the distributions of macropolitical behavior, there is no purely inductive basis for classifying political events or their causal structure, other than nominal distinctions. For instance, distinctions commonly made in everyday discourse, such as viewing political events as "local" versus "national," or "domestic" versus "international" are mostly nominal distinctions that cannot be used for systematic purposes.

Instead, I use two independent theoretical categories to systematize the variety of political events and their causal structure: (i) the first logic orders of the causal structure (conjunction–disjunction versus disjunction-conjunction) and (ii) the temporal context for the occurrence (static versus kinematic). These criteria give rise to the taxonomy shown in table 7.1.

By the first criterion, the first logic orders of the causal structure of a political event can be either conjunctive–disjunctive or disjunctive–conjunction, as illustrated in figures 7.1 and 7.2.[2] The first two levels of causal order are especially important because, as I discuss below (section 7.3.1),

---

[1] Several other important reasons exist for maintaining the two modes theoretically separate, the validity of the several-among-some principle notwithstanding. First, as I demonstrate in the final chapter through unified principles (theorems 8.1 and 8.2), conjunction and disjunction give rise to qualitatively different types of aggregate macro-political behavior. Second, from a more technical perspective, a unified treatment using the several-among-some principle alone comes at a high mathematical cost (basing all derivations on equation 6.34), which is feasible but not insightful from a substantive political standpoint.

[2] The event tree methodology I use is outlined in appendix 4.

Table 7.1. *Taxonomy of political events*

	Static $\Psi = \Psi(\mathbb{X}s \text{ and } \mathbb{Z}s)$	Kinematic $\Psi = \Psi(\mathbb{X}s \text{ and } \mathbb{Z}s; \tau)$
Conjunctive–disjunctive	Class 1 models:	Class 3 models:
First-order necessary events, second-order sufficient modes (figure 7.1)	$$\mathbb{Y} = \bigwedge_{i=1}^{n}\left(\bigvee_{j=1}^{m} \mathbb{Z}_j\right)$$ Examples: • Political communication with redundant channel components • Policy implementation with parallel subprograms • Political behavior in the willingness–opportunity framework • Functional political system with parallel structures	Same as class 1 models, with time-dependent causal probabilities
Disjunctive–conjunctive	Class 2 models:	Class 4 models:
First-order sufficient modes, second-order necessary events (figure 7.2)	$$\mathbb{Y} = \bigvee_{j=1}^{m}\left(\bigwedge_{i=1}^{n} \mathbb{X}_i\right)$$ Examples: • Redundant deterrence legs (threats), each with requisites • Political decision making through alternate mechanisms (table 1.1) • Political integration with parallel strategies • Political failure in a Lasswell–Kaplan system	Same as class 2 models, with time-dependent causal probabilities

Source: Prepared by the author.

they often contain theoretical (unobservable) and empirical (observable) events, respectively. However, recall that any compound referent political event can and often should be decomposed down to elemental events defined as decisional acts and states of nature (section 5.2). (This can be often accomplished in two levels, as I demonstrate below, although sometimes additional levels are needed in order to anchor the referent event on elemental decisional acts or states of nature.) The first case (figure 7.1) applies to the class of political events that occur by a conjunction of necessary or required conditions (first-order conjunction), each of which in

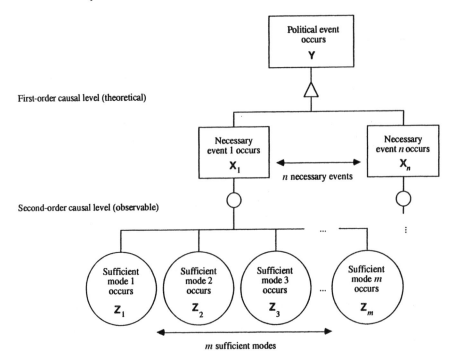

First-order causal level (theoretical)

Second-order causal level (observable)

Figure 7.1. Event tree for a conjunctive–disjunctive political event

turn occurs in a variety of alternative or redundant modes (second-order disjunction). The second class (figure 7.2) applies to political events that occur by a disjunction of alternative modes (first-order disjunction), each of which in turn occurs through a set of necessary events or conditions (second-order conjunction). Each case is explored in greater detail in this chapter. In addition, I should note that the first causal level of a political event (in either mode) is usually expressed in theoretical form and not as a set of observable events, whereas the second level (in either mode) is often observable or "operational."

By the second criterion, the occurrence of a political event may be examined statically or kinematically. I use time as the second criterion because this is a fundamental feature linked to the occurrence ("in time") of any political event – in this sense politics resembles natural history more than it resembles physics. Paraphrasing Harold Lasswell (1936), issues of when are as politically significant as those of who gets what or how. More specifically, the occurrence of political events and the special micropolitical principles that explain their uncertainty can be established from two distinct perspectives: static (based on time-independence) and kinematic

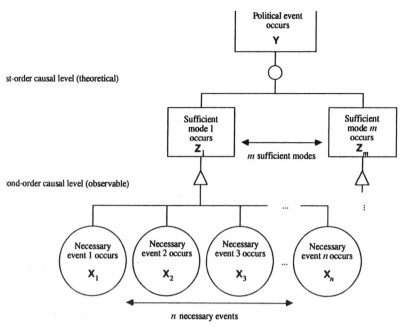

Figure 7.2. Event tree for a disjunctive–conjunctive political event

(based on time-dependence). These two perspectives are roughly analogous to analyzing politics "cross-sectionally" as opposed to "longitudinally" (Bartolini 1993), or "synchronically" as opposed to "diachronically" (Cortés 1974; Galtung 1969). I prefer the simpler terms "static" and "kinematic" because they refer explicitly to the role of time and are therefore better suited for a general theory of political occurrences.

Static special principles for political events are expressed independent of time because all the probabilities are assumed to be constant or instantaneous. Static principles are like a "snapshot" of the structure of political uncertainty – the "photography," so to speak. These have the usual general functional form that I have discussed thus far:

$$\mathbb{Y} = \Psi(\mathbb{X}_1, \mathbb{X}_2, \mathbb{X}_3, \ldots),$$ (event function for event $\mathbb{Y}$)

and

$$\mathbf{P}(\mathbb{Y}) = f[\mathbf{P}(\mathbb{X}_1), \mathbf{P}(\mathbb{X}_2), \mathbf{P}(\mathbb{X}_3), \ldots]$$ (probability function for $\mathbb{Y}$)

or

$$\mathbf{P}(\mathbb{Y}) = f(X_1, X_2, X_3, \dots), \qquad \text{(probability function for } \mathbb{Y})$$

where $X_i = \mathbf{P}(\mathbb{X}_i)$.

By contrast, kinematic principles are time-dependent because event probabilities are assumed to vary as a function of time – a common feature of real-world political uncertainty caused by change. Kinematic principles are like a "movie" of the evolution of political uncertainty – the "cinematography," so to speak. These have the general functional form

$$\mathbf{P}(\mathbb{Y}; \tau) = f[X_1(\tau), X_2(\tau), X_3(\tau), \dots],$$

where the terms in the right-hand side of the equation, denoted by $X_i(\tau) = \mathbf{P}(\mathbb{X}_i; \tau)$, are now explicitly functions of time τ. Note that this time denoted by τ is not the same time as the random variable denoted by T earlier in chapters 2 through 4 at the macro level of analysis. Time τ is true historical time, like an index variable, and is also called "calendrical," "epochal," or "chronological" time.[3] By convention, time τ is expressed as a date, and the initial value is denoted by τ_0. Time T is a continuous random variable that refers to a duration and takes on values t in the open interval $(0, +\infty)$. By convention, the time T is measured in the usual system of units (hours, days, months, years, etc.). I deal with kinematic principles within this chapter, as opposed to dedicating a separate chapter, because this maintains the analysis of time as a special topic – giving rise to its own set of special micro principles – just as the details of causal structure are also a special topic. Both static-structural and kinematic-temporal aspects represent special topics within the general micro principles presented in chapter 6.

Static and kinematic models of political events are exhaustive and mutually exclusive; they therefore provide the taxonomy shown in table 7.1. This taxonomy has several advantages worth highlighting:

1 *Equal importance to static and kinematic perspectives.* Most investigations in political science are oriented toward the uncertain occurrence of political events from a static perspective – that is, without explicit consideration of changes in uncertainty over time. Even some of the most recent probabilistic models, such as logit or probit, approach the explanation of political events in a static mode. A kinematic perspective on politics is necessary because it contains new insights that are not available from a static perspective alone. Moreover, the two approaches combined provide a new perspective that makes sense to apply because political occurrences have both causal structural features (statics) and time dependence (kinematics).

---

[3] The term "epoch" is used by Feller (1968: 73), following J. Riordan.

2 *New areas of political inquiry.* The taxonomy also helps identify new models and principles for explaining political events that thus far have remained unexplored. For example, as I show later in this chapter, little research has been conducted using "cut set" analysis, a static modeling approach that I discuss in section 7.3. Also, little analysis has been done with nonlinear kinematic models (section 7.4). The overwhelming effort in political science thus far has been mostly on first-order static models, and even those have not been fully investigated to understand many basic properties of political uncertainty. This taxonomy – like the earlier taxonomy for macropolitics (section 4.2.1, figure 4.1) – is based on the form of the event function and provides an organizing framework for understanding a variety of forms of uncertainty involved directly in the occurrence of political events.

3 *Substantive political nature of the event function.* The two-level event function is well suited for theoretical purposes because it yields a viable and fruitful taxonomy of political event models. Rather than being based on a purely formal or mathematical (content-free) property – for example, a criterion based purely on the logic connectives – the basic form of the two-level structure (conjunctive–disjunctive versus disjunctive–conjunctive) and its static or kinematic form provide a substantive basis for the classification of political occurrences. In general, the first order addresses theoretical or unobservable causality (events such as "leaders are available to spearhead a collective action effort," or "one of several 'legs' of a deterrence triad is credible"), whereas the second order addresses operational causality ("members of the military leadership force a solution by imposing a curfew," or "the ICBM [intercontinental ballistic missile] strategic nuclear force is credible"), as detailed below (section 7.3.1). A two-level event function is therefore the minimally necessary specification for linking the abstract occurrence of political events to the real world.

4 *Toward a unified theory.* The taxonomy offers a theoretically based system for classifying and possibly unifying previously disconnected analyses of political events – "middle-range theories" (Plano et al. 1982) or "islands of theory" (Guetzkow 1996) – by proposing the four classes in table 7.1. In this chapter I illustrate this claim for some well-known areas of inquiry.

5 *Research programs.* The taxonomy offers a fruitful framework for designing new research programs aimed at investigating unexplored areas of political uncertainty for which causal complexity, intertwined logics, subjectivism, and kinematics intersect. This chapter outlines a set of puzzles that progress from simple statics to complex kinematics in the occurrence of political events.

6 *Policy significance*. From a policy perspective, the taxonomy highlights and ranks different political events that call for different approaches in planning and managing intervention. For example, political events that are governed by kinematic (time-dependent) probabilities require more complex intervention policies than events that are governed by mostly static (constant) probabilities. Alternatively, the policy analyst may want to know the pros and cons of different configurations for implementation (e.g. conjunction–disjunction versus disjunction–conjunction). Thus, public policy can be improved by developing a better understanding of political uncertainty under different static and kinematic conditions.

7.2.2   Progressive problemshifts

Problemshifts along two theoretical directions – the primary causal orders and the role of time – generate special micropolitical principles that shed additional new light on the uncertain occurrence of political events. In the static analysis (section 7.3) I shall decompose events once again into conditional and sequential logic to arrive at a more insightful understanding of the structure of uncertainty for the occurrence (or failure) of political events – an understanding that can be missed by the analysis of sequential logic as just a special case of conditional conjunctive logic. In the kinematic analysis (section 7.4) I shall consider the effect of time-dependent probabilities to derive special principles that explain the evolution of political uncertainty at the micro level. Kinematic principles can also incorporate special features from static analysis, such as several logic orders (section 7.3.1), combined causal logics (sequential and conditional, section 7.3.3), or subjective probabilities (section 7.3.4), which examine the problem of political uncertainty as actors might see it. Statics precede kinematics in understanding the uncertainty of political events.

7.3 Static principles: the structure of political occurrences

Recall the static model for the occurrence of a political event with general form as I have discussed thus far (chapter 6), namely:

$$\mathbb{Y} = \Psi(\mathbb{X}_1, \mathbb{X}_2, \mathbb{X}_3, \dots),$$

where Ψ is the event function and $\mathbb{X}_1, \mathbb{X}_2, \mathbb{X}_3, \dots$ are the causal events. Depending on the specific causal assumptions represented by Ψ, this event model yields a corresponding special principle, with probability model of the general form

$$\mathbf{P}(\mathbb{Y}) = f[\mathbf{P}(\mathbb{X}_1), \mathbf{P}(\mathbb{X}_2), \mathbf{P}(\mathbb{X}_3), \ldots] = f(X_1, X_2, X_3, \ldots),$$

where $X_i = \mathbf{P}(\mathbb{X}_i)$ denotes the probability of the ith causal event.

I now cover four topics from a static perspective: causal ordering, complexity reduction, combined logics, and subjective probabilism. These are treated in order of increasing complexity and generality because each topic also incorporates features of the previous one. For instance, the analysis of combined logics presupposes an understanding of causal ordering and complexity reduction, whereas subjective probabilism is best approached after the other puzzles have been treated in some detail.

7.3.1   Causal orders

The first area of special static micropolitical principles concerns the orders of political complexity to understand uncertainty. The causal order for a given political event refers to the depth of explanatory detail – the degree of causal resolution. As I mentioned earlier, the first two levels of causal order are especially important because these often contain theoretical (first level; unobservable) and empirical (second level; observable) events, as illustrated below. Formally, the causal order is expressed by the argument of the associated event function. Graphically, the causal order refers to the levels of the event tree that visually represent the event function of a political event (e.g. figures 7.1 and 7.2, and other figures in this chapter). In chapter 6, I considered only the first-order causality of political events, as in tables 6.1 and 6.3. The higher-order (deeper) structure of a political event is established in the same way as the first-order structure: by asking "how can or why does this event occur?" and expressing the answer in the formal logic form of an event function Ψ.

A problemshift occurs when Ψ is expressed in a higher-order form, to capture the deeper causal structure that governs political uncertainty – what lies "beneath the tip of the iceberg," so to speak. The next examples illustrate the higher-order causal structure of some of the events I have discussed in the earlier chapters, such as the variety of events in table 6.3. In each case, the structure function of the referent political event ("deterrence works," "a coalition forms," and so forth) is translated into a corresponding event tree that highlights the causal structure and facilitates a better understanding of the event as well as comparisons across events. While the choice of the last level of causal specification is an unsolvable (and arguably philosophical, not scientific) problem of reductionism (Eulau 1969: 131–2), a useful rule that I proposed earlier (chapters 1 and 5) is to develop the causal argument of Ψ to a level where elemental decisional acts and states of nature are encountered. This procedure tends to develop more explicit

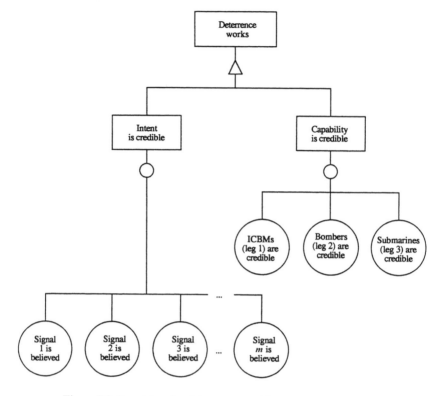

Figure 7.3. Event tree for deterrence working

microfoundations for what is politically relevant, which is a theoretically desirable result.

Example 7.1 (deterrence). Credibility of intent and credibility of capability ($\mathbb{X}_{intent}$ AND $\mathbb{X}_{capability}$) are necessary conditions for deterrence to work (first-order causal event function of $\mathbb{Y}_{deterrence}$), as shown in figure 7.3. By the conjunctive principle (theorem 6.3), therefore:

$$\mathbb{Y}_{det} = \Psi_\wedge(\mathbb{X}_{intent}, \mathbb{X}_{cap}) = \mathbb{X}_{intent} \wedge \mathbb{X}_{cap} \qquad [7.1]$$

$$\mathbf{P}(\mathbb{Y}_{det}) = \mathbf{P}(\mathbb{X}_{intent})\,\mathbf{P}(\mathbb{X}_{cap}) = p_{intent}\,p_{cap}. \qquad [7.2]$$

This is the first-order causal structure of deterrence, composed of mostly theoretical (unobservable) events (the occurrence of credible intent and capability). Typically, these first-order events concerning credibility of intent and credibility of capability emerge from decisions (i.e. events such as $\mathbb{X}_{intent}$ and $\mathbb{X}_{cap}$ are, technically, decisional acts, not states of nature) based on intelligence estimates. In turn, credibility of intent is communicated by issuing redundant signals, while credibility of capability is implemented through the active deployment of redundant "triad legs" (Bendor 1985; Cohen 1981; Landau 1969, 1973). Thus, by applying the disjunctive principle (theorem 6.4), the problem of modeling $\mathbb{Y}_{det}$, Ψ_{det}, and $\mathbf{P}(\mathbb{Y}_{det})$ now shifts to the second-order model given by:

$$\mathbb{Y}_{det} = \Psi_{\wedge}[\Psi_{\vee}(\mathbb{Z}_{intent}), \Psi_{\vee}(\mathbb{Z}_{cap})]$$
$$= (\mathbb{X}_{sig\ 1} \vee \mathbb{X}_{sig\ 2} \vee \mathbb{X}_{sig\ 3} \vee \ldots) \wedge (\mathbb{X}_{leg\ 1} \vee \mathbb{X}_{leg\ 2} \vee \mathbb{X}_{leg\ 3})$$
$$[7.3]$$

$$\mathbf{P}(\mathbb{Y}_{det}) = \mathbf{P}(\mathbb{X}_{sig\ 1} \vee \mathbb{X}_{sig\ 2} \vee \mathbb{X}_{sig\ 3} \vee \ldots)\,\mathbf{P}(\mathbb{X}_{leg\ 1} \vee \mathbb{X}_{leg\ 2} \vee \mathbb{X}_{leg\ 3})$$
$$= [1 - (1 - p_{sig\ 1})(1 - p_{sig\ 2})(1 - p_{sig\ 3})\ldots] \times$$
$$\times\, [1 - (1 - p_{leg\ 1})(1 - p_{leg\ 2})(1 - p_{leg\ 3})]$$
$$= [1 - (1 - Q_{signals})^{\sigma}]\,[1 - (1 - Q_{legs})^{3}],\qquad [7.4]$$

where $Q_{signals}$ and Q_{legs} represent the probabilities of individual signals and individual legs being credible, respectively, and $\sigma = 1, 2, 3, \ldots, m$, represents the number of redundant signals transmitted to the adversary. This is the second-order structure of deterrence, this time composed of mostly empirical (observable) events (weapons systems and signals). In this example the second-order events are viewed more as states of nature than as decisional acts.

Example 7.2 (coalition formation). Consider the event $\mathbb{Y} = $ "a three-member coalition forms." The first-order causal structure of this event can be expressed by the following simple conjunction of decisional acts (see figure 7.4): "member 1 decides to join" AND "member 2 decides to join" AND "member 3 decides to join."[4] The three decisional acts provide the conditions for a coalition to exist among members. Without these key decisions there would not be a coalition. In turn, to address the second-order causal structure we need to ask how each of these events (decisional acts) occurs. In other words, how exactly (i.e. operationally) does each member decide to join? The second-order structure specifies the causes of the first-level events and can be given by an exclusive disjunction based on alternative decisional mechanisms or modes for political choice (recall section 1.2, table 1.1): EITHER "decision mode 1 is used" OR "decision mode 2 is used" OR "decision mode 3 is used" OR ... OR "decision mode m is used," where m

---

[4] Note that, in general, the first-level conjunction need not be conditional, so a sequential logic Boolean AND is not required in figure 7.4. However, if allied decisions are interdependent, then this can be denoted by sequential logic AND connectors to represent conditionality. When sequential and conditional, the probability of the top event is still given by the conjunctive principle (chapter 6).

denotes the variety of decision modes potentially available to each coalition member.[5] From the perspective of uncertainty, a significant feature of the political decision to join the coalition is that such a decision occurs through a variety of choice mechanisms (as those identified earlier in table 1.1), not through a single unique mode. As a consequence there is hyperprobability, which increases the overall probability of coalition formation. The third-order causality would address how these subsequent events occur. For instance, the event "decision mode 3 (by expected utility; table 1.1 in section 1.2) is used" would have a structure function to specify the set of necessary conditions for this mode to occur (i.e. "a set of alternatives [decisional acts] is considered" AND "a set of outcomes is estimated for each alternative," AND ...). Note that each decisional mechanism has hypoprobability because each is based on causal conjunction. The expected utility mechanism, in particular, is based on numerous requirements (i.e. existence of alternatives, preferences, utility estimates, probability estimates, computations, and so on), producing a significant degree of hypoprobability. In turn, each of these events can usually be modeled as the effect of states of nature (unless they are induced by other actors' decisions), at which point the political analysis can rest if no subsequent events are caused by putatively purposive political decisions.

Example 7.3 (opportunity and willingness). In the opportunity-willingness framework pioneered by Harold and Margaret Sprout (1969), and developed more recently by Harvey Starr (1978, 1997; see also Cioffi-Revilla and Starr 1995), political behavior occurs as a result of the uncertain occurrence of willingness to act and opportunity to do so (see figure 7.5). Letting $\mathbb{Y}$ = "political behavior occurs," then the first-order causal structure is given by the following conjunction: "willingness is formed" AND "opportunity exists," without any particular sequence. These events are both unobservable, theoretical constructs. In turn, however, each event occurs in "substitutable" (i.e. equivalent or redundant) modes, according to the

---

[5] The discussion in chapter 1 identified decision making mechanisms generally available to political actors (section 1.2, table 1.1). Information on the precise *type* of coalition (e.g. government cabinet, collective action leadership group, war alliance, and so on) can help determine the probability of each decision mode being used. For example, a deontic logic mechanism (number 2 in table 1.1) may have the highest probability of being used under conditions of perceived moral obligation and the need to establish a high ethical standard of conduct, such as those confronting principled leaders in collective revolutionary action. By contrast, an economic utilitarian mechanism (number 3 in table 1.1) may have a greater probability of being used under conditions allowing for more time and information on the other members' preferences, such as those confronting political parties attempting to form a governmental coalition. War coalitions are often decided under conditions of considerable uncertainty, limited information regarding the specific preferences of adversaries, and past historical record, resulting in a satisficing decisional mode (number 5 in table 1.1).

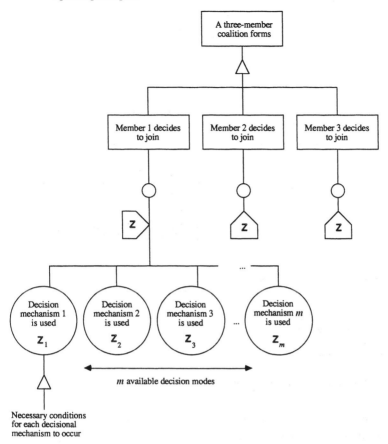

Figure 7.4. Event tree for coalition formation

following second-order causal structure: "willingness is formed" = "one of n substitutable empirical modes of willingness occurs," and "opportunity exists" = "one of m substitutable empirical modes of opportunity occurs." This second-order causal structure is disjunctive and contains observable events. Thus, the United States counter-attacked Iraq ($\mathbb{Y}$) with the support of a broad coalition (willingness) and a multinational military force (opportunity). Neither the actual coalition that formed nor the actual military force that was used were unique for producing the required willingness and opportunity. The first-order causal structure of an opportunity–willingness model of politics is conjunctive, and the second-order causality is disjunctive. Again, note that whereas the first-order events are theoretical, the second-order events are observable. Opportunity modes commonly occur

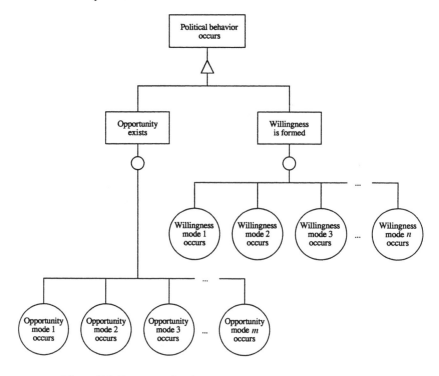

Figure 7.5. Event tree for the opportunity–willingness framework

as states of nature (e.g. availability of resources), whereas willingness modes often occur as decisional acts (e.g. decision to form a coalition).

Example 7.4 (collective action). Consider the occurrence of collective action in any one of its specific contexts (see figure 7.6). Let $\mathbb{Y}$ = "actors take collective action." How does collective action occur? All forms of collective action require some kind of leadership and coordination among leaders and commoners, as pointed out earlier in example 6.16. Thus, the first-order causal structure can be specified as: "Leaders of collective action emerge" AND "followers follow leaders." Note that the AND connector in this case is sequential, since for commoners to follow leaders the latter must first emerge. In turn, the second-order causal structure addresses the next question: how or why would leaders and followers emerge? Namely, under conditions of opportunity and willingness for each type of actor. The event tree in figure 7.6 is specified down to the level of decisional acts and states of nature concerning the multiple (substitutable) modes in which opportunity and willingness actually occur. (Note that decision-making by expected utility is one among several mechanisms, as already highlighted in table 1.1.) The standard game-theoretic analysis of collective action addresses only the first levels, whereas the underlying casual structure gives a precise account for the emergence of complexity.

I draw the following points from the preceding examples. (i) Political events have a deeper causal structure, which lies beneath the first conjunctive or disjunctive events that are commonly addressed by the general principles already examined in chapter 6. (ii) From a political uncertainty perspective, the causal structure reaches as deep as the most elemental decisional acts and states of nature that can be identified as having political significance, obviously while avoiding an infinite regression (individual decisional acts offer a natural resting place for explaining political events). (iii) Most extant theoretical explanations address only the first-order causal structure, a few address the second order, but third-order and deeper structures are addressed only in rare cases, or are simply unexplored. (iv) An event tree can highlight some important qualitative features, such as bottlenecks, cycles, symmetries, and so on, that are not apparent otherwise, and not even so clearly in the event function Ψ. (v) The event tree for the occurrence of two or more empirically distinct political events can show a set of important similarities and differences that might otherwise go unnoticed. For example, from the event tree structures in figures 7.1 and 7.3, it is immediately apparent that the essence of deterrence reduces to a special case of the willingness–opportunity model, an idea worth exploring. In turn, the opportunity–willingness model is a special case of the conjunction–disjunction case (figure 7.1), for the special case where $n = 2$ necessary conditions and an unequal number of sufficient modes. Therefore the conjunctive–disjunctive structure is common to both deterrence and willingness–opportunity. Similarly, the analysis of collective action (example 7.4, figure 7.6) highlighted important causal properties – e.g. hypoprobability of individual decisional mechanisms, of leaders and followers emerging, of overall collective action occurring; hyperprobability of opportunity and willingness for both leaders and followers; causal symmetries down to at least four causal levels; and so on – that have been previously unknown in the extant game-theoretic approaches that acknowledge alternative solutions to collective action problems (Lichbach 1996: 19–21; Sandler 1992: 58–61; Taylor 1987: 21–30). These and other aspects can be investigated further.

The variety and complexity of political events in the real world – a diversity that is arguably only remotely exemplified by the relatively simple event trees in figures 7.2–7.6 – is too rich to explore in toto. Special theoretical principles are needed to reduce this complexity to a smaller class of important structures, which can give rise to canonical variations in the empirical world. The principles that follow apply to the two symmetric cases of second-order probabilistic causality: conjunction–disjunction (similar to examples 7.1, 7.2, and 7.3) and disjunction–conjunction (alternative decisional mechanisms in each example).[6] As I argued earlier, the first two causal levels are important because quite often the first level applies to a set of theoretical, unobservable causes, whereas the latter level often refers to empirical, observable events in the form of decisional acts or basic states of nature.

Political events that occur by conjunction–disjunction. The following principles govern the class of political events that occur, endure, or fail by first-order conjunction and second-order disjunction. The general event tree for this class was shown in figure 7.1.

Theorem 7.1 (conjunctive–disjunctive principle). *A political event that occurs by first-order n-degree conjunction and second-order m-degree disjunction, with general event function given by*

$$\mathbb{Y} = \bigwedge_{i=1}^{n} \left(\bigvee_{j=1}^{m} \mathbb{Z}_j \right) \tag{7.5}$$

and event tree as in figure 7.1 has probability given by the equation

$$\mathbf{P}(\mathbb{Y}) = \{1 - [1 - \mathbf{P}(\mathbb{Z}_j)]^{\Gamma}\}^{\Theta} \tag{7.6}$$

$$= [1 - (1 - Q)^{\Gamma}]^{\Theta}, \tag{7.7}$$

where Q denotes the probability of the Γ sufficient modes $\mathbb{Z}_j$ ($\Gamma = 1, 2, 3, \ldots, m$) and Θ denotes the number of necessary events for $\mathbb{Y}$ ($\Theta = 1, 2, 3, \ldots, n$).

Note that the uncertainty of a conjunctive–disjunctive political event is affected by both hypoprobability and hyperprobability. Deterrence (figure 7.3), coalition formation (figure 7.4), world politics based on opportunity and willingness (figure 7.5), and the emergence of leaders and followers in collective action situations (figure 7.6, below events $\mathbb{L}$ and $\mathbb{F}$), are political areas governed by this special principle. The first-order causes make the event difficult, so to speak, because the event has to meet a set of requirements. This is caused by hypoprobability. However, the second-order conditions facilitate occurrence because of the alternate modes available. This is caused by hyperprobability.

The natural puzzle that comes from this mixed situation concerns the

---

[6] The reader may wish to derive parallel special principles for the pure cases of second-order conjunction and disjunction, including sensitivity and dominance theorems.

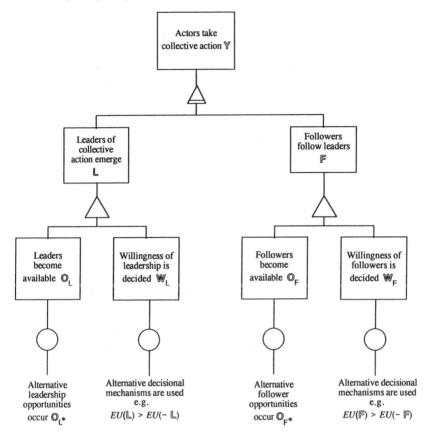

Figure 7.6. Event tree for occurrence of collective action

differentiated dependence of the probability of a conjunctive–disjunctive political event with respect to the probability of the alternate modes, to the number of modes, and to the number of necessary conditions (the independent variables in equation 7.7). The following principles address these properties.

Corollary 7.1 (dependence of a conjunctive-disjunctive political event on the probability of alternate modes Q). *The rate of change in the probability of a conjunctive–disjunctive political event with respect to a change in the probability of the second-order sufficient or redundant events Q is given by the expression:*

$$\frac{\partial \mathbf{P}(\mathbb{Y})}{\partial Q} = \Theta \Gamma (1 - Q)^{\Gamma - 1} [1 - (1 - Q)^{\Gamma}]^{\Theta - 1}, \qquad [7.8]$$

which is always positive and greater than 1, so $\mathbf{P}(\mathbb{Y})$ *is concave with respect to* Q.

Corollary 7.2 (dependence of a conjunctive–disjunctive political event on the number of necessary conditions Θ). *The rate of change in the probability of a conjunctive–disjunctive political event with respect to a change in the number of first-order necessary conditions Θ is given by the expression:*

$$D_\Theta \mathbf{P}(\mathbb{Y}) = -(1 - Q)^\Gamma [1 - (1 - Q)^\Gamma]^\Theta, \qquad [7.9]$$

which is always negative, so $\mathbf{P}(\mathbb{Y})$ *is convex with respect to Θ.*

Corollary 7.3 (dependence of a conjunctive–disjunctive political event on the number of alternate modes Γ). *The rate of change in the probability of a conjunctive-disjunctive political event with respect to a change in the number of second-order sufficient conditions Γ is given by the expression:*

$$D_\Gamma \mathbf{P}(\mathbb{Y}) = [1 - (1 - Q)^{\Gamma + 1}]^\Theta - [1 - (1 - Q)^\Gamma]^\Theta, \qquad [7.10]$$

which is always positive and smaller than 1, so $\mathbf{P}(\mathbb{Y})$ *is concave with respect to Γ.*

Informally, the preceding results establish the following basic properties: the probability of any political event that occurs by first-order conjunction and second-order disjunction (i) increases as the probability of alternate modes increases (corollary 7.1); (ii) decreases as the number of necessary conditions increases (corollary 7.2); (iii) increases as the number of alternate modes increases (corollary 7.3); and (iv) although the general qualitative direction of these changes may be intuitive, all the changes occur in nonlinear ways that are not always intuitive. This last claim, in particular, confirms and highlights the potential for surprise in the occurrence of political events.

Given these differentiated effects on the probability of a conjunctive–disjunctive political event, the next natural question regards the exact impact of each effect, a question that has no intuitive answer. Consider the following questions, each of which has immediate theoretical and policy importance:

1 How is deterrence more affected: by increasing the number of legs, by decreasing the overall requirements, or by increasing the credibility of each leg?
2 How is the probability of policy implementation (Pressman and Wildavsky 1973) most affected: by decreasing the implementation stages, or by increasing the number or the probability of the alternate steps taken in implementation? The same question applies to the problem of low

reliability in any multistage political sequential process (recall examples
in table 6.1).

3 How is the endurance and further development of a political system
more effectively enhanced: by reducing its basic operational requirements, by increasing the redundancy of its operations, or by increasing
the probability of its operational performance? These and similar questions are also at the heart of the "size-of-government debate" between
liberals and conservatives.

The answer to this class of questions is established by the following
dominance principle, obtained from the preceding results (corollaries
7.1–7.3):

Corollary 7.4 (dominance principle for a conjunctive–disjunctive political
event). *The probability of a conjunctive–disjunctive political event is most
sensitive to change in the probability Q of the second-order alternate modes,
less sensitive to the number Γ of modes, and least sensitive to the number Θ of
first-order necessary conditions. Formally,*

$$s_Q > s_\Gamma > s_\Theta \qquad\qquad [7.11]$$

in terms of the respective sensitivities (see appendix 4).

Informally, this dominance result establishes that the probability of any
political event that occurs by first-order conjunction and second-order
disjunction is most affected by changes in the probability of the alternate
modes (Q), followed by changes in the number of alternate modes (Γ),
followed by changes in the number of necessary conditions (Θ). Although
the general qualitative direction of each change may have been intuitive,
this ordinal property is not intuitive. This property also explains the
potential for surprise in the occurrence of political events.

In reference to the earlier questions, using the dominance principle:

1 Deterrence is most significantly affected by changes in the probability of
the redundant operational requirements working (Q), followed by
changes in the number of redundant legs in the triad (Γ), followed by
changes in the number of necessary conditions that each triad has to
meet (Θ).

2 The probability of a policy being implemented is most affected by
increasing the probability and then the number of the alternate programs used in implementation, followed by decreasing the number of
implementation requirements. The same solution applies to the problem
of low reliability in any multistage policy implementation process
(examples in table 6.1): the overall probability of implementation is most

critically affected by the probability of the alternate or redundant activities taken to implementation at every level (federal, state, local), followed by the number of redundant activities, followed by the total number of stages in the process.

3 The performance of a political system is most effectively enhanced by increasing the performance probability of the existing basic functions that have redundancy, followed by a reduction in the number of minimally required functions, followed by an increase in the existing redundancy. In terms of the "size-of-government debate," assuming such a debate is captured by this question (the debate is arguably more complex!), it is best to improve the efficiency of existing governmental operations first (by reducing corruption and incompetence, improving the efficiency and education of government officials, and so forth). It is least effective (although effective to some degree) to attempt to reduce the number of basic functions that are needed to maintain the system of government. Increasing the redundancy of government operations lies somewhere in between these two strategies.

Political events that occur by disjunction–conjunction. The following dual principles govern the other class of political events that have first-order disjunction and second-order conjunction. The general event tree for this class was shown in figure 7.2.

Theorem 7.2 (disjunctive–conjunctive principle). *A political event that occurs by first-order m-degree disjunction and second-order n-degree conjunction, with general event function given by*

$$\mathbb{Y} = \bigvee_{j=1}^{m} \left(\bigwedge_{j=1}^{n} \mathbb{X}_i \right)$$ [7.12]

and event tree as in figure 7.2 has probability given by the equation

$$\mathbf{P}(\mathbb{Y}) = 1 - \{1 - [\mathbf{P}(\mathbb{X}_i)]^{\Theta}\}^{\Gamma}$$ [7.13]

$$= 1 - (1 - P^{\Theta})^{\Gamma},$$ [7.14]

where P denotes the probability of the Θ necessary events $\mathbb{X}_i$ ($\Theta = 1, 2, 3, \ldots, n$) and Γ denotes the number of sufficient modes for $\mathbb{Y}$ ($\Gamma = 1, 2, 3, \ldots, m$).

Note that this time the uncertainty of a disjunctive–conjunctive political event is also affected by hypoprobability and hyperprobability, but in reverse order. Policy decisions when alternate mechanisms are available (viz., deontic, utilitarian, incrementalist, and so on), political communication with redundant channels, and similar political events are areas governed by this special principle. In this case the first-order causes make the event likely, so to speak, because it can occur in a variety of modes. This is caused by hyperprobability. However, the second-order conditions make the occurrence difficult, so to speak, because of the requirements that must be met. This is caused by hypoprobability.

Here too, the natural puzzle that comes from this mixed situation concerns the differentiated dependence of the probability of a disjunctive–conjunctive political event with respect to the probability of the necessary conditions being met, to the number of modes, and to the number of necessary conditions (the independent variables in equation 7.14). The following principles address these properties.

Corollary 7.5 (dependence of a disjunctive–conjunctive political event on the probability of necessary conditions P). *The rate of change in the probability of a disjunctive–conjunctive political event with respect to a change in the probability of the second-order necessary conditions P is given by the expression:*

$$\frac{\partial \mathbf{P}(\mathbb{Y})}{\partial P} = \Theta \Gamma P^{\Theta - 1}(1 - P^{\Theta})^{\Gamma - 1} \qquad [7.15]$$

which is always positive and greater than 1, so $\mathbf{P}(\mathbb{Y})$ *is concave with respect to* P.

Corollary 7.6 (dependence of a disjunctive–conjunctive political event on Θ). *The rate of change in the probability of a disjunctive–conjunctive political event with respect to a change in the number of second-order necessary conditions* Θ *is given by the expression:*

$$D_{\Theta}\mathbf{P}(\mathbb{Y}) = (1 - P^{\Theta})^{\Gamma} - (1 - P^{\Theta + 1})^{\Gamma} \qquad [7.16]$$

which is always negative, so $\mathbf{P}(\mathbb{Y})$ *is convex with respect to* Θ.

Corollary 7.7 (dependence of a disjunctive–conjunctive political event on Γ). *The rate of change in the probability of a disjunctive–conjunctive political event with respect to a change in the number of first-order sufficient modes* Γ *is given by the expression:*

$$D_{\Gamma}\mathbf{P}(\mathbb{Y}) = (1 - P^{\Theta})^{\Gamma}\, [1 - (1 - P^{\Theta})^{\Gamma}] \qquad [7.17]$$

which is always positive and smaller than 1, so $\mathbf{P}(\mathbb{Y})$ *is concave with respect to* Γ.

Informally, the preceding results establish the following basic properties: the probability of any political event that occurs by first-order disjunction and second-order conjunction (i) increases as the probability of necessary conditions increases (corollary 7.5); (ii) decreases as the number of necessary conditions increases (corollary 7.6); (iii) increases as the number of alternate modes increases (corollary 7.7); and (iv) although the general qualitative direction of these changes is again intuitive, all these changes occur in nonlinear ways that are not always intuitive.

Given these differentiated effects on the probability of a disjunctive–conjunctive political event, consider the following questions, each with its own theoretical and policy significance:

1 How is political communication most affected: by increasing the number of redundant channels, by decreasing the overall requirements of signal processing within each channel, or by increasing the reliability of each stage in the signal processing requirements?
2 How is the probability of a policy decision increased: by increasing the number of available decisional mechanisms, by increasing the probability of each decisional requirement being met under each particular mechanism, or by decreasing the number of requirements in each mechanism?
3 How is the probability of political integration based on multiple strategies (e.g. top-down federalism, functionalist spillover, mass mobilization, or other common strategies) most directly affected: by increasing the number of strategies, by the integration probability of each strategy, or by the variety of conditions that each strategy must satisfy?

The answer to this class of questions is established by the following dominance principle, obtained from the preceding results (corollaries 7.5–7.7).

Corollary 7.8 (dominance principle for a disjunctive–conjunctive political event). *The probability of a disjunctive–conjunctive political event is most sensitive to change in the probability P of the second-order necessary conditions, less sensitive to the number Γ of modes, and least sensitive to the number Θ of second-order necessary conditions. Formally,*

$$s_P > s_\Gamma > s_\Theta \qquad [7.18]$$

in terms of the respective sensitivities.

Informally, this dominance result establishes that the probability of any political event that occurs by first-order disjunction and second-order conjunction is most affected by changes in the probability of the necessary conditions (P), followed by changes in the number of alternate modes (Γ), followed by changes in the number of necessary conditions (Θ). Although the general qualitative direction of each change was intuitive, this ordinal property is again not intuitive.

I note immediately that this ordinal result parallels the earlier result for the dual principle in the conjunctive–disjunctive mode (corollary 7.4). Therefore the three variables of probability (either P or Q), sufficiency (Γ), and necessity (Θ) affect the occurrence of political events in ways that are ordinally similar, although their exact impact varies considerably qualitatively as well as quantitatively. The probability of the second-order causal events is most important, followed by the number of sufficient conditions, followed by the number of necessary conditions.

In reference to the earlier questions, using the dominance principle:

1′ Political communication is most affected by the reliability of each stage in the signal processing requirements, followed by the number of redundant channels, followed by the number of requirements of signal processing within each channel.
2′ The probability of a policy decision (and also of a willingness decision in a collective action situation; events W_L and W_F in figure 7.6) is mostly affected by changes in the probability of each requirement obtaining within each decisional mechanism, followed by changes in the number of alternative decisional mechanisms, followed by changes in the number of requirements within the individual decisional mechanisms.
3′ Political integration based on multiple strategies is most directly affected by changes that increase the integration probability of each individual strategy, followed by the number of alternative strategies being actively pursued, followed by the variety of conditions that each strategy must satisfy in order to achieve integration.

This concludes my treatment of the special static micropolitical principles for the occurrence of political events, as given by first-order and second-order causal events. Additional principles can be derived by considering third- and higher-order events (down to decisional acts and basic states of nature), as is sometimes useful for understanding political events from the perspective of their deeper causal structure – for example, for understanding collective action when the fourth level causes are those at the bottom of figure 7.6. These special principles will in turn provide foundations for the next problemshifts, just as these were obtained from the general principles introduced in chapter 6.

7.3.2   *Reduced political complexity*

The preceding set of special static micropolitical principles addressed some relatively simple situations of political uncertainty for which the events in question lacked significant complexity, particularly in the deep structure of several causal orders. A second area of special static micropolitical principles that I analyze concerns the reduction of political complexity to understand uncertainty when analyzing deeper causal structures. I explore this topic by first presenting the basic concepts and then illustrating the reduction of political complexity in the political system modeled by Harold Lasswell and Abraham Kaplan (Lasswell and Kaplan 1950).

Critical modes and deepest causes. How important are communications channels for maintaining political performance in a polity? Which are the critical ways (failure modes or occurence modes) in which a political system can fail? These critical modes for occurrence or for failure refer to key sequences or combinations that lead to a given political event. Here I derive some qualitative results that provide insights for political systems that operate with a complex structure, as most of them do in the real world. These results can be generalized to the occurrence or failure of complex political events – not necessarily systems in a strict sense – with many levels of causation and different combinations of conjunction and disjunction leading down to decisional acts and elemental states of nature.

A theoretically equivalent way to investigate critical modes is to consider the event tree of a particularly complex political occurrence, and then ask questions such as the following. Is it possible to rigorously derive a logically equivalent tree that is simpler than the original complicated tree? For example, given the event tree for the endurance of a political system and several causal layers of other events beneath, which are the critical failure modes? Conversely, given a tree for the occurrence of a political event, which are the dominant modes of failure? What is the effect of dependent or mutually exclusive events? How can different political events be compared with regard to their occurrence modes? Which are the "critical paths" in a complex political occurrence? How do we discover these?

In the following example the critical modes for occurrence and failure are obvious because the political event is simple. I use this example because its simplicity highlights some properties that are essential for understanding significantly more complicated political occurrences.

Example 7.5 (coalition failure). Consider a three-member political coalition with members A, B, C, where each member is considered to be pivotal. The event "the coalition endures ($\mathbb{Y}$)" occurs when "A provides support ($\mathbb{A}$)" AND "B provides support ($\mathbb{B}$)" AND "C provides support ($\mathbb{C}$)." Suppose in turn that $\mathbb{A}$ occurs when *either* A will join with B and C for domestic reasons (event $\mathbb{D}$), *or* when A will coalesce with B and C because of fear of some other actor(s) in the system (event $\mathbb{E}$). In other words, member A has two separate motivations for adhering to the coalition, a common situation. In this case, using logic notation,

$$\mathbb{Y} = \mathbb{M}_1 + \mathbb{M}_2, \qquad \text{(by the equivalence rule)} \qquad [7.19]$$

where

$$\mathbb{M}_1 = \mathbb{B} \wedge \mathbb{C} \wedge \mathbb{D} \text{ and } \mathbb{M}_2 = \mathbb{B} \wedge \mathbb{C} \wedge \mathbb{E}. \qquad [7.20]$$

Therefore, the coalition will be maintained in only two modes, $\mathbb{M}_1$ and $\mathbb{M}_2$, as in equation 7.20. Formally, these two modes define what is called the path set for the occurrence of $\mathbb{Y}$. (When the modes represent failure events then this is called a cut set.) To maintain the coalition it is therefore sufficient to obtain $\mathbb{B}$ AND $\mathbb{C}$ AND $\mathbb{D}$ OR $\mathbb{E}$. The path set of $\mathbb{Y}$ is represented using the standard notation:

$$\begin{Bmatrix} \mathbb{BCD} \\ \mathbb{BCE} \end{Bmatrix} \qquad [7.21]$$

The preceding ideas can be extended to any political event that has a specified event structure. Note that the occurrence modes in the path set of a political event (or in the cut set for a failure) represent mutually exclusive conjunctions. However, these are not necessarily independent. Qualitatively, one can think of these modes as "alternative scenarios" for the occurrence of a political event because the alternative scenarios commonly describe multiple or substitutable ways in which a political occurrence may happen. In addition, every event tree has a unique path set. The general form of a path set is therefore governed by the disjunction–conjunction principle (theorem 7.2) as it applies to exclusive disjunction at the first causal level.

Case study: political failure in a Lasswell–Kaplan polity. In general, the composition of the separate sets of events that are contained within the path set for a political occurrence, such as for the sets $\mathbb{BCD}$ and $\mathbb{BCE}$ in example 7.5, may not be readily apparent from plain inspection of an event tree. This is obviously true when the tree is large, or is given by a complex event function, or when the causes include some events that appear more than once (called common causes). For example, in a system of public administration for the implementation of governmental policy, communications failures, as well as miscalculations of resources, incompetence, corruption, fraud, and other common recurrences in bureaucratic systems may occur at many junctures. Most political events of interest have this characteristic of being affected by common causes.

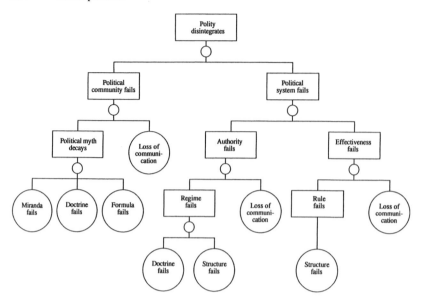

Figure 7.7. Event tree for polity disintegration in a Lasswell–Kaplan system

To understand how the preceding ideas are used to derive the causal essence of a complex political event, consider the occurrence of failure in a large political system such as the Lasswell–Kaplan (1950) framework, one of the few polity models to specify conditions for maintaining political performance.[7] Lasswell's (1935, 1936) pioneering interest in the emergence of political complexity (Eulau 1969, 1996) also makes this model of the political system particularly appropriate for the investigation of uncertainty. Few other models are as detailed and explicit in terms of operating conditions. Also, as I will show, the reconstructed Lasswell–Kaplan system that emerges from this analysis suggests new lines of investigation beyond those explored by the original researchers.

A close study of the complicated framework described in *Power and*

---

[7] Similar analyses can be carried out for other models of the political system, such as those developed by David Easton (1965, 1979), Samuel N. Eisenstadt (1993), Talcott Parsons (1969), or Morton A. Kaplan (1957). The case of the Lasswell–Kaplan model was suggested to me by Richard L. Merritt some years ago as a challenging test for the application of the special logic principles. Merritt trained under Harold Lasswell and used the Lasswellian framework extensively. The Lasswell–Kaplan framework described in *Power and Society* (Lasswell and Kaplan 1950) played an influential role in the development of contemporary political theory as one of the first systematic propositional inventories (Finifter 1983, 1993). According to Almond (1990: 301), "among its noteworthy contents was the elaborated version of Lasswell's classification of base values."

Society yields a causal structure consisting of at least four levels, as shown in figure 7.7. The top event is "polity disintegrates" ($\mathbb{Y}$) and, following the standard convention (see appendix 4), the primary events that define the tree's resolution are denoted by circles. Accordingly, in the Lasswell–Kaplan framework a polity functions when it is able to maintain in good order both its political community and its political system, otherwise the polity experiences failure.[8] Below these first-order causal events are many other events that also occur by disjunction. An interesting feature of this tree is that several events occur more than once, as common causes of political disintegration: "loss of communication," "structure fails," and "doctrine fails." How does the existence of common causes affect political failure in this complicated framework? How sensitive is the probability of polity endurance to changes in any of the probabilities of the primary events? Questions like these and others are important for understanding how a political system works – the Lasswell–Kaplan system, along with others as well – but the complexity of the framework, as shown in figure 7.7, prevents any straightforward answers. To derive the necessary political principles for this, let:

$\mathbb{Y}$ = "polity disintegrates"
$\mathbb{B}$ = "political community fails"
$\mathbb{C}$ = "political myth decays"
$\mathbb{D}$ = "miranda fails"
$\mathbb{E}$ = "formula fails"
$\mathbb{F}$ = "political system fails"
$\mathbb{G}$ = "authority fails"
$\mathbb{H}$ = "regime fails"
$\mathbb{I}$ = "doctrine fails"
$\mathbb{J}$ = "effectiveness fails"
$\mathbb{K}$ = "loss of communication"
$\mathbb{L}$ = "rule fails"
$\mathbb{M}$ = "structure fails"

The preceding events and their symbols comprise all those shown in figure 7.7. First, note that $\mathbb{B} = \mathbb{C} + \mathbb{K}$. However, $\mathbb{C} = \mathbb{D} + \mathbb{I} + \mathbb{E}$, so

$$\mathbb{B} = \mathbb{D} + \mathbb{I} + \mathbb{E} + \mathbb{K}. \qquad [7.22]$$

Now consider how the political system fails, $\mathbb{F}$. One way is by $\mathbb{G}$, which in turn is an event that occurs by $\mathbb{H} + \mathbb{K}$. But also $\mathbb{H} = \mathbb{I} + \mathbb{M}$, so

---

[8] See Lasswell and Kaplan (1950) for the definitions of terms such as "polity," "miranda," "formula," and so forth. The reader can assume that each term is well defined and distinct; otherwise, any attempt to take the Lasswell–Kaplan framework seriously would be unwarranted.

$$\mathbb{G} = \mathbb{I} + \mathbb{M} + \mathbb{K}. \tag{7.23}$$

The other way in which $\mathbb{F}$ occurs is by $\mathbb{J} = \mathbb{L} + \mathbb{K}$. But also $\mathbb{L} = \mathbb{M}$, so

$$\mathbb{J} = \mathbb{M} + \mathbb{K}. \tag{7.24}$$

From equations 7.23 and 7.24, it immediately follows that

$$\begin{aligned}
\mathbb{F} &= \mathbb{G} + \mathbb{J} \\
&= \mathbb{I} + \mathbb{M} + \mathbb{K} + \mathbb{M} + \mathbb{K} \\
&= \mathbb{I} + \mathbb{M} + \mathbb{K}
\end{aligned} \tag{7.25}$$

after reducing $\mathbb{M}$ and $\mathbb{K}$ by the identity rule. Finally, since $\mathbb{Y} = \mathbb{B} + \mathbb{F}$, substituting equations 7.22 and 7.25 into the parts of the top event yields

$$\mathbb{Y} = \mathbb{D} + \mathbb{E} + \mathbb{I} + \mathbb{K} + \mathbb{M}. \tag{7.26}$$

Accordingly, since equation 7.26 shows no conjunctions for the top event $\mathbb{Y}$ to occur, it follows that the set of critical modes (path set) for this seemingly complicated framework is simply:

$$\left\{ \begin{matrix} \mathbb{D} \\ \mathbb{E} \\ \mathbb{I} \\ \mathbb{K} \\ \mathbb{M} \end{matrix} \right\}. \tag{7.27}$$

Therefore, a Lasswell–Kaplan polity disintegrates in any of these five modes, a conclusion that is nowhere stated in *Power and Society*.[9] A further important implication of this result is that we can now prune the original tree that was derived from the original narrative (figure 7.7) and construct a new tree that contains essentially the same causal structure, expressed in the more parsimonious form of the path set (figure 7.8).

To conclude this analysis of the Lasswell–Kaplan framework, the probability of polity disintegration is given by

---

[9] I suspect that neither Lasswell nor Kaplan realized this result; otherwise, it is difficult to imagine why the framework in *Power and Society* was stated in such a complicated way. Of the two scholars, Kaplan certainly had the necessary background in formal logic (he was a philosopher by training), and this at least in principle could have allowed him to derive similar results, had he tried.

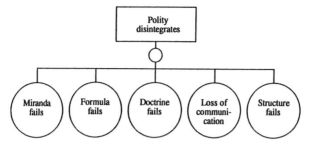

Figure 7.8. Reconstructed event tree for polity disintegration in a Lasswell–Kaplan system

$$\mathbf{P}(\mathbb{Y}) = 1 - [1 - \mathbf{P}(\mathbb{D})]\,[1 - \mathbf{P}(\mathbb{E})]\,[1 - \mathbf{P}(\mathbb{I})] \times$$
$$\times [1 - \mathbf{P}(\mathbb{K})]\,[1 - \mathbf{P}(\mathbb{M})], \qquad\qquad [7.28]$$

which is a special case of the general disjunctive principle (theorem 6.4) for $\Gamma = 5$ alternate modes. As such, polity disintegration in the Lasswell–Kaplan framework is strongly hyperprobable, meaning that disintegration is more probable than even the most likely of the five failure modes, regardless of which one that may be. For example, assuming each critical mode is "unlikely" to occur, or $Q \approx 0.2$, we get $\mathbf{P}(\mathbb{Y}) = 0.67 \approx$ "likely or close to certain," which is not an intuitive inference from each mode being merely "unlikely."[10] None of this deeply embedded instability nor other results that explain political uncertainty seem apparent in *Power and Society*.

Finally, the reconstructed event tree in figure 7.8 suggests questions concerning the occurrence of each individual disintegration mode. For example, how does miranda fail? How is communication lost? Are these events decisional acts or states of nature? Questions such as these and others have not previously been addressed from the political uncertainty perspective.

The same principles of complexity reduction can be applied to other complicated frameworks to derive those truly critical events that may be embedded deeply within the causal structure. When the event function or the tree of a political event contains one or more common causes (as for the Lasswell–Kaplan polity and others), it is important to carry out the reduction of complexity because common causes generally affect a top event in *stronger* ways than other presumably "unique" events in the causal structure.

[10] The verbal values of probability are translated using the semantic equivalents derived by Barclay, Beyth-Marom, and others, reported by Maoz (1990: 254). See also table 7.2. In section 7.3.4, I discuss verbal values of probability in greater detail.

In designing a political system or in planning a political event, it is desirable to avoid as much as possible the presence of common causes. Some measures for ensuring that common causes do not arise or for minimizing their effects when they are inevitable include diversifying resources (if one resource is lost not all events are affected), increasing security (not telling the left hand what the right is doing), separating procedures (increasing redundancy), isolating some critical events (making them causally independent), and other design strategies. The theoretical reason why these measures are effective and commonly used is that they tend to significantly reduce the propagation of problems in the causal structure of a political event.

7.3.3   Combined logics

So far I have examined the principles for mixed causality for up to two orders (section 7.3.1) and the principles for reducing complexity for up to any order (7.3.2). A third area of special static micropolitical principles concerns the combination of sequential and conditional logics. As reminded by the epigraph at the beginning of this chapter, politics is as much about the past as about the present and the future, so the logics of politics must somehow be unified by uniform principles capable of capturing this duality and increasing our understanding of political uncertainty.

Conditional–sequential combination. To approach the conditional–sequential problem, consider the combined event tree illustrated in figure 7.9. Given a conditional event function Ψ_C for the political event Y,

$$Y = \Psi_C(\{X_i\}), \tag{7.29}$$

where the argument of Ψ_C is of whatever form (conjunction or disjunction), one can model the sequential causality of events in the argument of Ψ_C to obtain the general conditional–sequential form

$$Y = \Psi_C[\Psi_{Sj}(\{X_{ij}\})], \tag{7.30}$$

where i and j are indexes that denote the conditional and sequential causal events in the argument of Ψ_C and Ψ_{Sj}, respectively. For example, for n conditional requirements for a candidate to win an election (such as by conjunctive successes in winning the support of voters across a spectrum of issues), a sequential event function Ψ_{Sj} is used to model the occurrence of each requirement as the outcome of a sequential branching process (how each form of support is secured). Similarly, for n conditional requirements for conflict to occur (such as by disjunctive failures of deterrence, fear, miscalculation, plain aggression, or some other), a sequential event func-

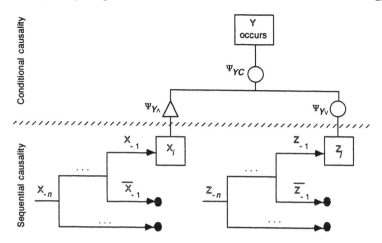

Figure 7.9. Conditional political causality (upper part) with embedded sequential causality (lower part)

tion Ψ_{sj} models the occurrence of each requirement as the outcome of a sequential branching process (how each cause of conflict originates). The event function 7.30 captures the idea of a political event caused by a set of prior causes, each of which is one among several possible outcomes in the process of other prior developments.

This way of combining logics embeds a sequential logic process within each causal event in the argument of a conditional logic structure. In this case the probability of the referent political event is given by the usual principles, namely conjunctive and disjunctive principles for the conditional portion first, followed by the sequential principles needed for each conditional event. Principles for dependence and sensitivity similar to the earlier corollaries can also be derived for this combined logic structure, following the procedures employed earlier.

Sequential–conditional combination. Conversely, consider figure 7.10, the dual political situation of figure 7.9. Given a sequential event function Ψ_s for the occurrence of a political event $\mathbb{Y}$,

$$\mathbb{Y} = \Psi_s[\mathbb{X}_{-1}, \mathbb{X}_{-2}, \ldots, \mathbb{X}_{-n+1}, \mathbb{X}_{-n}], \qquad [7.31]$$

there exists a conditional event function Ψ_c for each event in the argument of Ψ_s:

$$\mathbb{Y} = \Psi_s[\Psi_{cj}(\{\mathbb{X}_{ij}\})], \qquad [7.32]$$

where j indexes the sequential events $\mathbb{X}_{-n}, \mathbb{X}_{-n+1}, \ldots, \mathbb{X}_{-2}, \mathbb{X}_{-1}$, in the

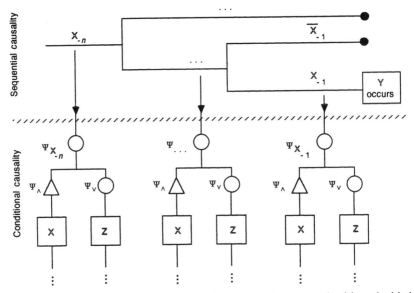

Figure 7.10. Sequential political causality (upper part) with embedded conditional causality (lower part)

argument of Ψ_{Cj}. For example, given the sequential logic Ψ_S of policy enactment in figure 6.1 (the sequential political process: $\mathbb{A} \to \mathbb{B} \to \mathbb{C} \to \mathbb{D}$), a conditional logic event function Ψ_C can be developed for each of the individual requisite events $\mathbb{A}$, $\mathbb{B}$, $\mathbb{C}$, and $\mathbb{D}$ in the process of policy production. Similarly, given the sequential logic Ψ_S of conflict onset in figure 6.2 (the escalatory sequence to civil or international war: $\mathbb{A} \to \mathbb{B} \to \mathbb{C} \to \mathbb{D}$), the conditional event function Ψ_C can be developed for each of the individual prewar events in the process of escalation toward war.

This way of combining logics embeds (or "hangs") a conditional causal structure onto each event in the argument of a sequential logic branching process. In this case the probability of the referent political event is also given by the usual principles, namely the sequential principles for the sequential branching portion first, followed by the conjunction and disjunction principles needed for each individual sequential event. Principles for dependence and sensitivity similar to the earlier corollaries can also be derived for this combined logic structure, following the same procedures used before.

A political event expressed by combined logics (such as the cases of policy production, war onset, or others) will almost inevitably give rise to a more complicated event function and corresponding event tree. Consequently, the event will also have a more complicated probability equation, although the same principles will remain valid and applicable. In particular, the presence of common causes (e.g. the need to form coalitions in the policy process, or the occurrence of misperception on various occasions on the road to war) requires the application of reduction principles to obtain critical modes discussed in section 7.3.2.

Other assumptions about the combined logic of political events can generate other problemshifts and results (theorems and corollaries). Conditional and sequential explanations of politics support each other – through dual principles – and combine to provide a better understanding of political uncertainty. The resulting models of $\Psi(\mathbb{Y})$ and $\mathbf{P}(\mathbb{Y})$ – which explain political events and their probabilities, based on both logics – are richer and more insightful than single-logic models.

7.3.4   *Subjective probabilism*

Like most individuals, neither decision makers nor scholars have an exact command of probabilistic calculations, unless these are assisted by rigorous procedures. The social science field of subjective uncertainty and prospect theory (Kahneman and Tversky 1979, 1982; Levy 1992; Tversky and Kahneman 1974, 1981) attests to this feature of the real world. The implications of subjective probabilism for politics are important, particularly when incorporated with the principles of political uncertainty. Perceptions often define reality and the reverse is rather uncommon. Even fairly marked phenomena, such as hypoprobability and hyperprobability, are not easily recognized as real-world features. What is the effect of subjective probabilism on political uncertainty? How do these principles operate when subjective – rather than objective or quantitative – probability values are used? My discussion in this section is based on the claim that political actors and analysts alike often use subjective probabilities and therefore any realistic approach to a theory of political uncertainty must establish some links in this area. However, I recognize that a full treatment of these aspects would require a more lengthy analysis. What follows merely attempts to begin to lay some foundations.

There are at least two ways to introduce subjective elements into a theory of political uncertainty to derive additional results, particularly about the perception of political occurrences: using subjective estimates of probability values from prospect theory and using verbal probability values from experimental semantics. I call these prospect probabilities and verbal probabilities, respectively.[11]

---

[11] Other intriguing implications of subjectivism and perceptions for political uncertainty can also be explored through the application of power functions due to Eisler (1976), Stevens (1951), and others discussed in Bittinger (1976: 360–1).

Prospect probabilities. Research results from prospect theory, particularly the Kahneman–Tversky experimental curve (figure 7.11), can be used to transform objective probability values into subjective probability estimates and then examine the results of the probability of a political event in the light of the standard principles and concepts derived thus far. As illustrated in figure 7.11, the experimental function for objective and subjective values of probability, the function $S(P)$, has the following properties: (i) all subjective values are greater than the objective values (individuals tend to overestimate) for low levels of objectively unlikely events ($p < 0.3$); (ii) all subjective values are smaller than the objective values (individuals tend to underestimate) for objectively moderate to high probability events ($p > 0.3$); (iii) the misperception is greatest for the lowest values of objective probability (as $p \to 0^+$) and for mid-range values of objective probability ($0.5 < p < 0.75$); and (iv) the function is not well behaved for extreme values of objective probability that mean either impossibility (0, 0) or certainty (1, 1). The diagonal line between the point of impossibility (0, 0) and the point of certainty (1, 1) represents an ideal function with perfectly correct estimation, in other words, $S(\mathbb{Y}) = P(\mathbb{Y})$ exactly.

To illustrate some possible relationships between my theory of political uncertainty and the prospect probability of political events, without any attempt to provide an exhaustive treatment, consider the case of deterrence stability.

Example 7.6 (prospect probabilities and deterrence stability). Consider a deterrence system based on first-order conjunction, as is common to model such systems (table 6.3). The probability of a highly likely event (even when the event in question may be a deterrence-related disaster, such as failure in command and control) is underestimated, whereas the probability of a very improbable event (such as a pre-emptive enemy strike "out of the blue") is overestimated. As shown in figure 7.11, the estimate for the latter may be off by as much as a factor of 10.

The implications of prospect probabilities for a proper understanding of hypoprobability in deterrence threats (or compellence, the dual phenomenon) remains mostly unexplored (Cioffi-Revilla 1989). For instance, little is known about the link between these cognitive phenomena and the prevention of overt violent conflict (the main goal of deterrence). The confirmed existence of prospect probabilities suggests that the net effect of hypoprobability must vary depending on the level of probability with respect to the threshold $p \approx 0.25$. Because decision makers overestimate in the range (0, 0.25), hypoprobability is greatest in this interval and increases as a power function as $p \to 0^+$ (see figure 7.11). Conversely, the effect is less pronounced (and tends to vanish) in the upper range (0.25, 1.0) because

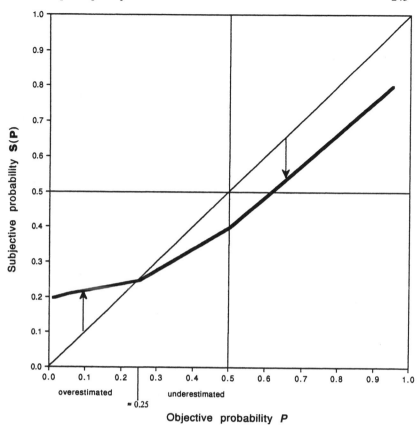

Figure 7.11. Experimental function for objective and subjective probability values

there the subjective underestimation of objectively high probability tends to balance the hypoprobability effect. The middle case in the range (0.5, 0.75) is interesting, because there subjective underestimation reaches its maximum, so the net result can approximate the objective probability values. For a decision maker, therefore, the magnitude of the hypoprobability effect (the variable K in section 6.2.3) varies, depending on the objective value of probability (and on the decision maker's personal estimation function). In any case, the joint occurrence of low and high probability events, in war and peace decisions commonly associated with deterrence, may easily result in miscalculation. The static principles I have presented, and the kinematic principles developed in the next section, provide a new objective baseline for assessing these political phenomena.

Table 7.2. *Semantic equivalents for estimating the subjective probability of political events*

"Certainly, for sure, always"		1.0
"Very high chance, most likely, almost certainly"	0.91–1.00$^-$:	0.95
"High chance, close to certain, or very good chance"	0.71–0.90:	0.80
"Likely, reasonable to assume, one should assume, reasonable chance, it seems to me, can expect, it seems, better than even, we believe, or probable"	0.51 – 0.70:	0.60
"It could be, even-odds, fifty-fifty"		0.50
"Perhaps, may happen, or chance not great"	0.31 – 0.49:	0.40
"Small chance, doubtful, improbable, or unlikely"	0.11–0.30:	0.20
"Very small chance, poor chance, highly unlikely, or little chance"	0.00$^+$–0.10:	0.05
"Impossible, never"		0.00

Source: Prepared by the author, combining data from Beyth-Marom (1982: 267), Maoz (1990: 254), and Wallsten et al. (1986).

The same insights that obtain for deterrence also obtain for other political phenomena belonging to the same class (i.e. all political events that occur by first-order conjunctive structure, including collective action, political systems performance, coalition formation, and others identified in tables 6.1 and 6.3). Similar results can also be derived for other classes of events that occur with other event structures. The main generalization to be drawn from the effect of prospect probabilities in the deterrence case is that the occurrence of very low or moderately high probability events (i.e. those events that are either rare or quite probable) is something that must be carefully considered when subjective probability assessments are involved. When using personal probability assessments to apply the principles of political uncertainty, it is necessary to compensate for over- and underestimation of such values; otherwise, the assessment of the political event will be in error.

Verbal probabilities. Another way to examine the role of subjective probability in understanding political uncertainty is to use the semantic qualitative equivalents of the standard quantitative probability values, also called verbal or lexical probabilities. Table 7.2 provides a scale of such values, based on experimental evidence reported by Maoz (1990: 250–9) and others. The existence of these verbal-to-quantitative equivalences – and other related experimental results that are likely to obtain in the future, this being a significant area of investigation in psychology and cognitive science – clearly is due to its potential use in many applied analyses where exact quantitative estimates of causal probability are impossible or impractical, but verbal or lexical values are available or can be estimated. As shown in the table, the verbal probability values range from political events that are seen as "impossible" or "never" occurring, to those that are "certain," will happen "for sure," or "always" occur.

To illustrate some possible uses of verbal probabilities in this theory of political uncertainty, consider again the case of deterrence.

Example 7.7 (verbal probabilities and deterrence stability). Consider again a deterrence system based on first-order conjunction. For instance, in Wohlstetter's (1959) classical model for an effective retaliatory threat sufficient to deter, $\Theta = 6$ conjunctive events (necessary "hurdles" to be overcome). Using the verbal probability values in table 7.2, this yields the following results for overall deterrence success $\mathbf{P}(\mathbb{Y})$ under different levels of probability P:

1 Simply "likely" or "probable" performance in the necessary operational conditions (i.e. in overcoming the Wohlstetter "hurdles") yields nothing better than an overall "highly unlikely" success (because $0.60^6 = 0.05$).
2 It is only by attaining something like "very high chance" or "almost certainty" that one gets "a high chance" of success (because $0.95^6 = 0.74$).

In the above cases probabilities were reduced from 0.60 to 0.05, and from 0.95 to 0.74, respectively. This strong effect of hypoprobability is just as active when assigning verbal probabilities as it is when working with the standard quantitative values.

Beyond the case of deterrence, some of the most important principles presented thus far yield similar or dual symmetric results when these are solved for semantically equivalent values, rather than the standard numerical probability values. The use of verbal probability values also permits us to explore possible linkages between this theory of political uncertainty and fledging approaches in artificial intelligence and related fields.

7.4 Kinematic principles: the evolution of political occurrences

A general theory of political uncertainty cannot be complete without an analysis of probabilities that change over time and how this affects political occurrences. In the macropolitical part of this theory I already examined how changes in the probability of a political event (e.g. changes in the probability of conflict onset; chapter 2) occur as a result of changes in the hazard forces that operate on a set of actors. I now consider changes that occur as a function of time τ, following the taxonomy of political events outlined in the introduction to this chapter (section 7.2, table 7.1).[12] As I

---

[12] Recall that τ denotes historical, calendrical, or chronological time.

have demonstrated with the dominance principles (corollaries 6.8, 6.12, 7.4, 7.8), variations in the causal probabilities have even greater effect on the overall probability of a political event than changes in structural conditions (necessity Θ or sufficiency Γ). The analysis of temporal variation is a fertile area of exploration that may be viewed as "orthogonal" to the earlier analysis of structural variation (Bartolini 1993).

More specifically, I shall now examine what happens to the probability $\mathbf{P}(\mathbb{Y})$ of a political event $\mathbb{Y}$ when the causal probabilities P and Q change over time, rising or falling. Formally, the class of puzzles I address may be stated as follows: given the time-dependent functions

$$P = P(\tau; a_i) \quad \text{and} \quad Q = Q(\tau; b_j), \qquad [7.33]$$

where a_i and b_j are constants (parameters), what will be the behavior of $\mathbf{P}(\mathbb{Y})$ as a function of τ? Informally, what new insights can be derived about the occurrence of political events when probabilistic causes change over time? The answer to this class of puzzles is found through the application of the general and special principles discussed thus far, with the addition of time-dependent probability functions.

Notationally, the independent variable $\mathbf{P}(\mathbb{Y})$ should now be denoted by an expression such as: $\mathbf{P}[(\mathbb{Y}); \tau]$. However, in the interest of simplicity and without risk of confusion, I leave the time variable τ implicit in the standard expression $\mathbf{P}(\mathbb{Y})$.

The first thing I note is that in the real world, the causal probabilities of $\mathbf{P}(\mathbb{Y})$ can vary according to many patterns (different functions of time) that need obey only a mild condition, namely that probability values must always be in the interval $[0, 1]$. Other than this, the causal probabilities that affect political occurrences can rise, decline, remain constant, oscillate, or even fluctuate randomly (according to the distribution of second-order stochasticity). Interestingly, the main qualitative features of the kinematic principles are largely invariant to these patterns of behavior. Therefore, as detailed below, I limit my analysis to two basic kinematic cases that highlight the more general properties of other situations: (i) the simple case of linear increase as a function of τ in the causal probabilities P and Q, as in a "ramp" toward occurrence; and (ii) a case of "rise and fall," which I model by a simple parabola.

In the next sections, I address the kinematics of political occurrences using first- and second-order causal levels only, as I did earlier in the presentation of static principles (section 7.3). Results for deeper levels can be derived using similar procedures, although the principal patterns that arise from kinematic variation are readily identifiable from the first levels. For each topic I include a case study to illustrate the main results in somewhat more familiar and less abstract contexts.

7.4.1   *First-order kinematics*

General properties. The simplest variation in time is linear. For example, in reference to the probability of coalition formation (or other examples in tables 6.1 and 6.3), this linear variation means that the adhesion probabilities of each pivotal member rise or decline steadily over some time horizon. In the case of war onset (figure 6.1), this linear situation would correspond to the steady increase or decrease in the probability of the events leading to escalation. For policy implementation, this case would mean that the probability of successful implementation at each stage would be rising or declining over time.

In the general linear case the causal probabilities P or Q (independent variables) rise steadily at some constant rate, as in a straight upward ramp.[13] This is the classical case of the "rise," "development," or "emergence" of a political event, as understood by social scientists and historians.[14] Moreover, without loss of generality I shall assume that the increase in the causal probability is from an initial value of 0 (when for some reason the causal events of $\mathbb{Y}$ are impossible, at $\tau_0 = 0$), to a final probability value of 1.0 (when the causal events are *certain*, at $\tau_f = 1.0$). How does the probability of political occurrence, $\mathbf{P}(\mathbb{Y})$, behave during this linear evolution that goes from impossibility to certainty in the causes of $\mathbb{Y}$? Formally, the linear case is based on the following kinematic equations:

$$P(\tau) = a_1 + a_2\tau \quad \text{and} \quad Q(\tau) = b_1 + b_2\tau \qquad [7.34]$$

so

$$P(\tau) = Q(\tau) = \tau \qquad [7.35]$$

when $a_1 = b_1 = 0$ (initial impossibility) and $a_2 = b_2 = 1.0$ (final certainty).

As I have already shown, the first-order causal structure of a political event can be either by conjunction or by disjunction (theorem 6.2). Using the linear kinematic equations 7.34 and 7.35, we obtain the following probability equations for the occurrence of $\mathbb{Y}$:

$$\mathbf{P}(\mathbb{Y}_\wedge) = \tau^\Theta \qquad [7.36]$$

$$\mathbf{P}(\mathbb{Y}_\vee) = 1 - (1 - \tau)^\Gamma \qquad [7.37]$$

for the cases of conjunction ($\mathbb{Y}_\wedge$) and disjunction ($\mathbb{Y}_\vee$), respectively, and $\tau \leq 1$ units of time (days, months, years, or some other).

---

[13] As I discuss below, this analysis also applies for the steady decline in causal probabilities, as in a straight downward incline.

[14] This focus on the "rise," "development," or "emergence" of a political event is shared by the following influential works in different disciplines: Axelrod (1981), Carneiro (1970), Ford (1898), Haas (1982), Huot et al. (1990), McKay and Scott (1983), Merriman (1962), Service (1975), Upham (1990), and Willey (1991).

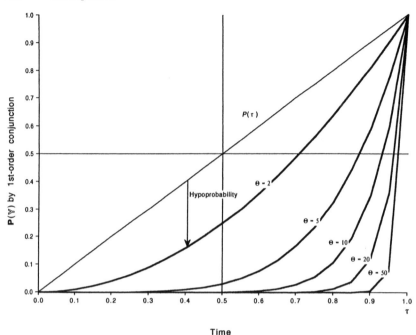

Figure 7.12. Kinematic political occurrence by conjunction

Figure 7.12 illustrates the family of parametric trajectories in the probability $\mathbf{P}(\mathbb{Y}_\wedge)$ for a conjunctive political occurrence (thick curves), as given by equation 7.36, when the causal probabilities P increase linearly (thin diagonal line), as in equation 7.34a. The main qualitative features exhibited by this case can be summarized as follows:

1 *Different probabilistic behaviors.* Although the causal probability P increases linearly, the response (effect) in the probability of the conjunctive political event is to increase curvilinearly (with concavity). In other words, the probabilistic behavior of political events at the two levels (i.e. first-order causes $\mathbb{X}$ and their corresponding effects $\mathbb{Y}$) differs fundamentally throughout the entire time span. The two levels obey different kinematics in the behavior of political uncertainty. This is indicative of "emergent" – as opposed to merely "resultant" – behavior in political complexity (Eulau 1969, 1996; Lasswell 1935, 1936), an important idea which recurs later as well as in chapter 8.
2 *Delay in conjunctive political occurrence.* This cross-level incongruence is fundamental. In practice it means that an observer may well be able to correctly identify and closely monitor the rise in the causes of a given

political event (e.g. in assessing the adhesion probabilities of pivotal allies; the $\mathbb{X}$'s in equation 6.19) and still be genuinely surprised by the delayed timing in the occurrence (the event $\mathbb{Y}$). This is because the causal probability P (rising linearly) always will reach high levels before the probability of the referent political event (rising curvilinearly below the diagonal in figure 7.12). For example, in reference to figure 7.12, halfway through the interval at time $\tau = 0.5$ (center of the graph), the causal probability P has already reached a value of 0.5 (even-odds). However, $\mathbf{P}(\mathbb{Y}_\wedge)$ will not reach such a value until a later time ($\tau' > 0.5$). Therefore, the occurrence of the event $\mathbb{Y}_\wedge$ is delayed relative to the probability of its causes.

3 *Hypoprobability as the cause of delay.* The cause of this delay or asynchrony in the two probabilities, and therefore the discrepancy in the occurrence of causes and effects, is the hypoprobability effect, which always induces a drop in the value of $\mathbf{P}(\mathbb{Y}_\wedge)$ relative to the value of P at each instant of time τ between 0 and 1. This delay in occurrence, and therefore the potential surprise on the part of an observer, is a fundamental property of this case of political uncertainty and cannot be eliminated so long as the first-order structure for the referent political event is conjunctive.

4 *The magnitude of the asynchrony under conjunction.* As illustrated in figure 7.12, the magnitude of the incongruence between the causal probability P and referent event probability $\mathbf{P}(\mathbb{Y}_\wedge)$ is proportional to the number of necessary conditions Θ. Therefore, the larger the number of requirements for deterrence to be credible, or the larger the number of conditions to maintain political performance, or the larger the number of pivotal actors to form a coalition or solve a collective action problem, the greater the gap between the probabilities of the causes and the probability of the referent political event (deterrence working or a coalition forming). Because this incongruence is also proportional to the observed delay in the occurrence of the referent event, this gap is useful to measure. Formally, as can be seen in figure 7.12, the area A_Θ between the linear diagonal trajectory of $P(\tau)$ and the curvilinear trajectory of $\mathbf{P}(\mathbb{Y}_\wedge)$ provides a measure of the asynchrony for a conjunctive political event occurring with Θ necessary conditions. That is,

$$A_\Theta = \left(\int_0^1 P(\tau)\, d\tau \right) - \left(\int_0^1 \mathbf{P}[(\mathbb{Y}_\wedge);\, \tau]d\tau \right) \qquad [7.38]$$

$$= \int_0^1 \tau\, d\tau - \int_0^1 \tau^\Theta\, d\tau$$

$$= 0.5 - 1/(\Theta + 1). \hspace{3cm} [7.39]$$

I note immediately that the behavior of A with respect to the number Θ of necessary conditions is nonlinear (hyperbolic), so as the number of necessary conditions varies, the asynchrony of this political situation (delays in occurrence, incongruent probability values) will vary in nonintuitive ways. Recalling that this is the simplest of cases (linear), it follows that all real world cases involving nonlinear changes in the causal probabilities (P) will result in nonlinear and therefore nonintuitive behavior in the probability of political occurrences [$\mathbf{P}(\mathbb{Y}_\wedge)$].

5 *"Last-minute rush"* to political occurrence. The preceding phenomena can be summarized by something akin to a "last-minute rush" for the referent political event $\mathbb{Y}$ to occur, as seen in figure 7.12 for the pattern of increasingly steep trajectories for the probability of the referent political event (compare this to the steady slope of the causal probability P). Whereas the slope of $P(\tau)$ remains *constant*, the slope of $\mathbf{P}(\mathbb{Y}_\wedge)$ *increases* (i.e. the $\mathbf{P}(\mathbb{Y}_\wedge)$ trajectories are accelerating, since $\partial^2 \mathbf{P}(\mathbb{Y}_\wedge)/\partial\tau^2 > 0$), because the probability of the referent political event has to spring a "last-minute rush" to catch up with $P(\tau)$ at the final point of certainty (1, 1), where the two trajectories intersect.

The preceding analysis is symmetrically valid for the opposite case when the "ramp" is declining, by pivoting the diagonal trajectory in figure 7.12 around the central point (0.5, 0.5). This change in political perspective occurs when the causal probability P drops linearly from a value of 1 (certainty) at $\tau_0 = 0$ to a value of 0 (impossibility) at $\tau_f = 1$, as in a straight downward incline. This is the dual classical case involving the "fall," "decline," or "collapse" of a political situation as understood by social scientists and historians.[15] The above four features remain valid, only now the asynchrony between levels means that the political occurrence will likely cease *sooner* than an observer would imagine by just tracking the trajectory of $P(\tau)$ while disregarding the number of necessary events Θ. This phenomenon too can be a cause of surprise and it is an effect that is not apparent from the simplicity of the underlying causal situation. In the next example I show how this reverse phenomenon works.

Example 7.8 (sudden change in a political system: fall of the Berlin Wall). The dual phenomenon regarding the sudden drop in the probability of a conjunctive political event (the opposite pattern of the "last-minute rush" to occurrence) in spite of a gradual drop (linear) in the causal probability, could well explain the surprising fall of the Berlin Wall. As explained by

[15] See Culbert (1973), Gibon (1946), Gurr (1985), Petrocik (1981), Renfrew (1979), Seton-Watson (1985), Taylor (1962), Weigel (1992).

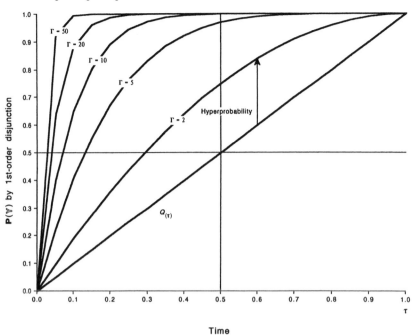

Figure 7.13. Kinematic political occurrence by disjunction

this theory, throughout the Cold War the Berlin Wall (more generally, the iron curtain) had endured because the East German regime had managed to maintain a large set of necessary conditions (conjunctions), such as a strong state, fear of insubordination by the population, little communication with the West, elite compliance with the regime, and other conditions that are commonly necessary for a totalitarian state to survive. (How this was done is also of interest, but constitutes a second-order issue.) However, by the late 1980s such conditions began to erode, so when the probability P of meeting so many conjunctive conditions (five at the very least, according to the Lasswell–Kaplan polity model; see figure 7.8) began to slowly decrease (see the nearly vertical slope of the probability function for high values of Θ) the result was a precipitous drop in the probability of the Wall remaining in place and, consequently, an equally sudden burst in the probability of it collapsing (and with it the East European regime). A diferent (slower) tempo of political change may have occurred had the number of conjunctive conditions been fewer (< 5, according to the Lasswell–Kaplan polity model) or the component probabilities $P(\tau)$ declined at a slower rate. The theory therefore accounts for the observed surprise in the fall of the Berlin Wall and related events.

More generally, the same phenomenon of surprise change occurs every time the endurance of a political event (like the continued existence of the Berlin Wall) is contingent upon the occurrence of many conjunctions and a process of gradual erosion in the causal probabilities begins, no matter how gradual the erosion might be.

The kinematics I have discussed so far pertain to first-order conjunctive political occurrences. The disjunctive case has dual properties. Figure 7.13 illustrates the family of parametric trajectories in the probability $\mathbf{P}(\mathbb{Y}_\vee)$ for a disjunctive political occurrence (thick curves), as given by equation 7.37, when the causal probabilities Q increase linearly (thin diagonal line), as in equation 7.34b. The main qualitative features of this case parallel those discussed earlier but in an opposite sense, and can be summarized as follows:

1 *Different probabilistic behaviors.* Although the causal probability Q increases linearly, the response (effect) in the probability of the disjunctive political event is to increase curvilinearly (this time with convexity). Again, the probabilistic behavior of political events at the two levels (i.e. first-order causes $\mathbb{Z}$ and their effects $\mathbb{Y}$) differs fundamentally throughout the entire time span, confirming that the two levels obey different kinematics in the behavior of political uncertainty. This is again a form of emergent complexity in political uncertainty (Eulau 1969, 1996; Lasswell 1935, 1936).

2 *Anticipation in disjunctive political occurrence.* In this case the practical meaning of the cross-level incongruence is that an observer may again be able to correctly identify and closely monitor the rise in the causes of a given political event (e.g. in the probabilities of redundant policy strategies working; formally, the $\mathbb{Z}$'s in equation 6.20) and still be surprised by the anticipated timing in the occurrence (the event $\mathbb{Y}$). This is because the causal probability Q (rising linearly) always will reach high levels after the probability of the referent political event (rising curvilinearly above the diagonal in figure 7.13). For example, in reference to figure 7.13, halfway through the interval at time $\tau = 0.5$ (center of the graph), the causal probability Q has reached a value of 0.5 (even-odds), but $\mathbf{P}(\mathbb{Y}_\vee)$ had already reached such a value at an earlier time and at this point it is much higher, so the occurrence of the event $\mathbb{Y}_\vee$ is anticipated relative to the probability of its causes.

3 *Hyperprobability as the cause of anticipation.* The cause of the anticipation in the two probabilities, and therefore in the occurrence of causes and effects (asynchrony), is the hyperprobability effect, which always induces a rise in the value of $\mathbf{P}(\mathbb{Y}_\vee)$ relative to the value of Q at each instant of time τ between 0 and 1. This anticipation in occurrence, and

therefore the almost certain surprise by an observer, is again a fundamental property of political uncertainty and cannot be eliminated so long as the first-order structure for the referent political event is disjunctive.

4 *The magnitude of the asynchrony under disjunction.* The magnitude of the incongruence between the causal probability Q and referent event probability $P(\mathbb{Y}_\vee)$ is proportional to the number of sufficient conditions (redundant modes) Γ. Therefore, the larger the number of redundant signals for a political communication to be credible, or the larger the number of causes of political disintegration (recall the reduced Lasswell–Kaplan conditions in section 7.3.2, figure 7.8), or the number of alternative government strategies to achieve policy implementation, the greater the gap between the probabilities of the causes and the probability of the referent political event (communications working or policies being implemented). For example, $\Gamma = 5$ conditions in the reduced Lasswell–Kaplan polity, which produces a highly asynchronous effect in figure 7.13. Because this incongruence is also proportional to the observed anticipation in the occurrence of the referent event, the gap between the probability functions is useful to measure. Similar to the earlier situation, this can be measured by the area A_Γ between the linear diagonal trajectory of $Q(\tau)$ and the curvilinear trajectory of $P(\mathbb{Y}_\vee)$, for a disjunctive political event occurring with Γ sufficient conditions. That is,

$$A_\Gamma = \left(\int_0^1 Q(\tau)\, d\tau \right) - \left(\int_0^1 P[(\mathbb{Y}_\vee); \tau]\, d\tau \right) \qquad [7.40]$$

$$= \int_0^1 \tau\, d\tau - \int_0^1 [1 - (1 - \tau)^\Gamma]\, d\tau$$

$$= 0.5 - 1/(\Gamma + 1), \qquad [7.41]$$

which is isomorphic to the earlier dual result as a function of Θ (equation 7.39), and proves that necessity and sufficiency have the same effect on the asynchrony of first-order kinematics in political occurrences. Note that this result holds true even though the form of the probability equations 7.36 and 7.37 is markedly different, meaning that the magnitude of these temporal effects (delay and anticipation) are invariant with respect to the specific form of probabilistic causality (conjunction or disjunction) and the effects depend exclusively on the degree or complexity (Θ and Γ) of their first order. Also, as before, the behavior of A_Γ, as a measure of occurrence anticipation, is nonlinear (hyperbolic); therefore, as the number of sufficient conditions varies, the asynchrony of this political situation (anticipation, incongruence) will vary in nonintuitive ways. Again, these phenomena are enhanced in real-world political occurrences, where the trajectories of the causal probabilities (Q) will not likely be linear and the resulting probability of the referent political event $[\mathbf{P}(\mathbb{Y}_\vee)]$ will be strongly nonlinear and therefore less intuitive.

5 *"First-instant spring"* to political occurrence. The preceding dual phenomena can be summarized by something akin to a "first-instant spring" for the referent political event $\mathbb{Y}_\vee$ to occur, as seen in figure 7.13 by the pattern of steep trajectories for the probability of the referent political event (compare this to the steady slope of the causal probability Q). Whereas the slope of $Q(\tau)$ remains constant, the slope of $\mathbf{P}(\mathbb{Y}_\vee)$ undergoes an initial "burst" (i.e. now the $\mathbf{P}(\mathbb{Y}_\vee)$ trajectories have decreasing slopes, since $\partial^2\mathbf{P}(\mathbb{Y}_\vee)/\partial\Gamma\partial\tau < 0$), because the probability of the referent political event undergoes an initial "first-instant spring," distancing itself from $Q(\tau)$ after the initial point of impossibility $(0, 0)$, where the two trajectories intersect.

To complete my treatment of this duality, I note that the preceding analysis is symmetrically valid for the case when the "ramp" is reversed, by again pivoting the diagonal trajectory in figure 7.13 around the central point $(0.5, 0.5)$. This change in political perspective occurs when the causal probability Q drops linearly from a value of 1 (certainty) at $\tau_0 = 0$ to a value of 0 (impossibility) at $\tau_f = 1$, as in a straight downward incline. Again, the above four features remain valid, only now the asynchrony between levels means that the political occurrence will likely cease later than an observer would imagine by just tracking the trajectory of $Q(\tau)$ while disregarding the redundancy Γ. This phenomenon too can be a cause of surprise and it is an effect that is not apparent from the simplicity of the underlying causal situation. The next example illustrates how this reverse phenomenon works.

Example 7.9 (resilient change in a political system: endurance of the Castro regime). The enduring resilience in the probability of a disjunctive political event (the opposite of the rapid rise illustrated in figure 7.13) in spite of a gradual linear drop in the causal probability, may explain why Fidel Castro's Communist regime in Cuba has been so resilient to change, more so than the East German regime. As explained by this theory, throughout the Cold War Castro's regime endured because it managed to successfully maintain a large set of redundant structures of totalitarian government (disjunctions), such as a strong military and police state obeying a single party, a ubiquitous condition of fear in the population, effective ideological indoctrination in schools, elite compliance with the regime (among those not in exile), and other conditions. Note that each of these conditions acts to increase the likelihood of satisfying the Lasswell–Kaplan conditions for polity endurance. In a relatively small political system such as that of Cuba, under significantly weaker net international pressure (actually receiving support from European Community members and some Latin American countries), these conditions were to a large extent redundant for maintaining the totalitarian order.[16] (Again, how this was done is also of interest, but represents a second-order issue.) However, by the late 1980s and early 1990s the probability of maintaining such conditions began to erode (e.g. loss of massive Soviet financial subsidy), but when the probability Q of meeting these many disjunctive conditions began to slowly decrease (see the nearly horizontal slope of the probability function for high values of Γ) the result was only a negligible decline in the probability of the regime remaining in power and, consequently, a virtually trivial increase in the probability of the regime collapsing. Again, a different (faster) tempo of political change may have occurred had the number of disjunctive conditions been fewer or the causal probabilities declined at a faster rate. The theory therefore accounts for the observed resilience of Castro's regime. The regime would collapse quickly if the current supports were to evolve from a status of redundancy (as they have been) to one of necessity (as they were in East Germany) – hypoprobability would provide the fundamental cause of collapse. This could occur by increasing the pressure to a level comparable to the pressure that eventually was brought to bear on the East German regime (e.g. increased coordinated pressure through the United States, the Roman Catholic Church, the European Union, and members of the Organization of American States, including Canada and Mexico), in which case most redundancy would vanish and the set of regime-maintenance conditions would become conjunctive and no longer disjunctive. If such a change does not occur, the slow erosion of the causal probabilities will still eventually cause a collapse, but it will take much longer.

---

[16] The reason for viewing the former East German regime as based on a conjunction of stability conditions and the Cuban regime as based on a disjunction is based on the different pressures brought to bear on each regime. In East Germany, with a population many times larger than Cuba's (hence greater revolutionary potential, ceteris paribus) and under relentless political and economic pressure from NATO, the European Community, and the Church, most or all of these regime-maintenance conditions eventually became absolutely necessary (i.e. no longer redundant) for the Communist order not to collapse (conjunction). By contrast, in Cuba, with a much smaller population (hence lower revolutionary potential, ceteris paribus), only hesitant American pressure (versus significant European, Canadian, and Mexican support, with Church acquiescence), several of the regime maintenance conditions remain redundant (disjunct). Formally, East Germany was at one extreme of the v-out-of-m redundancy situation ($v \to 1$ or just a few), whereas Cuba was at the other ($v \to m$ or most).

More generally, the same phenomenon of resilience to change occurs every time the endurance of a political event (such as the continued existence of Castro's regime) is contingent upon the occurrence of many disjunctions and a process of gradual erosion in the causal probabilities begins, no matter how steep the erosion might be.

Case study: rise and fall in the probability of a political event. My analysis has been limited to the class of political situations in which the probability kinematics always move in one direction (monotonic), rising or declining. In addition, the general situation I examined involved only linear change in the causal probabilities, P or Q. I now consider one of the next simplest political cases in first-order kinematics, the situation in which the causal probabilities have a trajectory reminiscent of a process of "rise and fall." This political situation is important – theoretically and practically – because very often causal probabilities such as P and Q obey the "ebb and flow" of other factors, such as economic, technological, social, or demographic conditions whose net effect is indeed a process of rise and fall in the causal probabilities of political occurrences. This is the classical combined case that looks at a complete cycle in the evolution of a political occurrence, a type of analysis that has ancient and established traditions in both social science and history.[17] For example, as popular economic expectations rise and actual economic conditions decline, the probability of new demands on the political process increases (e.g. Russia in the 1990s), sometimes exceding a regime's capacity to maintain governability. However, when living conditions improve rapidly and expectations do not grow as rapidly, the probability of radical political change is decreased or remains low (e.g. the United States in the 1950s).

One of the simplest cases of "rise-and-fall" variation that is also non-linear is shown by the parabolic trajectory in figure 7.14. For example, in reference to the probability of coalition formation (and other examples in tables 2.1 [temporal variables], 6.1, and 6.3), the parabola can be interpreted as the time-path of the adhesion probability of each of the pivotal members – rising, peaking, and declining over the time horizon – while the coalition is in power.[18] Or, in the case of conflict onset (figure 6.1 and the subsequent process of conflict duration and termination), this political situation would correspond to the rise and fall in the probability of the events that cause conflict and its termination. Similarly, for policy imple-

---

[17] See, for example, Adams (1959), Dacey (1970), Dawson (1978), Eisenstadt (1993), Flannery (1972), Hibbert (1980), Kennedy (1987), Marcus (1992), McClelland (1972), Roberts (1993), Shirer (1960), Taagepera (1979), Tapie (1971), Thompson (1954), and Thompson (1985).

[18] In chapters 3 and 4, I provided references to the literature on governmental coalitions. See also the duration variables in table 2.1, which contains cases such as riots, alliances, wars, rivalries, and other macro processes subject to the same principles.

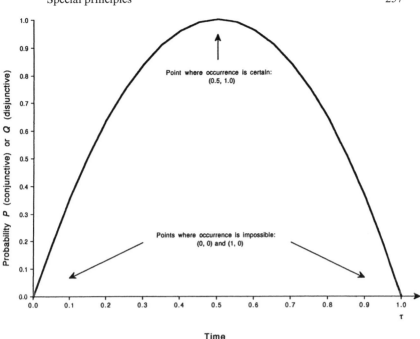

Figure 7.14. Rise and fall in the probability of causal events

mentation as the referent political event, this case would correspond to the rise and fall in the causal probabilities that sustain implementation at various levels of government (federal, state, local) over a given time interval. In general, in a collective action situation, this case corresponds to the rise and fall in the causal probabilities of decisional acts (willingness) and states of nature (opportunities) over a time interval from the rise of the problem to its solution.

In the general parabolic case the causal probabilities P or Q follow a convex trajectory of rise and fall.[19] Moreover, without loss of generality I shall now assume that the rise in the causal probability is from an initial value of 0 (when for some reason the causal events that can produce $\mathbb{Y}$ are impossible, at $\tau_0 = 0$), to a mid-term probability value of 1.0 (when the causal events are certain and $\mathbb{Y}$ actually occurs, at $\tau_m = 0.5$), and finally again to a probability value of 0 (when the causal events are again impossible, at $\tau_f = 1.0$). The entire cycle therefore comprises the three phases of

[19] An analysis similar to this can be derived for the dual opposite case, when P and Q fall and then rise again, as in a concave trajectory. The political interpretation of such a case ($P_0 = 1$, $P_\tau \to 0$, and $P_f = 1$) would correspond to the cycle of cessation and recurrence.

"rise," "endurance," and "decline."[20] How does the probability of political occurrence, $\mathbf{P}(\mathbb{Y})$, behave during the complete evolution that goes from impossibility to certainty and back to impossibility in the causes of $\mathbb{Y}$? Formally, the parabolic case is based on the following general kinematic equations:

$$P(\tau) = a_1 + a_2\tau + a_3\tau^2 \quad \text{or} \quad Q(\tau) = b_1 + b_2\tau + b_3\tau^2 \quad [7.42]$$

which require further political specification to model the rise and fall in causal probabilities P and Q. In reference to the parabola in figure 7.14, the political situation requires that the probabilistic trajectory pass through the following three points that define a "rise-and-fall" process:

(0, 0) : initial impossibility of occurrence
(0.5, 1) : mid-period certainty of occurrence
(1, 0): final impossibility of occurrence

These three points (political conditions) are thus the solutions to the system of simultaneous equations that yields

$$P(\tau) = Q(\tau) = 4\tau - 4\tau^2 \quad [7.43]$$

as the kinematic equation for modeling the rise and fall in political occurrence.

Using the kinematic equation 7.43 for the trajectory of the causal probabilities, we get the following probability equations for the occurrence of $\mathbb{Y}$:

$$\mathbf{P}(\mathbb{Y}_\wedge) = (4\tau - 4\tau^2)^\Theta \quad [7.44]$$

$$\mathbf{P}(\mathbb{Y}_\vee) = 1 - (1 - 4\tau + 4\tau^2)^\Gamma \quad [7.45]$$

for conjunction ($\mathbb{Y}_\wedge$) and disjunction ($\mathbb{Y}_\vee$), respectively.

Figure 7.15 illustrates the trajectories in the probabilities $\mathbf{P}(\mathbb{Y}_\wedge)$ and $\mathbf{P}(\mathbb{Y}_\vee)$ for conjunctive and a disjunctive political occurrences (thick curves for $\Theta = 5$ and $\Gamma = 5$, respectively), as given by equations 7.44 and 7.45, when the causal probabilities P and Q rise and fall (the thinner curve), as in equation 7.43.

[20] The "cyclical" nature of the process I am postulating is only for theoretical purposes and does not imply any constant periodicity. That a rise-and-fall process can be viewed as a cycle only means that the causal probabilities of the political event evolve from low to high and back to low again, as commonly occurs in the real world. Several other functions of time also have unexplored properties that are worth examining for the occurrence of political events. These include, for example, the simple sine function or the hyperbolic secant, as well as more complicated periodic patterns such as the catenary curve, the cycloid, the trochoid, the tractrix, or the witch of Agnesi. I use the parabolic model because it (i) captures the essence of the rise-and-fall process, (ii) is the simplest nonlinear trajectory to justify (smallest number of political assumptions), and (iii) is sufficiently rich to provide insights.

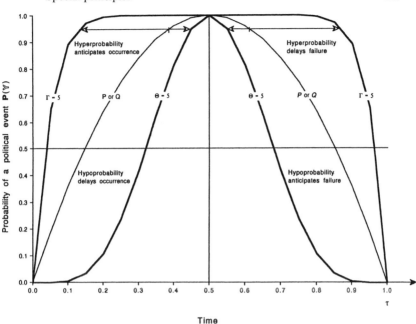

Figure 7.15. Rise and fall in the probability of a political event

The main qualitative features exhibited by this case of parabolic rise and fall essentially replicate, although in somewhat more accentuated form, the features obtained earlier for the linear monotonic case. The effects of hypo- and hyperprobability are clearly visible, as can be seen by the marked asynchronous behavior of the two sets of probability trajectories (emergence).

Beyond the replication of some of the earlier behavior, a new and interesting qualitative feature in these kinematics is the appearance of inflection points in the trajectories of the overall probabilities $P(\mathbb{Y}_\wedge)$ and $P(\mathbb{Y}_\vee)$. Politically, this means that while the causal probabilities undergo a constant deceleration as they peak at the point of certainty (0.5, 1), and later as they accelerate constantly all the way down toward the final point (1, 0), the overall probabilities $P(\mathbb{Y}_\wedge)$ and $P(\mathbb{Y}_\vee)$ undergo a rise and fall process that contains more complicated stages of acceleration and deceleration (absent in the underlying causal probabilities) – the overall top event level of the referent political occurrence $\mathbb{Y}$ therefore shows richer behavior than the lower level from which it originates (emergence). The different causal structures are responsible for this. As shown in the inner curve in figure 7.15, the inflection points are particularly pronounced in the case of conjunctive political events (e.g. collective action by leaders and followers, deterrence by requirements, coalitions with pivotal members, political systems with critical functions, and the like). In figure 7.15 the inflection points for the conjunctive case occur closer to the midperiod (i.e. closer to the time of occurrence) than to the initial or final points, so the circumstances surrounding the occurrence of these events are more complex, in probabilistic terms, close to the time of occurrence. By contrast, the occurrence of disjunctive events tends to take place much earlier, because of hyperprobability.

This concludes my treatment of the first-order kinematics of political events. Beyond the linear and parabolic cases, the principles I have presented can be used to explore other political situations in which the first-order causal probabilities P and Q vary over time, affecting the overall probability of political occurrences. By extension, it is also possible to consider temporal variations in the structural parameters Θ and Γ. However, as I showed with the dominance principles (corollaries 6.8, 6.12, 7.4, and 7.8) variations in the causal probabilities P and Q have greater effect on the probability of a political event.

7.4.2   Second-order kinematics

Second-order kinematics in the occurrence of a political event involve the evolution of political occurrences as affected by temporal changes in twice-removed causes. For example, second-order kinematics are involved in the following political occurrences:

1 collective action (referent political event) as a function of willingness and opportunity (second-order causes) occurring for both leaders and followers;
2 coalition formation (referent political event) in terms of negotiated variations in the agreement conditions for each pivotal actor (second-order causes);
3 political system performance (referent political event) as a function of temporal changes in the operational processes that make each basic function of a political system work (second-order causes);
4 conflict onset, continuation, or termination in terms of changes in the empirical operational conditions that make these events more or less likely;
5 the occurrence of political agreement (referent political event) as a function of changes in each party's operational requirements (second order causes) as caused by bargaining, changing images, or other processes that characterize any pre-accord phase.

The second-order causes that undergo change in time can refer either to necessary or to sufficient conditions. Second-order kinematics, as I highlighted earlier, are a significant area of investigation because they link the analytical occurrence of political events (theoretical level) to their operational causes (observable level).

General properties. How does the probability of war change as changes occur in the operational conditions (necessary or sufficient) for war? How does the probability of political integration vary as historical changes take place in the detailed events that take place as part of the implementation of alternative strategies, such as federalism, functionalism, or mass mobilization? Second-order kinematics cover the effects of time-dependency on the core class of the mixed political situations that I have discussed earlier, namely, (i) the cases of mixed causal structures, by conjunction–disjunction (theorem 7.1) and by disjunction–conjunction (theorem 7.2); and (ii) the cases of mixed causal logics, by sequential–conditional and by conditional–sequential.

Earlier in this chapter I discussed the second-order static principles that govern these political situations. In a kinematic analysis, the basic question becomes: how is the probability of a political occurrence, $P(\mathbb{Y})$, affected by temporal variations that occur in the trajectory of causal probabilities or other parameters at the second (and deeper) levels of causation?

The answer to this general second-order kinematic question comes directly from the foundations I have established thus far. $P(\mathbb{Y})$ is determined exclusively by two defining features of the political situation regarding the occurrence: (i) the form of the structure function Ψ, and (ii) the form of the kinematic trajectories for the dependent causal probability functions $P(\tau)$ and $Q(\tau)$, where P and Q denote the probabilities of necessary and sufficient conditions, respectively. From a purely theoretical perspective, second-order kinematics are only an extension of first-order kinematics, viewing the behavior of $P(\mathbb{Y})$ as dependent on deeper (second-order) causes. However, quite often the second-order has greater political interest than the first, because the former tends to be more abstract (nonobservable) whereas the latter tends to be more operational (observable), as I show next.

Case study: turbulence in the post-Cold War system. Earlier in this chapter I treated the opportunity–willingness idea as a special case of general political behavior that is caused by first-order conjunction and second-order disjunction. Thus, political events that occur by opportunity and willingness (arguably a vast class of events in world politics) are uniformly governed by the conjunctive–disjunctive principle (theorem 7.1) and associated results regarding sensitivities, dominance, and other fundamental properties (corollaries 7.1–7.4). I now show how a kinematic analysis of the opportunity–willingness idea in the light of the theoretical principles I have developed can help explain the onset and diffusion of "turbulence" worldwide during the post-Cold War era,[21] particularly in Eastern Europe and the former Soviet Union (Dawisha and Parrott 1994). Aspects of this analysis can also be extended to account for the ethnic violence in the Balkans, following the disintegration of the former Yugoslavia.

According to the opportunity–willingness axiom, political events occur by the conjunction of two necessary conditions: (i) the opportunity for behavior to manifest itself (accordingly, acts of collective defiance to regime authority cannot occur under tightly controlled security conditions because the coordination they require is prevented by the regime), and (ii) the willingness on the part of actors to engage in the behavior in question (thus, not all capable actors in a repressive regime always decide to act because of multiple reasons, including fear for one's life). In turn, each of these conditions occurs in substitutable forms: opportunities are enhanced by a variety of means, willingness is enhanced by more decisional options becoming available. Although opportunity and willingness are theoretical constructs (first-order causal level), their substitutable forms are observable (second-order causal level).

When the Cold War ended in the late 1980s and early 1990s, a significant increase took place in the variety and frequency of political events worldwide, particularly in the former Soviet area: regime changes, ethnic cleansing, public demonstrations and riots, overt challenges to authority, open elections, foreign interventions, unpunished defections, declarations of secession, unreciprocated acts of anti-regime violence, and many other forms of political behavior that had been unthinkable a few years earlier – punishable by death. Beside this burst in frequency and variety, a characteristic feature of this turbulence was (is) that these political events were (are) being carried out by "new" actors that just a few years before would never have contemplated, let alone actually manifested, such behavior. Any unauthorized individual approaching the Berlin Wall from East to West anytime between 1961 and 1989 would have been killed by one or more of the following means (sufficient causes): machine gun fire (from redundant sources), land mines (of various types), imprisonment (accompanied by torture), and other means of physical termination (classified for greater deterrent effectiveness). By contrast, in 1989 thousands of individuals approached the same Wall and destroyed it with complete impunity. Over

---

[21] Gaddis (1992), Rosenau (1990, 1992), Russett and Sutterlin (1991), Singer and Wildavsky (1993).

the whole former Soviet area the empirical repertoire of behavior suddenly exploded with great diversity; and political activity was happening where once only the totalitarian ruling party elite was allowed to be politically active. Elsewhere in the world – in Africa, the Americas, and Asia – some changes took place, but the increase in political activity was not as dramatic as in the former Soviet area. Why?

An explanation of this post-Cold War turbulence, including its differentiated impact across world regions, can be provided by considering the probabilistic kinematics of political events. For each potentially active individual or group in a society, political behavior of a given form (the referent political event $\mathbb{Y}$) occurs according to the event equation

$$\mathbb{Y} = \left(\bigvee_{i=1}^{m} \mathbb{L}_i \right) \wedge \left(\bigvee_{j=1}^{n} \mathbb{O}_j \right),$$
[7.46]

where $\mathbb{L}_i$ is the ith substitutable form of willingness ($i = 1, 2, 3, \ldots, m$), $\mathbb{O}_j$ is the jth substitutable form of opportunity ($j = 1, 2, 3, \ldots, n$), and the corresponding event tree has the familiar form already shown in figure 7.5. Using the conjunctive–disjunctive principle (theorem 6.1), the static probability of political behavior will therefore be given by the equation

$$\mathbf{P}(\mathbb{Y}) = \{1 - [1 - \mathbf{P}(\mathbb{L}_i)]^M\} \times \{1 - [1 - \mathbf{P}(\mathbb{O}_j)]^N\}$$
[7.47]

$$= [1 - (1 - Q)^\Gamma]^2,$$
[7.48]

where Q denotes the probability of $\mathbb{L}_i$ and $\mathbb{O}_j$, with $\mathbf{P}(\mathbb{L}_i) = \mathbf{P}(\mathbb{O}_j)$, and the structural parameter $\Gamma = M = N$ denotes the number of alternate modes for $\mathbb{L}_i$ and $\mathbb{O}_j$. (The simplifying assumptions involved in reducing equation 7.47 to 7.48 are inconsequential to the main results.)

During the Cold War, the same Soviet-area individuals and groups that later became highly active were at the time (in the late 1940s to late 1980s) in a political situation with the following characteristics:

1 Virtually no safe opportunities existed to manifest diverse political behavior (only state-sanctioned behavior was allowed, and the police state prevented all threatening deviations). There were also few sources of willingness to engage in diverse forms of political behavior, given the harsh consequences, such as imprisonment in the Lubianka dungeons, deportation to Siberian labor camps, execution by a KGB squad, reprisals on family members, and other common methods of state terror that were organized to maintain effective repression. Thus, the value of Γ was low or near 0.

2 It was also very rare for individuals or groups to seize any of the few available opportunities, for many of the same reasons already given and

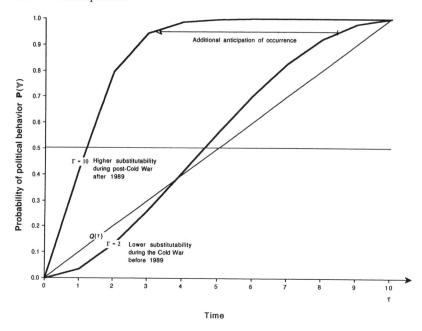

Figure 7.16. Onset of turbulence in world politics during and after the Cold War

for others (knowledge of virtually sure extermination). For example, during the entire Cold War only a couple hundred individuals died from unauthorized attempts to cross the Berlin Wall, a rather small number considering the duration of the conflict, the size of the population at risk, and the means deployed (many more people die every year crossing the streets of US cities). Thus, the value of Q also was low, if not quite zero (acts of courageous defiance are in the historical record).

As shown in figure 7.16, turbulence has occurred since the end of the Cold War because these conditions have changed dramatically since the war's termination. Accordingly:

1′ There are now numerous opportunities for individuals and groups to manifest themselves through diverse forms of political behavior (the state no longer decides on what is permissible, except within broad liberal boundaries established by democratically approved laws). Moreover, there are also numerous sources of willingness to act politically, particularly because the consequences of doing so are now trivial (at worse there are fines, reprimands, public ridicule, and so on) compared to the earlier risk of death inflicted by the state. The availability of technical means of political mobilization, such as a free mass media, has also increased the number of willingness and opportunity modes. Thus, Γ has increased dramatically since the end of the Cold War.

2' Individuals and groups have slowly awakened to this new reality, gradually increasing the probability of seizing the new opportunities and realizing the new incentives that promote willingness to act. After all, the sudden availability of opportunities or good reasons for acting does not translate immediately in a high probability of such opportunities being seized. Attitudes, perceptions, belief systems, and all else that motivates political action are complex cognitive and emotional entities that change only slowly. Thus, the value of Q has also increased gradually and steadily since the end of the Cold War.

As shown by the change in figure 7.16, during the Cold War the variety in substitutable modes of opportunity and willingness was low (say as low as $\Gamma = 2$; the exact number does not matter) and under such conditions the behavior of the probability of political events was quite close to being the same as – with the differences already noted – the causal probability Q of willingness or opportunity occurring. However, as the Cold War ended and the number of substitutable modes of opportunity and of willingness increased dramatically (say, to $\Gamma = 10$, for the sake of argument, the exact new level not being important), the probability of political behavior jumped to levels of virtual certainty, even for levels of Q below the even-odds value. The root cause of this phenomenon is hyperprobability, which grew intensely with the increase in substitutability (Γ). Add to this the rise in the probability Q, and the result is an extraordinary rise in the frequency and variety of political events occurring – i.e. turbulence in world politics.

Why has turbulence occurred mostly in the former Soviet area, including the ethnic wars raging in the Balkans, and less so or not at all in the Americas, Africa, or Asia? Because it is mostly in the former Soviet area that substitutability in the availability of modes of opportunity and of willingness has undergone the greatest change, while the same parameter has remained largely unchanged (and traditionally fairly high) in the other areas. Compared to the former Soviet area, there have been relatively fewer changes in the opportunities and motivations for willingness in the Americas, Africa, and Asia. However, where basic parametric changes in Γ or in Q have occurred (e.g. South Africa, Mexico, Nicaragua, Rwanda, Palestine), the same turbulence has resulted. This recent pattern of political uncertainty in the post-Cold War system is therefore explained by the kinematic behavior of the conjunctive–disjunctive principle (equations 7.46–7.48). Other features of world politics await investigation by similar or related principles of political uncertainty.

7.5   Conclusions

In this chapter I applied the set of general micropolitical principles developed in chapter 6 to a succession of more specific situations of occurrence that commonly govern political events. From a systematic perspective, I distinguished between static and kinematic models, as well as among various levels of causal structure. Empirically, as already indicated in earlier chapters, these models are also developed and tested using case methods similar to those used in decision models[22] and game models.[23]

Static principles (section 7.3) explain a political occurrence by focusing on the underlying causal structure, independent of any changes that may happen in time. For theoretical purposes, I considered only the first two causal levels because these are the most common and – by induction and simple substitution – similar static principles can be derived for any greater depth of resolution. The main examples in this section were drawn from the study of deterrence, coalitions, the prisoner's dilemma game, and the opportunity–willingness framework. Considering first the case of a political event that occurs by first-order conjunction and second-order disjunction, the main results were the conjunctive–disjunctive principle (theorem 7.1), the conjunctive–disjunctive dependence principles (corollaries 7.1–7.3), and the dominance principle for conjunction–disjunction (corollary 7.4). Considering next the case of a political event that occurs by first-order disjunction and second-order conjunction, the main results were the disjunctive–conjunctive principle (theorem 7.2), the dependence principles for disjunction–conjunction (corollaries 7.5–7.7) and the dominance principle for disjunction–conjunction (corollary 7.8).

The fledgling complexity suggested by the preceding analysis motivated the need to reduce all political complexity that turns out to be causally irrelevant for understanding uncertainty. For this I introduced the concepts of critical modes and minimal paths. I demonstrated these principles by applying them in a case study that focused on the occurrence of endurance or disintegration in the political system model due to Harold Lasswell and Abraham Kaplan, one of the few polity models with specific conditions for maintaining political performance. The analysis showed how the Lasswell–Kaplan system reduces to a very simple form in spite of its original forbidding complexity. The minimal Lasswell–Kaplan conditions were also used later in the chapter to analyze domestic political change in the post-Cold War.

Going beyond the conjunctive–disjunctive and disjunctive–conjunctive

[22] Allison (1971), Bueno de Mesquita and Lalman (1992), Hernes (1975), and Saris and Saris-Gallhoffer (1975).

[23] Brams (1985, 1994), Brams and Kilgour (1988), Morrow (1994), Ordeshook (1986), Snyder and Diesing (1977), and Zagare (1984).

combinations, I next examined the combination of the more general logic modes. By embedding sequential and conditional logic within each other I was able to obtain integrated models that contain both dimensions. The corresponding special principles for these combined cases involve the selective application of the principles discussed for sequential, conditional, conjunctive, and disjunctive portions of the event tree.

The last context in which I considered static principles concerned the use of subjective probabilities, replacing the standard objective probabilities. My treatment developed in two directions, that associated with the Kahneman–Tversky prospect probabilities, and another consisting of verbal probabilities. I illustrated some of the principles involved in each case in the more specific context of deterrence.

Kinematic principles (section 7.4) explain a political occurrence by focusing on the joint effects of underlying causal structure and any changes in time that might occur either in the causal probabilities or in the causal structure itself. I developed my treatment of kinematics by examining the evolution in the probability of political occurrences according to first- and second-order principles. In terms of first-order kinematic principles, I analyzed the conjunctive case and examined the occurrence of sudden change in political regime, as illustrated by the fall of the Berlin Wall. I also analyzed the disjunctive case and applied it to the resistance to change in a political system, as illustrated by the endurance of the Castro regime in Cuba. The generalization of these cases led to analysis in the rise and fall in the probability of a political event, an important evolutionary process that has attracted significant scholarly attention in political science and elsewhere (e.g. history, economics, anthropology, archeology).

In terms of second-order kinematics, I motivated the significance of these based on several examples, followed by the presentation of basic governing principles. The case study that I examined consisted of the onset of "turbulence" in post-Cold War politics, a term coined by James N. Rosenau. I explained this recent phenomenon by the co-occurrence of a sharp increase in the availability of substitutable modes for political behavior, in the diversity of potentially active political agents, and in the slow rise in the probability of sufficient willingness to act politically.

Part IV

Conclusions

8   Synthesis

Macro level phenomena, then, are not mere epiphenomena or in any sense less "real" than micro level phenomena. The behavior involved, whatever the level of analysis, is the same.

Heinz Eulau, *Micro-Macro Political Analysis*

8.1   Introduction

Coalitions, policy outcomes, conflicts, collective action, and other core political phenomena have both macro level properties and micro level foundations – nothing significant in politics ever "comes out of the blue." In politics, what is the relationship between the behavior of aggregate variables at the macro level of analysis and the occurrence of individual events at the micro level? More specifically, how can we link macropolitical behavior to microfoundations consisting of states of nature and acts of choice? Are these levels connected and, if so, how? How are the two branches of this theory of political uncertainty related? How does the internal structure of the black box at the micro level of individual events account directly for aggregate macro behavior? In causal Lasswellian terms (1935, 1936; Eulau 1969: 128), is macropolitical behavior a "resultant" or an "emergent" effect of events at the micro level? In the former case, macropolitics is simply the sum of micropolitics; in the latter case macropolitics is qualitatively different or complex. As already anticipated by the discussion of the levels of analysis (axiom 1) in chapter 1, these and related questions represent an enduring puzzle in political science, beyond the specific set of intriguing questions raised by each level of analysis separately. Since the antiquity of the levels of analysis puzzle can be dated back to Aristotle and continues to attract significant attention as a foundational puzzle in politics (Eulau 1996), to claim to have complete answers to these questions would be overreaching. In this chapter I outline some feasible and tentative solutions by way of conclusions.

In this chapter I demonstrate a plausible integration of the ideas in part II (uncertainty of macropolitics) and part III (uncertainty of micropolitics), as promised in the first chapter. I say "plausible" because there are probably other approaches to achieving similar results and only future research will tell whether the approach I am suggesting here will stand the test of talent and time applied to these topics by others. In doing this, I shall first recapitulate some of the essential ideas covered in previous chapters (section 8.2), focusing primarily on those that are indispensable here to link the two levels of analysis. I shall then present an integration of the macro and micro levels, first theoretically (section 8.3) and then more practically (section 8.4), by analyzing several unified aspects of the theory as derived from the set of recurring examples I have been discussing (primarily coalitions and conflict). The purpose of this chapter is to synthesize the theory by showing how the "black box" of aggregate macropolitical behavior (presented in part II) can be accounted for by the micropolitical events which occur within the black box (part III) – and vice versa, how the microprocesses that take place within the black box (presented in part III), consisting of states of nature and acts of choice, give rise to the observed macro behavior of the black box (in part II).

8.2   Recapitulation

I began this book with the claim that uncertainty is ubiquitous, consequential, and ineradicable in political life. In the preceding chapters I have explored this idea from a variety of perspectives, namely at the macro and micro levels of analysis in chapters 2 through 4 and 5 through 7, respectively. Before addressing directly the connection that may exist between separate levels of analysis, I shall highlight the essential ideas that are necessary to provide such a synthesis.

The first part of this book (chapter 1) was dedicated to establishing that uncertainty is a core substantive quality of politics, not simply a result of some measurement inaccuracy or something which must remain a mystery. Stripping politics of its uncertainty – by ignoring, or trivializing it – means depriving political life of one of the fundamental characteristics that makes it so scientifically intriguing and challenging. The theory outlined in this book – incomplete as it may be, but arguably fertile with many directions for future investigation – aims at providing some foundations for advancing our scientific understanding of politics through a systematic treatment of political uncertainty. The core puzzles of the research program are to causally explain two related phenomena: (i) the uncertain behavior of aggregate political variables (macropolitics, in chapters 2, 3, and 4; part II) and (ii) the uncertain occurrence of individual political events (micropolitics, in chapters 5, 6, and 7; part III). The formal analytical tools for exploring these new concepts, assumptions, and principles consist of sets, logic, and probability, with basic calculus to obtain new insights on the sensitivity of uncertainty to changes that occur in political conditions.

Conflict, deterrence, collective action, and coalition behavior – cases of core political phenomena (identified in figure 1.1) from both domestic and international domains – were used as running examples to illustrate general and specific principles at both levels of analysis. Using these core cases, the scope of the theory was established on broader general grounds.

The second part of the book addressed aggregate political behavior at the macro level of analysis, as a black box (without details on the occurrence of individual realizations). Though probabilistic, hazard forces acting on political actors, decision makers, systems, or processes are defined and exactly specified. These hazard forces have calculable causal effects on observed patterns of political uncertainty. Among the general macro principles, the distributions principle (theorem 3.1) establishes the exact causal relationship between the hazard force acting on individuals or groups and the political behavior that such individuals or groups will produce. Other principles as well add to a more precise and insightful understanding of political uncertainty at the macro level. From simple to more complex, progressive problemshifts analyze a succession of qualitatively different hazard forces, each generating a set of special principles of political behavior. These have been applied and tested in areas such as coalition dynamics, political integration, and war and peace.

At the macro level, implicit models explain political behavior in terms of aggregate causal forces without specific reference to their substantive origin (economic, demographic, social, or other). Four progressive problemshifts were considered, using the onset of war in recent centuries as the principal illustrative example. Hazard force was shown to be approximately constant for large, heterogeneous populations of realizations under diverse political conditions. This explained the widespread applicability of the Poisson model in a variety of areas of political and social science. Conversely, hazard force was shown to be variable (not constant) for smaller, more homogeneous populations of realizations under narrower political conditions. This was associated with different, non-Poisson patterns of uncertainty, such as those modeled by the Weibull and other distributions.

Explicit models explained political behavior in terms of substantive hazard forces, such as economic, demographic, social, or other – as when situational and other factors are hypothesized to produce effects on patterns of conflict behavior. The empirical implementation of these models involves the use of event history analysis and other survival analysis methods. However, these are examined here under a new theoretical light provided by principles and concepts similar to those derived for the implicit models. The theory of political uncertainty also uses these models to explain several anomalies in the literature, such as the cross-century reversal of war correlates in international relations.

The third part of this book addressed individual political events at the micro level (looking inside the black box to examine the causal detail), explaining their uncertain occurrence through sequential and conditional causal logics. Sequential logic explained a political event as a contingent outcome in the sample space of a branching process, a process that moves from the uncertain occurrence of initial conditions for a potential political event to occur, to the actual realization or failure of such a potential. Examples discussed included the occurrence of collective action; the formulation of public policy by government, in response to socioeconomic disturbances; the downfall of a coalition government as caused by an initial threat to withdraw pivotal support; and the onset of warfare from a provocation to violence escalation.

The conditional logic approach explained the occurrence of a political event as a function of causally necessary or sufficient conditions. Hypoprobability, hyperprobability, cut sets, and kinematics were explored as central aspects of political uncertainty at this micro level – important structural and temporal phenomena which occur within the black box. General principles (theorems) unambiguously relate the causal logic of a political event to its corresponding probability. Progressive problemshifts use general principles to generate special principles: by successive decomposition of events, by synergistic interaction between sequential and conditional logics, and by making probabilities time-dependent or dependent on other variables. This part of the theory of political uncertainty has also been applied to areas such as collective action, conflict, deterrence, coalitions, integration, and political communication.

This two-level exploration of political uncertainty logically raises the question of the relationship between levels – the puzzle in Heinz Eulau's epigraph at the beginning of this chapter. As I have already indicated (and now will demonstrate in detail) events and variables – the two core elements in the puzzle of political uncertainty – are causally linked. Informally, this is because events and their probabilities – based on either conditional logic or sequential logic – are governed by hazard forces acting to produce the components of events: acts of choice, states of nature, or combinations as compound events. An event model of conflict onset and termination contains events and probabilities of escalation, diffusion, and so on, that are governed by hazard forces acting on belligerents. Similarly, conflict onset and termination are events determined by the causal logic of domestic and international processes, and by environmental and internal hazards. Links in the theory can provide us with a better understanding of the dual causal connection between political events and hazard forces acting on individuals, institutions, and collectivities.

8.3   Unified theoretical principles

Consider an aggregate political behavior variable Y with distribution functions $p(y)$ and $\Phi(y)$ at the macro level, as these terms were defined in chapter 2. In addition, consider that Y has a set of corresponding individual realizations of the event $\mathbb{Y}$ specified by an event function Ψ at the micro level, as defined in chapter 5. The two principles which follow integrate macro and micro levels of analysis under the most elementary political conditions: pure conjunction, pure disjunction, and independent exponentially distributed individual events with constant hazard force at the micro level. Recall that conjunction and disjunction are exhaustive and mutually exclusive causal modes (section 6.3), so the principles which follow provide important building blocks to explore other situations that contain greater complexity and realism. Although simple, these elementary conditions are important because the principles they produce (theorems 8.1 and 8.2 below) constitute the foundation for deriving further results. Other unified principles can be derived through similar theoretical procedures in future investigations, as I suggest in section 8.4.

8.3.1   Unified principle for conjunction

The first unified principle addresses the relationship between levels of analysis when the causal structure is based on the conjunction of more elementary necessary events. For example, this applies to the class of political cases in table 6.1 and table 6.3, column 2, such as collective action through requirements that must occur, coalitions based on pivotal actors, political integration occurring by necessary conditions, and other applications discussed in earlier chapters.

Theorem 8.1 (unified principle for conjunction of constant hazard forces). *Given a political event $\mathbb{Y}$ that is caused by the conjunction* (Boolean logic AND) *of n necessary conditions at the micro level of analysis* $(\mathbb{X}_1, \mathbb{X}_2, \mathbb{X}_3, \ldots, \mathbb{X}_n)$, *with each condition occurring with exponential probability distribution* (constant hazard forces k_i)

$$\Phi_i(y) = 1 - e^{-k_i y}, \qquad\qquad\qquad [8.1]$$

where $i = 1, 2, 3, \ldots, n$, then the aggregate properties of political behavior Y at the macro level of analysis are given by the equations:

$$\Phi(y) = 1 - e^{-(k_1 + k_2 + k_3 + \ldots + k_n)y}$$

$$= 1 - e^{-(\Sigma_i k_i)y} \tag{8.2}$$

$$p(y) = (k_1 + k_2 + k_3 + \ldots + k_n)\, e^{-(k_1 + k_2 + k_3 + \ldots + k_n)y}$$
$$= (\textstyle\sum_i k_i)\, e^{-(\Sigma_i\, k_i)y} \tag{8.3}$$

$$E(Y) = 1/(k_1 + k_2 + k_3 + \ldots + k_n)$$
$$= 1/\textstyle\sum_i k_i \tag{8.4}$$

$$H(y) = k_1 + k_2 + k_3 + \ldots + k_n$$
$$= \textstyle\sum_i k_i \tag{8.5}$$

and when $k_1 = k_2 = k_3 = \ldots = k_n = k$, then

$$\Phi(y) = 1 - e^{-\Theta k y} \tag{8.2$'$}$$

$$p(y) = \Theta k\, e^{-\Theta k y} \tag{8.3$'$}$$

$$E(Y) = 1/\Theta k \tag{8.4$'$}$$

$$H(y) = \Theta k, \tag{8.5$'$}$$

where $1 < \Theta < n$ is the number of necessary conditions at the micro level.

I note immediately that equations 8.2–8.5 and 8.2$'$–8.5$'$ each express a dependent macro level variable as a function of independent micro level variables.[1] The core result contained in this principle is that the aggregate properties of political behavior Y at the macro level will be exponentially (Poisson) distributed whenever the causal events that produce the individual realizations of Y are all necessary conditions (event function is AND-based) and each condition is exponentially distributed at the micro level (equations 8.2, 8.3, 8.2$'$, and 8.3$'$). The exponential constant at the macro level equals the sum of exponential constants acting at the micro level. This is the first unified result which addresses the relationship between the two levels of analysis. The principle expresses how individual micro level events are synthesized to produce aggregate macro level behavior – how macro behavior is affected by micro occurrences.

In Lasswellian terms (Eulau 1969: 128; 1996: 180–1) the unified principle for conjunction states that macro behavior in this case is a "resultant" effect of micro level event occurrences, not an "emergent" property. (As I will demonstrate below, the same is not true for the disjunctive case.)

The aggregate expected value $E(Y)$ of political behavior Y at the macro level (equations 8.4 and 8.4$'$) is inversely proportional to the number of necessary conditions Θ, as well as to the intensity of the individual hazard forces k_i acting at the micro level. This is similar to the special expectation principle for constant hazard force (theorem 4.1), consistent with the

---

[1] Prime marks ($'$) indicate equivalent equations expressed in more general form, assuming that all hazard rates are equal, $k_1 = k_2 = k_3 = \ldots = k_n = k$, and $1 < \Theta < n$.

"resultant" property just noted, only enhanced by the structural variable Θ. Politically, this means that both k and Θ have the greatest effect on E when they are small (weak forces and few necessary conditions), with monotone declining effects as they increase.

By theorem 8.1, the aggregate hazard force at the macro level, $H(y)$, is monotone, constant, and a linear combination of the individual hazard forces $H(y_i)$ acting at the micro level of events (equations 8.5 and 8.5'). Accordingly, in this conjunctive case the macro level hazard force $H(y)$ is directly proportional to the micro level hazard forces acting on the individual causal events $(\mathbb{X}_1, \mathbb{X}_2, \mathbb{X}_3, \ldots, \mathbb{X}_n)$, for all values of Y.

More generally, the individual equations of this unified principle are reminiscent of theorem 4.1 at the macro level, the special principle for aggregate political behavior caused by constant hazard force. However, as indicated by the primed equations 8.2'–8.5', the micro causal structure is now made explicit by including the number of necessary conditions Θ for the individual realizations of Y. Thus, in a sense, theorem 8.1 looks inside the black box examined earlier by theorem 4.1, showing the direct effect of micro causal structure.

Theorem 8.1 states that a set of exponential distributions for events occurring at the micro level causes an exponentially distributed behavior at the macro level (when the causal structure is purely conjunctive). Does the opposite result of theorem 8.1 also hold true? In other words, given an aggregate exponential distribution observed at the macro level, can it be inferred that this must be caused by a set of exponential distributions at the micro level? To answer this question we must examine the next unified principle.

8.3.2   Unified principle for disjunction

The second unified principle addresses the relationship between levels of analysis when the causal structure is based on the disjunction of more elementary sufficient events. For example, this applies to the class of political cases in table 6.3, column 3, including multiple sufficient solutions for solving collective action problems, deterrence and compellence (in general, political power relations) based on multiple threats, political communication through redundant signals, and other applications identified earlier.

Theorem 8.2 (unified principle for disjunction of constant hazard forces). *Given a political event $\mathbb{Y}$ that is caused by the disjunction (Boolean logic OR) of m sufficient conditions at the micro level of analysis $(\mathbb{Z}_1, \mathbb{Z}_2, \mathbb{Z}_3, \ldots, \mathbb{Z}_m)$, with each condition occurring with exponential probability distribution (constant hazard forces k_j)*

$$\Phi_j(y) = 1 - e^{-k_j y}, \qquad\qquad [8.6]$$

where $j = 1, 2, 3, \ldots, m$, *then the aggregate properties of political behavior* Y *at the* macro *level of analysis are given by the equations*:

$$\Phi(y) = 1 - e^{-k_1 y} - e^{-k_2 y} - e^{-k_3 y} - \ldots - e^{-k_m y} +$$
$$+ e^{-(k_1 + k_2 + k_3 + \ldots + k_m)y}$$
$$= 1 - (\textstyle\sum_j e^{-k_j y}) + e^{-(\Sigma_j k_j)y} \qquad\qquad [8.7]$$

$$p(y) = k_1 e^{-k_1 y} + k_2 e^{-k_2 y} + k_3 e^{-k_3 y} + \ldots + k_m e^{-k_m y}$$
$$- (k_1 + k_2 + k_3 + \ldots + k_m) e^{-(k_1 + k_2 + k_3 + \ldots + k_m)y}$$
$$= (\textstyle\sum_j k_j e^{-k_j y}) - (\textstyle\sum_j k_j) e^{-(\Sigma_j k_j)y} \qquad\qquad [8.8]$$

$$E(Y) = 1/k_1 + 1/k_2 + 1/k_3 + \ldots + 1/k_m - 1/(k_1 + k_2 + k_3 + \ldots + k_m)$$
$$= (\textstyle\sum_j 1/k_j) - 1/\textstyle\sum_j k_j \qquad\qquad [8.9]$$

$$H(y) = \frac{k_1 e^{-k_1 y} + \ldots + k_m e^{-k_m y} - (k_1 + \ldots + k_m)e^{-(k_1 + \ldots + k_m)y}}{e^{-k_1 y} + \ldots + e^{-k_m y} - e^{-(k_1 + \ldots + k_m)y}}$$

$$= \frac{(\textstyle\sum_j k_j e^{-k_j y}) - (\textstyle\sum_j k_j) \, e^{-(\Sigma_j k_j)y}}{(\textstyle\sum_j e^{-k_j y}) + e^{-(\Sigma_j k_j)y}} \qquad\qquad [8.10]$$

and when $k_1 = k_2 = k_3 = \ldots = k_m = k$, *then*

$$\Phi(y) = 1 - \Gamma e^{-ky} + e^{-\Gamma ky} \qquad\qquad [8.7']$$

$$p(y) = \Gamma k(e^{-ky} - e^{-\Gamma ky}) \qquad\qquad [8.8']$$

$$E(Y) = (\Gamma - 1/\Gamma)/k \qquad\qquad [8.9']$$

$$H(y) = \frac{\Gamma k \, (e^{-ky} - e^{-\Gamma ky})}{\Gamma e^{-ky} - e^{-\Gamma ky}}, \qquad\qquad [8.10']$$

where $1 < \Gamma < m$ *is the number of sufficient conditions at the micro level.*

As may have been anticipated by a close examination of the earlier disjunctive principles in chapters 6 and 7, this is a somewhat more complex situation. The core result expressed by this principle is that the aggregate properties of political behavior Y at the macro level will not be exponentially (Poisson) distributed when the causal events to produce the individual realizations of Y are all disjunctive conditions (event function is Boolean OR-based) and these are exponentially distributed at the micro level (equations 8.7, 8.8, 8.7′, and 8.8′). This is the second fundamental result which addresses the relationship between the two levels of analysis. Again, the principle expresses how individual micro level events are synthesized to produce aggregate macro level behavior – how macro is affected by micro – only now under a disjunctive structure of sufficient conditions.

In Lasswellian terms – and contrary to the earlier case of conjunction – the unified principle for causal disjunction states that macro political behavior in this case is indeed an "emergent" phenomenon, not merely a "resultant" phenomenon lacking complexity. This can be readily seen by comparing the cross-level isomorphic functions in theorem 8.1 with the cross-level non-isomorphic functions in theorem 8.2. I shall return to this critical qualitative difference below.

In terms of the aggregate expected value $E(Y)$ of political behavior Y at the macro level (equations 8.9 and 8.9′), this remains – exactly – inversely proportional to the intensity of the individual hazard forces k acting at the micro level. Thus, aggregate mean behavior increases as forces decrease; and vice versa. However, in this case the micro structure affects the aggregate expected value by a relationship that is more complicated in terms of the number of sufficient conditions Γ (compare equations 8.9 and 8.9′ with the corresponding equations 8.4 and 8.4′ in theorem 8.1). In this case the causal complexity (Γ) has both increasing and decreasing effects on $E(Y)$, as indicated in equation 8.9′, depending on the value of Γ. For small values of Γ the aggregate mean behavior is mostly inversely affected by Γ (low redundancy decreases the aggregate expected value), whereas for large values of Γ the aggregate mean behavior is mostly proportional to Γ (high redundancy increases the aggregate expected value). Overall, therefore, aggregate mean behavior in this disjunctive case is similar to the special expectation principle for constant hazard force (theorem 4.1) only with respect to the individual level hazard forces, and is more complicated with respect to the effect of the structural variable Γ.

By theorem 8.1, the aggregate hazard force at the macro level $H(y)$ is no longer a simple monotone function of the hazard forces $H(y_i)$ acting at the micro level of events $\mathbb{Z}_1, \mathbb{Z}_2, \mathbb{Z}_3, \ldots, \mathbb{Z}_m$ (compare equations 8.10 and 8.10′ with equations 8.5 and 8.5′ earlier in theorem 8.1). In this case the aggregate hazard rate produced by individual hazard forces acting at the component event level is far more complex and nowhere nearly linear additive. In fact, the aggregate $H(y)$ is not even monotone with respect to y.

Overall, what does the aggregate political behavior look like at the macro level in this case of simple disjunction and exponentially driven individual events at the micro level? The equations of this unified principle (theorem 8.2) are not reminiscent of any of the previous results, but as I argue in the next section they provide new insights on political uncertainty by detailing the emergence of complexity.

8.3.3   The macro–micro puzzle

The macro–micro puzzle in political science has many intriguing aspects, most of which remain mysteriously challenging. In the preceding chapters I have addressed aspects of political uncertainty at separate levels of analysis, combined here in an integrated way to gain further insights into this puzzle.

Macro behavior from micro events. The unified principles I have just presented demonstrate that aggregate political behavior at the macro level can be deduced (synthesized) from knowledge of individual events which occur at the micro level. As I have just shown for the two most fundamental cases, given a distribution function (equations 8.1 and 8.6) and an event function Ψ at the micro level it is possible to derive the exact characteristics (distribution functions and special values) at the macro level. More complex situations of individual event occurrences (e.g. Weibull or lognormally distributed) or more complicated event structures (e.g. various levels with mixed conjunction and disjunction) only make the resulting aggregate properties more complicated, but not less tractable. (In the next section (8.4) I discuss some of what is involved in the context of coalitions and conflict.) Thus, this part of the macro–micro puzzle – how and why does micro give rise to macro – is in principle solved, at least in broad theoretical terms.

More specifically, the synthesis provided by each principle clearly indicates that the conjunction of events at the micro level gives rise to resultant (linear additive) political behavior at the macro level; whereas the disjunction produces emergent (nonlinear complex) political behavior at the macro level. Symbolically, we may write

$$\text{micro } \Psi_\wedge \to resultant \text{ (linear additive) macro behavior}$$

and

$$\text{micro } \Psi_\vee \to emergent \text{ (nonlinear complex) macro behavior,}$$

where $\Psi_\wedge$ and $\Psi_\vee$ denote conjunctive and disjunctive causal structures, respectively. Moreover, as can be shown by extending the analysis beyond the case of identically distributed Poisson variables (the conditions in theorems 8.1 and 8.2), similar results obtain for the case when individual events at the micro level occur with a Weibull (i.e. generally not Poisson) distribution.[2] Here again, conjunction yields resultant behavior (also Weibull distributed) whereas disjunction yields emergent behavior (neither Weibull nor Poisson). A general conclusion to be drawn from these theoretical results is that a sure source of complexity in political uncertainty at the macro level lies in the occurrence of causal disjunction at the micro level of analysis.

---

[2] I am grateful to Anne M. Dougherty and John A. Williamson for suggesting this extension.

Micro events from macro behavior. What about the reverse version of the same puzzle? How can information about the macro level tell us something about the micro level? Another important insight provided by these unified principles has to do with this inferential question raised earlier in this chapter (section 8.2.1), concerning what might be the possible micro structure of an aggregate form of political behavior Y which is empirically known to be, say, exponentially distributed. For example, as I discussed in earlier chapters, many forms of aggregate political conflict, from both domestic and international domains (riots, *coups*, wars), have been tested to see whether the Poisson or exponential distribution is empirically supported (references cited in chapters 2, 3, and 4). Indeed, according to some, "the use of the Poisson and related stochastic distributions to model formally domestic political conflict is a truly cumulative research approach" (Lichbach 1992: 348). If political conflict is exponentially distributed at the macro level, can we infer anything about the micro level? In other words, applying these unified principles in reverse, can we make micro level inferences based upon observed macro behavior? The answer is yes, albeit only conditionally, by elimination of alternatives.

To understand why this is so (it sounds like a violation of basic logic), recall the exhaustive and mutually exclusive nature of the causal conditions examined by the two unified principles – conjunction and disjunction as the only fundamental causal alternatives which exist (chapter 6). This is an essential premise, otherwise my claim is not warranted even as a weak inference. Given the fact that the two principles cover the only two possible causal situations, if the aggregate political behavior at the macro level is known to be exponentially distributed, then the individual event occurrences at the micro level must also be exponentially distributed, but only conditionally upon them being also conjunctive. Alternatively, if the aggregate political behavior at the macro level is known to be exponentially distributed, then the individual event occurrences at the micro level must be causally organized as a conjunction, but only conditionally upon them being also exponentially distributed. In other words, the two properties (form of event structure and form of behavioral distributions or hazard forces) are fundamentally linked by means of an uncertainty relationship: we either know the individual event distributions or hazard forces and assume the causal structure, or know the causal structure and assume the distributions. What we cannot do is to infer both structural and distributional properties simultaneously with only knowledge about the macro distribution; hence the weak character of this inference. Although weak, this is another important insight derived from the unified principles; another step in solving the macro–micro puzzle. I discuss some empirical implications of this in the next section.

Given this result, what is the corresponding micro structure to the succession of aggregate models (models I – VII) at the macro level? Political behavior Y in models I and V–VII is always exponentially distributed with intensity k, so the previous discussion applies to them as well. For these cases the underlying causal structure can be assumed to be affected by constant hazard forces acting in conjunction. On the other hand, the other models await further investigation, applying theorems 8.1 and 8.2 to infer plausible micro properties. Most likely, these other macro models are based on disjunctions and different hazard forces acting at the micro level.

Macro–micro invariance. Finally, another insightful step in solving the macro–micro puzzle in politics concerns the intriguing relationships given in the two unified principles (theorems 8.1 and 8.2), between aggregate mean behavior at the macro level, $E(Y)$, and the causal properties of individual event realizations at the micro level. Specifically, in both structural cases (conjunction and disjunction), aggregate mean political behavior $E(Y)$ is an inverse function of k, the hazard force operating at the micro level (compare equations 8.4′ and 8.9′). The causal structure does not matter, an invariance property which only the mean value seems to poses. Politically, this means that structural types of causation at the micro level – whether the aggregate behavior is caused by necessary or by sufficient conditions in the event function Ψ – have no effect on the way in which individual hazard forces produce mean aggregate behavior, whereas other aggregate properties (distributions, aggregate hazard rate, and so on) are – as intuitively expected – significantly affected by causal structure. This is another insight on the macro–micro puzzle. The explanation of this invariance phenomenon – the micro forces which produce mean aggregate behavior act independently of causal structure – awaits further investigation. For now, however, we can be certain of its existence.

8.4   Applications, interpretations, insights

As I have been discussing since the introductory chapter (section 1.1.1, figure 1.1), coalitions and warfare represent core areas of general politics affected by uncertainty, covering both domestic and international domains. Both also exemplify important features of collective action. Since both topics have numerous intriguing aspects connected with aggregate behavior (Y) and with individual events ($\mathbb{Y}$), I have used them throughout this book to illustrate the theory of political uncertainty at macro (part II) and micro (part III) levels of analysis. I shall now use these same topics to illustrate some aspects of the applications, interpretations, and insights which can be obtained through unified principles such as those just discussed.

Bearing in mind the nature of coalitions and warfare, it should be noted that these and other cases which call for coordinated cooperation by members of a collectivity are instances of collective action. In the case of coalitions, collective action is manifested initially in the formation process, and subsequently in maintaining the coalition together. Leaders and followers must emerge, and coordinate among themselves, for collective action in coalition behavior to occur. In the case of warfare, actors must initially coordinate in order to resist an adversary or to undertake aggression against others, and subsequently they must cooperate to carry on the war effort. This is true of domestic coalitions, international alliances, civil wars, or international wars, so the precise political domain – domestic or international – is secondary in this context of general politics. Therefore, the discussion which follows extends – more generally – to aspects of political uncertainty in the theory of collective action.

8.4.1   *Coalitions: government cabinets and international alliances*

As I discussed earlier in chapter 2 (example 2.1), at the macro level of analysis the process of formation and dissolution of coalitions – the aggregate coalition process – is a multidimensional phenomenon described by a set of dependent variables with individual values that occur on the historical timeline τ (the n-tuple in figure 2.1). At the macro level of analysis, a coalition n-tuple consists of time of formation $t \in T$, size $s \in S$, support $r \in R$, duration $\delta \in D$, policy orientation $o \in O$, degree of cohesion $c \in C$, and other dimensions. The behavior of each variable Y is viewed as a black box that is governed by the hazard forces discussed in chapters 2 through 4. Some coalition processes are governed by implicit hazard forces (classes 1 and 2 in table 4.1), others by explicit forces (classes 3 and 4 in table 4.1). For example, recent studies have shown that the duration D of coalition governments in parliamentary democracies is governed not only by intrinsic hazard forces, as it was once supposed (Browne et al. 1986; Cioffi-Revilla 1984), but also by other contextual forces as well (King et al. 1990). Therefore, our current understanding is that coalition duration D in parliamentary democracies is exponentially distributed with aggregate rate k.

At the micro level of analysis, a coalition forms ($\mathbb{C}$) when pivotal members join, and falls apart ($\mathbb{F}$) when one or more pivotal members leave. A coalition forms when a set of pivotal members decide to join and other political and constitutional requirements are met. Causally, this means that the event function for $\mathbb{C}$ is conjunctive, with $\mathbb{X}_1$, $\mathbb{X}_2$, $\mathbb{X}_3$, ..., $\mathbb{X}_n$ describing the necessary events. For example, in the case of governmental coalition, the event $\mathbb{C}$ requires (i) pivotal members deciding to join, (ii) a coalition leader or prime minister being available, (iii) passing the initial vote of confidence in Parliament, and so forth. Similarly, for an international alliance, $\mathbb{C}$ requires (i) a leading state to emerge, (ii) allies deciding to join, (iii) some international machinery to coordinate the allied work, and so forth. Accordingly, by theorem 8.1 (unified principle for conjunction of constant hazard forces), if each of the necessary events for coalition formation occurs with exponential distribution, then the formation process T will also be exponentially distributed. In a pioneering study of international alliances, McGowan and Rood (1975) reported a very satisfactory empirical fit for the exponential distribution (Poisson process), but without much substantive theoretical explanation. The micro level analysis just offered provides a causally plausible theoretical explanation for observing how international alliances form with exponential distribution. Similar studies could be undertaken for the formation process of domestic coalitions, adding a new theoretical dimension to the extant studies of coalition duration in parliamentary democracies.

Examining the process from a different perspective, the dissolution of a coalition (determining an individual duration $\delta \in D$) is marked by the occurrence of an event $\mathbb{F}$ ("coalition dissolves") with conjunctive function, where each event ($\mathbb{X}_1$, $\mathbb{X}_2$, $\mathbb{X}_3$, ..., $\mathbb{X}_n$) now marks the occurrence of necessary events for coalition termination (e.g. departure of one or more pivotal coalition members, prime minister fails to mend fences, head of state accepts resignation, and so forth). Here the conditions of theorem 8.1 may not be met, primarily because some of these events may not occur independently (e.g. the probability of a head of state accepting the resignation of a cabinet government is likely to be significantly influenced by the prior events.) In spite of this, empirical studies show strong support for the exponential distribution, with (King et al. 1990) and without (Browne et al. 1986; Cioffi-Revilla 1984) explicit hazard forces. Under this conjunctive argument – a set of necessary conditions must be met for a coalition to terminate – then (by theorem 8.1) the expected aggregate distribution for duration D at the macro level would be exponential, as observed, if the individual distributions for the necessary events were also exponential. Causally, coalition dissolution $\mathbb{F}$ is mostly governed by defection decision rates, so the theory predicts that these must be exponentially distributed as well.

To sum up, the unified principles which link the two levels of analysis can be used to investigate political coalitions from new macro and micro perspectives, with the two levels related, to gain a better understanding of their uncertainty properties. Specifically, we may use individual event structures at the micro level to account for observed distributions at the macro level; or, we may use aggregate empirical distributions at the aggregate level to explore inferences about what may be occurring at the micro level, inside the black box. At a minimum, these principles should assist us in developing new causal theories of coalitions, founded on the individual occurrence of events, composed of states of nature (e.g. situational attributes, such as polarization) and decisional acts (e.g. decisions to join, remain, or defect), with their related, observable aggregate properties at the macro level.

8.4.2   Conflict: domestic violence and international war

In chapter 2 (example 2.2), I proposed a macro level perspective on the process of warfare – the aggregate process of onset, duration, and termination – as a multidimensional phenomenon described by a set of dependent variables with individual values that occur on the historical timeline τ (the n-tuple in figure 2.2). Although I developed the example of international (world) war, the same theoretical perspective is valid for domestic political violence (e.g. riots) and civil war. At the macro level of analysis, warfare (domestic or international) is an n-tuple consisting of onset times $t \in T$, magnitude $\mu \in M$, size $s \in S$, duration $\delta \in D$, and other dimensions discussed in chapter 2. Here the behavior of a conflict variable Y is viewed as a black box that is governed by the hazard forces discussed in chapters 3 and 4. Some warfare processes are governed by implicit hazard forces (classes 1 and 2 in table 4.1), while others are affected by explicit forces (classes 3 and 4 in table 4.1). For example, recent studies have shown that the onset T of riots in urban areas is governed not only by intrinsic hazard forces, as early investigations had reported (Midlarsky 1978; Spilerman 1970, 1971), but also by other contextual forces as well (Olzak et al. 1996). A similar phenomenon is reported for the duration D of interstate rivalries (Cioffi-Revilla 1998), which is also exponentially distributed with other specified hazard factors (section 4.4.2). Overall, our current understanding is that the aggregate dimensions of political conflict and warfare are often exponentially distributed, or sometimes Weibull distributed with shape parameter α close to the Poisson case.

At the micro level of analysis, warfare breaks out ($\mathbb{W}$) when a conflict escalates (figure 6.2), and terminates ($\mathbb{T}$) when the fighting ceases. War onset occurs when a set of necessary conditions are met, including the escalation of force, persistence of and resistance to provocation events. In the case of conflict, most of these events are decisional outcomes, not states of nature. Causally, this means that the event function for $\mathbb{W}$ is conjunctive, with $\mathbb{X}_1, \mathbb{X}_2, \mathbb{X}_3, \ldots, \mathbb{X}_n$ describing the necessary events (e.g. the sequential logic events in figure 6.2). Not surprisingly, conjunctions of decisional acts are often modeled as game-theoretic situations. Now, by theorem 8.1, if each of these necessary events occurs with exponential distribution, then the onset process T will also be exponentially distributed. Richardson's (1960) pioneering study of deadly quarrels – including domestic and international warfare – reported a high degree of empirical fit for the exponential distribution (Poisson process), as I discussed in chapter 4. The micro level analysis based on individual event occurrences offers a causally plausible theoretical explanation for observing conflicts occur with exponential distribution. Aggregate onset behavior may be caused by a variety of constant hazard forces (of different intensity k_i) acting to escalate various security issues, any one of which can produce war.

Other studies should be undertaken to explore the underlying causal structure of the Weibull distribution at the micro level and better understand its complexity. Based on the unified results discussed in the previous section (8.2), an aggregate Weibull distribution for war onset at the macro level can be caused by a set of Weibull-distributed hazard forces with individual intensity (k) and shape (α) parameters at the micro level arranged in conjunction. A plausible political interpretation of this situation would be to distinguish different types of security threats (e.g. territorial, symbolic, resources, and so on), each affected by its own distinct hazard force with individual intensity and shape. This diverse array can still be synthesized by the same methods as in theorems 8.1 and 8.2. For domestic political conflict, a similar situation can be interpreted, considering multiple but differentiated threats to internal stability. These and other micro level structures can provide new insights to better understand onsets of conflict that are observed at the macro level.

Viewing the warfare process from a different perspective, the duration of war (producing an individual duration $\delta \in D$) is marked by the occurrence of an event $\mathbb{D}$ ("war terminates") with event function Ψ, where each event ($\mathbb{X}_1$, $\mathbb{X}_2$, $\mathbb{X}_3$, ..., $\mathbb{X}_n$) marks the occurrence of necessary and sufficient events for war termination (e.g. cessation of hostilities on both sides, and so forth). The conditions of theorem 8.1 must be closely examined, because some of these events may not occur independently (e.g. cessation by one side may be conditional on cessation by the other). As I have discussed elsewhere (Cioffi-Revilla 1989), empirical studies beginning with Horvath (1968) and Weiss (1963) have reported strong support for the Weibull distribution. Under which causal argument at the micro level – which event function for a set of necessary and sufficient conditions for war to terminate – would the duration D at the macro level be Weibull distributed? One possibility already mentioned is that the micro level – inside the black box – consists of a conjunction of Weibull occurrences with different intensities (k_i) and shapes (α_i). This and similar cross-level questions can be explored further through unified principles.

The unified principles which link the two levels of analysis can be used to investigate political conflict from new macro and micro perspectives, with the two levels related, to gain a better understanding of their uncertainty properties. We may use individual event structures at the micro level to account for observed distributions at the macro level; or, we may use macro empirical distributions at the aggregate level to explore inferences about what may be occurring at the micro level, inside the black box. At a minimum, these principles should assist us in developing new causal theories of conflict, founded on the individual occurrence of events, composed of states of nature (e.g. situational attributes, such as alliance configurations) and decisional acts (e.g. decisions to resist, persist, and escalate), with their related, observable aggregate properties at the macro level.

8.5   Conclusions

The theoretical motivation for this chapter consisted in the need to explore and develop plausible linkages across levels of analysis, particularly in the light of the concepts and principles of political uncertainty discussed in earlier chapters. As an ancient puzzle, the levels of analysis problem persists as an enduring challenge in contemporary political science, as well as in the other social sciences such as anthropology, economics, psychology, and sociology. Given its complexity and diverse manifestations, in all likelihood this puzzle will continue to defy any definitive solution. However, its occurrence in the context of political uncertainty at both levels – macro and micro – coupled with the derivation of a set of principles at both levels suggests some plausible solutions or at least partial answers that can advance our understanding.

In this final chapter I attempted to suggest some new ways in which to relate the uncertainty of politics across different levels of analysis. I examined two fundamental situations which are analytically simple but theoretically insightful: aggregate macro political behavior which results from individual micro occurrences with constant hazard forces operating under pure conjunction and pure disjunction. The two unified principles derived in this chapter for conjunction and disjunction, respectively, showed that macro political behavior in both cases can be unambiguously synthesized from micro political events. In terms of complexity – and earlier ideas explored by Lasswell, Eulau, and others more recently – the case of causal conjunction at the micro level was shown to give rise to resultant (linear additive) behavior at the macro level; whereas disjunction gives rise to emergent (truly complex) behavior.

I also explored the reverse level of analysis problem – what can be inferred about the micro level, given some knowledge about the macro level? – showing that only weak inferences may be drawn, under special conditions, but even these can be insightful in spite of their more limited scope. Uncertainty exists across levels of analysis because we either assume an underlying causal structure and are thereby able to infer the micro level distributions or, alternatively, assume the micro level distributions and are thereby able to infer the underlying causal structure. We cannot infer both micro properties simultaneously, no matter how complete is our knowledge of aggregate political behavior at the macro level.

Although ubiquitous, consequential, and ineradicable, the uncertainty of politics is scientifically tractable and has numerous intriguing properties which can be systematically explored, as I have attempted to demonstrate throughout this book. General and special principles exist that can account for the properties of political uncertainty, yielding new insights and suggesting future lines of investigation. This theory seeks to understand politics with all its uncertainty, proposing implications for other theories where political events and their probabilities are elemental but left as axiomatic. Political events and their probabilities should also be analyzed with greater rigor in decisional and game models, to improve our understanding of uncertainty in situations of interdependent decision making. From this perspective, an obvious area for applying these principles is in the probabilistic stability of game equilibria (e.g. mutual cooperation in the game of prisoner's dilemma, or deadlock in the game of chicken) where uncertainty and its purposive political manipulation play a significant role.

In comparative terms, the theory requires further evaluation across different sets of political conditions and historical eras containing diverse political actors, processes, or systems, all of them affected by different forces but governed by the same uniform principles. Future research may also contribute to our scientific understanding of whether the uncertain character of politics in the present age – how the lives, fortunes, and government of collectivities is patterned – bears resemblance to previous eras. Such knowledge could help explain where the global polity may be directed, perhaps in time to rethink its course if need be.

Appendix 1: Glossary

This appendix provides a survey of the principal terms that are used in the theory of political uncertainty, as well as some other auxiliary terms from logic, probability, or methodology. More rigorous definitions are provided in the text and in appendix 4.

Causal mechanism. Process linking causes and effects. See also *Deterministic causality* and *Probabilistic causality.*

Causal probability. Probability of a causal event, usually treated as an independent variable for obtaining the probability of a referent political event (dependent variable).

Common cause. Causal event that occurs more than once in the event function of a political event.

Conditional logic. Specification of the causal occurrence of a political event as explained by a set of necessary or sufficient conditions.

Conditional–sequential logic. Specification of the occurrence of a political event explained in conditional logic, for which the necessary or sufficient events are in turn explained as outcomes in sequential logic.

Conjunction. Political occurrence by necessary conditions.

Conjunctive principle. Theorem that provides the probability of a political event in terms of the probabilities of its necessary conditions.

Cumulative probability function. Relationship that relates the values of a political variable and their corresponding cumulative probability of occurring.

Determinism. Situation whereby, having complete information regarding the structure of a system and its initial condition, it is possible to predict with total certainty the future behavior of the system (Laplace).

Deterministic causality. Causal mechanism based on determinism.

Dimensionality. Property of aggregate political behavior concerning the variables (dimensions) that can be defined to characterize it.

Disjunction. Political occurrence by sufficient conditions.

Disjunctive principle. Theorem that provides the probability of a political event in terms of the probabilities of its sufficient conditions.

Distributions principle. Macro principle that relates the aggregate distributions of a political variable to the causal hazard forces.

Dominance principles. Logic principles that establish the relative sensitivity in the probability of a political event to changes in independent variables.

Duality of politics. Politics as consisting fundamentally of aggregate behavioral dimensions (variables at the macro level) and individual occurrences (events at the micro level).

Emergent property. Macro level political property caused by the nonlinear aggregation of micro level effects. See also *Resultant property.*

Event. Set of sample (elemental) points drawn from a sample space consisting of decisional acts and states of nature. See *Sample space.*

Event function. Causal proposition that specifies the occurrence of a political event in either sequential or conditional logic, based on necessary and sufficient event conditions.

Event tree. Graphic representation of the event function of a political event.

Expectation principle. Macro principle that relates the moments of a political variable to the causal hazard forces.

Explicit hazard force model. Model of political behavior based on a set of exogenous hazard forces, such as causally relevant social, economic, or other contextual conditions.

Force. See *Hazard force.*

Hazard force. Probabilistic propensity, intensity, or tension for the occurrence of a given value of a political variable. Causal agent that accounts for aggregate political behavior through probabilistic causality. Independent variable at the macro level of the theory of political uncertainty.

Hazard force function. Function that specifies a set of hazard rate values for values of an associated political variable.

Hyperexponential distribution. The probability distribution of a political behavior that has greater variance than mean value.

Hyperprobability. Probability surplus that occurs in political events that are caused by disjunction of sufficient conditions. The larger probability of a referent political event compared to the probability of its sufficient causes.

Hypoexponential distribution. The probability distribution of a political behavior that has smaller variance than mean value.

Hypoprobability. Probability deficiency that occurs in political events that are caused by conjunction of necessary conditions. The smaller probability of a referent political event compared to the probability of its necessary causes.

Implicit hazard force model. Model of political behavior based on endogenous hazard force, without detailing other variables external to the political behavior.

Initiating event. The first event defined in the sequential logic occurrence of a political event.

Integrated logic. Specification of the occurrence of a political event explained as a combination of sequential and conditional logics.

Intensity variable. Dimension of political behavior associated with a significant magnitude, for example, level of domestic political violence, size of a coalition, or voter turnout at an election.

Kaplan–Meier estimate. Empirical value of a function obtained by interpolation between midpoints. Used in the estimation of empirical probability functions such as the density function and the hazard rate function.

Kinematic principles. Principles of political uncertainty that explain changes in the probability of a political event as a function of changes in independent variables over time.

Kinematics. Theory of change based on the passage of time.

Logic. Causal structure of necessary (conjunctive) and sufficient (disjunctive) conditions for the occurrence of a political event.

Logic order. Level of causal remoteness for the occurrence of a referent political event. Immediate causes are first order, followed by second order, third order, and so on, as a result of asking the conditional logic question: how can or how does this occur?

Macro level of analysis. Theoretical level of analysis that explains aggregate political behavior based on hazard forces as the causal agents.

Measurability. Property of a political variable to be measured.

Median principle. Macro principle that relates the median value of a political variable to the causal hazard forces.

Median value. Value of a political variable that has even-odds of occurring.

Micro level of analysis. Theoretical level of analysis that explains individual political events based on necessary and sufficient occurrences as the causal agents.

Modal principle. Macro principle that relates the modal value of a political variable to the causal hazard forces.

Modal value. The value of a political variable having the highest probability of occurrence.

Moments of a political variable. The expected value (expectation or arithmetic mean), the variance, and other statistics that describe the distribution of a political variable.

Moments principle. Macro principle that relates the moments of a political variable to the causal hazard forces.

Monocausal model. Model of political behavior based on a single hazard force.

Multicausal model. Model of political behavior based on a set of several causal hazard forces.

Poisson model. Probability model first developed by the French mathematician Siméon Denis Poisson during the French Revolution to describe the probability of obtaining an erroneous conviction by a jury.

Politics. Social phenomena (variables or events) that affect the lives, fortunes, or governance of a collectivity of individuals, including the allocation of values and solving collective action problems.

Probabilistic causality. Causal mechanism based on a probabilistic realization or occurrence.

Probability. Formal measure of the uncertainty of occurrence associated with a given event.

Probability density function. Relationship that specifies the set of values of a political variable and the probability density of each value.

Random variable. A variable that has a probability value associated to each of the values it may assume.

Resultant property. Macro level property caused by the linear aggregation of effects at the micro level. See also *Emergent property.*

Sample space. Universal set of all possible elemental events used to define an event. A political sample space is often defined in terms of decisional acts and states of nature related to or affecting the governance of a collectivity.

Sensitivity principles. Political uncertainty principles that account for changes in the probability of a political event as a function of changes in other causal factors (independent variables).

Sequential–conditional logic. Specification of the occurrence of a political event explained in sequential logic, with each prior event explained in terms of its own conditional logic for occurrence.

Sequential logic. Specification of the occurrence of a political event explained as an outcome from prior events.

Sequential principle. Micropolitical principle that relates the probability of a political event to the probabilities of its sequential logic causes.

Several-among-some principle. Micropolitical principle that provides the probability of a political event when occurrence is caused by several necessary (conjunctive) conditions that can be drawn as a combination from a larger set of other alternative (disjunctive) causes.

Special values. Set of values that have properties of general interest in the uncertain behavior of a political variable at the macro level of analysis. See also *Median value*; *Modal value*; *Moments of a political variable*.

State of nature. An event that is generally not produced by human choice. For example, "rain" versus "sunshine" are states of nature, as are "high" versus "low" government ratings in public opinion.

Statics. Theory of causes independent of time.

Surprisability. Measure of political uncertainty. The ratio of the standard deviation to the mean value of a political variable.

Temporal variable. Dimension of political behavior associated with the onset or duration of a political event, such as for onset and duration of coalitions, conflicts, or other aggregate phenomena that take place over time.

Theory of political uncertainty. Framework for explaining the behavior of political variables and the occurrence of political events according to probabilistic causality, based on general, special, and unified principles.

Top event. Event at the top of an event tree in conditional logic. Referent political event in conditional logic.

Uncertainty. Property of politics that accounts for the random behavior of political variables and events in terms of their probability, as calculated from causes (hazard forces or other necessary and sufficient conditions).

Unified principle. Principle of political uncertainty that relates the macro level of aggregate behavior in variables to the micro level of individual behavior in event occurrences.

Weibull model. Model of political behavior with a single implicit hazard force (implicit–multicausal model) that can increase, decrease, or remain constant.

Appendix 2: Notation

The system of notation I use in this book mostly follows the standard conventions (American Mathematical Society 1984; *Chicago Manual of Style* 1983: ch. 13; James 1992) with only minor exceptions.

Variables are denoted by upper-case Roman letters in italics (X), values of variables by lower case (x), events and sets by hollow Gothic letters ($\mathbb{X}$), and vectors by bold-face letters ($\mathbf{x}$). I use the same symbol for an event as for a set because my theory of political uncertainty conceptualizes (defines) an event as a point set, consistent with standard practice in modern probability theory. Following a similar convention for dependent and independent variables, the main political variable or event to be being explained (the referent *explanandum*) is generally denoted by the symbols Y or $\mathbb{Y}$, respectively. By contrast, other variables or events that are considered as causal or explanatory (the *explanans*) are denoted by symbols such as $X, Z, \mathbb{X},$ or $\mathbb{Z}$.

No special symbol is used to denote a random variable (r.v.), as opposed to a deterministic variable, because all variables in the macro level of the theory (chapters 2, 3, and 4) are random. The symbol "$\mathbf{P}(\ )$" always denotes the probability of the event within the parentheses. When treating a probability as a variable, the symbol X is used to mean the same as $\mathbf{P}(\mathbb{X})$.

The following listing includes those symbols that are used generally more than once. Conventional symbols from logic, set theory, probability, and calculus are assumed (e.g. $d/dx, f, \lim, \approx, e, \hat{\ }$), so I do not list these. See also appendices 3 and 4.

A	area between kinematic probability trajectories
a, b, c	parameters in macropolitical model IV
D	war duration; coalition duration; duration variable
$D_x(Y)$	first-order difference of Y with respect to X
E	expected value; first moment
$E_A(\mathbb{X})$	A's expected utility of act $\mathbb{X}$
H	behavioral force (hazard rate)
$I(y)$	input function for political behavior
K	gap between P and $\mathbf{P}(\mathbb{Y})$ caused by hypo- or hyperprobability
k	war onset rate; Poisson constant in model I
L	canonically transformed behavioral force
M	war magnitude
$M(\alpha)$	moment-generating function
P	probability of a conjunctive causal event

$\mathbf{P}(\mathbb{X})$	probability of a conjunctive causal event
$\mathbf{P}(\mathbb{Y})$	probability of a referent political event
$\mathbf{P}(\mathbb{Z})$	probability of a disjunctive causal event
$\mathbf{P}(y)$	probability of value $y \in Y$
$p(y)$	probability density function (p.d.f.) of variable Y
p_i	probability of the ith prior event in sequential logic ($i = 1, 2, 3, \ldots, n$)
Q	probability of a disjunctive causal event
q_j	probability of the jth disjunctive causal event ($j = 1, 2, 3, \ldots, m$)
S	coalition size; war size; size variable
s	value of coalition size; value of war size; value of size variable
$s_x(Y)$	sensitivity of Y with respect to X
$\mathbf{S}(\mathbb{X})$	subjective probability of event $\mathbb{X}$
$S(y)$	survival function of variable Y
T	time between events (dependent variable)
t	value of time between events
V	variance; second moment
$\mathbb{W}$	event "war onset"
X	generic independent variable
X_i	ith generic independent variable
x	value of a generic independent variable
$\mathbb{X}$	causal conjunctive explanatory event qua independent variable
Y	political behavior variable; generic dependent variable
y	value of political behavior variable; value of generic dependent variable
$\mathbb{Y}$	political event, referent political event, main event of interest
$\mathbb{Z}$	causal disjunctive explanatory event qua independent variable
α	generic parameter; qualitative adversity in model III
β	generic parameter
Γ, γ	number of disjunctive, sufficient, or OR-related events
Δ	interval
δ	value of duration variable
ε	error term in a regression equation
ζ	$\ln 2 \approx 0.69$; semiprobability constant
Θ, θ	number of conjunctive, necessary, OR Boolean AND events
κ	hazard intensity in model III
Λ, λ	length of a sequential process leading to a political event
μ	value of war magnitude
v	number of requisites in several-among-some (v-out-of-m) causality
$\hat{v}$	estimate of relative frequency
ρ	slope of hazard rate in model II
$\sum$	set of special values of a political variable
σ	standard deviation
τ	time (calendrical, chronological)
Φ	cumulative probability density
$\Phi(y)$	cumulative density function (c.d.f.) of variable Y
ϕ	initial value of hazard rate in model II
Ψ	event function
Ψ_c	conditional logic event function

Ψ_s	sequential logic event function
$\Psi_\cup$	conditional logic disjunctive event function
$\Psi_\cap$	conditional logic conjunctive event function
ψ	median value of political behavior
Ω	sample space of political events
ω	modal value of political behavior

References

American Mathematical Society. 1984. *A Manual for Authors of Mathematical Papers*. Providence, RI: American Mathematical Society.

James, Robert C., ed. 1992. *Mathematics Dictionary*. Princeton, New Jersey: D. Van Nostrand Reinhold.

The Chicago Manual of Style. 1994. 14th edition. Chicago: University of Chicago Press.

Appendix 3: Proofs

MACRO PRINCIPLES

THEOREM 3.1 (distributions principle)

Proof: this proof consists of two stages (Cioffi-Revilla 1984, 1985a, 1985b). Equation 3.2 is derived first, followed by equation 3.1. First, by the standard definitions of the probability density and cumulative functions (eqaution 2.10),

$$p(y) = \frac{d}{dy} \Phi(y)$$

$$= \frac{d}{dy} \left[\int_{-\infty}^{y} p(u) du \right].$$

Taking derivatives on both sides of this expression and rearranging terms yields

$$\frac{d}{dy} [1 - \Phi(y)] = -p(y).$$

Solving for $p(y)$ in this last expression and substituting for the definition of hazard force (equation 2.19) yields

$$H(y) = - \left[\frac{\frac{d}{dy}[1 - \Phi(y)]}{1 - \Phi(y)} \right].$$

Integrating both sides of this expression from 0 to y, since $H(y) \geq 0$, we obtain

$$\int_{0}^{y} H(u) du = - \int_{0}^{y} \left[\frac{\frac{d}{du}[1 - \Phi(u)]}{1 - \Phi(u)} \right] du$$

$$= \ln [1 - \Phi(y)].$$

Finally, solving this last expression for $\Phi(y)$ yields

$$\Phi(y) = 1 - \exp\left[-\int_0^y H(u)du \right],$$

which is equation 3.2 in the distributions principle (theorem 3.1). Second, taking derivatives on both sides of equation 3.2 yields

$$\Phi'(y) = 1 - \frac{d}{dy}\left[-\int_0^y H(u)du \right],$$

which reduces to equation 3.1. $\square$

THEOREM 3.2 (moments principle)

Proof: equation 3.3 follows from direct substitution of equation 3.2 into the standard definition of the moment generating function $M(\alpha)$ and simplifying the result. $\square$

THEOREM 3.3 (expectation principle)

Proof: equation 3.4 obtains from direct substitution of equation 3.2 into the standard definition of the first moment,

$$E(Y) = \int_{-\infty}^{+\infty} y\,p(y)\,dy.$$

Equation 3.5 is the standard definition of the second moment. $\square$

THEOREM 3.4 (median principle)

Proof: by the definition of the median value (definition 2.3), $\Phi(\psi) = 1/2$. Using equation 3.2 to replace $\Phi(\psi)$ with $H(\psi)$ yields equation 3.6:

$$1 - \exp\left[-\int_0^\psi H(y)dy \right] = 1/2$$

$$-\int_0^\psi H(y)dy = \ln 1 - \ln 2$$

$$= -\zeta. \qquad \square$$

THEOREM 3.5 (modal principle)

Proof: by the definition of the modal value (definition 2.4), $dp(y)/dy = 0$ for $y = \omega$. Equation 3.7 obtains by applying the chain rule to equation 3.2, symplifying the result, and equating it to zero. The complete solution follows by solving for ω.

THEOREM 4.1 (special principles of model I)

Proof: equations 4.2 to 4.6 are obtained by assigning a constant value k to $H(y)$ in all the preceding results and simplifying the expressions. □

THEOREM 4.2 (special principles of model III)

Proof: equations 4.10 to 4.14 are obtained by substituting equation 4.9 into the same equations that earlier (theorem 4.1) resulted in equations 4.2 to 4.6. □

MICRO PRINCIPLES

THEOREM 6.1 (sequential probability principle of a political event)

Proof: equation 6.2 is the event function for a compound event consisting of prior conditionals. Equation 6.3 follows directly from the multiplication theorem for the probability of a compound event. Note that probabilities will multiply even if the events are conditional. QED. Equation 6.4 is a shorthand simplication of equation 6.3 obtained by assuming that all the probabilities of the Λ events that lead to $\mathbb{Y}$ have the same value P. □

COROLLARY 6.1 (sequential hypoprobability principle of a political event)

Proof: the product of any two numbers in the open interval $(0, 1)$ is always smaller than the smallest of the two. Since $1 < p < 0$, except in trivial cases (when $p = 0$ or 1, corresponding to impossibility and certainty, respectively), it follows that $\mathbf{P}(\mathbb{Y})$ must be smaller than the smallest of the two probabilities. □

COROLLARY 6.4 (nonlinear sequential probability of a political event)

Proof: the inequalities in this theorem follow directly from the elasticities of $\mathbf{P}(\mathbb{Y})$ with respect to P and Λ in the range of values $0 < P < 1$ and $\Lambda > 1$. □

THEOREM 6.2 (existence and nonuniqueness principle of political event logics)

Proof: if $\mathbb{Y}$ is a nonempty point set, then it must be susceptible to at least one partition. □

THEOREMS 6.3 AND 6.4 (probabilities of conjunctive and disjunctive political events)

Proof: theorems 6.3 and 6.4 obtain from the application of the theorem for the probability of a compound event. $\square$

COROLLARIES 6.8 AND 6.9 (elasticities of conjunctive and disjunctive political events)

Proof: these corollaries follow the proof of Corollary 6.2. $\square$

UNIFIED PRINCIPLES

THEOREM 8.1 (unified principle for conjunction of constant hazard forces)

Proof: this proof is constructed in two stages. First, recall the survival function $S(y)$ of the r.v. Y (discussed in section 3.3.1), given by

$$S(y) = 1 - \Phi(y) = \mathbf{P}(Y > y),$$

which defines the probability of a value larger than y being realized. When Y is a time variable D or T, then S represents the probability of lasting longer than δ, or

$$S(\delta) = \mathbf{P}(D > \delta) = 1 - \mathbf{P}(D \le \delta).$$

In a conjunctive mode, for $\mathbb{Y}$ to endure $(D > \delta)$ it is necessary that all the n necessary events also endure. Thus (by the conjunctive principle), for the event $\mathbb{Y}$,

$$S_Y(\delta) = S_1(\delta) \cdot S_2(\delta) \cdot S_3(\delta) \cdot \ldots \cdot S_n(\delta).$$

Now, equation 8.1 is

$$\begin{aligned}\Phi_i(y) &= 1 - e^{k_i y} \\ &= 1 - S_i(\delta)\end{aligned}$$

so

$$S_i(\delta) = e^{-k_i y}$$

and therefore

$$\begin{aligned}S_Y(\delta) &= e^{-k_1 y} \cdot e^{-k_2 y} \cdot e^{-k_3 y} \cdot \ldots \cdot e^{-k_n y} \\ &= 1 - \Phi_Y(y).\end{aligned}$$

Second, this last expression is solved for $\Phi(y)$ and simplified to yield equation 8.2. From this, equations 8.3, 8.4, and 8.5 are derived by applying the standard general principles for distribution functions and special values in chapter 5. $\square$

THEOREM 8.2 (unified principle for disjunction of constant hazard forces)

Proof: this proof is similar to the previous, constructed in two stages. Under disjunction, for $\mathbb{Y}$ to endure $(D > \delta)$ it is sufficient that one of the m events also endures. Thus (by the disjunctive principle), for the event $\mathbb{Y}$,

$$S_Y(\delta) = 1 - [1 - S_1(\delta)] \cdot [1 - S_2(\delta)] \cdot [1 - S_3(\delta)] \cdot \ldots \cdot [1 - S_m(\delta)]$$

The rest of the proof is by the same substitutions as before. Note: In general, the distribution and special value functions (e.g. equations 8.2–8.5 and 8.7–8.10) are derived by first constructing the appropriate survival function and then carrying out the necessary substitutions. □

Appendix 4: Methods

This appendix highlights some methodological tools used in theoretical politics for deriving results and exploring aspects of political uncertainty. In general, but not exclusively, continuous methods are used primarily at the aggregate macro level, whereas discrete methods are used primarily at the micro level of events. However, important insights are obtained in reverse (e.g. sensitivity and dominance principles at the micro level). Unified principles require the combined application of most of these methods.

Consider a continuous function in several independent variables and parameters, with general form:

$$Y = Y(X_1, X_2, X_3, \ldots; \alpha, \beta, \gamma, \ldots).$$

Several mathematical tools exist to analyze the behavior of such a function with respect to changes in the independent variables or in the parameters. For example, one may want to compare how Y is affected by changes in several variables (e.g. X_1 and X_3) contained in the argument of the function. In general, these tools are essential to gain a better understanding of the dependence of a variable Y on any set of independent variables or parameters, particularly in the case of nonlinear functions such as is common with political uncertainty and probabilistic causality. In deriving several of the theoretical principles I applied analytical techniques from elementary multivariate analysis, including derivatives, elasticities, gradients, and the Laplacian (Kaplan 1984; Lang 1992). These tools are based on the following standard concepts.

FUNCTIONS AS INPUT–OUTPUT SYSTEMS

A real-valued function $Y = f(X)$ is a mapping of values x_1, x_2, x_3, …, from a domain $\{X\}$ to a range $\{Y\}$ with values y_1, y_2, y_3, … Such a mapping can also be represented as as an input-output system with general form:

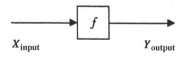

This approach is used in chapter 3 to represent a set of nonlinear functions (general macropolitical principles), using different block symbols to indicate functional operations (addition, multiplication, exponentiation, integration). Although the original mathematical expression for each function is complicated (equations

3.1–3.7), the input–output graphic representation is much simpler becaused it is based on qualitatively similar basic functional forms that are used in various combinations. This method is used to obtain simpler canonical forms (equations 3.1′–3.7′) without loss of essential detail.

OBTAINING CAUSAL DEPENDENCIES

CONTINUOUS VARIABLES

The derivative of Y with respect to X, denoted by $\partial Y/\partial X$, is interpreted as the rate of change of Y with respect to change in X. The derivative is the most common mathematical tool for analyzing change. In political science, derivatives have been widely used in arms race theory (Olinick 1978; Schrodt 1976), and are used widely in conjunction with all continuous models (e.g. Ordeshook 1986; Rapoport 1983). The value of a derivative is also used to obtain the qualitative form of a function (concave, convex), or if it changes periodically (harmonic). An increasing function has a positive first derivative; a decreasing function has a negative first derivative. A concave function has cup-form ("∪") and a positive second derivative; a convex function has dome-form ("∩") and a negative second derivative. Several derivatives can be compared whenever they are expressed in the same units (comparing "apples with apples" and "oranges with oranges").[1]

DISCRETE VARIABLES

Strictly speaking, derivatives can be used only when both Y and X are continuous variables. When they are not, as when X denotes the number of events or the length Λ of a sequential branching process, then the difference is used. This is defined as

$$D_X(Y) = Y_{X+1} - Y_X.$$

COMPARING CAUSAL DEPENDENCIES

The sensitivity of Y with respect to X, denoted by $s_X(Y)$, is a relative or standardized rate of change, expressed in percentage units. This is necessary when the changes in the independent variables being compared are expressed in different units. For two continuous variables, sensitivity is an extension of the concept of the derivative and is defined as the percentage change in Y with respect to a percentage change in X. Formally,

---

[1] Economists use the term "comparative statics," meaning the derivatives of a multivariate function. I do not use this term because (i) derivatives are often expressed in different units, making the rates of change incomparable; and (ii) time (the least static of all properties!) is often one of the independent variables, making the derivative $\partial Y/\partial t$ a rather strange "comparative static."

$$s_X(Y) \equiv \frac{\dfrac{\Delta Y}{Y} \times 100}{\dfrac{\Delta X}{X} \times 100} = \left(\frac{\Delta Y}{Y}\right)\left(\frac{X}{\Delta X}\right)$$

$$= \frac{\partial Y}{\partial X}\left(\frac{X}{Y}\right).$$

Alternatively, when the independent variable X is discrete (e.g. Λ, Θ, and Γ are discrete variables in the micro theory of political events), then the first-order difference replaces the derivative, as follows:

$$s_X(Y) = (Y_{X+1} - Y_X)\left(\frac{X}{Y}\right).$$

Sensitivities are always directly comparable because they are expressed in pure numbers, whereas derivatives are not always comparable because they can be expressed in different unit (comparing "apples with oranges").

VECTOR FIELDS

Common derivatives and sensitivities are scalar quantities; they have no direction. The gradient of Y, denoted by $\vec{\nabla} Y$, is a vector (i.e. a magnitude with direction) that always points in the direction of greatest change in Y. The gradient of Y is defined as follows:

$$\vec{\nabla} Y \equiv \frac{\partial Y}{\partial X_1}\, \mathbf{e}_1 + \frac{\partial Y}{\partial X_2}\, \mathbf{e}_2 + \frac{\partial Y}{\partial X_3}\, \mathbf{e}_3 + \dots,$$

where $\mathbf{e}_1$, $\mathbf{e}_2$, $\mathbf{e}_3$, ..., are orthogonal unit vectors (sometimes also called versors) defined on the space of continuous variables $X_1, X_2, X_3, \dots$.

The Laplacian of Y, denoted by $\nabla^2 Y$, is a scalar quantity obtained from the second derivatives. This is defined as follows:

$$\nabla^2 Y \equiv \frac{\partial^2 Y}{\partial X_1^2} + \frac{\partial^2 Y}{\partial X_2^2} + \frac{\partial^2 Y}{\partial X_3^2} + \dots .$$

The Laplacian is a quantity commonly used to detect if Y shows any harmonic behavior with respect to an independent variable X.

EVENT TREES

A conditional logic tree is a graphic model of the event function of a political occurrence. A tree consists of component events ($\mathbb{Y}$, $\mathbb{X}$s, $\mathbb{Z}$s) and connectives (also called "logic gates" in the terminology of circuitry theory) that express a unique causal structure. The referent political event $\mathbb{Y}$, or main event of interest, is called

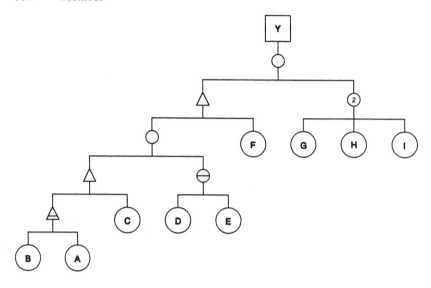

Figure A4.1. Event tree for the occurrence of a political event

the top event and is represented by a rectangle or square, as in figure A4.1. The most detailed events (often representing decisional acts and basic states of nature) are called primary events and are represented within circles.

I use the following symbols for representing the two basic Boolean logic connectives:

$\triangle$ for the Boolean AND, set intersection, conjunction, or necessity, and
$\bigcirc$ for the Boolean OR, set union, disjunction, redundancy, or sufficiency.

The first of the operations corresponds to the logic addition (+), and the latter corresponds to the dot product (•). The dot is omitted when the product is unambiguous. This formal system obeys the following laws:

Commutative law:	$A + B = B + A$
	$AB = BA$
Distributive law:	$A(B + C) = AB + AC$
Identity law:	$A + A = A$
	$AA = A$
Laws of complements (de Morgan's):	$\overline{A} + \overline{B} = \overline{(AB)}$
	$\overline{A}\,\overline{B} = \overline{(A + B)}$

In addition, I use the following auxiliary symbols to represent some recurring and important variants of the basic conjunction and disjunction operations:

$\triangle$ for the "sequential AND"

$\ominus$ for the "exclusive OR", or the English common language "either"

$\textcircled{v}$ for the "v-out-of-m OR", or combinatorial disjunction

where v is the number of sufficient conditions among m available conditions. The "sequential AND" is also used for representing the sequential conjunction and conditional occurrences. The exclusive OR means "EITHER A OR B," whereas the more common (inclusive) OR means "either A OR B or both A AND B." The "v-out-of-m" connective has two logic limits: (i) reducing to the simple "AND" as $v \to m$, and (ii) reducing to the simple (inclusive) "OR" as $v \to 1$.

Using these symbols, it is possible to translate any event equation or structure function Ψ in formal logic or set theoretic form into a conditional event tree. This is particularly useful for highlighting in visual form the complete causal structure for the occurrence or failure of a political event to a given degree of resolution. For example, consider some political event that has the following complicated event function:

$$\mathbb{Y} = \Psi(\mathbb{A}, \mathbb{B}, \mathbb{C}, \mathbb{D}, \mathbb{E}, \mathbb{F}, \mathbb{G}, \mathbb{H}, \mathbb{I})$$

$$= \{[(\mathbb{A}|\mathbb{B} \wedge \mathbb{C}) \vee (\mathbb{D} \veebar \mathbb{E})] \wedge \mathbb{F}\} \vee [(\mathbb{G} \vee \mathbb{H} \vee \mathbb{I})_2]$$

$$= \{[(\mathbb{A}|\mathbb{B} \wedge \mathbb{C}) \vee (\mathbb{D} \veebar \mathbb{E})] \wedge \mathbb{F}\} \vee [(\mathbb{G} \wedge \mathbb{H}) \vee (\mathbb{H} \vee \mathbb{I}) \vee (\mathbb{G} \wedge \mathbb{I})]$$

Using the above notation, this structure translates into the event tree shown in figure A4.1.

Event trees are useful tools for many purposes: (i) identifying common causal patterns across different political events (compare examples 7.1–7.4); (ii) obtaining the degree of resolution (causal order) for a given political event or for a theory concerning its occurrence; and (iii) finding common causes or "cut sets" (for failure events) and "path sets" (for occurrence events) in a complicated political occurrence.

References

Aalen, Odd O. 1978. "Nonparametric inference for a family of counting processes," *Annals of Statistics* 6: 701–26.

Abbott, Edwin A. 1952. *Flatland: A Romance of Many Dimensions*. New York: Dover.

Abelson, Robert P. 1959. "Modes of resolution of belief dilemmas," *Journal of Conflict Resolution* 3: 343–52.

Aberle, David. 1950. "The functional prerequisites of a society." *Ethics* 60: 100–11.

Adams, Brooks. 1959 [1896]. *The Law of Civilization and Decay*. New York: Vintage Books.

Allison, Graham. 1971. *The Essence of Decision: Explaining the Cuban Missiles Crisis*. Boston: Little, Brown.

Allison, Paul D. 1984. *Event History Analysis: Regression for Longitudinal Event Data*. Beverly Hills, CA: Sage.

Almond, Gabriel A. 1960. "A functional approach to comparative politics." In James S. Coleman (ed.), *The Politics of Developing Areas*. Princeton, NJ: Princeton University Press.

  1990. *A Discipline Divided*. Newbury Park, CA: Sage.

Almond, Gabriel A., and G. Bingham Powell, Jr. 1978. *Comparative Politics: System, Process, and Policy*, 2nd edn. Boston: Little, Brown.

Almond, Gabriel A., and Steven J. Genco. 1977. "Clouds, clocks, and the study of politics," *World Politics* 29: 489–522.

Almond, Gabriel A., G. Bingham Powell, Jr., and Robert J. Mundt. 1996. *Comparative Politics: A Theoretical Framework*, 2nd edn. New York: HarperCollins.

Anderson, John R. 1983. "A spreading activation theory of memory," *Journal of Verbal Learning and Verbal Behavior* 22: 261–95.

Aracil, Javier, and Miguel Toro. 1984. "A case study of qualitative change in system dynamics," *International Journal of Systems Science* 15(6): 575–99.

Archibald, G. C., and Richard G. Lipsey. 1976. *An Introduction to Mathematical Economics: Methods and Applications*. New York: Harper and Row.

Aristotle. 1941. *Nicomachean Ethics*. New York: Random House.

Arrow, Kenneth J. 1951. *Social Choice and Individual Values*. New Haven, CT: Yale University Press.

  1956. "Mathematical models in the social sciences," *General Systems: Yearbook of the Society for General Systems Research* 1: 29–34.

Arthur, W. Brian. 1989. "Competing technologies, increasing returns, and lock-in by historical events," *Economic Journal* 99: 116–31.

Ashby, W. Ross. 1956. *Introduction to Cybernetics*. New York: Wiley and Sons.

Avenhaus, Rudolf, Steven J. Brams, John Fitchner, and D. Marc Kilgour. 1989. "The probability of nuclear war," *Journal of Peace Research* 26: 91–9.

Axelrod, Robert. 1967. "Conflict of interest: an axiomatic approach," *Journal of Conflict Resolution* 11: 87–99.

1973. "Schema theory: an information processing model of perception and cognition," *American Political Science Review* 67: 1248–66.

1981. "The emergence of cooperation among egoists," *American Political Science Review* 75: 306–18.

Azar, Edward E. 1980. "The Conflict and Peace Data Bank (COPDAB) project," *Journal of Conflict Resolution* 24: 143–52.

Azar, Edward E., and Joseph D. Ben-Dak, eds. 1975. *Theory and Practice of Events Research*. London: Gordon and Breach.

Bak, Per, and Kan Chen. 1991. "Self-organized criticality," *Scientific American* 264: 46–53.

Baloyra-Herp, Enrique. 1995. "When things fall apart: a preliminary Boolean analysis of regime transitions." Paper presented at the XIII World Congress of Sociology, 18–23 July, 1994, Bielefeld, Germany.

Baron, David P. 1996. "A dynamic theory of collective goods programs," *American Political Science Review* 90: 316–30.

Bartholomew, D. J. 1982. *Stochastic Models for Social Processes*. New York: Wiley.

Bartolini, Stefano. 1993. "On time and comparative research," *Journal of Theoretical Politics* 5: 131–67.

Bayes, Thomas. 1764/65. "An essay toward solving a problem in the doctrine of chance," *Philosophical Transactions of the Royal Society* 53: 370–418, and 54: 296–325; reprinted in *Biometrika* 1958, 45: 293–315.

Beck, Nathaniel. 1983. "Time-varying parameter regression models," *American Journal of Political Science* 27: 557–600.

1991. "The illusion of cycles in international relations," *International Studies Quarterly* 35: 455–76.

1996. "Reporting heteroskedasticity consistent standard errors," *Political Methodologist* 7: 4–6.

Beck, Nathaniel, and Jonathan N. Katz. 1995 "What to do (and not to do) with time-series cross-section data," *American Political Science Review* 89: 634–47.

Beer, Francis A., Alice F. Healy, Grant P. Sinclair, and Lyle E. Bourne, Jr. 1987. "War cues and foreign policy acts," *American Political Science Review* 81: 701–15.

1995. "Peace agreement, intractable conflict, escalation trajectory: a psychological laboratory experiment," *International Studies Quarterly* 39: 297–312.

Bendor, Jonathan B. 1985. *Parallel Systems: Redundancy in Government*. Berkeley, CA: University of California Press.

Bendor, Jonathan B., and Terry M. Moe. 1985. "An adaptive model of bureaucratic politics," *American Political Science Review* 79: 755–74.

Bermann, George A. 1989. "The Single European Act: a new constitution for the Community?" *Columbia Journal of Transnational Law* 27: 529–87.

Berry, Frances Stokes, and William D. Berry. 1990. "State lottery adoptions as policy innovations: an event history analysis," *American Political Science Review* 84: 395–416.

Beyth-Marom, R. 1982. "How probable is probable? A numerical translation of verbal probability expressions," *Journal of Forecasting* 1: 257–69.

Bienen, Henry, and Nicolas van de Walle. 1989. "Time and power in Africa," *American Political Science Review* 83: 19–34.

Binford, Lewis R. 1965. "Archaeological systematics and the study of culture change," *American Antiquity* 31: 203–10.

Bishir, John W., and Donald W. Drewes. 1970. *Mathematics in the Behavioral and Social Sciences*. New York: Harcourt, Brace and World.

Bittinger, Marvin L. 1976. *Calculus: A Modeling Approach*. Reading, MA: Addison-Wesley.

Bittinger, Marvin L., and J. C. Crown. 1982. *Mathematics: a Modeling Approach*. Reading, MA: Addison-Wesley.

Black, Duncan. 1958. *Theory of Committees and Elections*. Cambridge, UK: Cambridge University Press.

Blainey, Geoffrey. 1973. *The Causes of War*. New York: Macmillan.

Blalock, Hubert M., Jr. 1964. *Causal Inferences in Nonexperimental Research*. Chapel Hill, NC: University of North Carolina Press.

1989. *Power and Conflict*. Newbury Park, CA: Sage.

Blondel, Jean. 1968. "Party systems and patterns of government in Western democracies," *Canadian Journal of Political Science* 1: 180–203.

Blossfeld, Hans-Peter, and Goetz Rohwer. 1995. *Techniques of Event History Modeling*. New York: Lawrence Erlbaum.

Blossfeld, Hans-Peter, Alfred Hamerle, and Karl Ulrich Mayer. 1989. *Event History Analysis*. Hillsdale, NJ: Lawrence Erlbaum.

Bochner, Salomon. 1966. *The Role of Mathematics in the Rise of Science*. Princeton, NJ: Princeton University Press.

Bohm, David. 1957. *Causality and Chance in Modern Physics*. Philadelphia: University of Pennsylvania Press.

Boole, George. 1951 [1854]. *An Investigation of the Laws of Thought*. New York: Dover.

Boynton, G. Robert. 1980. *Mathematical Thinking about Politics*. New York: Longman.

Brams, Steven J. 1985. *Rational Politics*. Washington, DC: Congressional Quarterly Press.

1994. *A Theory of Moves*. New York and Cambridge, UK: Cambridge University Press.

Brams, Steven J., and Marc Kilgour. 1988. *Game Theory and National Security*. New York: Basil Blackwell.

Brand, Myles, ed. 1976. *The Nature of Causation*. Urbana, IL: University of Illinois Press.

Bremer, Stuart A. 1995. "Advancing the scientific study of war." In Stuart A. Bremer and Thomas R. Cusack (eds.), *The Process of War: Advancing the Scientific Study of War*. Luxembourg: Gordon and Breach.

Bremer, Stuart A., and Thomas R. Cusack, eds. 1995. *The Process of War: Advancing the Scientific Study of War*. Luxembourg: Gordon and Breach.

Brinton, Crane. 1938. *Anatomy of Revolution*. Englewood Cliffs, NJ: Prentice-Hall.

Brito, Dagobert L. 1972. "A dynamic model of an armaments race," *International Economic Review* 13: 359–75.

Brodie, Bernard. 1959. "The anatomy of deterrence," *World Politics* 11: 173.

1973. *War and Politics*. New York: Macmillan.

Bronowski, Jacob. 1978. *The Common Sense of Science*. Cambridge, MA: Harvard University Press.

Brookshire, R. G., and D. F. Duncan. 1986. "Survival in the US Congress." In M. Czudnowski and H. Clarke (eds.), *International Yearbook for Studies of Leaders and Leadership*. DeKalb, IL: Northern Illinois University Press.

Brown, Courtney. 1995. *Chaos and Catastrophe Theories*. Newbury Park, CA: Sage Publications.

Browne, Eric C. 1984. "An 'events' approach to the problem of cabinet stability," *Comparative Political Studies* 17: 167–97.

1988. "Contending models of cabinet stability: rejoinder," *American Political Science Review* 82: 930–41.

Browne, Eric C., John P. Frendreis, and Denis W. Gleiber. 1986. "The process of cabinet dissolution: an exponential model of duration and stability in Western democracies," *American Journal of Political Science* 30: 628–50.

Bruschi, Alessandro. 1990. *Conoscenza e Metodo. Introduzione alla Metodologia delle Scienze Sociali* [Knowledge and Method: Introduction to the Methodology of the Social Sciences]. Milan: Mondadori.

Brzezinski, Zbigniew. 1989. "Post-Communist nationalism," *Foreign Affairs* 68: 1–25.

1993. *Out of Control: Global Turmoil on the Eve of the 21st Century*. New York: Scribner's.

Buchanan, James M. 1968. *The Demand and Supply of Public Goods*. Chicago: Rand McNally.

Bueno de Mesquita, Bruce. 1978. "Systemic polarization and the occurrence and duration of war," *Journal of Conflict Resolution* 22: 241–67.

1981. *The War Trap*. New Haven, CT, and London: Yale University Press.

Bueno de Mesquita, Bruce, and David Lalman. 1986. "Reason and war," *American Political Science Review* 80: 113–29.

1992. *Reason and War*. New Haven, CT, and London: Yale University Press.

Bunge, Mario. 1979. *Causality and Modern Science*, 3rd revised edn. New York: Dover.

Burns, Arthur Lee. 1958. "The international consequences of expecting surprise," *World Politics* July: 512.

1960. "International theory and historical explanation," *History and Theory* 1: 55–74.

Cairns, Robert B., ed. 1979. *The Analysis of Social Interactions: Methods, Issues, and Illustrations*. New York: Halstead.

Callen, E., and H. Leidecker, Jr. 1971. "A mean life on the Supreme Court," *American Bar Association Journal* 57: 1188–92.

Carmines, Edward G., and Richard A. Zeller. 1979. *Reliability and Validity Assessment*. Beverly Hills, CA: Sage.

Carneiro, Robert. 1970. "A theory of the origin of the state," *Science* 169: 733–8.

Casstevens, Thomas W. 1970. "Turnover and tenure in the Canadian House of Commons, 1867–1968," *Canadian Journal of Political Science* 3: 655–61.

1974. "The Soviet Central Committee since Stalin: a longitudinal view," *American Journal of Political Science* 18: 559–68.

1980. "Birth and death processes of governmental bureaus in the United States," *Behavioral Science* 25: 161–5.

1984. "Population dynamics of governmental bureaus," *UMAP Journal* 5.

Casstevens, Thomas W., and Harold Casstevens II. 1989. "The circulation of elites: a review and critique of a class of models," *American Journal of Political Science* 33: 296–7.

Casti, John L. 1990. *Searching for Certainty: What Scientists Can Know about the Future.* New York: William Morrow.

Chan, Steve. 1979. "The intelligence of stupidity: understanding failures in strategic warning," *American Political Science Review* 73: 171–80.

1982. "Expert judgments under uncertainty: some evidence and suggestions," *Social Science Quarterly* 63: 428–44.

Chase-Dunn, Christopher, and Thomas D. Hall. 1996. *Rise and Demise: Comparing World-Systems.* Boulder, CO: Westview Press.

Chatterjee, Partha. 1972. "The classical balance of power theory," *Journal of Peace Research* 9: 51–61.

1973. "On the rational choice theory of limited strategic war," *Indian Journal of Political Science* 34: 157–72.

1975. *Arms, Alliances, and Stability: The Development of the Structure of International Politics.* New York and New Delhi: Halsted Press of John Wiley.

Chung, Kai Lai. 1979. *Elementary Probability Theory with Stochastic Processes.* New York: Springer-Verlag.

Cioffi-Revilla, Claudio. 1979. "Diplomatic communications theory: channels, signals, and networks," *International Interactions* 6: 209–65.

1981. "Fuzzy sets and models of international relations," *American Journal of Political Science* 25: 129–59.

1983. "A probability model of credibility: analyzing strategic nuclear deterrence systems," *Journal of Conflict Resolution* 27: 73–108.

1984. "The political reliability of Italian governments: an exponential survival model," *American Political Science Review* 78: 318–37.

1985a. "Political reliability theory and war in the international system," *American Journal of Political Science* 29: 657–78.

1985b. "European political cooperation: an application of political reliability theory to integration," *International Studies Quarterly* 28: 467–92.

1985c. "Great power war and political reliability theory, 1495–1975." Paper Presented at the Annual Meeting of the American Political Science Association, New Orleans.

1986. "Teoria polemologica e scienza dei conflitti [Conflict theory and the science of conflict]," *Progetto Pace. Rivista Quadrimestrale di Ricerche sulla Pace* [Italian Quarterly Journal of Peace Research] 2: 25–48.

1987. "Crises, war, and security reliability." In Claudio Cioffi-Revilla, Richard L. Merritt, and Dina A. Zinnes (eds.), *Communication and Interaction in Global Politics.* Beverly Hills, CA: Sage.

1989. "Mathematical contributions to the scientific understanding of war," *Mathematical and Computer Modeling* 12: 561–76; reprinted in Paul E. Johnson (ed.), *Formal Theories of Politics: Mathematical Modelling in Political Science.* Oxford: Pergamon Press, pp. 533–45.

1990. *The Scientific Measurement of International Conflict: Handbook of Datasets on Crises and Wars, 1495–1988 AD.* Boulder, CO: Lynne Rienner.

1991a. "On the likely magnitude, extent, and duration of an Iraq–UN war," *Journal of Conflict Resolution* 35: 387–411.

1991b. "Data resources for the study of interstate conflict: what we have and what we need." Report prepared for the Workshop on Advancing the Scientific Study of War, sponsored by the Wissenschaftszentrum Berlin für Sozialforschung, Washington, DC, 27–29 August.

1996. "Origin and evolution of war and politics," *International Studies Quarterly* 40: 1–22.

1998. "The political uncertainty of interstate rivalries: a punctuated equilibrium model." In Paul F. Diehl (ed.), *The Dynamics of Enduring Rivalries.* Urbana, IL: University of Illinois Press, pp. 64–97.

Cioffi-Revilla, Claudio, and Raymond Dacey. 1988. "The probability of war in the *N*-crises problem: modeling new alternatives to Wright's solution," *Synthese* 76: 285–306.

Cioffi-Revilla, Claudio, and Pierangelo Isernia. 1988. "Conflict among allies: the North Atlantic area, 1948–1978." Paper presented at the Annual Meeting of the International Studies Association, Washington, DC.

Cioffi-Revilla, Claudio, and David Lai. 1995. "War and politics in Ancient China, 2700–722 BC: measurement and comparative analysis." *Journal of Conflict Resolution* 39: 467–94.

Cioffi-Revilla, Claudio, and Todd Landman. 1996. "Rise and fall of Maya polities in the ancient Mesoamerican system." Working Paper. Long-Range Analysis of War (LORANOW) Project, University of Colorado, Boulder.

Cioffi-Revilla, Claudio, and Melanie Mason. 1991. "War and Politics in Ancient China, 722–222 BC: a probabilistic theory." Paper presented at the Annual Meeting of the International Studies Association, Vancouver, BC, March.

Cioffi-Revilla, Claudio, and Richard L. Merritt. 1982. "Communications research and the new international information order," *Journal of International Affairs* 35: 225–45.

Cioffi-Revilla, Claudio, and Henrik Sommer. 1993. "War and politics in ancient Mesopotamia: a tri-force theory of war." Paper presented at the Annual Meeting of the American Political Science Association, Washington, DC.

Cioffi-Revilla, Claudio, and Harvey Starr. 1995. "Opportunity, willingness, and political uncertainty: theoretical foundations of politics," *Journal of Theoretical Politics* 7: 447–76.

Claude, Inis. 1962. *Power and International Relations.* New York: Random House.

Cohen, M. D. 1981. "The power of parallel thinking," *Journal of Economic Behavior and Organization* 2: 285–306.

Cohen, Morris R. 1942. "Causation and its application to history," *Journal of the History of Ideas* 3: 12–29.

Cohen, R., and Elman R. Service, eds. 1978. *Origins of the State: The Anthropology of Political Evolution.* Philadelphia: Institute for the Study of Human Issues.

Coleman, James S. 1973. *The Mathematics of Collective Action.* Chicago: Aldine.
    1981. *Longitudinal Data Analysis.* New York: Basic.
Coleman, Stephen. 1975. *Measurement and Analysis of Political Systems.* New
    York: John Wiley.
Conybeare, John A. C. 1990. "A random walk down the road to war: war cycles,
    prices and causality," *Defense Economics* 1: 329–37.
Cortés, Fernando, Adam Przeworski, and John Sprague. 1974. *Systems Analysis for
    Social Scientists.* New York: John Wiley.
Coughlin, Peter J. 1992. *Probabilistic Voting Theory.* Cambridge: Cambridge University
    versity Press.
Cox, David R., and Valeris Isham. 1980. *Point Processes.* London: Chapman and
    Hall.
Cox, David R., and P. A. W. Lewis. 1966. *The Statistical Analysis of Series of Events.*
    London: Methuen.
Cox, David R., and David Oakes. 1984. *Analysis of Survival Data.* London: Chapman
    man and Hall.
Culbert, T. Patrick, ed. 1973. *The Classic Maya Collapse.* Albuquerque, NM:
    University of New Mexico Press.
Cusack, Thomas R., and Wolf-Dieter Eberwein. 1982. "Prelude to war: incidence,
    escalation, and intervention in international disputes, 1900–1976," *International
    national Interactions* 9: 9–28.
Dacey, Michael F. 1970. "A probability model for the rise and decline of states,"
    Peace Research Society (International) Papers 14: 147–53.
Dacey, Raymond. 1991. "Rational dishonesty and irrational honesty." Presented at
    the annual meeting of the Peace Science (International) Society, Ann Arbor.
    1995. "Two stage inquiry and the scientific enterprise." Paper presented at the
    Logic, Methology, and Philosophy of Science Congress, Florence, Italy, August
    gust 19–25, 1995.
Dahl, Robert A. 1984. *Modern Political Analysis*, 4th edn. Englewood Cliffs, NJ:
    Prentice-Hall.
Davies, J. C. 1962. "Toward a theory of revolution," *American Sociological Review*
    27: 5–19.
Davis, K. 1959. "The myth of functional analysis," *American Sociological Review* 24:
    757–72.
Davis, Otto A., M. A. H. Dempster, and Aaron Wildavsky. 1966. "A theory of the
    budgetary process," *American Political Science Review* 60: 529–47.
Dawisha, Karen, and Bruce Parrott. 1994. *Russia and the New States of Eurasia: the
    Politics of Upheaval.* New York: Cambridge University Press.
Dawson, Christopher. 1978. *Dynamics of World History.* La Salle, IL: Sherwood
    Sugden.
de Condorcet, Marie Jean Antoine Nicolas Caritat. 1785. *Essai sur l'application de
    l'analyse à probabilité des décisions rendues à la pluralité des voix.* Paris:
    Imprimerie Royale.
De Laet, Sigfried J. 1994. "From the beginnings of food production to the first
    states." In *History of Humanity.* Vol. I: *Prehistory and the Beginnings of
    Civilization*, ed. Sifried J. De Laet. London: Routledge, for UNESCO.
de Laplace, Pierre Simon. 1812. *Théorie analytique des probabilités.* Paris: Courcier.

de Pietri-Tonelli, Alfonso. 1941. "Per una teoria matematica del puro potere politico," *Rivista di Politica Economica*: 369–86.

1943. *Teoria Matematica delle Scelte Politiche* [A Mathematical Theory of Political Decision-making]. Padua: Casa Editrice Dott. Antonio Milani (CEDAM).

De Swaan, A. 1973. *Coalition Theories and Cabinet Formations*. Amsterdam: Elsevier.

Dessler, David. 1991. "Beyond correlations: toward a causal theory of war," *International Studies Quarterly* 35: 337–55.

Deutsch, Karl W. 1966. *The Nerves of Government*. New York: Free Press.

1978. *The Analysis of International Relations*. Englewood Cliffs, NJ: Prentice-Hall.

Devaney, Robert L. 1987. "Chaotic bursts in nonlinear dynamical systems," *Science* 235: 342–5.

Diehl, Paul, ed. 1998. *Dynamics of Enduring Rivalries*. Urbana, IL: University of Illinois Press. In press.

Dodd, Lawrence C. 1976. *Coalitions in Parliamentary Government*. Princeton, NJ: Princeton University Press.

Downes, Chauncey. 1976. "Functional explanations and intentions," *Philosophy of the Social Sciences* 6: 215–25.

Downs, Anthony. 1957. *An Economic Theory of Democracy*. New York: Harper and Row.

Dray, William. 1960. "Toynbee's search for historical laws," *History and Theory* 1: 32–54.

Dunlop, John B. 1993. *The Rise of Russia and the Fall of the Soviet Empire*. Princeton, NJ: Princeton University Press.

Duvall, Raymond. 1976. "An appraisal of the methodological and statistical procedures of the Correlates of War Project." In Francis W. Hoole and Dina A. Zinnes (eds.), *Quantitative International Politics: an Appraisal*. New York: Praeger, pp. 71–3.

Duverger, Maurice. 1954. *Political Parties*. New York: Wiley.

Easton, David. 1965. *A Framework for Political Analysis*. Englewood Cliffs, NJ: Prentice-Hall.

Eberwein, Wolf-Dieter. 1981. "The quantitative study of international conflict: quantity or quality? An assessment of empirical research," *Journal of Peace Research* 18: 19–38.

Eisenstadt, Samuel N. 1985. "Civilization formations and political dynamics," *Scandinavian Political Studies* 8: 231–51.

1993 [1963]. *The Political Systems of Empires*. New Brunswick, NJ: Transactions Press.

Eisenstadt, Samuel N., M. Abitbol, and N. Chazan. 1987. "Cultural premises, political structures and dynamics," *International Political Science Review* 8: 291–306.

Eisler, Hannes. 1976. "Experiments on subjective duration 1868–1975: a collection of power function exponents," *Psychological Bulletin* 83: 1154–71.

Elandt-Johnson, Virginia, and Norman L. Johnson. 1980. *Survival Models and Data Analysis*. New York: Wiley.

Elster, Jon. 1989. *Nuts and Bolts for the Social Sciences.* Cambridge, UK: Cambridge University Press.

1993. *Political Psychology.* Cambridge, UK: Cambridge University Press.

Emerson, John D. 1986. *Classifying Probability Distribution Functions.* Arlington, MA: Consortium for Mathematics and Applications COMAP.

Enelow, James, and Melvin J. Hinch. 1984. "Probabilistic voting and the importance of centrist ideologies in democratic elections," *Journal of Politics* 46: 459–78.

Enelow, James, J. W. Endersby, and Michael C. Munger. 1993. "A revised probabilistic spatial model of elections: theory and evidence." In Bernard Grofman (ed.), *Information, Participation and Choice.* Ann Arbor, MI: University of Michigan Press.

Erickson, Robert S., and David W. Romero. 1990. "Candidate equilibrium and the behavioral model of the vote," *American Political Science Review* 84: 1103–26.

1979 [1965]. *A Systems Analysis of Political Life.* Chicago: University of Chicago Press.

Eulau, Heinz. 1963. *The Behavioral Persuasion in Politics.* New York: Random House.

1969. *Micro-Macro Political Analysis: Accents of Inquiry.* Chicago. Aldine.

1996. *Micro–Macro Dilemmas in Political Science: Personal Pathways Through Complexity.* Norman, OK: University of Oklahoma Press.

Feller, William. 1968. *An Introduction to Probability Theory and its Applications.* New York: John Wiley.

Ferejohn, John A., and James H. Kuklinski, eds. 1990. *Information and Democratic Processes.* Urbana, IL: University of Illinois Press.

Finifter, Ada. 1983. *Political Science: The State of the Discipline.* Washington, DC: American Political Science Association.

1993. *Political Science: The State of the Discipline II.* Washington, DC: American Political Science Association.

Fischer, David Hackett. 1970. *Historian's Fallacies: Toward a Logic of Historical Thought.* New York: Harper and Row.

Fisher, Roger, and William Ury. 1983. *Getting to Yes: Negotiating Agreements Without Giving in.* Harmondsworth, UK: Penguin.

Flanigan, W., and E. Fogelman. 1965. "Functionalism in political science." In D. Martindale (ed.), *Functionalism in the Social Sciences.* Philadelphia: American Academy of Political and Social Science.

Flannery, Kent V. 1972. "The cultural evolution of civilizations," *Annual Review of Ecology and Systematics* 3: 399–426.

Floud, Roderick. 1973. *An Introduction to Quantitative Methods for Historians.* Princeton, NJ: Princeton University Press.

Ford, Henry Jones. 1898. *The Rise and Growth of American Politics.* New York: Macmillan.

French, Peter A., Theodore E. Euhling, Jr., and Howard K. Wettstein, eds. 1984. *Causation and Causal Theories.* Midwest Studies in Philosophy, vol. IX. Minneapolis, MN: University of Minnesota Press.

Frendreis, John P., Denis Gleiber, and Eric C. Browne. 1986. "The study of cabinet dissolutions in parliamentary democracies," *Legislative Studies Quarterly* 11: 619–28.

Friedman, Milton. 1953. "The methodology of positive economics." In *Essays in Positive Economics.* Chicago: University of Chicago Press.

Gaddis, John Lewis. 1992. *The United States and the End of the Cold War: Implications, Reconsiderations, Provocations.* New York: Oxford University Press.

Gaile, Gary L., and Cort J. Willmott, eds. 1984. *Spatial Statistics and Models.* Dordrecht, Holland: D. Reidel.

Gaines, B. R. 1978. "Fuzzy and probability uncertain logics," *Information and Control* 38: 154–69.

Galtung, Johan. 1969. "The social sciences: an essay on polarization and integration." In Klaus Knorr and James N. Rosenau (eds.), *Contending Approaches to International Politics.* Princeton, NJ: Princeton University Press.

Garnham, David. 1985. "The causes of war: systemic findings." In Alan Ned Sabrosky (ed.), *Polarity and War: The Changing Structure of International Conflict.* Boulder, CO: Westview Press.

George, Alexander L., and Richard Smoke. 1974. *Deterrence in American Foreign Policy.* New York: Columbia University Press.

Gerstein, Dean R., R. Duncan Luce, Neil J. Smelser, and Sonja Sperlich, eds. 1988. *The Behavioral and Social Sciences: Achievements and Opportunities.* Washington, DC: National Academy Press.

Gibbon, Edward. 1946. *The Decline and Fall of the Roman Empire.* Chicago: University of Chicago Press.

Giddens, Anthony. 1995. *Beyond Left and Right: The Future of Radical Politics.* Stanford, CA: Stanford University Press.

Gill, Graeme. 1994. *The Collapse of a Single Party System: the Disintegration of the Communist Party of the Soviet Union.* Cambridge, UK: Cambridge University Press.

Gillespie, John V., and Dina A. Zinnes. 1975. "Progressions in mathematical models of international conflict," *Synthese* 31: 289–321.

Gilliant, S. 1987. "Being political: a quarrelsome view," *International Political Science Review* 8: 367–84.

Gilpin, Robert. 1981. *War and Change in World Politics.* Cambridge, UK: Cambridge University Press.

Gnedenko, B. V. 1975. *The Theory of Probability.* Moscow: Mir.

Gochman, Charles S. 1995. "The evolution of disputes." In Stuart A. Bremer and Thomas R. Cusack (eds.), *The Process of War: Advancing the Scientific Study of War.* Luxembourg: Gordon and Breach.

Gochman, Charles S., and Zeev Maoz. 1984. "Militarized interstate disputes, 1816–1976: procedures, patterns, insights," *Journal of Conflict Resolution* 28: 585–615.

Goldstein, Larry, David I. Schneider, and Martha J. Siegel. 1991. *Finite Mathematics and Its Applications*, 4th edn. Englewood Cliffs, NJ: Prentice-Hall.

Good, I. J. 1961a, 1961b, 1962. "A causal calculus," *British Journal of Philosophy of Science* 11: 305–18; 12: 43–51; 13: 88.

   1966. "The probability of war," *Journal of the Royal Statistical Society*, Series A, 129(2): 268–9.

   1972. "Review of Patrick Suppes's, *A Probabilistic Theory of Causality*," *Journal of the American Statistical Association* 67, March: 245–6.

1980. "Some comments on probabilistic causality," *Pacific Philosophical Quarterly* 61: 301–4.

Graber, Doris. 1993. "Political communication." In Ada W. Finifter (ed.), *Political Communication: the State of the Discipline II*. Washington, DC: American Political Science Association.

Granger, Gilles-Gaston. 1956. *La mathématique sociale du marquis de Condorcet*. Paris: Presses Universitaires de France.

Green, Donald P., and Jan Shapiro. 1994. *Pathologies of Rational Choice Theory: A Critique of Applications in Political Science*. New Haven, CT: Yale University Press.

Grofman, Bernard, and Peter van Roozendaal, 1997. "Modelling cabinet durability and termination," *British Journal of Political Science* 27: 419–51.

Groom, A. J. R. 1978. "Integration." In A. J. R. Groom and C. R. Mitchell (eds.), *International Relations Theory: a Bibliography*. New York: Nichols.

Gross, Alan J., and Virginia A. Clark. 1975. *Survival Distributions*. New York: Wiley.

Guetzkow, Harold. 1996 [1950]. "Long range research in international relations." In John A. Vasquez (ed.), *Classics of International Relations*, 3rd edn. Englewood Cliffs, NJ: Prentice-Hall, pp. 67–75.

Gulick, Edward V. 1955. *Europe's Classical Balance of Power*. Ithaca, NY: Cornell University Press.

Gurr, Ted Robert. 1970. *Why Men Rebel*. Princeton, NJ: Princeton University Press.

1985. "On the political consequences of scarcity and economic decline," *International Studies Quarterly* 29: 51–75.

Haas, Ernst B. 1964. *Beyond the Nation State*. Stanford, CA: Stanford University Press.

Haas, Jonathan. 1982. *The Evolution of the Prehistoric State*. New York: Columbia University Press.

Haken, Hermann. 1978. *Synergetics: an Introduction*. New York: Springer-Verlag.

Harsanyi, John C. 1962. "Mathematical models for the genesis of war," *World Politics* 14: 687–99.

Hayes, Richard E. 1973. "Identifying and measuring changes in the frequency of event data," *International Studies Quarterly* 17: 471–93.

Heider, Fritz. 1958. *The Psychology of Interpersonal Relations*. New York: Wiley.

Hempel, Carl G. 1959. "The logic of functional analysis." In L. Gross (ed.), *Symposium on Sociological Theory*. Evanston, IL: Row, Peterson, pp. 271–307.

1965. *Aspects of Scientific Explanation*. New York: Free Press.

Hernes, Helga. 1975. "Formal theories of international relations," *European Journal of Political Research* 3: 69–83.

Herz, John. 1957. *Political Realism and Political Idealism*. Chicago: University of Chicago Press.

Heyman, Edward S. 1979. "Monitoring the diffusion of transnational terrorism: a conceptual framework and methodology." Unpublished MA thesis. Department of Political Science, University of North Carolina, Chapel Hill.

Hibbert, Christopher. 1980. *The House of Medici: its Rise and Fall*. New York: Morrow Quill.

Hilpinen, Risto, ed. 1971. *Deontic Logic: Introductory and Systematic Readings.* Dordrecht, Holland: D. Reidel.

1981. *New Studies in Deontic Logic.* Dordrecht, Holland: D. Reidel.

Holsti, Kalevi J. 1991. *Peace and War: Armed Conflicts and International Order, 1648–1989.* Cambridge, UK, and New York: Cambridge University Press.

Holt, Robert T. 1965. "A proposed structural-functional framework for political science." In D. Martindale (ed.), *Functionalism in the Social Sciences.* Philadelphia: American Academy of Political and Social Science.

Hopmann, Terrence. 1967. "International conflict and cohesion in the Communist system," *International Studies Quarterly* 11: 212–36.

Horowitz, Donald L. 1985. *Ethnic Groups in Conflict.* Berkeley, CA: University of California Press.

Horvath, William J. 1968. "A statistical model for the duration of wars and strikes," *Behavioral Science* 13: 18–28.

Horvath, William J., and Caxton C. Foster. 1963. "Stochastic models of war alliances," *Journal of Conflict Resolution* 7: 110–16.

Howard, Sir Michael. 1983. *The Causes of War and Other Essays.* Cambridge, MA: Harvard University Press.

Howeling, Henke W., and J. B. Kuné. 1984. "Do outbreaks of war follow a Poisson process?" *Journal of Conflict Resolution* 28: 51–62.

Howeling, Henke W., and Jan G. Siccama. 1985. "The epidemiology of war, 1816–1980," *Journal of Conflict Resolution* 29: 641–63.

Huckfeldt, R. Robert. 1989. "Noncompliance and the limits of coercion: the problematic enforcement of unpopular laws," *Mathematical and Computer Modelling* 12: 533–45.

Huckfeldt, R. Robert, C. W. Kohfeld, and Thomas L. Likens. 1982. *Dynamic Modeling: an Introduction.* Beverly Hills, CA: Sage.

Huot, Jean-Louis, Jean-Paul Thalman, and Dominique Valbelle. 1990. *Naissance des cités* [The birth of cities]. Paris: Éditions Nathan.

Hussein, Seif M. 1987. "Modeling war and peace," *American Political Science Review* 81: 221–30.

Huth, Paul. 1988. *Extended Deterrence and the Prevention of War.* New Haven, CT: Yale University Press.

Huth, Paul, and Bruce M. Russett. 1984. "What makes deterrence work? Cases from 1900 to 1980," *World Politics* 36: 496–526.

1988. "Deterrence failure and crisis escalation," *International Studies Quarterly* 32: 29–45.

Ikle, Fred C. 1973. "Can nuclear deterrence last out the century?" *Foreign Affairs* 51: 267–85.

Isaacs, Herbert H. 1963. "Sensitivity of decisions to probability estimation errors," *Operations Research* 11: 536–52.

James, Patrick. 1993. "Neorealism as a research enterprise: toward elaborated structural realism," *International Political Science Review* 14: 123–48.

Jeffrey, Richard. 1983. *The Logic of Decision.* Chicago: University of Chicago Press.

Jillson, Calvin. 1981. "Constitution-making: alignment and realignment in the Federal Convention of 1787," *American Political Science Review* 75: 598–612.

1994. "Patterns and periodicity in American national politics." In Lawrence C. Dodd and Calvin Jillson (eds.), *The Dynamics of American Politics: Approaches and Interpretations.* Boulder, CO: Westview.

Job, Brian L. 1976. "Membership in inter-nation alliances, 1815–1965: an exploration utilizing mathematical probability models." In Dina A. Zinnes and John V. Gillespie (eds.), *Mathematical Models in International Relations.* New York: Praeger, pp. 74–109.

Jones, Bryan, ed. 1995. *The New American Politics: Reflections on Change and the Clinton Administration.* Boulder, CO: Westview Press.

Judd, Charles M., and Gary H. McClelland. 1989. *Data Analysis: A Model-Comparison Approach.* New York: Harcourt, Brace and Jovanovich.

Kahneman, Daniel, and Amos Tversky. 1979. "Prospect theory: an analysis of decision under risk," *Econometrica* 47: 263–91.

1982. "The psychology of preferences," *Scientific American* 246: 160–73.

Kalbfleisch, John D. and Ross L. Prentice. 1980. *The Statistical Analysis of Failure Time Data.* New York: Wiley.

Kaplan, E. L., and P. Meier. 1958. "Non-parametric estimation from incomplete observations," *Journal of the American Statistical Association* 53: 457–81.

Kaplan, Morton A. 1957. *System and Process in International Politics.* New York: John Wiley.

1958. "The calculus of nuclear deterrence," *World Politics* 11: 20–43.

1969. *Macropolitics: Selected Essays on the Philosophy and Science of Politics.* Chicago: Aldine.

Kaplan, Wilfred. 1984. *Advanced Calculus,* 3rd edn. Reading, MA: Addison-Wesley.

Kaufmann, Arnold, D. Grouchko, and R. Cruon. 1977. *Mathematical Models for the Study of the Reliability of Systems.* New York: Academic Press.

Kegley, Charles Jr., ed. 1991. *The Long Postwar Peace.* New York: HarperCollins.

Kegley, Charles Jr., Gregory A. Raymond, Robert M. Rood, and Richard A. Skinner, eds. 1975. *International Events and the Comparative Analysis of Foreign Policy.* Columbia, SC: University of South Carolina Press.

Kennedy, Paul. 1987. *The Rise and Fall of the Great Powers: Economic Change and Military Conflict from 1500 to 2000.* New York: Random House.

Keohane, Robert. 1984. *After Hegemony.* Princeton, NJ: Princeton University Press.

King, Gary. 1989a. *Unifying Political Methodology: the Likelihood Theory Approach.* New York: Cambridge University Press.

1989b. Computer Program to Estimate an Empirical Density Function.

King, Gary, James E. Alt, Nancy E. Burns, and Michael Laver. 1990. "A unified model of cabinet dissolution in parliamentary democracies," *American Journal of Political Science* 34: 846–71.

King, Gary, Robert O. Keohane, and Sidney Verba. 1994. *Designing Social Inquiry: Scientific Inference in Qualitative Research.* Princeton, NJ: Princeton University Press.

Kingdon, John W. 1984. *Agendas, Alternatives, and Public Policies.* Boston: Little, Brown.

1989. *Congressmen's Voting Decisions,* 3rd edn. Ann Arbor, MI: Michigan University Press.

Kline, Morris. 1985. *Mathematics and the Search for Knowledge*. Oxford: Oxford University Press.

Klosko, George. 1990. "The moral force of political obligations," *American Political Science Review* 84: 1235–48.

Kovalenko, I. N., N. Yu. Kuznetsov, and V. M. Shurenkov. 1996. *Models of Random Processes: a Handbook for Mathematicians and Engineers*. Boca Raton, FL: CRC Press.

Kramer, Gerald. 1971. "Short-term fluctuations in US voting behavior, 1896–1964," *American Political Science Review* 65: 131–43.

Krejcí, Jaroslav. 1983. *Great Revolutions Compared: the Search for a Theory*. New York: St Martin's Press.

Kugler, Jacek, and A. F. Kenneth Organski. 1989. "The power transition: a retrospective and prospective evaluation." In Manus I. Midlarsky (ed.), *Handbook of War Studies*. Boston: Unwin Hyman.

Lakatos, Imre. 1973. "Falsification and the methodology of scientific research programs." In Imre Lakatos and Alan Musgrave (eds.), *Criticism and the Growth of Knowledge*. Cambridge, UK: Cambridge University Press.

Lalman, David, Joe Oppenheimer, and Piotr Swistak. 1993. "Formal rational choice theory: a cumulative science of politics." In Ada W. Finifter (ed.), *The State of the Disciplibe II*. Washington, DC: American Political Science Association.

Landau, Martin. 1968. "On the use of functional analysis in political science," *Social Research* 35: 48–75.

1969. "Redundancy, rationality, and the problem of duplication and overlap," *Public Administration Review* 29: 346–58.

1973. "Federalism, redundancy, and systems reliability," *Publius* 3: 173–96.

1979. *Political Theory and Political Science: Studies in the Methodology of Political Inquiry*. Atlantic Highlands, NJ: Humanities Press.

Landy, Marc K., and Martin Levin. 1995. *The New Politics of Public Policy*. Baltimore, MD: Johns Hopkins University Press.

Lang, Serge. 1992. *Calculus of Several Variables*. Reading, MA: Addison-Wesley.

Lasswell, Harold. 1935. *World Politics and Personal Insecurity*. New York: McGraw-Hill.

1936. *Politics: Who Gets What, When, and How*. New York: McGraw-Hill.

Lasswell, Harold, and Abraham Kaplan. 1950. *Power and Society*. New Haven, CT: Yale University Press.

Leege, David C., and Wayne L. Francis. 1974. *Political Research: Design, Measurement, and Analysis*. New York: Basic Books.

Leng, Russell. 1993. *Interstate Crisis Behavior, 1816–1980*. Cambridge, UK, and New York: Cambridge University Press.

Levi, Werner. 1981. *The Coming End of War*. Beverly Hills, CA: Sage.

Levy, Jack S. 1983. *War in the Modern Great Power System, 1495–1975*. Lexington, KY: University Press of Kentucky.

1992. "An introduction to prospect theory," *Political Psychology* 13: 171–86.

1996. "Loss aversion, framing, and bargaining: the implications of prospect theory for international conflict," *International Political Science Review* 17: 179–95.

Levy, Marion. 1950. *The Structure of Society*. Princeton, NJ: Princeton University Press.

Lew, Darryl S. 1989. "The EEC legislative process: an evolving balance," *Columbia Journal of Transnational Law* 27: 679–719.

Li, Richard, and William R. Thompson. 1975. "The coup contagion hypothesis," *Journal of Conflict Resolution* 19: 63–88.

Liao, Tim Futing. 1994. *Interpreting Probability Models: Logit, Probit, and Other Generalized Linear Models*. Newbury Park, CA: Sage.

Lichbach, Mark Irving. 1989. "An evaluation of 'does economic inequality breed political conflict' studies," *World Politics* 41: 431–70.

1992. "Nobody cites nobody else: mathematical models of domestic political conflict," *Defense Economics* 3: 341–57.

1995. *The Rebel's Dilemma*. Ann Arbor, MI: University of Michigan Press.

1996. *The Cooperator's Dilemma*. Ann Arbor, MI: University of Michigan Press.

Lindley, D. V. 1987. "The probability approach to the treatment of uncertainty in artificial intelligence and expert systems," *Statistical Science* 2: 17–24.

Lijphart, Arend. 1994. *Electoral Systems and Party Systems*. Oxford, UK: Oxford University Press.

Machiavelli, Niccolò. 1965 [1512]. *Machiavelli: The Chief Works and Others*, vol. II. Trans. Allan Gilbert. Durham, NC: Duke University Press.

1977. *The Prince*. Transl. Robert M. Adams. New York: W. W. Norton.

Majone, Giandomenico. 1975a. "On the notion of political feasibility," *European Journal of Political Research* 3: 259–74.

1975b. "The feasibility of social policies," *Policy Sciences* 6: 49–69.

Mancini, G. Federico. 1989. "The making of a constitution for Europe," *Common Market Law Review* 26: 595–614.

Mandelbaum, Maurice. 1942. "Causal analysis in history," *Journal of the History of Ideas* 3: 30–50.

Manin, Philippe. 1987. "The European Communities and the Vienna Convention on the Law of Treaties between States and International Organizations or between International Organizations," *Common Market Law Review* 24: 457–81.

Mansfield, Edward. 1988. "The distribution of wars over time," *World Politics* 41: 21–51.

Maoz, Zeev. 1982. *Paths to Conflict: International Dispute Initiation, 1816–1976*. Boulder, CO: Westview Press.

1990. *National Choices and International Processes*. New York: Cambridge University Press.

1994. "The onset and initiation of disputes." In Stuart A. Bremer and Thomas R. Cusack (eds.), *Advancing the Scientific Study of War*. New York and London: Gordon and Breach.

Marcus, Joyce. 1992. "Dynamic cycles of Mesoamerican states", *National Geographic Research and Exploration* 8:392–411.

Masters, Roger D. 1989. *The Nature of Politics*. New Haven, CT: Yale University Press.

McCalla, Robert B. 1992. *Uncertain Perceptions: US Cold War Crisis Decision Making*. Ann Arbor, MI: University of Michigan Press.

McClelland, Charles A. 1961. "The acute international crisis," *World Politics* 14: 182–204.

1968. "Access to Berlin: the quantity and variety of events, 1948–1963." In J. David Singer (ed.), *Quantitative International Politics*. New York: Free Press, pp. 159–86.

1972. "The beginning, duration, and abatement of international crises: comparisons in two conflict areas." In Charles Hermann (ed.), *International Crises: Insights from Behavioral Research*. New York: Free Press.

1978. *World Events Interaction Survey*. World Events Interaction Survey (WEIS) Project, University of Southern California, Los Angeles, CA.

McGowan, Patrick J., and Robert M. Rood. 1975. "Alliance behavior in balance of power systems: applying the Poisson model to nineteenth century Europe," *American Political Science Review* 69: 859–70.

McIver, R. M. 1942. *Social Causation*. Boston: Ginn.

McKay, Derek, and H. M. Scott. 1983. *The Rise of the Great Powers, 1648–1815*. London: Longman.

McKelvey, Richard D., and Peter C. Ordeshook. 1986. "Sequential elections with limited information: a formal analysis," *Social Choice and Welfare* 3: 199–211.

1987. "Elections with limited information: a multidimensional model," *Mathematical Social Sciences* 14: 77–99.

Mclachlan, H. H. 1976. "Functionalism, causation, and explanation," *Philosophy of the Social Sciences* 6: 235–40.

McLaughlin, Robert, ed. 1982. *What? Where? When? Why? Essays on Induction, Space and Time, Explanation*. Boston: D. Reidel.

McNeill, William H. 1979. *A World History*. New York and Oxford: Oxford University Press.

Mearsheimer, John. 1983. *Conventional Deterrence*. Ithaca, NY: Cornell University Press.

1990. "Back to the future: instability in Europe after the Cold War," *International Security* 15: 5–56.

Merriam, Charles E. 1945. *Systematic Politics*. Chicago: University of Chicago Press.

1970. *New Aspects of Politics*. 3rd edn., enlarged. Chicago and London: Chicago University Press.

Merriman, Roger Bigelow. 1962. *The Rise of the Spanish Empire in the Old World and the New*. New York: Cooper Square.

Merritt, Richard L. 1972. *Communication in International Politics*. Urbana, IL: University of Illinois Press.

Merritt, Richard L, Robert G. Muncaster, and Dina A. Zinnes. 1993. *International Event-Data Development*. Ann Arbor, MI: University of Michigan Press.

Mershon, Carol A. 1996. "The costs of coalition: coalition theories and Italian government," *American Political Science Review* 90: 534–54.

Meyer, Paul L. 1970. *Introductory Probability and Statistical Applications*, 2nd edn. Reading, MA: Addison-Wesley.

Mezey, Michael L. 1979. *Comparative Legislatures*. Durham, NC: Duke University Press.

Midlarsky, Manus I. 1974. "Power, uncertainty, and the onset of international violence," *Journal of Conflict Resolution* 18: 395–431.

1975. *On War*. New York: Free Press.

1978. "Analyzing diffusion and contagion effects: the urban disorders of the 1960s," *American Political Science Review* 72: 996–1008.

1981. "Stochastic modeling in political science research." In C. Taillie, G. P. Patil, and Bruno Baldessari (eds.), *Statistical Distributions in Scientific Work*. Dordrecht, Holland: D. Reidel, pp. 139–40.

1983a. "Absence of memory in the nineteenth-century alliance system: perspectives from queuing theory and bivariate probability distributions," *American Journal of Political Science* 4: 762–84.

1983b. "The balance of power as a 'Just' Historical System," *Polity* 16: 181–200.

1986. "A hierarchical equilibrium theory of systemic war," *International Studies Quarterly* 30: 77–105.

1988a. *The Onset of World War*. Boston: Unwin Hyman.

1988b. "Theoretical foundations for the collection of *Major Power-Minor Power War* data," *International Interactions* 14: 187–90.

Milgram, Stanley. 1963. "Behavioral study of obedience," *Journal of Abnormal and Social Psychology* 67: 372–8.

1974. *Obedience to Authority: an experiment*. New York: Free Press.

Mill, John Stuart. 1952 [1859]. *On Liberty*. In Robert Maynard Hutchins (ed.), *Britannica Great Books of the Western World*, vol. XLIII. Chicago: Encyclopaedia Britannica.

Miller, Eugene F. 1979. "Metaphor and political knowledge," *American Political Science Review* 73: 155–70.

Mintz, Alex, and Phil A. Schrodt. 1987. "Distributional patterns of regional interactions: a test of the Poisson process as a null model." In Claudio Cioffi-Revilla, Richard L. Merritt, and Dina A. Zinnes (eds.), *Communication and Interaction in Global Politics*. Beverly Hills, CA: Sage.

Mitrany, David. 1948. "The functional approach to world organization," *International Affairs*. 24: 350–63.

1966. *A Working Peace System*. Chicago: Quadrangle Books.

1975. *The Functional Theory of Politics*. London: Martin Robertson.

Moe, Terry. 1979. "On the scientific status of rational choice theory," *American Journal of Political Science* 23: 215–43.

1990. "The politics of structural choice: toward a theory of public bureacracy." In Oliver Wilson (ed.), *Organization Theory: From Chester Barnard to the Present and Beyond*. New York: Oxford University Press.

Moe, Terry, and Scott Wilson. 1994. "Presidents and the politics of structure," *Law and Contemporary Problems* 57: 1–44.

Mohr, Lawrence. 1982. *Explaining Organization Behavior*. San Francisco: Jossey Bass.

Morgan, Granger M., and Max Henrion. 1990. *Uncertainty: a Guide to Dealing with Uncertainty in Quantitative Risk and Policy Analysis*. Cambridge, UK: Cambridge University Press.

Morgan, Patrick M. 1983. *Deterrence: a Conceptual Analysis*, 2nd edn. Beverly Hills, CA: Sage.

Morgenthau, Hans, and Kenneth W. Thompson. 1985. *Politics Among Nations: The Struggle for Power and Peace*, 6th edn. New York: Alfred A. Knopf.

Morris, Charles. 1914. *One Hundred Years of Conflict Between the Nations of Europe: the Causes and Issues of the Great War*. London: L. T. Myers.

Morrow, James D. 1994. *Game Theory for Political Scientists*. Princeton, NJ: Princeton University Press.

Most, Benjamin A., and Harvey Starr. 1982. "Case selection, conceptualizations and basic logic in the study of war," *American Journal of Political Science* 26: 834–56.

1989. *Inquiry, Logic, and International Politics*. Columbia, SC: University of South Carolina Press.

Moyal, J. 1949. "The distribution of wars in time," *Journal of the Royal Statistical Society* (Series A) 112: 446–69.

Mueller, John. 1989. *Retreat from Doomsday: the Obsolescence of Major War*. New York: Basic Books.

Munch, Peter A. 1976. "The concept of 'function' and functional analysis in sociology," *Philosophy of the Social Sciences* 6: 193–213.

Murthy, V. K. 1974. *The General Point Process: Applications to Structural Fatigue, Bioscience, and Medical Research*. Reading, MA: Addison-Wesley.

Nadelmann, Ethan A. 1990. "Global prohibition regimes: the evolution of norms in international society," *International Organization* 44: 479–526.

Nagel, Jack H. 1975. *The Descriptive Analysis of Power*. New Haven, CT, and London: Yale University Press.

Newbold, Paul, and Theodore Bos. 1985. *Stochastic Parameter Regression Models*. Beverly Hills, CA: Sage.

Newman, Robert P. 1975. "Communication pathologies of intelligence systems," *Speech Monographs* 42: 271–90.

Nicholson, Michael. 1989. *Formal Theories in International Relations*. Cambridge, UK: Cambridge University Press.

1992. *Rationality and the Analysis of International Conflict*. Cambridge, UK: Cambridge University Press.

Niemi, Richard G., and Herbert F. Weisberg, eds. 1972. *Probability Models of Collective Decision Making*. Columbus, OH: Charles E. Merrill.

Niou, Emerson M. S., and Peter C. Ordeshook. 1990. "Stability in anarchic international systems," *American Political Science Review* 84: 1208–34.

1994. "Alliances in anarchic international systems," *International Studies Quarterly* 38: 167–91.

Nowakowska, M. 1977. "Methodological problems of measurement of fuzzy concepts in the social sciences," *Behavioral Science* 22: 107–15.

Nurmi, H. 1984. "Probabilistic voting: a fuzzy interpretation and extension," *Political Methodology* 10: 81–95.

Nye, Joseph S. 1968. "Comparative regional integration," *International Organization* 22: 875.

Olinick, Michael. 1978. *An Introduction to Mathematical Models in the Social and Life Sciences*. Reading, MA: Addison-Wesley.

Olson Jr., Mancur. 1965. *The Logic of Collective Action: Public Goods and the Theory of Goods*. Cambridge, MA: Harvard University Press.

1982. *The Rise and Decline of Nations: Economic Growth, Stagflation, and Social Rigidities.* New Haven, CT: Yale University Press.

Olzak, Susan, Suzanne Shanahan, and Elizabeth H. McEneany. 1996. "Poverty, segregation, and race riots: 1960 to 1993," *American Sociological Review* 61: 590–613.

Ordeshook, Peter C. 1986. *Game Theory and Political Theory.* Cambridge, UK: Cambridge University Press.

Ore, Oystein. 1953. *Cardano: the Gambling Scholar.* Princeton, NJ: Princeton University Press.

Organski, A. F. Kenneth, and Jacek Kugler. 1980. *The War Ledger.* Chicago: University of Chicago Press.

Ornstein, D. S. 1989. "Ergodic theory, randomness, and chaos," *Science* 243: 182–7.

Ortega y Gasset, José. 1957 [1930]. *The Revolt of the Masses.* New York: W. W. Norton.

Ostrom, Charles W., Jr., and Francis A. Hoole. 1978. "Alliances and war revisited: a research note," *International Studies Quarterly* 22: 215–35.

Ostrom, Elinor. 1990. *Governing the Commons: the Evolution of Institutions for Collective Action.* Cambridge, UK: Cambridge University Press.

1991. "Rational choice theory and institutional analysis: toward complementarity," *American Political Science Review* 85: 237–43.

Pareto, Vilfredo. 1897. *Cours d'economie politique* [A course in political economy]. Lausanne, Switzerland: Rouge.

Parsons, Talcott. 1969. *Politics and Social Structure.* New York: Free Press.

Parzen, Emanuel. 1960. *Modern Probability Theory and Its Applications.* New York: John Wiley and Sons.

1962. *Stochastic Processes.* San Francisco: Holden-Day.

Petersen, Ib Damgaard. 1987. "The Weibull distribution in the study of international conflict." In P. G. Bennett (ed.), *Analyzing Conflict and its Resolution: some Mathematical Contributions.* Oxford: Clarendon Press, pp. 177–91.

1991. "The world war pattern: outbreak of international wars 1823–1989 as stochastic diffusion processes," *Cooperation and Conflict* 26: 1–20.

Petrocik, John R. 1981. *Party Coalitions: Realignments and the Decline of the New Deal Party System.* Chicago and London: University of Chicago Press.

Petty, Sir William. 1690. *Political Arithmetick.* London: Peacock and Hen.

Plano, Jack C., Robert E. Riggs, and Helenan S. Robin. 1982. *The Dictionary of Political Analysis*, 2nd edn. Santa Barbara, CA: ABC-CLIO.

Plender, Richard. 1986. "The role of consent in the termination of treaties," *British Yearbook of International Law* 57: 133–67.

Poisson, Siméon Denis. 1837. *Recherches sur la probabilité des jugements en matière criminelle et en matière civile, précédés des règles générales du calcul des probabilités.* Paris: Bachelier.

1853. "Recherches sur la probabilité de jugements, principalment en matière criminelle," *Comptes rendus Hebdomadaires Académie des Sciences* 1: 473–94.

Polacek, Solomon W. 1980. "Conflict and trade," *Journal of Conflict Resolution* 24: 55–78.

Polsby, Nelson, and Fred Greenstein, eds. 1975. *Handbook of Political Science.* Reading, MA: Addison-Wesley.

Pool, Robert. 1989. "Is it chaos, or is it just noise?" *Science* 243: 25–8.

Pressman, J. L., and Aaron Wildavsky. 1973. *Implementation: How Great Expectations in Washington are Dashed in Oakland.* Berkeley, CA: University of California Press.

Quattrone, George A., and Amos Tversky. 1988. "Contrasting rational and psychological analyses of political choice," *American Political Science Review* 82: 719–36.

Quigley, Carroll. 1961. *The Evolution of Civilizations.* New York: Macmillan.

Rae, Douglas W. 1971. *The Political Consequences of Electoral Laws,* 2nd edn. New Haven, CT: Yale University Press.

Ragin, Charles C. 1987. *The Comparative Method: Moving Beyond Qualitative and Quantitative Strategies.* Berkeley, CA: University of California Press.

Rapoport, Anatol. 1960. *Fights, Games and Debates.* Ann Arbor, MI: University of Michigan Press.

    1983. *Mathematical Models in the Social and Behavioral Sciences.* New York: John Wiley and Sons.

Rapoport, Anatol, and Albert M. Chammah. 1965. *Prisoner's Dilemma: a Study in Conflict and Cooperation.* Ann Arbor, MI: University of Michigan Press.

Raser, John. 1969. "Theories of deterrence," *Peace Research Reviews* 3.

Rawls, John. 1971. *A Theory of Justice.* Cambridge, MA: Harvard University Press.

Reich, Utz-Peter. 1968. "Conflict of interest: a pragmatic approach," *Journal of Peace Research* 5: 211–15.

Reichenbach, H. 1956. *The Direction of Time.* Berkeley, CA: University of California Press.

Renfrew, Colin. 1979. "System collapse as social transformation." In *Transformations: Mathematical Approaches to Culture Change.* New York and London: Academic Press, pp. 481–506.

    1984. *Social Approaches to Social Archaeology.* Cambridge, MA: Harvard University Press.

Richards, T. 1989. *Clausal Form Logic: an Introduction to the Logic of Computer Reasoning.* Reading, MA: Addison-Wesley.

Richardson, Lewis Fry. 1919. "The mathematical psychology of war." Manuscript in British copyright libraries.

    1941. "Frequency and occurrence of wars and other fatal quarrels," *Nature* 148: 598.

    1945a. "The distribution of wars in time," *Journal of the Royal Statistical Society* (Series A) 107(3–4): 242–50.

    1945b. "The distribution of wars in time," *Nature* 155: 610.

    1952. "Is it possible to prove any general statements about historical fact?" *British Journal of Sociology* 3: 77–84.

    1960a. *Arms and Insecurity.* Pacific Grove, CA: Boxwood Press.

    1960b. *Statistics of Deadly Quarrels.* Pacific Grove, CA: Boxwood Press.

Riker, William H. 1962. *The Theory of Political Coalitions.* New Haven, CT: Yale University Press.

    1990. "Political science and rational choice." In James E. Alt and Kenneth A. Shepsle (eds.), *Perspectives on Positive Political Economy.* Cambridge UK: Cambridge University Press.

Riker, William H., and Peter C. Ordeshook. 1973. *An Introduction to Positive Political Theory*. Englewood Cliffs, NJ: Prentice-Hall.

Roberts, J. M. 1993. *History of the World*. New York and Oxford: Oxford University Press.

Rogers, Roberts. 1971. *Mathematical Logic and Formalized Theories*. New York: American Elsevier.

Rohwer, Götz. 1993. *Transition Data Analysis*. Software and Working Paper 1–1. Institut für Empirische und Augewandte Sociologie, University of Bremer, Germany.

Rood, Robert. 1978. "The contagion/heterogeneity problem revisited: a problem for stochastic modeling," *International Interactions* 4: 265–78.

Rosenau, James N. 1987. "Toward single-country theories of foreign policy: the case of the USSR." In Charles F. Hermann, Charles W. Kegley Jr., and James N. Rosenau (eds.), *New Directions in the Study of Foreign Policy*. Boston: Allen and Unwin.

1990. *Turbulence in World Politics: a Theory of Change in World Politics*. Princeton, NJ: Princeton University Press.

1992. *The United Nations in a Turbulent World*. Boulder, CO, and London: Lynne Rienner.

Ross, Sheldon M. 1985. *Introduction to Probability Models*. New York: Academic Press.

Rotberg, Robert I., and Theodore Rabb, eds. 1989. *The Origin and Prevention of Major Wars*. New York and Cambridge: Cambridge University Press.

Ruíz-Palá, Ernesto, Carlos Avila-Beloso, and William Hines. 1967. *Waiting-Line Models*. New York: Reinhold.

Russett, Bruce M. 1962. "Cause, surprise, and no escape," *Journal of Politics* 24(1). 1963. "The calculus of deterrence," *Journal of Conflict Resolution* 7: 97–109.

1993. *Grasping the Democratic Peace: Principles for a Post-Cold War World*. Princeton, NJ: Princeton University Press.

Russett, Bruce M. and Starr, Harvey. 1996. *World Politics: the Menu for Choice*. 5th edn. San Francisco: W. H. Freeman.

Russett, Bruce M., and James S. Sutterlin. 1991. "The UN in a New World Order," *Foreign Affairs* 70: 69–83.

Saaty, Thomas L., and M. W. Khouja. 1976. "A measure of world influence," *Journal of Peace Science* 2: 31–48.

Sabatier, Paul. 1991. "Toward better theories of the policy process," *Political Science and Politics* 24: 147–56.

Sabrosky, Alan Ned, ed. 1985. *Polarity and War*. Boulder, CO: Westview Press.

Salmon, Wesley C. 1971. *Statistical Explanation and Statistical Relevance*. Pittsburgh, PA: University of Pittsburgh Press.

1980. "Probabilistic causality," *Pacific Philosophical Quarterly* 61: 50–74.

Samuelson, Paul Anthony. 1965 [1947]. *Foundations of Economic Analysis*. Cambridge, MA: Harvard University Press.

Sanders, D., and V. Herman. 1977. "The stability and survival of governments in Western democracies," *Acta Politica* 12: 346–77.

Sandler, Todd. 1992. *Collective Action: Theory and Applications*. Ann Arbor, MI: University of Michigan Press.

Sanjian, Gregory S. 1988a. "Arms export decision-making: a fuzzy control model," *International Interactions* 14: 243–65.

1988b. "Fuzzy set theory and US arms transfers: modeling the decision-making process," *American Journal of Political Science* 32: 1018–46.

1989. "Great power arms transfers: an empirical test of a fuzzy decision-making model," Annual Meeting of the Midwest Political Science Association, Chicago.

Saris, W. E., and I. N. Saris-Gallhoffer. 1975. "L'application d'un modele de decisions a des donnes historiques," *Revue Française de Science Politique* 25: 473–501.

Sartori, Giovanni. 1973. "What is 'politics'?" *Political Theory* 1: 5–26.

1974. "Philosophy, theory and politics," *Political Theory* 2: 133–62.

1976. *Parties and Party Systems*. Cambridge, UK: Cambridge University Press.

1991. "Comparing and miscomparing," *Journal of Theoretical Politics* 3: 243–57.

Savage, Leonard J. 1951. "The theory of statistical decisions," *Journal of the American Statistical Association* 46: 55–67.

Schelling, Thomas C. 1978. *Micromotives and Macrobehavior*. New York: Norton.

Schlager, Edella. 1995. "Policy making and collective action: defining coalitions within the advocacy coalition framework," *Policy Sciences* 28: 243–70.

Schlager, Edella, and William Blomquist, 1996. "A comparison of three emerging theories of the policy process," *Political Research Quarterly* 49: 651–78.

Schofield, Norman J. 1975. "A game theoretic analysis of Olson's game of collective action," *Journal of Conflict Resolution* 19: 441–61.

Schrodt, Philip A. 1976. "Richardson's model as a Markov process." In Dina A. Zinnes and John V. Gillespie (eds.), *Mathematical Models in International Relations*. New York: Praeger.

1985. "The role of stochastic models in international relations research." In Michael D. Ward (ed.), *Theories, Models and Simulations in International Relations*. Boulder, CO: Westview Press.

Schroeder, Paul W. 1972. "World War I as Galloping Gertie: a reply to Joachim Remak," *Journal of Modern History* 44: 319–45.

Selten, Reinhard, and Reinhard Tietz. 1966a. "Security equilibria." In Richard N. Rosecrance (ed.), *The Future of the International Strategic System*. San Francisco, CA: Chandler.

Selten, Reinhard, and Reinhard Tietz. 1966b. "Appendix: a formal theory of security equilibria." In Richard N. Rosecrance (ed.), *The Future of the International Strategic System*. San Francisco, CA: Chandler.

Service, Elman R. 1975. *Origins of the State and Civilization: the Processes of Cultural Evolution*. New York: W. W. Norton.

Seton-Watson, Hugh. 1985. *The Decline of Imperial Russia*. Boulder, CO: Westview Press.

Shannon, Claude E. 1951. "Prediction and entropy of written English," *Bell Systems Technical Journal* 5: 50–64.

Shannon, Claude E., and Warren Weaver. 1949. *A Mathematical Theory of Communication*. Urbana, IL: University of Illinois Press.

Shepsle, Kenneth A. 1974. "On the size of winning coalitions," *American Political Science Review* 68: 505–18.

1979. "Institutional arrangements and equilibrium in multi-dimensional voting models," *American Journal of Political Science* 23: 27–59.

Shepsle, Kenneth A, and Barry R. Weingast. 1987. "The institutional foundations of committee power," *American Journal of Political Science* 81: 85–104.

Shils, Edward A., ed. 1968. *International Encyclopedia of the Social Sciences*. New York: Free Press.

Shirer, William L. 1960. *The Rise and Fall of the Third Reich*. New York: Simon and Schuster.

Shively, Philip. 1989. *The Craft of Political Research*. Englewood Cliffs, NJ: Prentice-Hall.

Sienkiewicz, Stanley. 1982. "Observations on the impact of uncertainty in strategic analysis." In John F. Reichart and Steven R. Sturm (eds.), *American Defense Policy*. Baltimore and London: Johns Hopkins University Press, pp. 217–27.

Silverman, B. W. 1986. *Density Estimation for Statistics and Data Analysis*. London: Chapman and Hall.

Simon, Herbert A. 1955. "A behavioral model of rational choice," *Quarterly Journal of Economics* 69: 99–118.

1956. "Rational choice and the structure of the environment," *Psychological Review* 63: 129–38.

Singer, J. David. 1958. "Threat perception and the armament-tension dilemma," *Journal of Conflict Resolution* 2: 90–105.

1961. "The level of analysis problem in international relations." In Klaus Knorr and Sidney Verba (eds.), *The International System: Theoretical Essays*. Princeton, NJ: Princeton University Press.

1981. "Accounting for international war: the state of the discipline," *Journal of Peace Research* 18: 1–18.

1989. "System structure, decision processes, and the incidence of international war." In Manus I. Midlarsky (ed.), *Handbook of War Studies*. Boston: Unwin Hyman, pp. 1–21.

Singer, J. David, and Melvin Small. 1968. "Alliance aggregation and the onset of war, 1815–1945." In J. David Singer (ed.), *Quantitative International Politics*. New York: Free Press, pp. 247–86.

1972. *The Wages of War, 1816–1965: a Statistical Handbook*. New York: Wiley.

1984. *The Wages of War, 1816–1980: Augmented with Disputes and Civil War Data*. ICPSR Dataset 9044. Ann Arbor, MI: Inter-University Consortium for Political and Social Research.

Singer, J. David, Stuart A. Bremer, and John Stuckey. 1972. "Capability distribution, uncertainty, and major power war, 1820–1965." In Bruce M. Russett (ed.), *Peace, War, and Numbers*. Beverly Hills, CA: Sage, pp. 19–48.

Singer, Max, and Aaron Wildavsky. 1993. *The Real World Order: Zones of Peace, Zones of Turmoil*. Chatham, NJ: Chatham House Publishers.

Siverson, Randolph M., and George T. Duncan. 1976. "Stochastic models of international alliance initiation, 1885–1965." In Dina A. Zinnes and John V. Gillespie (eds.), *Mathematical Models in International Relations*. New York: Praeger, pp. 110–31.

Siverson, Randolph M., and Michael Tennefoss. 1982. "Interstate conflicts: 1815–1965," *International Interactions* 9: 147–78.

Skocpol, Theda. 1979. *States and Social Revolutions*. Cambridge, UK: Cambridge University Press.

Skocpol, Theda, and Margaret Somers. 1980. "The uses of comparative history in macrosocial inquiry," *Comparative Studies in Society and History* 22: 174–97.

Small, Melvin, and J. David Singer. 1983. *Resort to Arms: International and Civil Wars, 1816-1980*. Beverly Hills, CA: Sage.

Snyder, Glenn H. 1960. "Deterrence and power," *Journal of Conflict Resolution* 4: 163–78.

1971. "Prisoner's dilemma and chicken models in international politics," *International Studies Quarterly* 15: 66–103.

1996. "Process Variables in Neorealist Theory," *Security Studies* 5: 167–92.

Snyder, Glenn H., and Paul Diesing. 1977. *Conflict Among Nations: Bargaining, Decisionmaking, and System Structure in International Crises*. Princeton, NJ: Princeton University Press.

Sorokin, Pitirim A. 1937. *Fluctuations of Social Relationships, War, and Revolution*, vol. III. New York: American Book Company.

Spilerman, Seymour. 1970. "The causes of racial disturbances: a comparison of alternative explanations," *American Sociological Review* 35: 627–49.

1971. "The causes of racial disturbances: tests of an explanation," *American Sociological Review* 36: 427–42.

1972. "Strategic considerations in analyzing the distribution of racial disturbances," *American Sociological Review* 37: 493–9.

Sprout, Harold, and Margaret Sprout. 1969. "Environmental factors in the study of international politics." In James N. Rosenau (ed.), *International Politics and Foreign Policy*. New York: Free Press.

Starr, Harvey. 1978. "'Opportunity' and 'willingness' as ordering concepts in the study of war," *International Interactions* 4: 363–87.

1997. *Anarchy, Order, and Integration: How to Manage Interdependence*. Ann Arbor, MI: University of Michigan Press.

Stevens, S. S. 1951. *Mathematics, Measurement, and Psychophysics: Handbook of Experimental Psychology*. New York: Wiley, pp. 1–49.

Stimson, James A. 1991. *Public Opinion in America*. Boulder, CO: Westview Press.

Stimson, James A., ed. 1989. *Political Analysis*. Ann Arbor, MI: University of Michigan Press.

Stoll, Richard J., and Michael D. Ward, eds. 1989. *Power in World Politics*. Boulder, CO: Lynne Rienner.

Stone, Walter J., Ronald B. Rapoport, and Lonna Rae Atkenson. 1995. "A simulation model of presidential nomination choice," *American Journal of Political Science* 39: 135–61.

Strom, Kaare. 1988. "Contending models of cabinet stability", *American Political Science Review* 82: 923–41.

Stuart, Alan, and J. Keith Ord, eds. 1991. *Advanced Theory of Statistics*, 5th edn, 2 vols. New York: Oxford University Press.

Suppes, Patrick. 1957. *Introduction to Logic*. New York: Van Nostrand.

1970. *A Probabilistic Theory of Causality*. Amsterdam: North-Holland.

1981. *Logique du probable*. Paris: Flammarion.

1984. *Probabilistic Metaphysics*. New York and Oxford: Basil Blackwell.

Taagepera, Rein. 1979. "Size and duration of empires: growth–decline curves, 600 BC to AD 600," *Social Science History* 3: 115–38.

1986. "Reformulating the cube law for proportional representation elections," *American Political Science Review* 80: 489–504.

Taagepera, Rein, and Bernard Grofman. 1985. "Rethinking Duverger's law: predicting the effective number of parties in plurality and PR systems," *European Journal of Political Research* 13: 341–52.

Taagepera, Rein, and James P. Hayes. 1977. "How trade/GNP ratio decreases with country size," *Social Science Research* 6: 108–32.

Taber, Charles S., and Richard Timpone. 1994. "Computational modeling in political science." SUNY at Stony Brook. Unpublished manuscript.

1996. *Computational Modeling.* Thousand Oaks, CA: Sage Publications.

Tapie, Victor L. 1971. *The Rise and Fall of the Hapsburg Monarchy.* New York: Praeger.

Taylor, Charles Lewis, and David A. Jodice. 1983. *World Handbook of Political and Social Indicators.* vol. II: Political Protest and Government Change. New Haven, CT, and London: Yale University Press.

Taylor, Edmond. 1962. *The Fall of the Dynasties.* Garden City, NJ: Doubleday.

Taylor, Michael. 1987. *The Possibility of Cooperation.* Cambridge, UK: Cambridge University Press.

Taylor, Michael, and V. M. Herman. 1971. "Party systems and government stability," *American Political Science Review* 65: 28–37.

Taylor, Michael, and Michael Laver. 1973. "Government coalitions in Western Europe," *European Journal of Political Research* 1: 205–48.

1971. "Party systems and government stability," *American Political Science Review* 65: 28–37.

Teggart, Frederick J. 1942. "Causation in historical events," *Journal of the History of Ideas* 3: 3–11.

1977 [1925]. *Theory and Processes of History.* Berkeley, CA: University of California Press.

Thom, René. 1975. *Structural Stability and Morphogenesis.* Trans. David H. Fowler. Reading, MA: Addison-Wesley.

Thomas, George B. 1992. *Calculus and Analytic Geometry,* 8th edn. Reading, MA: Addison-Wesley.

Thompson, J. E. S. 1954. *The Rise and Fall of Maya Civilization.* Norman, OK: University of Oklahoma Press.

Thompson, William R. 1985. "Cycles of general, hegemonic, and global war." In Urs Luterbacher and Michael D. Ward (eds.), *Dynamic Models of International Conflict.* Boulder, CO: Lynne Rienner.

1988. *On Global War: Historical-Structural Approaches to World Politics.* Columbia, SC: University of South Carolina Press.

Truman, David B. 1951. *The Government Process.* New York: Alfred Knopf.

Tsebelis, George. 1989. "The abuse of probability in political analysis: the Robinson Crusoe fallacy," *American Political Science Review* 83: 77–91.

Tsebelis, George, and John Sprague. 1989. "Coercion and revolution: variations on a predator–prey model," *Mathematical and Computer Modelling* 12: 547–59.

Tsipis, Kosta. 1975. "Physics and the calculus of countercity and counterforce nuclear attacks," *Science* 187: 393–7.

Tufte, Edward R. 1974. *Data Analysis for Politics and Policy.* Englewood Cliffs, NJ: Prentice Hall.

Tuma, Nancy, and Michael T. Hannan. 1984. *Social Dynamics: Models and Methods.* New York: Academic Press.

Tversky, Amos. 1972. "Elimination by aspects: a theory of choice," *Psychological Review* 79: 281–99.

Tversky, Amos, and Daniel Kahneman. 1974. "Judgment under uncertainty: heuristics and biases," *Science* 185: 1124–31.

1981. "The framing of decisions and the psychology of choice," *Science* 211: 453–8.

1992. "Advances in prospect theory: cumulative representation of uncertainty," *Journal of Risk and Uncertainty* 5: 297–323.

Ulmer, S. S. 1982. "Supreme Court appointments as a Poisson distribution," *American Journal of Political Science* 26: 113–16.

Upham, Steadman, ed. 1990. *The Evolution of Political Systems: Sociopolitics in Small-Scale Sedentary Societies.* Cambridge and New York: Cambridge University Press.

van den Berghe, Pierre L. 1990. *State Violence and Ethnicity.* Niwot, CO: University Press of Colorado.

Vasquez, John A. 1993. *The War Puzzle.* Cambridge and New York: Cambridge University Press.

Viertl, Reinhard. 1996. *Statistical Methods for Non-Precise Data.* Boca Raton, FL: CRC Press.

Voevodsky, John. 1969a. "Quantitative behavior of warring nations," *Journal of Psychology* 72.

1969b. "Quantitative analysis of nations at war," *Peace Research Reviews* 3(5): 1–63.

von Clausewitz, Carl. 1976 [1832] *On War.* Trans. Michael Howard and Peter Paret. Princeton, NJ: Princeton University Press.

von Mises, Richard. 1957. *Probability, Statistics, and Truth.* New York: George Allen and Unwin.

Von Neumann, John, and Oscar Morgenstern. 1972 [1947]. *The Theory of Games and Economic Behavior,* 3rd edn. Princeton, NJ: Princeton University Press.

von Wright, Georg Henrik. 1951. "Deontic logic," *Mind* 60: 1–15.

1971. "A new system of deontic logic." In Risto Hilpinen (ed.) *Deontic Logic: Introductory and Systematic Readings.* Dordrecht, Holland: D. Reidel.

Vuchinich, Samuel, and Jay Teachman. 1993. "Influences on the duration of wars, strikes, riots, and family arguments," *Journal of Conflict Resolution* 37: 544–69.

Wagner, Harrison. 1994. "Peace, war, and the balance of power," *American Political Science Review* 88: 593–607.

Wallis, W. A. 1936. "The Poisson distribution and the Supreme Court," *Journal of the American Statistical Association* 31: 376–80.

Wallsten, T. S., D. V. Badescu, A. Rapoport, R. Zwick, and B. Forsyth. 1986. "Measuring the vague meanings of probability terms," *Journal of Experimental Psychology, General* 115: 348–65.

Waltz, Kenneth N. 1955. *Man, the State, and War.* New York: Columbia University Press.

1989. "The origins of war in neorealist theory." In Robert I. Rotberg and Theodore K. Rabb (eds.), *The Origin and Prevention of Major Wars*. Cambridge and New York: Cambridge University Press, pp. 39–52.

Ward, Michael D. 1982. "Differential paths to parity: a study of the contemporary arms race," *American Political Science Review* 78: 297–317.

1988. "Things fall apart," *International Interactions* 15: 65–79.

Warwick, Paul. 1979. "The durability of coalition governments in parliamentary democracies," *Comparative Political Studies* 11: 465–98.

Warwick, Paul, and Stephen T. Easton. 1992. "The cabinet stability controversy: new perspectives on a classic problem," *American Journal of Political Science* 36: 122–46.

Weber, Max. 1949. *Methodology of the Social Sciences*. Trans. Edward A. Shils and H. A. Finch. Glencoe, IL: Free Press.

Weisberg, Herbert F., ed. 1986. *Political Science: the Science of Politics*. New York: Agathon Press.

1995. *Democracy's Feast: Elections in America*. Chatham, NJ: Chatham House.

Weiss, Herbert K. 1963. "Stochastic models for the duration and magnitude of a deadly quarrel," *Operations Research* 11: 101–21.

Wiegel, George. 1992. *The Final Revolution: the Resistance Church and the Collapse of Communism*. Oxford and New York: Oxford University Press.

Wigner, Eugene P. 1969 [1960]. "The unreasonable effectiveness of mathematics in natural science." In Thomas L. Saaty and F. Joachim Weyl (eds.), *The Spirit and Uses of the Mathematical Sciences*. New York: McGraw-Hill, pp. 123–40.

Wilkinson, David. 1980. *Deadly Quarrels: Lewis F. Richardson and the Statistical Study of War*. Berkeley, CA: University of California Press.

Willey, Gordon. 1991. "Horizontal integration and regional diversity: an alternating process in the rise of civilizations," *American Antiquity* 56: 197–215.

Williamson, Paul, John Warner, and Stephen A. Hopkins. 1988. "A model of international dispute onsets with preliminary application to the impact of nuclear weapons." Unpublished manuscript. Correlates of War (COW) Project, University of Michigan, Ann Arbor.

Wohlstetter, Albert. 1959. "The delicate balance of terror," *Foreign Affairs* 37: 211–34.

Wright, Henry T. 1977. "Recent research on the origin of the state," *Annual Review of Anthropology* 6: 379–97.

Wright, Quincy. 1942. *A Study of War*. Chicago: University of Chicago Press.

1965. "The escalation of international conflicts," *Journal of Conflict Resolution* 9: 434–49.

Yost, David S. 1981. "The French defense debate," *Survival* 23: 19–30.

Zadeh, Lofti A. 1965. "Fuzzy sets," *Information and Control* 8: 338–53.

1968. "Probability measures of fuzzy events," *Journal of Mathematical Analysis* 10: 421–7.

1973. "Outline of a new approach to the analysis of complex systems and decision processes," *IEEE Transactions on Systems, Man, and Cybernetics* SMC-3: 28–44.

Zagare, Frank C. 1984. *Game Theory: Concepts and Applications*. Beverly Hills, CA: Sage.

1987. *The Dynamics of Deterrence*. Chicago: University of Chicago Press.

Index

Aalen, Odd O., 127
Abbott, Edwin A., 30
Abelson, Robert P., 17 (table)
Aberle, David, 176 (table)
Adams, Brooks, 14n., 256n.
Adenauer, Konrad, 48
Africa, 263, 265
aggregate political behavior, *see*
　macropolitical behavior
Agnesi, witch of, 258
Allison, Graham, 266n.
Allison, Paul D., 74n., 111 (table), 127
Almond, Gabriel A., 5n., 11, 20, 35, 37, 49n.,
　150, 158n., 162 (table), 172n., 176
　(table), 234n.
Anderson, John R., 12, 17 (table)
Aracil, Javier, 22n.
Aristotle, 5, 7, 17 (table), 271
Arrow, Kenneth J., 9n., 11n., 15, 17 (table)
Arthur, W. Brian, 172
Art of War, The (Sun-Tzu), 7
Ashby, W. Ross, 31
Asia, 263, 265
Avenhaus, Rudolf, 16n.
Axelrod, Robert, 52 (table), 175n., 177
　(table), 247n.
Azar, Edward E., 49n., 141

Bak, Per, 117n.
balance of power, 178 (table)
Balkans, 262, 265
Baloyra-Herp, Enrique, 205
Barclay, S., 237n.
Baron, David P., 10
Bartholomew, D. J., 74n., 111 (table)
Bartolini, Stefano, 209, 213, 246
Bayes, Thomas, 17 (table)
Bayesian decision model, 17 (table), 18
Beck, Nathaniel, 26n., 71
Beer, Francis A., 10, 17 (table)
Behavioral Correlates of War (BCOW)

Project, 141
behavioral force, 293
　see also hazard (rate) forces
Ben-Dak, Joseph D., 49n.
Bendor, Jonathan B., 20, 192, 219
Berlin Wall, 89, 90n., 150, 248, 251, 252, 262,
　264, 267
Bermann, George A., 162 (table)
Berry, Frances Stokes, 109 (table), 111
　(table)
Berry, William D., 109 (table), 111 (table)
Beyth-Marom, R., 22n., 163n., 237n., 244
　(table)
Bienen, Henry, 74n., 109 (table), 111 (table)
Binford, Lewis R., 14n.
Bishir, John W., 48n.
Bismarck, Otto von, 197
Bittinger, Marvin L., 48n., 85n., 241n.
Black, Duncan, 9n., 11n., 17 (table)
Blainey, Geoffrey, 5n., 178 (table)
Blalock, Hubert M., Jr., 10n., 15n., 32
Blomquist, William, 21
Blondel, Jean, 12
Blossfeld, Hans-Peter, 127, 119 (table)
Bochner, Salomon, 8, 88n.
Bohm, David, 11, 22n.
Boole, George, 147n.
Boolean logic, 23, 147n., 179, 277, 304
Bos, Theodore, 38, 71
Brams, Steven J., 5, 11n., 15, 52 (table), 177
　(table), 266n.
Brand, Myles, 22n.
Bremer, Stuart A., 32n., 45, 126
Brinton, Crane, 162 (table), 176 (table)
Brodie, Bernard, 23, 152, 177 (table)
Bronowski, Jacob, 22n., 31n., 88n.
Brookshire, R. G., 114n.
Brown, Courtney, 22n.
Browne, Eric C., 52 (table), 114n., 131, 162
　(table), 283, 284
Bruschi, Alessandro, 34n., 139
Brzezinski, Zbigniew, 120, 170